# PRAISE FOR *SOCIAL ENTREPRENEURSHIP IN PRACTICE*



'This book offers a clear and compelling exploration of social enterprises, combining authoritative research with practice from leading contributors. Readers are guided through the theories and practicalities of starting and running a social enterprise in an engaging and accessible way. Essential reading for students, practitioners and anyone passionate about social enterprises.'

**Prof Rob Blackburn, Director, Brett Centre for Entrepreneurship, University of Liverpool, UK**

'A timely and thoughtful academic exploration of how entrepreneurial practice which is focused toward social endeavour holds the capacity to reshaping the intersection between business and social change. With compelling real-world examples, grounded frameworks and clear insights, this book doesn't just define what social entrepreneurship is – it shows what it looks like in action. A must-read for students, teachers and leaders who believe that impact and social change go hand in hand. Whether you're launching a purpose-driven startup or transforming a traditional organization from within, this book offers the roadmap – and the inspiration – you need to make meaningful, measurable change.'

**Dr David Higgins, Senior Lecturer in Management, University of Liverpool, UK**

'This expertly crafted textbook fills a critical gap by embracing the hybrid school approach to social entrepreneurship, demonstrating how social missions and financial sustainability can work synergistically rather than in tension. The authors' emphasis on dual logic provides educators with a robust pedagogical framework while offering students and practitioners the essential skills to build viable social enterprises that create lasting impact. The integration of mainstream entrepreneurship principles with social innovation makes this an indispensable resource for anyone seeking to develop sustainable solutions to pressing social and environmental challenges. A practical, research-grounded guide that transforms good intentions into successful enterprises.'

**Dr Magdalena Plesa, Lecturer of Strategy and Entrepreneurship, University of Liverpool, UK**

'An invaluable resource that bridges theory and practice. Its "Stop and think" boxes and "Key research" features are blended seamlessly, encouraging critical reflection while grounding learning in evidence. Educators will find it a structured teaching tool, students gain practical insights and practitioners benefit from guidance on designing and managing social enterprises. This book not only explains social entrepreneurship but also empowers readers to create meaningful impact.'

**Dr Begüm Seray Samur-Teraman, Course Lead, BSc Business and Entrepreneurship, Birmingham City University, UK**

'This book is a timely and invaluable contribution to the field of social entrepreneurship. It skilfully bridges the continuum from theoretical foundations to real-world application, offering insights that resonate with both novice and seasoned scholars. With its engaging spotlights on key research, thought-provoking prompts and practical examples, it provides a holistic and accessible resource for deepening understanding and advancing practice.'

**Dr Beth Edwards, Enterprise Education Development Co-ordinator, Bangor University, UK**

'Educating social entrepreneurs so that they can have a valuable societal impact on their communities is an essential task for entrepreneurship programs worldwide. Conceptualizing, leading and growing such enterprises is not the same as launching a for-profit venture. It requires different knowledge, skills, and competencies that make social entrepreneurship a unique activity, one that necessitates its own specialized learning techniques. *Social Entrepreneurship in Practice* steps into the void by providing the groundwork that helps educators design and develop programmes, enabling students to engage in this form of entrepreneurial endeavour.'

**Dr Luke Pittaway, Copeland Professor of Entrepreneurship, Ohio University, USA**

'The intersection between theoretical understanding and practical application in social enterprise venture creation is a critical area of development. Given the complexity involved in establishing and managing social enterprises, the knowledge presented in this book provides aspiring founders with valuable insights and a strong foundation to increase their chances of success.'

**Dr David Bozward, Director of Employability and Entrepreneurship, Global Banking School, UK**

'An excellent resource that thoughtfully integrates theory with application. Covering essential themes such as developing your understanding of social enterprise, theoretical debates, intention formation, CSR and social innovation and value creation, the book equips readers with both conceptual insights and hands-on tools. With practical guidance on starting a social enterprise, crafting a social value proposition, business modelling, entrepreneurial learning and financing, it serves as a comprehensive text for students,

educators and practitioners alike. This book stands out as a highly usable and research-informed guide to advancing knowledge and practice in social entrepreneurship.'
**Prof Track Dinning, Professor of Entrepreneurship Education, Liverpool John Moores University, UK**

'An outstanding textbook that equips educators with the tools and real-world insights needed to inspire the next generation of changemakers. Its engaging blend of real-world examples, pedagogical frameworks and global perspectives makes it ideal for teaching both the theory and application of social entrepreneurship. A must-have resource for lecturers designing courses that connect enterprise with impact.'
**Dr Trudie Murray, Lecturer in Entrepreneurship and Economics, Munster Technological University, Ireland**

'This is without a doubt a timely and thought-provoking contribution to the field. By blending theory with real-world application, it illuminates the transformative potential of social entrepreneurship. Equipping readers with conceptual tools and practical insights while inspiring action, the book is an invaluable resource for students, educators, practitioners, policymakers and anyone committed to driving sustainable social change through entrepreneurship.'
**Dr Chinthaka Aluthgama-Baduge, Senior Lecturer in Enterprise and Entrepreneurship, University of Derby, UK**

'*Social Entrepreneurship in Practice* lands at just the right moment – a world grappling with inequality, sustainability and an uncertain transition to Industry 5.0, so the need for a guide of this kind could not be clearer. Practical without being dry, and inspirational while still firmly rooted in reality, Djebali and her contributing authors bring a passion for social entrepreneurship, with grounded advice that is forward-looking, and deeply human. I recommend this book to students studying social entrepreneurship, but also those interested in sustainability, inclusive technologies and innovation in more technical fields. It is exactly the sort of text that belongs in the hands of the next generation as they prepare to do good in an increasingly VUCA world.'
**Prof Andrew King, Associate Dean for Entrepreneurship and Enterprise Hub, Taicang Entrepreneur College, China**

# Social Entrepreneurship in Practice

## Learn how to create and manage a successful social enterprise

Zeineb Djebali

KoganPage

First published in Great Britain and the United States in 2026 by Kogan Page Limited



**Kogan Page**
Kogan Page Ltd, 2nd Floor, 45 Gee Street, London EC1V 3RS, United Kingdom
Kogan Page Inc, 8 W 38th Street, Suite 902, New York, NY 10018, USA
www.koganpage.com

**EU Representative (GPSR)**
Authorised Rep Compliance Ltd, Ground Floor, 71 Baggot Street Lower, Dublin D02 P593, Ireland
www.arccompliance.com

Kogan Page books are printed on paper from sustainable forests.



**ISBNs**

| | |
|---|---|
| Hardback | 978 1 3986 1513 7 |
| Paperback | 978 1 3986 1511 3 |
| Ebook | 978 1 3986 1512 0 |

**British Library Cataloguing-in-Publication Data**
A CIP record for this book is available from the British Library.

**Library of Congress Control Number**
2025041091

Typeset by Integra Software Services, Pondicherry
Print production managed by Jellyfish
Printed and bound by CPI Group (UK) Ltd, Croydon CR0 4YY

*Growing up in humble circumstances, I experienced hunger, poverty and deep frustration. But I've come to believe that education – and the good people we meet on our journey – are what keep us going. This book was born from a desire to inspire learners to make a meaningful difference in society.*

*To my daughters Thalia and Yasmine*

# CONTENTS

*Contributors* xiii
*Acknowledgements* xvi
*How to use this book* xvii
*Walkthrough of textbook features and online resources* xxiii

**01 Developing your understanding of social entrepreneurship** 1
*Dr Zeineb Djebali*
Introduction 1
Social entrepreneurship – definitional problems 3
Schools of thought 6
The Industrial Revolution as a catalyst for social entrepreneurialism 10
Emergence of social entrepreneurship in Europe 13
Legal structures for social enterprises 16
Summary and key learning points 19
References 23

**02 Theoretical debates on social enterprise** 29
*Dr Simon Adderley*
Introduction 31
Definitional debates 31
Drivers of social innovation 37
Resource-based view 40
Stakeholder theory 43
Network theory 46
Institutional theory 48
Summary and key learning points 53
References 59

**03 Intention formation in social entrepreneurship** 68
*Dr Peter McLuskie*
Introduction 69
Personal drivers 70
Social drivers 75
Start-up theory 78
Summary and key learning points 83
References 85

**04** **Social or commercial business?** 90
*Lucy Findlay MBE*
Introduction **90**
Common drivers for social enterprises **91**
What do we mean by trading in a social vs commercial context? **95**
Procurement, commissioning and social value **99**
The case for accreditations **101**
Growth models and journey to sustainability for social enterprises **107**
Summary and key learning points **111**
References **113**

**05** **Corporate social responsibility and social enterprise** 117
*Dr Zeineb Djebali*
Introduction **119**
Corporate social responsibility **120**
Understanding social enterprise **125**
CSR and social enterprises – overlaps and differences **127**
CSR challenges **129**
Social enterprise challenges **132**
Summary and key learning points **134**
References **137**

**06** **Social innovation and social value creation** 146
*Dr Richard Tomlins*
Introduction **147**
Social enterprises and social innovation **148**
Social value **154**
Measurement challenges and methodologies **159**
Summary and key learning points **170**
References **174**

**07** **Starting a social enterprise** 179
*Dr Luna Dou*
Introduction **180**
Social start-up skills **181**
Problem identification **183**
Problem Statement Canvas **184**
Opportunity recognition **188**
Engagement principles and tools **191**
Summary and key learning points **195**
References **199**

**08** **Social value proposition** 203
*Dr Zeineb Djebali*
Introduction 207
Conceptual definitions of social enterprise 208
Social entrepreneurs 209
Social value creation and its tensions 212
Social entrepreneurial opportunity 213
Social value proposition 220
Summary and key learning points 225
References 229

**09** **Social business modelling** 235
*Dr Sarah Preedy*
Introduction 237
Balancing social mission with revenue generation 237
Business modelling 239
Innovation 241
Social business modelling 242
Social business modelling approaches 245
Reflection on the application of social business modelling 252
Summary and key learning points 254
References 259

**10** **Social entrepreneurial learning** 261
*Dr Kelly Smith*
Introduction to entrepreneurial learning 261
Experiential learning 263
The social nature of entrepreneurial learning 265
Entrepreneurial learning for social enterprise 268
Development of entrepreneurial competencies 269
Mechanisms of learning 272
Summary and key learning points 279
References 282

**11** **Social financing** 287
*Dr Ekaterina Murzacheva*
Introduction 287
Key finance sources for social enterprises 289
Blockchain applications in social finance 295
Social impact investment 298

Social bonds and social impact bonds 302
Social enterprise funding model 304
The choice factors of social finance and key challenges 307
Summary and key learning points 311
References 313

12 **Conclusions and future directions for social entrepreneurship** 319
*Dr Zeineb Djebali*
Introduction 319
Current state of social entrepreneurship – theoretical debates 320
Regulatory and policy environment for SEs 322
The process of starting up a social enterprise 323
Challenges ahead for nascent social entrepreneurs 325
Forward-looking perspectives on the evolving nature of social entrepreneurship 327
Concluding reflections for aspiring social entrepreneurs 332
References 333

*Index* 341

# CONTRIBUTORS

**Zeineb Djebali**, BA, MALit, MBA, PGCE, PhD, is a Senior Lecturer of Entrepreneurship at the Brett Centre for Entrepreneurship, University of Liverpool Management School, University of Liverpool (UK) and a Senior Fellow of the UK's Higher Education Academy. Djebali has a strong track record of teaching and curriculum design and development across undergraduate and postgraduate programmes, with particular expertise in social entrepreneurship, business modelling and innovation, corporate entrepreneurship, business planning and becoming entrepreneurial, as well as supervising Master's and MBA dissertations. Her scholarly work on social entrepreneurship has been published in leading journals, including *International Small Business Journal* and *International Journal of Entrepreneurial Behaviour and Research*. She has also contributed to edited volumes on qualitative research methods and reflective practice. Djebali also brings practical experience, having founded and managed entrepreneurial ventures both in the UK and overseas.

**Dr Simon Adderley** is a Senior Lecturer and Subject Coordinator in Enterprise and Entrepreneurship at Oxford Brookes University (UK). He specializes in the intersections of entrepreneurship, innovation and organizational behaviour, with a focus on paradox theory, social value creation and entrepreneurial identity. Adderley has taught across undergraduate, postgraduate and executive programmes, and has supervised numerous Master's and doctoral dissertations. He has published in peer-reviewed journals, contributed to edited academic volumes and is the author of *Harnessing the Entrepreneurial Paradox*, a monograph exploring the unresolved tensions at the heart of entrepreneurial identity and decision-making.

**Dr Luna Dou** is a Lecturer in Business Management at the University of Buckingham Business School (UK), specializing in Entrepreneurship and Human Resource Management. She chairs the School's Assessment, Learning and Teaching Committee and leads key modules on Research Methods and Final-Year Projects. With a background in Engineering and industry experience as an HR Manager in the hospitality sector, Dou brings both analytical rigour and practical insight to her teaching. Passionate about pedagogy and student experience, she continually reflects on and refines her teaching to create meaningful and impactful learning environments.

**Lucy Findlay MBE** is a distinguished social entrepreneur and campaigner based in Devon, UK. She was the founding force behind Social Enterprise Mark CIC, the world's first accreditation standard specifically for social enterprises. With over three decades of hands-on and strategic experience, Findlay has played a pivotal role in shaping policy and strengthening the global social enterprise ecosystem. She has collaborated with a range of universities – including Westminster, Plymouth Marjon, Solent, Salford, Cardiff Metropolitan, Northampton, Coventry and Winchester – to foster environments that actively support social enterprise growth and development. Findlay is particularly passionate about issues surrounding gender equality, disability inclusion and access to social finance, and she has mentored numerous students and social entrepreneurs throughout her career. She is also an engaged member of the Co-operative Party, advocating for the advancement of co-operatives and social enterprises at the political level.

**Dr Ekaterina Murzacheva** is a Senior Lecturer in Entrepreneurship & Innovation, the Head of Enterprise and leads the Digital Economy, Entrepreneurship & Innovation Discipline at Surrey Business School, University of Surrey, UK. With extensive experience in teaching entrepreneurship and supporting both new and established ventures in their development and growth, Murzacheva actively engages with industry to connect businesses with students and academics. Her expertise focuses on entrepreneurship within disadvantaged communities, entrepreneurial finance and women's entrepreneurship. Murzacheva is also a founding member of the Surrey Women's Entrepreneurship Network. In this capacity, she supports women entrepreneurs in enhancing their finance readiness through mentorship, event organization, mastermind sessions and creating matching opportunities.

**Dr Peter McLuskie** is a Lecturer in Business and Enterprise at University College Birmingham, UK. Peter has taught enterprise, entrepreneurship and innovation for over 10 years and has published widely on the topic of entrepreneurship education and entrepreneurial intentions. Prior to taking up an academic role, McLuskie worked extensively in business support and sector development in the creative industries and is an accredited business advisor and mentor. He is a Senior Fellow of the Higher Education Academy, a Member of the Enterprise Educators UK Advisory Council, a Certified Management and Business Educator for the Chartered Association of Business Schools, and an International Enterprise Educators Fellow (IEEP).

**Dr Sarah Preedy** is a Lecturer in Enterprise at the Faculty of Arts, Humanities and Business, Plymouth Business School, University of Plymouth (UK). She teaches across a range of Business modules with a specialism in enterprise, entrepreneurship and innovation. Her research to date focuses on the role, value and impact of enterprise education (both in- and extra-curricular), the development of entrepreneurial identity and intention, social enterprise and female entrepreneurship. She is a Senior Fellow of the Higher Education Academy, Fellow of Enterprise Educators UK, Member of the Enterprise Educators UK Advisory Council, and a Certified Management and Business Educator for the Chartered Association of Business Schools.

**Dr Kelly Smith** is an Associate Professor in Entrepreneurship at the Department of Management, Birmingham Business School, University of Birmingham (UK). Smith is an experienced enterprise educator having led institutional and regional student and graduate business and social enterprise start-up support initiatives, in addition to developing and leading undergraduate-level credit-bearing Venture Creation Programmes. Smith is a nationally and internationally recognized leader in enterprise and entrepreneurship education and policy, having held leadership positions for Enterprise Educators UK and the Institute for Small Business and Entrepreneurship, and is a Principal Fellow of the UK's Higher Education Academy.

**Chaitanya Sagar, MBA,** is a purpose-driven Project Management Specialist with over five years of experience leading digital transformation across the fintech, healthcare and retail sectors. He played a key role in advancing digital payments at Paytm and scaling Amazon P2M at Pine Labs, contributing to financial inclusion and product innovation. Passionate about social entrepreneurship, he supports UK-based social enterprises through voluntary and freelance work, helping them scale through strategic planning, digital enablement and operational improvement. Bridging academic insight with practical experience, he brings a systems-thinking approach to social impact, focusing on sustainable growth, inclusive innovation and delivering meaningful change in complex, fast-evolving environments.

**Dr Richard Tomlins** is the Coventry University Group Regional Director for UK and Europe. His work is rooted in a belief in the power of people, community and business and the scope for that social value to become a driver of societal change. He draws on his hybrid business and academic career experience, having started work as a housing officer and later moving into academia – taking on the post of Professor of Race, Diversity and Housing at De Montfort University – before running his own company Cohesia and subsequently returning to academic work. He now groups his teaching, learning and project interventions within a design thinking framework with much of his current work in Ukraine.

# ACKNOWLEDGEMENTS

We would like to thank Kogan Page Publishing for their encouragement and invaluable support throughout the development of this textbook. Particular thanks go to Anne-Marie Heeney at Kogan Page for her unwavering support and guidance throughout the writing process. Her insightful reviews and consistent encouragement were instrumental in bringing this work to completion.

We are especially grateful to all the contributors of this textbook for their commitment and belief in its overall vision: to equip learners with a practical, hands-on approach to creating meaningful impact on society through viable, innovative solutions.

We are also thankful to our reviewers, whose constructive feedback played a key role in shaping the content and structures of the chapters. We extend our particular thanks to Thalia Cox for her careful and constructive feedback, which greatly enhanced the quality and clarity of the texts.

Finally, my heartfelt thanks to my two daughters Thalia and Yasmine, and my colleagues Prof MariaLaura Di Domenico and Prof Mark NK Saunders, for their constant encouragement and support throughout this journey.

# HOW TO USE THIS BOOK

This textbook is structured with a progressive logic, meaning that all terms and concepts related to social entrepreneurship are defined when they are first introduced. We recommend that readers proceed sequentially through the chapters, engaging with the Key Research boxes, Stop and Think boxes, Expert Views boxes, Call to Action exercises and real-world examples. However, the order in which you navigate the textbook may vary depending on your specific needs and objectives. Below are some suggestions on how you might use this textbook effectively.

## As part of a social entrepreneurship course/module

If you are using this textbook as part of a social entrepreneurship course or module, the order in which you should read the chapters will likely be prescribed by your instructor, tailored to their understanding of your learning needs. Alternatively, if you are an aspiring social entrepreneur or involved in the field, you may prefer to read the chapters in an order that suits your specific interests. Regardless of your purpose, the order in which you approach the content of this textbook will depend on your background and practical experience. For students, particularly those pursuing an undergraduate or postgraduate degree in business management or other similar disciplines, it is likely that you will follow the order of the chapters closely.

In this textbook, you can read certain chapters as a group without significantly disrupting the logical flow. These chapters are: Starting a Social Enterprise (Chapter 7), Social Value Proposition (Chapter 8), Social Business Modelling (Chapter 9) and Social Financing (Chapter 11). Throughout the textbook, we emphasize the importance of completing the Call to Action questions to reinforce your understanding of key concepts explored in the textbook.

## As a guide to your social start-up

If you intend to use this textbook as a guide to your social start-up, we recommend reading the entire book before embarking on your social entrepreneurial journey. This will provide you with a critical understanding of the key theoretical debates surrounding social entrepreneurship (Chapters 2 and 3), and of the differences between social enterprises and profit-seeking businesses (Chapter 5). You will also develop a good understanding of key social entrepreneurial tools, such as the 'Problem Statement Canvas' (Chapter 7), the 'Social Value Proposition Canvas' (Chapter 8) and the 'Triple Layered Business Model Canvas' (Chapter 9). Following an initial reading, we suggest you revisit 'Starting a Social Enterprise' (Chapter 7) to enable you to define the problem you are solving and the processes required to create a solution that addresses the needs of your beneficiaries as well as your paying customers. Following this, we suggest you revisit Chapter 8 to build a compelling social value proposition that aligns the needs of beneficiaries, customers and overall social or environmental outcomes. Of equal importance, 'Social Business Modelling' (Chapter 9) enables you to understand the key components of your social business model, and how well you can articulate the positive impact you generate out of your social enterprise activities. Accessing finance is a key part of the start-up process, and hence we recommend you revisit Chapter 12 to gain an understanding of the range of social financing options you can access, including the challenges you may encounter as a nascent social entrepreneur.

This approach ensures that you fully understand the material contained in each chapter before applying it to your social start-up. If you encounter any challenges regarding any of the concepts, models and theories presented, pay particular attention to the 'Key Research boxes' within the text. The chapters also include real-world examples that illustrate how real-life social entrepreneurs address social and/or environmental challenges and the broader social impact they create. Additionally, the boxes on 'Key Research' present relevant scholarly debates on social entrepreneurship that have been published in peer reviewed journals. This will provide you with insights into current research practices related to the field of social entrepreneurship. All of the references included in each chapter can be easily accessed via online databases that your university or organization may have access to, which will offer you a deeper understanding of the most pertinent discourses on social entrepreneurship.

## Our approach to social entrepreneurship

Social entrepreneurship is a broad field that has attracted the attention of researchers and policy makers. Broadly, there exist two streams of research into social entrepreneurship, split between the 'innovation school' and the 'hybrid school'. The innovation school of thought takes a broader view of the field, examining the key characteristics that enable social entrepreneurs to succeed, as well as emphasizing the role social entrepreneurs play in developing innovative approaches to social problems; in contrast, the hybrid school focuses on the structural aspects of social entrepreneurship, examining specifically the hybrid structure of social enterprises (SEs): balancing business and social logics. Whilst we acknowledge the multifaceted conceptualizations of social entrepreneurship, we adopt the hybrid school view of social entrepreneurship, which describes the role social entrepreneurs play in developing innovative approaches to social or environmental challenges through market-based mechanisms.

This indicates that this textbook, including the entrepreneurial tools presented, involves building a social enterprise on a dual logic: a social mission with financial sustainability. The knowledge, skills and competencies that you will cultivate in this textbook are therefore designed to support you in building such a social enterprise. This approach is grounded in our belief that developing an innovative solution to social and environmental challenges requires an understanding of the pivotal role of financial sustainability. There is substantial evidence in mainstream entrepreneurship literature that underscores the interplay between identifying the right entrepreneurial opportunity and building a viable business to ensure success. Hence, we encourage you to consider balancing your social mission with financial sustainability to ensure the long-term success of your enterprise.

## Structure of the textbook

**Chapter 1** explores the foundational concepts and definitional debates related to social entrepreneurship, highlighting its key characteristics. The chapter also explores the two dominant schools of thought: The **Social Innovation School**, which puts emphasis on innovative solutions to social and/or environmental problems across various organizational types, and the **Hybrid School**, which focuses specifically on social enterprises that balance a social mission with financial sustainability. This chapter also examines the historical roots of social entrepreneurship, particularly foregrounding the English Industrial Revolution (1760–1840) and the corresponding emergence of the cooperative movement, whose principles of collective action, trade of goods and services, and limited profit generation can be seen as an early form of modern social enterprise. Finally, it outlines the legal structures available for social enterprises, emphasizing how these choices reflect different approaches to the social mission and revenue generation.

**Chapter 2** looks at the key theoretical debates surrounding social entrepreneurship. It explores the drivers for social innovation and the role social entrepreneurs play in bringing novel approaches to social or environmental challenges. The chapter also examines the hybridity of SEs and how these organizations balance their social mission with their financial sustainability. Finally, the chapter explores key theoretical frameworks and their application to the SEs' context. This chapter covers the resource-based view, stakeholder theory, network theory and institutional theory, and their relevance to the SEs' context including the limitations and challenges.

**Chapter 3** looks at the antecedents of social entrepreneurship. One of the key theoretical debates in entrepreneurship literature is whether entrepreneurs are born with certain characteristics or shaped by other factors that influence their entrepreneurial intentions. This chapter therefore raises the question, 'How are social entrepreneurial intentions formed?', and explores the personal drives that shape social intentions such as compassion, need for achievement and embedded agency. It also explores the social drivers such as gender, age and social capital and their role in shaping social entrepreneurial intentions. The chapter concludes with examining the 'start-up theory', paying particular attention to the role of opportunity recognition, effectuation and bricolage in the social entrepreneurial start-up process.

**Chapter 4** explores the motivations behind the creation of social enterprises, examining the key characteristics that distinguish them from shareholder-led organizations. The chapter also examines the rationale for accrediting social enterprises, focusing on the case of the Social Enterprise Mark CIC – the first UK-based social enterprise accrediting body. Drawing on insights from its 14 years of operation, the chapter reflects on the challenges, achievements and lessons from the founder's perspective, offering practical guidance for aspiring social entrepreneurs.

**Chapter 5** explores the evolution of corporate social responsibility (CSR) and its transformation into a strategic practice for for-profit shareholder organizations (i.e. corporations) to demonstrate their social and environmental responsibility. It examines the key regulatory and reporting frameworks such as the United Nations Global Compact (UNGC), the Global Reporting Initiative (GRI), the International Integrated Reporting Framework (IIRF) and the Environmental, Social and Governance (ESG) Investment Framework, all of which have shaped how corporations disclose their impact. The chapter also compares CSR practices with the mission-driven focus of social enterprises, highlighting both common goals and differences in how social value is created. The chapter concludes with a discussion on the limitations of CSR, including the risk of greenwashing and the challenges social enterprises face in measuring social impact.

**Chapter 6** builds on the role of social innovation in meeting social challenges and the creation of social value. Furthermore, it examines the barriers to social innovation, with a particular focus on resource constraints, such as financial and human resources, regulatory and institutional barriers, attitude to risk and challenges in measuring social impact. This chapter also introduces the concept of 'design thinking' as a human-centred approach, as well as examining the concept of social value and its role in public policy and practice. Lastly, the chapter examines the various frameworks available to measure social impact, such as the Social Return on Investment (SROI), while evaluating the challenges of quantifying social impact.

**Chapter 7** moves into the core blocks of the social start-up process. It explores the social entrepreneurial process and its components opportunity identification, evaluation and exploitation. The chapter also examines the processes involved in identifying and defining a social and/or environmental problem that is worth solving, presenting the 'Problem Statement Canvas' as one of the entrepreneurial tools that enables social entrepreneurs to define the problem, understand the context in which this problem occurs, and the impact it has on those affected. Finally, this chapter emphasizes the role of collecting data in gaining a deeper understanding of the problem identified and building a solution that meets the needs of beneficiaries.

**Chapter 8** explores the conceptual interpretations of social entrepreneurship, highlighting the lack of a universal definition but widespread consensus on its purpose of addressing social and/or environmental problems through innovative solutions. The chapter also explores the motivations of social entrepreneurs and the range of antecedents that shape their social entrepreneurial intentions. The chapter addresses the issue of mission drift that may arise from balancing a social mission with financial sustainability. It then introduces the key three stages of identifying social entrepreneurial opportunities – idea generation, experimentation and refinement – concluding by outlining how to build a strong social value proposition that aligns the needs of three distinct but intersecting groups: beneficiaries, customers and broader social outcomes.

**Chapter 9** takes up our own question – how does one build a social business model that successfully balances for-profit trading activities and a social mission? In particular, this chapter examines the key components of a social business model, including pricing, customer relationships, differentiation, vision and the approaches to social business modelling. This chapter introduces the Triple Layered Social Business Model as a tool that enables SEs to build a social business model that aligns the needs of their beneficiaries (individuals or the environment), financial sustainability and overall creation of social value.

**Chapter 10** introduces us to the concept of entrepreneurial learning, defined as a dynamic and continuous process where entrepreneurs develop the skills and knowledge necessary to start and manage a new business venture. It explores the importance of experiential learning, social networks and the context in which social entrepreneurs are embedded and how they play a key role in the learning process. The chapter also examines the role of critical incidents, mentors, formal and informal education, incubators, accelerators, business coaches and advisers as part of the ecosystem of entrepreneurial learning. Of equal importance, the chapter critically evaluates social entrepreneurial learning compared to traditional entrepreneurship. Throughout, the chapter underscores the role of critical reflection in enabling social entrepreneurs to assess injustices and develop solutions to address these.

**Chapter 11** moves into the relevant financing options available for SEs. It explores both internal and alternative financing sources. Additionally, it examines the variety of approaches to social financing, ranging from social bonds to social impact bonds and blockchain technologies. Finally, the chapter presents a social enterprise funding framework that explains SEs' funding cycles and the approaches available for social entrepreneurs to seek funding. This is followed by a realistic account of the key challenges faced by social entrepreneurs in accessing funding.

**Chapter 12** provides a summary of the core themes explored in this textbook. It begins by revisiting the key theoretical debates and the emergence of hybrid social enterprises that blend a social mission with business practices. It then examines the regulatory environment and its influence on the development of social enterprises, before reviewing the process of launching a social enterprise as well as outlining the key challenges of limited access to capital and social impact measurement. The chapter concludes with our forward-looking perspective, highlighting the role of corporate social intrapreneurs in driving social change within established organizations, as well as the potential of emerging technologies in advancing tech-driven solutions to social and environmental challenges.

# WALKTHROUGH OF TEXTBOOK FEATURES AND ONLINE RESOURCES

## Learning outcomes

A bulleted list at the beginning of each chapter summarizes what you can expect to learn, to help you to track your progress.

**LEARNING OUTCOMES**

By the end of this chapter, you should be able to:

- Identify the key theoretical debates related to social entrepreneurship.
- Identify the key characteristics of social enterprises.
- Compare and contrast the social innovation and hybrid schools of thought related to social entrepreneurship.

## Real-world examples and expert views

A range of examples and 'expert views' illustrate how key ideas and theories are operating in practice to help you to place the concepts discussed in real-life context.

**REAL-WORLD EXAMPLE** TOMS shoes – one-for-one business model

Several of the themes and issues covered in this chapter are exemplified and illustrated by our example, TOMS shoes. TOMS was founded by Blake Mycoskie in 2006 and is a renowned social enterprise that has transformed the footwear industry through its 'One-for-One' business model.

## 'Stop and Think' boxes

In each chapter, 'Stop and Think' boxes will encourage you to reflect critically on what you have read and reinforce what you have learnt.

**STOP AND THINK**

Do the personal qualities and traits described in this section mean that people who possess them are likely to be social entrepreneurs? What other professions seem to possess these qualities and traits? What other elements are needed to set a person on a social entrepreneurial mission?

## Key Research boxes

These highlight papers or researchers that may be of further interest for students in their studies.

**KEY RESEARCH**

In his 1989 seminal article, 'Who is an entrepreneur? is the wrong question', Gartner argues for a paradigm shift in understanding entrepreneurship. He notes that entrepreneurship is a multidimensional phenomenon and, therefore, the focus should be not just on examining the unique traits of the entrepreneur but also on a broader understanding of how organizations come into existence.

## Discussion questions

These can be used in tutorials or small study groups to stimulate debate and critical thinking:

Discussion questions:

1. How did Lucy Findlay MBE's leadership contribute to SEMCIC's success? What are the potential drawbacks of the social enterprise being associated solely with her name?
2. What were the main flaws in SEMCIC's initial pricing and business model? How could these be identified and addressed?

## Chapter summary and key learning points

Draws together the main threads of the chapter and summarizes the key learning points.

Key learning points at the end of each chapter summarize the main themes of the chapter and act as a useful revision tool:

Key learning points:

- There are a huge number of drivers for SE establishment but what holds them together is the need to set up a business that is truly focused on making a difference to people and planet rather than being driven by profit for individual shareholders. The business needs to be commercially viable, however, to carry out its mission.
- Social entrepreneurs when compared with traditional entrepreneurs often differ in their approach to a problem by seeing the social/environmental challenge as key and making money as secondary but necessary to mission implementation.

## References

Detailed references provide quick and easy access to the research and underpin sources behind the chapter.

## Online resources

This book includes online resources for lecturers and students, comprising:

- lecturer slides
- instructor guide
- further reading material

These resources can be accessed at www.koganpage.com/seip

# 01 Developing your understanding of social entrepreneurship

**ZEINEB DJEBALI**

**LEARNING OUTCOMES**

By the end of this chapter, you should be able to:

- Identify the key theoretical debates related to social entrepreneurship.
- Identify the key characteristics of social enterprises.
- Compare and contrast the social innovation and hybrid schools of thought related to social entrepreneurship.
- Evaluate the role of the English Industrial Revolution in driving social change.
- Identify the evolution of social entrepreneurship through the cooperative movement.
- Explain the most common legal structures for social enterprises.

## Introduction

As the topic has grown in importance over the last 20 years, there has been a steady increase in the number of textbooks dedicated to social entrepreneurship and social enterprise, including the management of small firms (Bornstein and Davis, 2010; Chahine, 2016; Collavo, 2022; Gunn and Durkin, 2010; Kickul and Lyons, 2012; Prazskier and Nowak, 2011). In this textbook, we take a distinctive approach to what is currently available. Whether you are an undergraduate or a postgraduate student, an aspiring or practising social entrepreneur, this textbook is designed to equip you with an understanding of the key theoretical debates related to social entrepreneurship and their application to real-world practice. More importantly, it provides you with the relevant entrepreneurial tools necessary to create a viable social enterprise that solves pressing societal and environmental problems. As such, the core approach of this textbook is a 'hands-on' approach that facilitates your understanding of how nascent social entrepreneurs identify, evaluate and exploit social entrepreneurship opportunities, both in the pre- and follow-up start-up stages.

After reading this textbook, you will have been introduced to a range of key theoretical debates related to social entrepreneurship (see Chapters 1, 2 and 3). Of equal importance, you will have been introduced to social entrepreneurial toolkits, including the 'Problem Statement Canvas' (see Chapter 7), 'Social Value Proposition Canvas' (see Chapter 8), and the 'Triple-Layered Business Model Canvas' (see Chapter 9), that enable you to design a viable social enterprise that balances a social mission with financial sustainability.

Furthermore, you will have gained a comprehensive understanding of the critical choices you will have to make when launching a social enterprise. These include areas such as social innovation (see Chapter 2), the antecedents to social entrepreneurship intentions (see Chapter 3), the choice of legal structures (see Chapter 1), the differences between commercial and social entrepreneurship (see Chapter 4), commonalities and differences between corporate social responsibility (CSR) and social enterprises (SEs) (see Chapter 5), social value creation and social impact measurement (see Chapter 6), social entrepreneurial learning (see Chapter 10) and social financing (see Chapter 11). In each of these chapters, you will also have been presented with real-world examples that illustrate how social entrepreneurs address social and environmental challenges through sustainable solutions.

Throughout your studies, you will inevitably read a wide range of textbooks and academic articles. In many of these sources, 'social entrepreneurship' and 'social enterprise' are often used interchangeably with terms like 'corporate social responsibility' (CSR), often led by 'profit-for-shareholders' (private commercial businesses) and 'not-for-profit' organizations (NFPs) (examples of NFPs: charities and non-governmental organizations (NGOs)). However, in this textbook, we are more precise in our use of these terms.

We define social entrepreneurship as a process that involves developing innovative solutions to address environmental and social needs and social entrepreneurs as individuals or groups of individuals who identify a social or environmental need and develop an innovative approach to create social value. We define social value, in this context, as the wider non-financial benefits that can be generated to improve the well-being of specific individuals and communities (i.e. beneficiaries) or, on a broader scale, benefit society and the environment at large (Santos et al, 2021). We recognize that there is no universal definition of social entrepreneurship; however, in this textbook, we use the term social enterprises (SEs) to describe 'hybrid' business organizations that are built on a dual logic: social mission and financial sustainability (Santos et al, 2015). We believe it is important to have a clear understanding of our definitions so you can make informed choices about the various pathways to social entrepreneurship.

This chapter is structured as follows: first, we provide a brief overview of the key definitional debates related to social entrepreneurship, which will be explored further in subsequent chapters (Chapters 2, 3 and 4). In this section, we also outline the key characteristics of SEs, followed by exploring the two schools of thought: the 'innovation school' and the 'hybrid school', from which the concept of social entrepreneurship took root, as well as conceptual convergences and divergences. Then, we explore the role of the English Industrial Revolution (IR) in driving social change. Initiatives such as philanthropic donations, charitable actions and particularly cooperatives emerged as a response to social challenges of the time, all of which led to the evolution of social entrepreneurship as a mechanism to solve unmet social needs. We explore the emergence of social entrepreneurship in Europe, including governments' responses to seeing this phenomenon as a potential solution to societal challenges. Next, we explore the most prominent legal structures that are available for SEs, followed by outlining the main learning outcomes of this chapter.

## Social entrepreneurship – definitional problems

In this section, we explore the research streams that have significantly contributed to our understanding of social entrepreneurship as a field of both academic enquiry and practice. The rise of social entrepreneurship is closely linked to the retrenchment of the role of government in delivering social and healthcare services, both in European and non-European countries, resulting in increased social welfare needs that cannot be met purely through traditional 'profit-for-shareholders' organizations and NFPs (Borgaza and Defourny, 2001).

As highlighted in Table 1.1, we describe profit-for-shareholder organizations as those that operate like commercial businesses. These organizations are, therefore, market-driven, serving customers through the sales of goods and services for the purpose of capturing financial value – that is, generating income and maximizing profits. Although these organizations can contribute to social good through CSR practices (see Chapter 5), their operation is primarily focused on maximizing shareholders' interests. On the other hand, NFPs such as charities and NGOs are defined as organizations that serve public interests (Salamon, 1999). These organizations are, therefore, most often devoid of any commercial interests and governmental

**Table 1.1** Sector-specific characteristics

| | Not-for-profit | Social enterprise | Profit-for-shareholders |
|---|---|---|---|
| **Purpose** | Charitable activities for public good | Dual objectives – economic and social value creation | Shareholder value maximization |
| **Who do they serve?** | Public good | Beneficiaries | Customers |
| **Activities** | Charitable, including campaigning, advocacy and research | Production and/or trade of goods and services; activities to serve a social mission | Production and/or trade of goods and services |
| **Role of profit** | Non-profit making | Reinvestment of surplus into social mission (retained earnings) | Profit maximization |
| **Sources of funding** | Grants and donations | Sales of goods/services; self-funding and social finance (incl. impact investment) | Sales of goods/services (internal)/banks, loans, shareholder equity (external) |
| **Governance** | Stakeholders | Stakeholders | Shareholders and management |
| **Driving factors** | Social need driven | Social need driven | Market driven |

control (Salamon and Anheir, 1992) and exist to support their beneficiaries and contribute to overall social good. However, compared to SEs that balance profit with a social mission, NFPs rely mainly on government subsidies and donations for their income (Dees, 1998; Di Domenico et al, 2010; Defourny and Nyssens, 2010; Stephan et al, 2015).

## *Unique characteristics of social enterprises*

Our discussion so far highlights that SEs have distinct characteristics when compared to both profit-for-shareholder organizations, whose primary mission is to maximize shareholder value and private wealth, and NFPs, who rely on public grants and philanthropic donations to contribute to social good. SEs are often spearheaded by social entrepreneurs who develop innovative approaches to social and environmental problems through entrepreneurial practices (Zahra et al, 2009). Nevertheless, the centrality of SEs extends beyond the individual social entrepreneur. This includes three core characteristics (see Figure 1.1): an explicit social mission, enterprising

**Figure 1.1** Unique characteristics of social enterprises

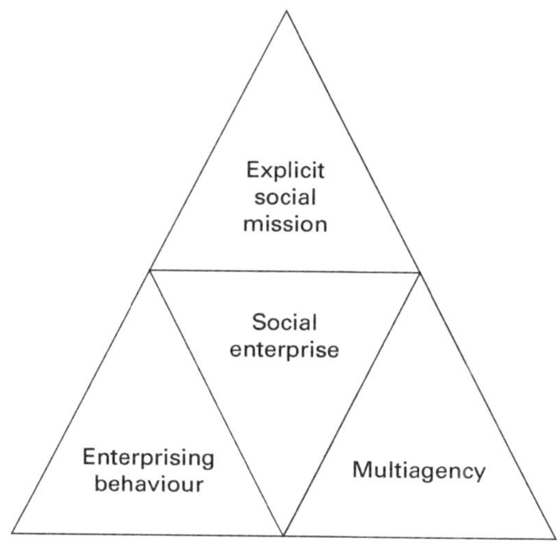


behaviour and multiagency (Dees, 2001; Dees and Elias, 1998; Martin and Osberg, 2007; Shaw and Carter, 2007; Weerawardena and Sullivan Mort, 2006):

- **Explicit social mission:** SEs are characterized by their explicit social and/or environmental mission. The term 'social' refers to how SEs address the needs of beneficiaries (those on whom the social mission is built), who are often underserved by profit-for-shareholder organizations and NFPs. The primary focus of SEs is therefore to serve the needs of beneficiaries and create social value at both social and environmental levels.
- **Enterprising behaviour:** SEs are defined as business organizations that trade goods or services for the purpose of generating revenue and yield profit (surplus) to ensure financial sustainability. SEs are autonomous organizations that do not rely on government subsidies, grants or philanthropic donations. The generated profits or surpluses (if any) are reinvested back into the SE to sustain the social mission.
- **Multiagency:** SEs are business organizations that are required to meet the needs of multiple stakeholders. These include beneficiaries (e.g. those disadvantaged) on whom the social mission is built; customers (e.g. customers buying fair trade products to benefit marginalized communities); and other stakeholders such as government, employees and communities.

Thus far, we have identified that social entrepreneurship is an approach to solving social and environmental needs and that SEs are hybrid organizations that balance a social mission alongside financial sustainability. Nevertheless, a review of the literature reveals the broad and diverse nature of the field, which can be categorized into two schools of thought: the innovation and hybrid schools of thought.

## Schools of thought

Despite growing interest from policymakers and scholars (Peattie and Morley, 2008; Roper and Cheney, 2005), the concept of social entrepreneurship remains ill-defined, with multiple conceptualizations (Peredo and Mclean, 2006; Weerawardena and Sullivan Mort, 2006). The most-used/useful conceptualizations have been categorized into two schools of thought, as we will now explore.

### *The social innovation school of thought*

This school of thought is deeply rooted in the work of Joseph Schumpeter (1947), who emphasized the 'unique' innovative characteristics of profit-oriented (commercial) entrepreneurs in identifying and exploiting entrepreneurial opportunities. According to Schumpeter, entrepreneurs are best defined as 'innovators' who disrupt the economic equilibrium by introducing novel products or services, production processes, organizational structures or markets that replace the older models. This brings us to his concept of 'Creative Destruction', which underscores the role entrepreneurs play as economic agents who are capable of creating innovative solutions that disrupt existing ones – take, for example, Netflix's subscription-based model disrupting Blockbuster's traditional brick-and-mortar business model. Innovation then is a critical component of entrepreneurship, crucial to building the competitive advantage and growth of organizations (Crossan and Apaydin, 2010; Lewrick et al, 2010).

Building on Schumpeter's definition of entrepreneurs as 'disruptive innovators', social entrepreneurs use their unique characteristics to play a pivotal role in developing innovative approaches to address pressing social and environmental challenges (Dees, 2001; Giovany, 2014; Mulgan, 2012; Phills et al, 2008). Bill Drayton, for instance – founder of Ashoka Innovators for the Public and credited with coining the term 'social entrepreneurship' – defines social entrepreneurs as powerful change agents who can make a positive difference in organizations, communities and countries, and who can catalyse social change by using their unique innovative characteristics (Ashoka, 2014).

The social innovation school of thought is thus built on the premise that social entrepreneurs are 'agents of change' who develop innovative approaches to social problems. This view is championed by both scholars and US-based organizations. Waddock and Post (1991), for instance, define social entrepreneurs as individuals who bring catalytic social change to the public sector agenda. In their study, they describe the 1980s 'Hands Across America' fundraising event as an action that was catalysed by social agents to bring awareness to social issues such as hunger and rough sleeping, which captured public attention and influenced social policies in the United States. Leadbeater (1997) argued similarly that social entrepreneurship emerged as a response to social needs that have been unmet by traditional welfare systems and therefore that social entrepreneurs play a critical role in innovating new welfare services and new ways of delivering these. Dees (2001), as pointed out in the following Key Research box, provides another definition of social entrepreneurs as 'rare breeds' and change agents.

### KEY RESEARCH

J. Gregory Dees – definition of the social entrepreneur

Dees (2001) describes social entrepreneurs as 'rare breeds' and change agents who play a critical role in developing innovative solutions to the increasingly complex social problems which state institutions have failed to address. He defines social entrepreneurs as those who:

- adopt a mission to create and sustain social value (not just private value)
- recognize and relentlessly pursue new opportunities to serve that mission
- engage in the process of continuous innovation, adaptation and learning
- act boldly without being limited by the resources currently at hand
- exhibit heightened accountability to the constituencies serviced and for the outcomes created

(Dees, 2001: 4).

Reflective questions:

1. What do you think are the main characteristics of social entrepreneurs as described by Dees?
2. What is the role of innovation in solving societal and/or environmental challenges?
3. What does accountability mean in this context?

Other global awarding organizations, such as the Skoll Foundation and the Schwab Foundation for Social Entrepreneurship, support social innovators worldwide and promote social entrepreneurship as an innovative approach to social problems. Muhammed Yunus, for instance, the founder of the Grameen Bank and Nobel Prize winner in 2006, is perceived as a social innovator who pioneered the concept of micro-financing as a revolutionary solution to the rampant poverty in rural Bangladesh.

In contrast to the hybrid school of thought, the social innovation school of thought takes a broader understanding of social entrepreneurship as a general process that develops innovative approaches to social and environmental challenges. Crucially, this process can be found in all types of organizations regardless of their legal or organizational structure (Dees, 2001; Johnson, 2000; Mair and Martí, 2006; Mulgan, 2012; Roper and Cheney, 2005). Social entrepreneurs exist, therefore, not only within SEs that adopt a hybrid structure, balancing a social mission with revenue-generating activities (Battilana and Lee, 2014), but also within 'profit-for-shareholders' organizations that are committed to doing social good as part of their CSR mission (see Chapter 5) but otherwise seek to maximize profit, as well as in NFPs that serve public interests and advocate social causes (see Chapter 8).

## The hybrid school of thought

The emergence of the hybrid school of thought has been driven by the increasing social and environmental problems that, the school argues, can only be solved through hybrid SEs that balance social and business objectives (Haigh et al, 2015). These organizations balance a social mission with for-profit trading activities to generate revenue and meet social objectives (Doherty et al, 2014; Defourny and Nyssens, 2010; Dacin and Dacin, 2011; Dacin et al, 2010; Saebi et al, 2019). In this context, SEs generate income and attract financial capital in ways that may be consistent with 'profit for shareholder' organizations. However, as explained earlier, despite the fact that 'profit for shareholder' organizations support social causes as part of their CSR mission, their primary purpose is to maximize shareholder value and private wealth (Cornforth, 2014; Martin and Osberg, 2007; Swanson and Di Zhang, 2010; Weerawardena and Sullivan Mort, 2006 – see more in Chapter 5).

In contrast, SEs differ from 'profit-for-shareholder' organizations due to their dual logic: a social mission alongside financial sustainability. This enables them to focus more completely on their social mission. The Big Issue, for instance (see Chapter 2), is a hybrid social enterprise that supports rough sleepers to improve their social and economic inclusion by selling the *Big Issue* magazine for a profit. However, the Big Issue adopts enterprising practices by generating revenues through the sales of the magazine to vendors as well as social trading.

In summary, both schools of thought have enhanced our understanding of social entrepreneurship. While the social innovation school emphasizes the role social entrepreneurs play in developing innovative approaches to social and/or environmental challenges, the hybrid school focuses on the dual objectives of SEs – that is, balancing a social mission with financial sustainability.

## Alternative research streams

Significant contributions have also been made in our understanding of the unique traits of social entrepreneurs that differentiate them from their commercial

(Schumpeterian) counterparts (see Chapter 3) (Austin et al, 2006). Social and commercial entrepreneurs both share common characteristics like innovativeness, creativity, proactivity, internal locus of control (a concept developed by Rotter (1966), referring to a person's perception of events in their lives as being the result of their own actions as opposed to luck, chance or fate), and self-efficacy (a person's belief that outcomes are dependent on their own judgement of how well they are able to perform a specific behaviour – see the work of Bandura (1977)) (Santos et al, 2021; Tiwari et al, 2020; To et al, 2020). However, social entrepreneurs are uniquely characterized by their salient prosocial characteristics, defined as the innate tendency to act for the benefit of others. These characteristics include empathy, altruism, compassion, moral and social responsibility, and integrity and honesty (Bacq and Alt, 2018; Bacq and Janssen, 2011; Douglas et al, 2021; Douglas and Prentice, 2019; Ernst, 2011; Mair and Noboa, 2006; Ip et al, 2021). Further studies demonstrate how personal attitudes and prior experience with social problems are unique characteristics of social entrepreneurs (Bacq et al, 2014; Cavazos-Arroyo et al, 2016; Hockerts, 2015, 2017).

Further research has also explored the influence of socio-economic, political and cultural contexts in fostering and enabling the growth of SEs (Canestrino et al, 2022; Haugh and Talwar, 2016; Ho and Yoon, 2022; Urban and Kujinga, 2017). These will be explored later in the textbook but include the broader economic activities of SEs (see Chapter 12), such as social financing (e.g. social impact investing) (Hochstader and Scheck, 2015) and the interplay between SEs and the 17 Sustainable Development Goals (SDGs) developed by the United Nations, highlighting how more and more SEs are solving social and environmental challenges related to SDG goals (Belz and Binder, 2017).

Further threads in the literature, as will be discussed in Chapters 7, 8 and 9, explore social entrepreneurship as an organizational activity by focusing on the process by which a social enterprise is created, including the role social entrepreneurs play in recognizing a social need in the market (pre-start-up stage), creating a hybrid social enterprise that balances a social mission with for-profit trading activities (start-up stage), and generating social value (post-start-up stage) (Cherrier et al, 2017; Di Domenico et al, 2010; Saebi et al, 2019; Zahra et al, 2009).

All of these concepts will be examined further in the textbook. However, despite these multiple interpretations, a common theme emerges: the concept of social value creation and the extent to which social entrepreneurship is a process that involves the development of innovative approaches to social and environmental challenges (Dees, 1998; Johnson, 2000; Peredo and McClean, 2006). To further understand how social entrepreneurship has evolved, it is important to look at its historical origin during the time of the English Industrial Revolution, in which social welfare practices formed the base of modern social entrepreneurship.

## The Industrial Revolution as a catalyst for social entrepreneurialism

Debates on the new ways of doing business often involve exploring the emergence of innovative social solutions that address social and/or environmental challenges alongside financial sustainability. Nevertheless, to fully understand the evolution of social entrepreneurship, we believe it is critical to explore how the English IR (1760–1840) played a role in catalysing movements that sought to tackle social change. Although the specific interest in social entrepreneurship arose in the 21st century, when looking at the definition in its broadest sense – developing innovative approaches to social and environmental problems – it is clear that it can apply to a wide range of traditional charitable practices which existed before (Defourny and Nyssens, 2010; McGowan and Westley, 2015; Peattie and Morley, 2008).

The English IR has been heralded as a period of significant progress, bringing about improvements in living standards (Pitman, 2018) such as increased employment opportunities, urbanization and advances in birth and life expectancy rates. Transitions from traditional farming systems to modern manufacturing processes have also contributed to efficiency, optimization and workplace productivity (Clark, 2001). Alongside these improvements, however, a range of social and environmental challenges were caused by industrialization (Flinn, 1984; Feinstein, 1998). For instance, the rapid urban migration of the working classes (mainly weavers, agricultural labourers and home-based micro-enterprises) led to them experiencing harsh working conditions, inadequate housing, poor nutrition, diseases and lower wages, which exacerbated income disparity and deepened the divide between social classes (Ashton, 1964; Crafts, 1985; Horrel, 1996; Williamson, 1984). Additionally, the expansion of factories in urban areas caused environmental pollution, which posed a health risk for the working classes who migrated in search of employment opportunities.

Due to the above challenges, social welfare provisions such as cooperatives, mutual societies, charities and philanthropic donations (Cornforth, 2003; Defourny and Nyssens, 2010) emerged as a response to social challenges that had not been met by traditional public service providers (Checkland, 1964; Owen, 1966), laying the foundations of modern social entrepreneurship. Of special interest is the cooperative movement, which was both a significant part of and contributor to the evolution of social entrepreneurship (Cornforth, 2003).

### The cooperative movement

In response to the harsh working conditions and lower wages that the new urban working class faced, cooperatives were formed to address their needs through collective actions. The Rochdale Society of Equitable Pioneers, for instance, was founded in 1844 by the social reformer Robert Owen (see Stop and Think box). It was the first cooperative to be formed (Thompson, 1994), and its membership consisted of 28 weavers and skilled workers based in Rochdale, Lancashire (UK) who owned and democratically controlled the cooperative, establishing a structure that continues to this day (Bailly et al, 2017; Perotin, 2012). The Rochdale Pioneers set up their first shop in the local community to sell affordable food and essential goods to support their local members. Additionally, they developed a set of cooperative principles, which included:

- open membership
- democratic control
- distribution of surplus in proportion to trade
- payment of limited interest on capital
- political and religious neutrality
- cash trading (no credit)
- promotion of education

(Ridley-Duff and Bull, 2011)

### STOP AND THINK

The Rochdale Pioneers – the birth of the consumer cooperative in the UK

Raising a capital of £28 (£1 contributed by each of the founding members), the Rochdale Pioneers developed an alternative form of business designed to serve the interests of its members. Members of the cooperative contributed by paying weekly subscription fees of approximately two to three pennies (50–70p in modern British pounds), and in turn they were compensated based on their transactions with the cooperative. Profits were shared in the form of dividends, with members receiving interest on their capital and dividends based on their purchases. This practice of paying dividends on purchases is a defining feature of cooperatives, distinguishing them from any other types of businesses.

Reflective question:

- Visit Table 1.3 and explain how the cooperative's form of dividends is different to SEs.

The cooperative movement quickly spread throughout Europe, leading to the formation of several other types of cooperatives across various countries. These included 'agriculture cooperatives', 'finance cooperatives', 'utilities cooperatives', 'health and social care cooperatives', 'cooperative schools', 'retail and food cooperatives', 'cooperative housing providers' and 'marketing cooperatives' (often used by farmers and artists). It was in Italy during the 1970s–1980s, however, that the cooperative movement took an especially strong hold, growing to play a pivotal role in the evolution of social entrepreneurship as a field of both research and practice in the 21st century.

During the 1970s Italy experienced a range of social challenges such as rising unemployment rates, drug addiction and homelessness, due to the oil crisis and slow economic growth. These growing social needs outstripped the capacity of traditional welfare systems and charitable actions to provide the relevant support for those affected. In response, the Italian government introduced a new legal structure for cooperatives, known as 'social solidarity cooperatives'. These cooperatives were designed to promote social integration, deliver social services and create employment opportunities for those disadvantaged (Vangen et al, 2014; Warhurst and Darr, 2006). Within this legal structure, a distinction was made between Type A and Type B cooperatives. Type A focused primarily on delivering social, health and educational support, often supported by the national solidarity funds. Type B cooperatives, however, can adopt a social enterprise status, benefiting from trading as a means to achieve their social mission, enabling a degree of independence from a struggling government. These social cooperatives were typically characterized by the following principles:

- managing social, healthcare and educational services
- providing employment opportunities for the disadvantaged
- democratic governance with a 'one person, one vote' rule
- partial non-profit distribution constraint: cannot distribute 70 per cent of their overall profits/surplus
- pursuit of the general interests of the community rather than individual members

This cooperative legal structure is therefore one of the first modern examples of an organization which balances collective actions and the social well-being of its members and community with the wider structural need for economic sustainability. Like these cooperatives, SEs also address social and environmental challenges and prioritize social value creation over profit. However, the distinction lies in the degree to which SEs integrate business logics into their organizational structure. While cooperatives, especially influenced by the traditions of the Rochdale Pioneers, tend to emphasize members' welfare with a democratic structure, SEs adopt business practices by trading goods and services to sustain themselves financially in the pursuit of their social mission (Bagnoli and Megali, 2011; Borgaza and Defourny, 2001). And it was precisely this greater structural incorporation of business logics that enabled SEs to address social needs unmet by governments and NFPs during a time of crisis, resulting in their growth and development in the rest of Europe.

## Emergence of social entrepreneurship in Europe

During the same time and continuing on through the 1990s, governments across Europe began to promote a shift in public service provision, seeking to offload the tasks of social and economic development onto external socially driven organizations (Ridley-Duff and Bull, 2011; European Union, 2015). A number of interrelated factors contributed to this, including increased urbanization and industrialization, alongside the rising costs of welfare provision, prompting governments to view these organizations as playing a role in delivering health and social care services. Although the interpretations of social organizations vary across Europe, they are broadly described as any organizational structure which serves the public interest, is independent of government control and operates on a not-for-profit basis (European Union, 2015). This encompasses a wide range of organizations, including charities, cooperatives, foundations, mutual associations, NGOs, grassroots groups, activist groups, faith-based organizations and SEs (World Economic Forum, 2013; VanDyck, 2017). Despite their diversity, these organizations are united in promoting social good, providing services for those underserved and promoting active citizenship (European Union, 2015).

While SEs are seen as part of the broader category of socially driven organizations, they have distinctive characteristics as already outlined in this chapter. SEs are built on dual objectives: balancing a social mission with financial sustainability. This means they operate independently and do not rely on government subsidies and philanthropic donations. Due to the growing pressure on state welfare systems, the comparative freedom of SEs prompted European governments to view them as a potential solution for addressing socio-economic challenges through innovative and sustainable solutions, such as tackling poverty and social exclusion, empowering underserved communities and fostering inclusive growth (European Union, 2015; Ridley-Duff and Bull, 2011).

As outlined in the Expert View box that follows, the UK government, for instance, perceived SEs as a vehicle to effectively deliver public services and address pressing social needs through market-based mechanisms (Cornforth, 2003; Defourny and Nyssens, 2010). The shift away from government welfare and towards a more market-oriented culture in the UK began under Conservative Prime Minister (PM) Margaret Thatcher (1975–1990), who reduced spending on social services such as education and housing and pursued a policy of privatization (Dodd and Anderson, 2001). However, it was during the New Labour Government under PM Tony Blair (1997–2007) that

SEs gained increased prominence for their potential in addressing social needs and building social capacity (Amin et al, 2002). In 2001 the Social Enterprise Coalition, led by the School of Social Entrepreneurs (SSE), Co-ops UK, Social Firm UK and the Development Trust Association (DTA), coined the term 'social enterprise' and advocated for its inclusion in the Small Business Service (SBS) – an initiative established by the Department of Trade and Industry (DTI) in 2000 aimed at providing business support services and promoting the role of small businesses within government (Dorey and Garnett, 2012).

By 2002, policy interest in SEs had risen, leading to the launch of the New Labour strategy titled 'Social Enterprise: A Strategy for Success'. Tony Blair emphasized the government's commitment to supporting the social enterprise sector to benefit the public (DTI, 2002). As part of its social policy agenda, the UK government identified specific areas where SEs could make significant contributions. These included driving competitiveness and economic productivity, creating wealth through sustainable economic activity, regenerating and revitalizing communities, reforming and delivering public services, and promoting social and financial inclusion (DTI, 2002).

**EXPERT VIEW**

Characteristics of social enterprises as defined by the UK government

The UK government defines an SE as a business with primarily social objectives whose surpluses are principally reinvested for that purpose in the business or in the community, rather than being driven by the need to maximize profits for shareholders and owners. SEs are characterized as follows:

- autonomous organizations through trading
- possess entrepreneurial, innovative and risk-taking behaviour
- adopt flexible and adaptable practices
- maintain focus on customers and communities
- promote stakeholder engagement
- encourage democratic participation
- deliver social, environmental and financial benefits through financially viable solutions by generating income through the sale of goods and products

(DTI, 2002: 16)

This interest in SEs continued to evolve with the introduction of a new Community Interest Company (CIC) legal structure in 2005 (see the next section). Community Development Finance Initiatives (CDFIs) were also established to further support the sector. For instance, under PM David Cameron (2010–2016), Big Society Capital (a wholesale bank) was launched in 2012, with £600 million in capital to help small-to-medium-sized charities and SEs access funding. Furthermore, Social Investment Tax Reliefs and Social Impact Bonds were introduced to attract private investments into social projects.

It is clear, then, that SEs are perceived as an innovative approach to addressing social challenges due to their market-based mechanisms (Di Domenico et al, 2010) and ability to bypass traditional needs for governmental funding. Nevertheless, due to the proximity of SEs to traditional profit-making organizations, a need for structures that ensured they remained focused on their social mission became crucial.

## *Reconciling social value creation with economic value creation*

As noted, profit-for-shareholder organizations contribute to social good through CSR practices. However, their primary mission remains directed at maximizing shareholder value (Brackman-Reiser, 2013; Swanson and DiZhang, 2010; Zahra et al, 2009). Consequently, these organizations are often measured according to their financial performance and metrics, such as sales, profits, returns on investment, market value and share prices. In contrast, SEs often face challenges in evaluating and measuring their social performance due to the complexities of the social problems being addressed (Buckland and Hehenberger, 2021). In addition, since they exist at the intersection of for-profit (market-driven) and not-for-profit (i.e. mission-driven), they often face tensions in balancing their social and business objectives. So-called 'mission drift' occurs when the business objectives are given priority over the social mission, or, less commonly, vice versa, when the social mission dominates at the expense of business objectives (Battilana and Lee, 2014; Cornforth, 2014; Haigh et al, 2015; Sabeti, 2011). There are several approaches that seek to help SEs avoid mission drift, with one such approach being the theory of change (ToC), as explored in the research box below.

**KEY RESEARCH**

The Theory of Change (ToC), which was first developed by Weiss in 1997, indicates that purpose-driven organizations, including SEs, are required to demonstrate how their intervention(s), (that is, the programme of activities aimed at supporting beneficiaries), lead to the intended social or environmental outcomes (Rogers, 2008).

The ToC involves mapping how inputs such as financial, physical and intellectual resources help support the SE's interventions, such as providing food, shelter and upskilling opportunities, all of which will result in short-term outputs for the beneficiaries. This is typically measured by the number of beneficiaries being served. Subsequently, these short-term outputs are expected, over time, to deliver long-term outcomes such as increased income, improved health and better social inclusion (Bickman, 1987; Chen and Rossi, 1983).

Of equal importance is the legal structure, which not only determines the orientation of a social enterprise – i.e. not-for-profit or hybrid – but also creates legal safeguards that help prevent mission drift, as discussed below.

## Legal structures for social enterprises

As we will further explore in Chapter 2, the stakeholder theory, which was first introduced by Freeman (1984), posits that the primary responsibility of corporations is to create value for all stakeholders beyond making profits (Carroll, 1991; Carroll and Shabana, 2010; Freeman,1984). Stakeholders, in this context, are defined as any group or individual who can affect or is affected by the corporation's actions, creating a broad group that includes, for instance, the board of directors, communities, employees, customers, political groups, trade unions, suppliers, lenders, government bodies and shareholders (Freeman, 1984; Phillips, 2003).

SEs therefore align closely with Freeman's stakeholder perspective, as they are primarily driven by meeting the needs of their beneficiaries (a key stakeholder in their social logic) alongside their financial sustainability (the business logic) (Battilana and Lee, 2014; Ebrahim et al, 2014; Mair and Martí, 2006; Mulgan, 2012). To accommodate this dual logic, many governments across European countries have taken active steps to introduce legal structures specifically designed to meet the needs of hybrid SEs (Santos et al, 2015), as noted in Table 1.2.

**Table 1.2** Examples of legal structures in Europe

| Country | Legal Framework |
|---|---|
| Belgium | **Société à Finalité Sociale** (social purpose company): incorporated into the 'Codes des Sociétés' in 1999. |
| Spain | **Cooperativa de Initiativa Social** (social initiative co-operative): established under law 27 in 1999, requires SEs to have a cooperative legal form to address unmet social needs. |

*(continued)*

**Table 1.2** (Continued)

| Country | Legal Framework |
|---|---|
| Italy | **Social Cooperatives**: Regulated since 1991. Includes:<br>• **A-Type Social Cooperatives:** focus on managing social, educational and healthcare services.<br>• **B-Type Social Cooperatives:** focus on work integration for disadvantaged individuals (e.g. former drug and alcohol addicts, prisoners and people with disabilities). Disadvantaged individuals must make up at least 30 per cent of the workforce, with their employment being the cooperative's primary mission. |
| France | **Société Coopérative d'Intérêt Collectif:** introduced in 2019, along with a new legal framework called 'Enterprise à Mission' (Enterprise with a Mission), allowing for-profit organizations to integrate social and environmental goals into their corporate structure. |
| Greece | **Koinonikos Syneterismos Periorismenis Eufthinis, KoiSPE:** (Limited Liability Social Cooperative): introduced in 2016, with criteria including one-member-one-vote decision making, profit distribution restrictions and limits on wage workers. |
| Finland | Recognizes any corporate legal form provided that the organization's social purpose is to offer employment to people with disabilities and those facing long-term unemployment. |

Adapted from various sources (Z. Djebali)

The UK, for instance, was one of the first European countries to regulate hybrid SEs by introducing the 'Community Interest Company' (CIC) legal structure in 2005. While a CIC legal structure is similar to a standard private limited company, which provides some advantages such as limited liability and payment of shares and dividends, it is subject to two specific legal and financial requirements to safeguard the social mission. These include:

- An 'asset lock', which restricts the transfer of assets to any private individuals or organizations. Instead, all assets must be transferred to organizations with a social purpose, such as a charity or another CIC.
- Capped dividends at approximately 35 per cent of distributable profits (Brackman-Reiser, 2013) to ensure that the surpluses are reinvested back into the business.

This specific CIC structure is but one of a range of other legal structures existing within the UK context (see Table 1.3), and the use of these structures depends on whether a social enterprise adopts a charitable model or a hybrid structure that includes the generation of revenues.

Some social enterprises operate without a legal structure, such as sole traders or self-employed and membership bodies (i.e. voluntary associations or community groups). However, these types of organizations have to navigate some of the drawbacks of unincorporated structures, particularly the personal liability of the founders or members for any debts incurred (UnLtd, 2024, see Table 1.3). Choosing an appropriate legal structure therefore offers several benefits: it enables SEs to meet the requirements of their stakeholder groups and protects the personal liability of founders in case of debts. The following are the most common existing legal structures within a UK context:

- **Unincorporated association (UA)** (can also be registered as a charity): This is a membership organization that is often led by voting members who determine its activities, such as a voluntary group or a sports club. This structure is ideal for small-scale enterprises that have no staff members and is regarded as the most simplistic since it is not regulated by the Charity Law. Nevertheless, UAs are often governed by a constitution that outlines their operational rules.
- **Company Limited by Guarantee (CLG)** (can also be registered as a charity): A CLG is incorporated and can be founded for charitable purposes with voting members. This structure does not allow income distribution to shareholders to ensure that all profits are reinvested back into the organization. It is regulated by Companies House, and hence it is legally bound to submit a governing document known as the 'Memorandum and Articles of Association'.
- **Company Limited by Shares (CLS):** A CLS is a corporate entity that is legally separate from any directors or shareholders. The term 'limited' often refers to shareholders' limited liability, as they are only responsible for the company's debt up to the value of their shares within the company. This legal structure is commonly used in profit-for-shareholder organizations that must file their governing document, known as the 'Articles of Association', to Companies House, as prescribed by the Companies Act 2006.
- **Industrial and Provident Society (IPS):** An IPS is owned and democratically controlled by its members. Profits generated by an IPS must be reinvested for community benefits; however, members can benefit from shares and interests. An IPS can register as a charity with the Financial Conduct Authority provided it has charitable aims and an asset lock to ensure all assets are transferred to another charity upon dissolution. This structure is particularly useful for communities that aim to manage some assets (e.g. buildings) and are typically funded through the sale of community shares.
- **Community Interest Company (CIC):** A CIC is a limited company which operates to benefit the community it serves. Hence, a CIC operates like any other limited company with a separate legal entity and is able to enter into contracts, own

assets, raise funds and directors can be paid and have similar rights and duties as any other directors. Nevertheless, CICs are subject to asset locks as explained above and regulated by both Companies House and CIC regulators.

## Summary and key learning points

This chapter began by exploring the definitional debates related to social entrepreneurship and identifying its key characteristics. We then discussed the two schools of thought: the social innovation school emphasizes the role social entrepreneurs play in developing innovative approaches to social and environmental challenges, and, hence, social entrepreneurship can exist in all types of organizations, including

**Table 1.3** Comparison of legal structures for your social enterprise

| Legal Structure | Key Features | Advantages | Disadvantages |
|---|---|---|---|
| Unincorporated Association (Voluntary/ community Associations) | • No legal incorporation.<br>• No distinct legal entity separate from members.<br>• Popular among voluntary and community associations.<br>• Governed by a constitution or the association rules. | • Simple governance.<br>• Not regulated by Companies House.<br>• Simple to set up and administer.<br>• Can own premises. | • Members personally liable for any debts incurred by the association.<br>• Potential corporation tax obligations and filing of tax return. |
| Registered Charity (Unincorporated Association) | • Must be registered with the Charity Commission.<br>• Must serve 1 or more of the 12 pre-determined charitable purposes and must benefit the community.<br>• Governed by a volunteer board of trustees. | • Facilitates fundraising activities from trusts or corporations.<br>• Potential tax exemptions and reliefs. | • Subject to additional regulations in exchange for tax benefits.<br>• Trustees cannot be paid but may be reimbursed for out-of-pocket expenses.<br>• Potential restriction on trading and entrepreneurial activities. |

*(continued)*

**Table 1.3** (Continued)

| Legal Structure | Key Features | Advantages | Disadvantages |
|---|---|---|---|
| Company Limited by Guarantee | • Common among the social sector.<br>• Governed by board of directors.<br>• Members' liability is limited to a specified amount (as little as £1).<br>• Separate legal entity, reducing personal liability for members/ directors (except in cases of fraud or mismanagement).<br>• Must register with Companies House and comply with annual reporting requirements.<br>• Can be incorporated with a single member. | • Separate legal entity from members and board of directors.<br>• Permitted to own premises and hold contracts.<br>• Directors can be paid. | • Subject to regulations by Companies House.<br>• Increased responsibility for the board of directors.<br>• Lack of asset protection without an asset lock. |
| Registered Charity (Company Limited by Guarantee) | • Must register with the Charity Commission.<br>• Must fulfil 1 or more of 12 pre-determined charitable purposes, and must benefit the community.<br>• Governed by a board of trustees. | • Facilitates fundraising/ access to grants/ corporation donations.<br>• Separate legal entity from members and directors.<br>• Can own property and hold contracts.<br>• Benefits of charitable status with limited liability.<br>• Potential tax exemptions and reliefs. | • Subject to dual regulations: Companies House and the Charity Commission.<br>• Trustees cannot be compensated beyond out-of-pocket expenses.<br>• Potential restrictions on trading and entrepreneurial activities. |

*(continued)*

**Table 1.3** (Continued)

| Legal Structure | Key Features | Advantages | Disadvantages |
|---|---|---|---|
| Company Limited by Shares | • Primarily used by corporate private entities.<br>• Governed by a board of directors.<br>• No limitations on dividends paid to shareholders.<br>• Members/ shareholders liability limited to their contributions, often as little as £1.<br>• Separate legal entity, reducing liability (except in cases of fraud and mismanagement).<br>• Must register with Companies House and comply with annual reporting.<br>• Can be incorporated with a single member. | • Attractive investment model due to potential shareholder dividends.<br>• Promotes entrepreneurial drive that benefits shareholders.<br>• Directors can be paid.<br>• Separate legal entity.<br>• Can own property or hold contracts. | • Regulated by Companies House.<br>• Potential conflicts between social objectives and shareholders' interests.<br>• Increased responsibility for directors.<br>• Self-financing model may limit fundraising through grants and donations.<br>• Unlike CIC, assets are not protected. |
| Industrial & Provident Society | • Typically used by cooperatives.<br>• Owned and operated by members.<br>• Can own property, enter into contracts, issue shares and take out loans.<br>• Regulated by the Financial Service Authority (FSA). | • Promotes democratic ownership and decision making.<br>• A separate legal entity from members. | • Less suitable for organizations with hierarchical structure.<br>• Limited recognition as a legal structure.<br>• Requires adherence to FSA formalities including filing accounts. |

*(continued)*

**Table 1.3** (Continued)

| Legal Structure | Key Features | Advantages | Disadvantages |
|---|---|---|---|
| Community Interest Company | • Can be a private company limited by guarantee or shares or public limited.<br>• May adopt cooperative, non-for-profit, or a commercial model.<br>• Must pass a community interest test to ensure it serves the community and manages profits appropriately.<br>• Subject to an asset lock to ensure it is not controlled by members.<br>• Must submit an annual community interest report with its accounts.<br>• CICs limited by shares may pay dividends but are subject to a cap. | • Distinct identity as an SE.<br>• Balances a social mission with for profit trading activities.<br>• Encourages democratic ownership, entrepreneurial activities.<br>• Protected by an asset lock.<br>• Directors can be paid.<br>• A separate legal entity from members.<br>• Enables property ownership and contract management. | • Subject to dual regulations: Companies Act and CIC Regulators.<br>• Increased responsibility for directors.<br>• Not suitable for non-SEs.<br>• Due to the trading arm, it may face potential to attract donations/grants.<br>• Cap on dividends may deter potential investors. |

(Adapted from various sources: UnLtd, 2024 and www.gov.uk: A Guide to Social Forms for Social Enterprise)

SEs. The hybrid school focuses on the hybrid structure of SEs in balancing a social mission with financial sustainability and is more specifically focused on the unique characteristics of SEs. We also considered the historical context by discussing the role of the English Industrial Revolution in catalysing social change movements and the corresponding rise of the cooperative movement as a response to social needs unmet by governments/public service providers. This historical development laid the ground for the evolution of modern social entrepreneurship in Europe. Finally, we reviewed the most common legal structures available for SEs.

The key takeaways are the following:

- Social entrepreneurship is a multifaceted concept, with multiple definitions and conceptualizations.

- Despite multiple definitions, SEs are often characterized by their explicit social mission, enterprising behaviour and multiagency.
- The social innovation school emphasizes the role of social entrepreneurs in developing innovative approaches to social and environmental problems.
- The hybrid school emphasizes the dual logic of social enterprises: blending a social mission with for-profit trading activities.
- The English IR played a key role in driving social change with the emergence of the cooperative movement as a mechanism for solving social needs, which laid the foundation for the evolution of social entrepreneurship.
- A variety of legal structures exist for SEs, but these are dependent on their overall social mission and approach to income generation. While some favour a charitable structure with limited trading, others may adopt a hybrid structure that balances a social mission with financial sustainability.

## References

Amin, A, Cameron, A and Hudson, R (2002) *Placing the Social Economy*, London: Routledge.

Ashoka (2014) https://www.ashoka.org/en-gb/about-ashoka (archived at https://perma.cc/U9NK-H8UV)

Ashton, T S (1964) *The Industrial Revolution, 1760-1830*, New York: Oxford University Press

Austin, J, Stevenson, H and Wei-Skillern, J (2006) Social and commercial entrepreneurship: Same, different or both? *Entrepreneurship: Theory and Practice*, 30: 1–22

Bacq, S and Alt, E (2018) Feeling capable and valued: a prosocial perspective on the link between empathy and social entrepreneurial intentions, *Journal of Business Venturing*, 33 (3): 333–50

Bacq, S, Hartog, C and Hoogendoorn, B (2014) Beyond the moral portrayal of social entrepreneurs: an empirical approach to who they are and what drives them, *Journal of Business Ethics*, 133: 703–18

Bacq, S and Janssen, F (2011) The multiple faces of social entrepreneurship: A review of definitional issues based on geographical and thematic criteria, *Entrepreneurship & Regional Development*, 23(5–6): 373–403

Bagnoli, L and Megali, C (2011) Measuring performance in social enterprises, *Nonprofit and Voluntary Sector Quarterly*, 40(1): 149–65

Bailly, F, Chapelle, K and Prouteau, L (2017) Wage differentials between conventional firms and non-worker cooperatives: Analysis of evidence from France, *Competition & Change*, 21(4), 321–41

Bandura, A (1977) *Social Learning Theory*, Englewood Cliffs, NJ: Prentice Hall

Battilana, J and Lee, M (2014) Advancing research on hybrid organizing – insights from the study of social enterprises, *Academy of Management Annals*, 8(1): 397–441

Belz, F M and Binder, J K (2017) Sustainable entrepreneurship: A convergent process model, *Business Strategy and the Environment*, 26(1): 1–17

Bickman, L (1987) The functions of program theory, *Evaluation and Artificial Intelligence*, 33: 5–18

Borgaza, C and Defourny, J (2001) *The Emergence of Social Enterprise*, London: Routledge

Bornstein, D and Davis, S (2010) *Social Entrepreneurship: What everyone needs to know*, UK: Oxford University Press

Brackman-Reiser, D (2010) Blended enterprise and the dual mission dilemma, *Vermont Law Review*, 35: 105–16

Brackman-Reiser, D (2013) Governing and financing blended enterprise, *Chicago-Kent Law Review*, 85(2): 619–55

Buckland, L and Hehenberger, L (2021) Measuring social impact can help foster a stronger European social economy, *Stanford Social Innovation Review*, https://doi.org/10.48558/T7W2-YR13 (archived at https://perma.cc/7AMR-Q2VC)

Canestrino, R, Magliocca, P, Cwiklicki, M and Pawelek, B (2022) Toward the emergence of 'Humane' entrepreneurial ecosystems: Evidence from different cultural contexts, *Journal of Intellectual Capital*, 24(1): 177–204

Carroll, A B (1991) The pyramid of corporate social responsibility: Toward the moral management of organizational stakeholders, *Business Horizons*, 34(4): 39–48

Carroll, A B and Shabana, K M (2010) The business case for corporate social responsibility: A review of concepts, research and practice, *International Journal of Management Reviews*, 12(1): 85–105

Cavazos-Arroyo, J, Puente-Diaz, R and Agarwal, N (2016) An examination of certain antecedents of social entrepreneurial intentions among Mexico residents, *Review of Business Management*, 19(64): 180–99

Chahine, T (2016) *Introduction to Social Entrepreneurship*, UK: Routledge

Checkland, S G (1964) The British industrial city as history: the Glasgow Case, *Urban Studies*, 1(1): 34–54

Chen, H T and Rossi, P H (1983) Evaluating with sense: The theory-driven approach, *Evaluation Review*, 7(3): 283–302

Cherrier, H, Goswami, P and Ray, S (2017) Social entrepreneurship: Creating value in the context of institutional complexity, *Journal of Business Research*, 86: 245–58

Clark, G (2001) The Secret History of the Industrial Revolution, https://www.researchgate.net/publication/228800335_The_secret_history_of_the_Industrial_Revolution (archived at https://perma.cc/28G7-3BZR)

Collavo, T (2022) *Foundations of Social Entrepreneurship: Theory, practical tools and skills*, London: Routledge

Cornforth, C (2003) *The Governance of Public and Non-Profit Organizations*, London: Routledge

Cornforth, C (2014) Understanding and combating mission drift in social enterprises, *Social Enterprise Journal*, 10(1): 3–20

Crafts, N F R (1985) *British Economic Growth During the Industrial Revolution*, New York: Oxford University Press

Crossan, M M and Apaydin, M (2010) A multi-dimensional framework of organizational innovation: a systematic literature review of the literature, *Journal of Management Studies*, 47(6): 1154–91

Dacin, M T and Dacin, P A (2011) Social entrepreneurship: A critique and future directions, *Organization Science*, 22(5): 1203–13

Dacin, P A, Dacin, M T and Matear, M (2010) Social entrepreneurship: Why we don't need a new theory and how we move forward from here, *Academy of Management Perspectives*, 24(3): 37–57

Dees, G (1998) The meaning of social entrepreneurship. Paper funded by the Kauffman Center for Entrepreneurial Leadership, https://web.stanford.edu/class/e145/2007_fall/materials/dees_SE.pdf (archived at https://perma.cc/WC53-G827)

Dees, J G (2001) The Meaning of 'Social Entrepreneurship', Centre for the Advancement of Social Entrepreneurship, https://case.fuqua.duke.edu/knowledge_items/the-meaning-of-social-entrepreneurship/ (archived at https://perma.cc/PN2Q-EM2P)

Dees, J G and Elias, J (1998) The challenges of combining social and commercial enterprise, *Business Ethics Quarterly*, 8(1): 165–78

Defourny, J and Nyssens, M (2010) Conceptions of social enterprise and social entrepreneurship in Europe and the United States: Convergences and divergences, *Journal of Social Entrepreneurship*, 1: 32–53

Department of Trade and Industry (2002) Social Enterprise: A strategy for success, http://webarchive.nationalarchives.gov.uk/+/http://www.cabinetoffice.gov.uk/media/cabinetoffice/third_sector/assets/se_strategy_2002.pdf (archived at https://perma.cc/4VPZ-JV6E)

Di Domenico, M L, Tracey, P and Haugh, H (2010) Social Bricolage: Theorizing social value creation in social enterprises, *Entrepreneurship Theory and Practice*, 34 (4): 681–703

Dodd, S D and Anderson, A R (2001) Understanding the enterprise culture paradigm: paradox and policy, *The International Journal of Entrepreneurship and Innovation*, 2(1): 13–26

Doherty, B, Haugh, H and Lyon, F (2014) Social enterprises as hybrid organizations: a review and research agenda, *International Journal Management Review*, 16(4): 417–36

Dorey, P and Garnett, M (2012) No such thing as the 'Big Society'? The Conservative Party's unnecessary search for 'narrative' in the 2010 general election, *British Politics*, 7 (4): 389–417

Douglas, E and Prentice, C (2019) Innovation and profit motivations for social entrepreneurship: a fuzz set analysis, *Journal of Business Research*, 99: 69–79

Douglas, E J, Shepherd, D and Venugopal, V (2021) A multi-motivational general model entrepreneurial intention, *Journal of Business Venturing*, 36(4): 106–07

Ebrahim, A, Battilana, J and Mair, J (2014) The governance of social enterprises: Mission drift and accountability challenges in hybrid organizations, *Research in Organizational Behavior*, 34: 81–100

Ernst, D K (2011) Heart over mind – an empirical analysis of social entrepreneurial intention formation on the basis of the theory of planned behaviour, Doctoral Dissertation Wuppertal, Germany: University of Wuppertal

European Union (2015) Building the Europe we want: Models for civil society involvement in the implementation of the Post-2015 agenda at the EU level, https://www.eesc.europa.eu/en/our-work/publications-other-work/publications/building-europe-we-want-models-civil-society-involvement-implementation-post-2015-agenda-eu-level#downloads (archived at https://perma.cc/BK2Y-S2S7)

Feinstein, C (1998) Pessimism perpetuated: real wages and the standard of living in Britain during and after the Industrial Revolution, *Journal of Economic History*, 58 (3): 625–58

Flinn, M W (1984) *The History of the British Coal Industry*, 1700–1830, Oxford: Clarendon Press

Freeman, R E (1984) *Strategic Management: A stakeholder approach*, Boston: Pitman

Giovany, C S (2014) Social innovation: moving the field forward. A conceptual framework, technological forecasting and social change, *Technological Forecasting and Social Change*, 82: 42–51

Gunn, R and Durkin, C (2010) *Social Entrepreneurship: A skills approach*, Bristol: Policy Press

Haigh, N, Walker, J, Bacq, S and Kickul, J (2015) Hybrid organizations: origins, strategies, impacts and implications, *California Management Review*, 57(3): 5–12

Haugh, H M and Talwar, A (2016) Linking social entrepreneurship and social change: the mediating role of empowerment, *Journal of Business Ethics*, 133: 643–58

Ho, J Y and Yoon, S (2022) Ambiguous roles of intermediaries in social entrepreneurship: The case of social innovation systems in South Korea, *Technological Forecasting and Social Change*, 175: 1–12

Hochstader, A and Scheck, B (2015) What's in a name: an analysis of impact investing understandings by academics and practitioners, *Journal of Business Ethics*, 132(2): 449–75

Hockerts, K (2015) Antecedents of social entrepreneurial intentions: a validation study, *Social Enterprise Journal*, 11(3): 260–80

Hockerts, K (2017) Determinants of social entrepreneurial intentions, *Entrepreneurship Theory and Practice*, 1: 105–30

Horrel, S (1996) Home demand and British industrialization, *The Journal of Economic History*, 56(3): 561–604

Ip, C Y, Liang, C and Lai, H J (2021) Determinants of social entrepreneurial intention: an alternative model based on social cognitive career theory, *Nonprofit Management and Leadership*, 31(4): 737–60

Johnson, S (2000) *Literature Review on Social Entrepreneurship*, Canadian Centre for Social Entrepreneurship, Edmonton

Kickul, J and Lyons, T S (2012) *Understanding Social Entrepreneurship: The relentless pursuit of mission in an ever changing world*, New York, NY: Routledge

Leadbeater, C (1997) The Rise of the Social Entrepreneur, DEMOS, https://demos.co.uk/wp-content/uploads/2023/03/theriseofthesocialentrepreneur.pdf (archived at https://perma.cc/7UNT-A2C3)

Lewrick, M, Omar, M, Raeside, R and Sailer, K (2010) Education for entrepreneurship and innovation: management capabilities for sustainable growth and success, *World Journal of Entrepreneurship, Management and Sustainable Development*, 6 (1–2): 1–18

Mair, J and Noboa, E (2006) Social entrepreneurship: how intentions to create a social venture are formed, in Mair, J, Robinson, J and Hockerts, K (eds) *Social Entrepreneurship*, London: Palgrave Macmillan, pp. 121–35

Mair, J and Martí, I (2006) Social entrepreneurship research: a source of explanation, prediction, and delight, *Journal of World Business*, 41: 36–44

Martin, R L and Osberg, S (2007) Social entrepreneurship: the case for definition, Stanford Social Innovation Review, https://ssir.org/articles/entry/social_entrepreneurship_the_case_for_definition (archived at https://perma.cc/2UY2-X9V3)

McGowan, K and Westley, F (2015) At the root of change: the history of social innovation, in Nicholls, A, Simon, J and Gabriel, M (eds) *New Frontiers in Social Innovation Research*, London: Palgrave Macmillan, pp. 52–68

Mulgan, G (2012) The theoretical foundations of social innovation, in Nicholls, A and Murdoch, A (eds) *Social Innovation-Blurring Boundaries to Reconfigure Markets*, New York: Palgrave Macmillan, pp. 33–65

Owen, W F (1966) The double development squeeze on agriculture, *The American Economic Review*, 56(1-2): 43–70

Peattie, K and Morley, A (2008) Eight paradoxes of the social enterprise research agenda, *Social Enterprise Journal*, 4(2): 91–107

Peredo, A M and McLean, M (2006) Social entrepreneurship: a critical review of the concept, *Journal of World Business*, 41(1): 56–65

Perotin, V (2012) The performance of workers' cooperatives, in Battilani, P and Schröter, H G (eds) *The Cooperative Business Movement 1950 to Present*, Cambridge: Cambridge University Press, pp. 195–221

Phillips, R (2003) *Stakeholder Theory and Organizational Ethics*, UK: Berrett-Koehler Publishers

Phills, J A, Deiglmeier, K and Miller, D T (2008) Rediscovering social innovation, *Stanford Social Innovation Review*, 6: 34–43

Pitman, L (2018) History of Cooperatives in the United States: An Overview, https://resources.uwcc.wisc.edu/History_of_Cooperatives.pdf (archived at https://perma.cc/W7G6-A399)

Prazskier, R and Nowak, A (2011) *Social Entrepreneurship: Theory and practice*, Cambridge: Cambridge University Press

Ridley-Duff, R and Bull, M (2011) *Understanding Social Enterprise*, London: Sage

Rogers, P J (2008) Using programme theory to evaluate complicated and complex aspects of interventions, *Evaluation*, 14(1): 29–48

Roper, J and Cheney, G (2005) The meanings of social entrepreneurship today, *Corporate Governance*, 5(3): 95–104

Rotter, J B (1966) Generalized expectancies for internal versus external locus of control of reinforcement, *Psychological Monographs*, 80: 1–28

Sabeti, H (2011) The for-benefit enterprise, *Harvard Business Review*, 1 November

Saebi, T, Foss, N J and Linder, S (2019) Social entrepreneurship research: past achievements and future promises, *Journal of Management*, 45: 70–95

Salamon, L M (1999) The nonprofit sector at a crossroads: the case of America, *International Journal of Voluntary and Nonprofit Organizations*, 10 (1): 5-23

Salamon, L M and Anheier, H K (1992) In search of the nonprofit sector: the question of definitions, Johns Hopkins Comparative Nonprofit Sector Project Working Paper2, Johns Hopkins University Institute for Policy Studies, Baltimore

Santos, F, Pache, A C and Birkholz, C (2015) Making hybrids work: aligning business models and organizational design for social enterprises, *California Management Review*, 57(3): 36–58

Santos, S C, Nikou, S and Brännback, M (2021) Are social and traditional entrepreneurial intentions really that different? *International Journal of Entrepreneurial Behavior & Research*, 27(7): 1891–911

Schumpeter, J A (1947) *Capitalism, Socialism and Democracy*, 2nd ed. New York: Harper and Bros

Shaw, E and Carter, S (2007) Social entrepreneurship: theoretical antecedents and empirical analysis of entrepreneurial processes and outcomes, *Journal of Small Business and Enterprise Development*, 14(3): 418–34

Stephan, U, Uhlaner, L M and Stride, C (2015) Institutions and social entrepreneurship: the role of institutional voids, institutional support, and institutional configurations, *Journal of International Business Studies*, 46: 308–31

Swanson, L A and Di Zhang, D (2010) The social entrepreneurship zone, *Journal of Nonprofit Public Sector Marketing*, 22(2): 71–88

Thompson, D J (1994) Weavers of Dreams: Founders of the modern co-operative movement, USA: Regents of the University of California

Tiwari, P, Bhat, A K and Tikoria, J (2020) Mediating role of prosocial motivation in predicting social entrepreneurial intentions, *Journal of Social Entrepreneurship*, 13(1): 118–41

To, C K, Martínez, J M G, and Orero-Blat, M (2020) Predicting motivational outcomes in social entrepreneurship: roles of entrepreneurial self-efficacy and situational fit, *Journal of Business Research*, 121: 209–22

UnLtd (2024) Determining the right legal structure for your social venture, https://www.unltd.org.uk/resources/social-entrepreneur/ (archived at https://perma.cc/LE7A-JX9X)

Urban, B and Kujinga, L (2017) The institutional environment and social entrepreneurship intentions, *International Journal of Entrepreneurial Behavior & Research*, 23(4): 638–55

VanDyck, C K (2017) Concept and definition of civil society sustainability, *Centre for Strategic and International Studies*, 1–5

Vangen, S, Hayes, J P and Cornforth, C (2014) Governing cross-sector, inter-organizational collaborations, *Public Management Review*, 17(9): 1237–60

Waddock, S A and Post, J E (1991) Social entrepreneurs and catalytic change, *Public Administration Review*, 51(5): 393–401

Warhurst, C and Darr, A (2006) From welfare to profit: the transformation of a trade union-owned firm, *Economic and Industrial Democracy*, 7(2): 285–309

Weerawardena, J and Sullivan Mort, G (2006) Investigating social entrepreneurship: a multidimensional model, *Journal of World Business*, 41: 21–35

Weiss, C H (1997) How can theory-based evaluation make greater headway? *Evaluation Review*, 21(4): 501–24

Williamson, J G (1984) Why was British growth so slow during the industrial revolution? *Journal of Economic History*, 44(3): 687–712

World Economic Forum (2013) Solving problems the civil society way, https://www.weforum.org/stories/2013/01/solving-problems-the-civil-society-way/ (archived at https://perma.cc/N9NW-TNEJ)

Zahra, S A, Gedajlovic, E, Neubaum, D O and Shulman, J M (2009) A typology of social entrepreneurs: Motives, search processes and ethical challenges, *Journal of Business Venturing*, 24, 519–32

# 02 Theoretical debates on social enterprise

SIMON ADDERLEY

## LEARNING OUTCOMES

By the end of this chapter, you should be able to:

- Identify and describe the major theoretical frameworks that underpin the study of social entrepreneurship.
- Compare and contrast various theoretical perspectives on social entrepreneurship, such as social innovation theory, institutional theory and stakeholder theory.
- Examine the key debates surrounding the definition and scope of social entrepreneurship.
- Discuss the tensions between social mission and economic sustainability within SEs.
- Compare the development and challenges of SEs in different cultural and economic contexts.
- Apply traditional strategic management theory to a social entrepreneurial context.

## REAL-WORLD EXAMPLE The Big Issue: a pioneering model of social innovation

Established in 1991 by John Bird and Gordon Roddick, the Big Issue is one of the most prominent social enterprises in the UK. Its primary aim is to combat rough sleeping and unemployment through a unique business model that offers rough sleepers the opportunity to become independent vendors. By selling the *Big Issue* magazine, individuals in or on the brink of rough sleeping can generate income and hopefully work towards financial self-sufficiency. The organization operates on the principle of providing a 'hand-up, not a handout', empowering vendors rather than creating dependency. Upon its inception in 1991, the Big Issue confronted several significant challenges, namely securing initial funding, establishing connections with a marginalized demographic, and persuading the public to buy their magazine (Bird, 2011). These were considerable obstacles that tested the viability and resilience of their business model. However, the innovative concept and strong leadership allowed the organization to turn these challenges into opportunities, thereby paving the way for its long-term success.

The Big Issue's core business model offers a distinctive approach to the issue of rough sleeping and unemployment, adopting a principle of empowerment over dependency. Vendors, mainly individuals on the brink of rough sleeping, buy the magazine at £2.00 and sell it for £4.00 to the public, keeping the profit (Bird, 2011). This model not only provides a source of income but also encourages self-worth and dignity, enabling individuals to step away from a cycle of dependency and reclaim control over their lives.

Over the years, the Big Issue has grown beyond magazine sales, launching Big Issue Invest in 2005, a social investment arm that supports other SEs. This marked a crucial step in the organization's development, expanding its impact from individual vendors to the broader social enterprise sector. While the Big Issue has faced some criticism, with some arguing that the model reinforces stereotypes of rough sleepers who need to 'earn' their support and further commodify their plight, according to a study by the University of Northampton (2022), in 2019, the Big Issue had worked with 4,000 unique vendors and supported, on average, 1,250 individuals each week. These figures underscore the social enterprise's substantial impact in helping individuals transition from rough sleeping and unemployment to self-employment. However, while these achievements are impressive, they also highlight the scale and persistence of the problem, suggesting a broader systemic failure that requires the attention of policymakers and other stakeholders.

Discussion questions:

1. How did the Big Issue's business model allow it to address the social issues of rough sleeping and unemployment differently to traditional charitable efforts?
2. Discuss the challenges the Big Issue faced during its inception phase and how it managed to overcome them. What lessons can be drawn from these experiences for future social entrepreneurs?
3. Evaluate the impact of Big Issue Invest on the broader social enterprise sector. How did it extend the Big Issue's influence beyond individual vendors?
4. Critically analyse the social impact of the Big Issue based on the figures provided by the University of Northampton study. How does the organization's success underline the scale and persistence of rough sleeping and unemployment problems?
5. How can you apply the key theoretical frameworks discussed in this chapter to the Big Issue?

(Indicative answers at the end of the chapter.)

# Introduction

The academic conversation regarding social enterprise (SE) has evolved significantly over the last two decades. While it may not boast a comprehensive theory or a singular dominant framework, it has transcended the exclusive domain of a handful of academics who initially examined it through the perspectives of unrelated disciplines. It is now a mainstream area of study. Nonetheless, it remains a distance away from a fully developed discourse, and many areas still need to be explored. Moreover, despite growing interest, social entrepreneurship is fraught with a lack of definitions and mis-conceptualizations (Dacin et al, 2011; Zahra et al, 2009). This chapter therefore provides students with relevant research strands and theoretical debates identified in the social entrepreneurship literature, from the social innovation views that focus on social value creation (Dees and Anderson, 2002; Mair and Martí, 2009; Martin and Osberg, 2007; Peredo and McLean, 2006; see Chapter 1) to the hybrid views of social entrepreneurship, balancing profit and social motives and creating sustainable solutions to social problems (Zaremohzzabieh et al, 2019; see Chapter 1).

While the notion of SE may still be relatively new and undefined (Alter, 2003; Dart, 2004; Defourny and Nyssens, 2006; Haugh, 2005; Hockerts, 2006; Kerlin, 2009; Mair and Martí, 2009; Peattie and Morley, 2008; Robinson et al, 2009; Spear, 2006; Thompson, 2008) for reasons that vary from region to region, the concept itself, along with two closely related notions, 'social entrepreneur' and 'social entrepreneurship', has, over the past two decades, become one of increasing interest to practitioners, policymakers and academics. In order to fully explore these ideas, this chapter deliberately chooses a definition that allows us to look at a wide range of activities and organizational typologies. Specifically, it follows the example of Doherty et al, (2014), who understand SEs as organizations that both span institutional boundaries and operate in multiple functional domains to alleviate social problems and catalyse social transformations.

In this chapter, we initially explain the core elements of social innovation theory. In the first sections, we will expand on some of the definitional debates raised in Chapter 1. Then we explore the drivers of social innovation, and then the remainder of the chapter explores a number of relevant theories before applying these to the world of SE. We will look at the Resource-Based View, Stakeholder Theory, Network Theory and Institutional Theory.

# Definitional debates

This definition is extremely wide and deliberately loose, and it reflects and acknowledges the fact that, as we have already mentioned and as will become clear throughout this textbook, SEs are multifaceted organizations subject to internal change themselves, let alone as a 'sector'. Nevertheless, SEs can be said to hold a series of shared objectives, including:

- *Mission-Driven Orientation:* As was shown in Chapter 1, at the heart of every SE lies a compelling mission to drive positive change. Unlike 'profit for shareholder' businesses solely focused on maximizing shareholder wealth, SEs articulate a clear social or environmental purpose that guides their operations. Whether tackling poverty, promoting education or advancing environmental conservation, the mission serves as the moral compass steering decision-making processes and shaping organizational goals (Komatsu Cipriani et al, 2020; Kulshresthat et al, 2022).
- *Innovative Business Models:* SEs are often highly innovative. In 2016, a report for the Office for Civil Society and Innovation showed that within the UK, the number of SEs introducing a new product or service within the last 12 months was at 50 per cent, compared to only 33 per cent within the for-profit sector (OCS&I, 2016). SEs often pioneer novel business models to address complex challenges effectively. They leverage creativity and adaptability to develop sustainable solutions that bridge market gaps while generating social value. As the various real-world examples in this textbook show, from microfinance institutions empowering underserved communities, such as the Grameen Bank, to fair trade cooperatives promoting ethical consumption, such as Divine Chocolate – these SEs epitomize the fusion of innovation and social impact (de Souza João-Roland, 2023).
- *Double or Triple Bottom Line:* Contrary to conventional profit-centric paradigms, SEs embrace a multidimensional approach to measuring success. While financial viability remains paramount, they also prioritize social and environmental outcomes, striving to achieve a triple bottom line of people, planet and profit (see more in Chapters 6, 8 and 9). This holistic perspective underscores their commitment to balancing economic prosperity with social equity and environmental stewardship, fostering sustainable development on multiple fronts (Zaharia and Zaharia, 2021).
- *Stakeholder Engagement and Collaboration:* As discussed in Chapters 1 and 5, SEs recognize the importance of inclusive multiagency stakeholder engagement in driving meaningful change. They actively involve diverse stakeholders, including beneficiaries, communities, investors and partners, in their decision-making processes, fostering transparency, accountability and shared ownership. By forging collaborative partnerships across sectors, SEs harness collective expertise and resources to amplify their impact and scale their initiatives effectively (Kulshrestha et al, 2022).
- *Impact Measurement and Evaluation:* Central to the ethos of SEs is an emphasis on impact measurement and evaluation. They employ a variety of metrics and assessment frameworks to gauge the effectiveness of their interventions and track

progress towards their social and environmental goals. By quantifying outcomes and learning from both successes and failures, SEs enhance their accountability, transparency and learning capacity, driving continuous improvement and maximizing their impact over time (Kah and Akenroye, 2020). In reality, however, it must be said that the exact nature of which metrics to use and how to measure concepts such as 'equality', 'fairness' and 'sustainability' remains contested, and this will be discussed further in Chapters 6 and 12.

- *Ethical Leadership and Governance:* Ethical leadership lies at the core of SE governance, guiding decision-making processes with integrity, empathy and social responsibility. Leaders of SEs demonstrate a deep commitment to ethical conduct, valuing principles such as fairness, inclusivity and sustainability. They uphold high standards of transparency, accountability and integrity in their interactions with stakeholders, fostering trust and credibility within their communities and beyond (Iskandar et al, 2023).
- *Flexibility and Adaptability:* In navigating the complex and ever-evolving landscape of social change, SEs exhibit remarkable flexibility and adaptability. They embrace innovation, experimentation and learning agility, pivoting their strategies and approaches in response to emerging challenges and opportunities. This adaptive capacity enables SEs to stay resilient, relevant and responsive to the evolving needs of their beneficiaries and the broader society (Iskandar et al, 2023).

## Hybridity

The distinctions between 'profit for shareholder' organizations and SEs are often discussed. However, a clear distinction must also be made between SEs and what in the UK are often called third-sector organizations (students from other areas may be more *au fait* with terms such as voluntary sector, non-governmental sector (NGO), charities or voluntary organizations). SEs operate at the intersection of the market and the social sector, blending profit-making activities with a social mission. Hybridity challenges traditional binary distinctions between for-profit and non-profit sectors, recognizing the diversity of organizational forms and logics that exist in practice.

Within this framework, and as we have seen in Chapter 1, SEs are viewed as hybrid entities that navigate tensions and trade-offs between economic sustainability and social impact. They must reconcile competing priorities, such as financial viability, social mission adherence and stakeholder expectations, while maintaining organizational identity and legitimacy. Hybridity sheds light on the strategies that SEs employ to manage these tensions, such as dual-mission alignment, resource diversification and boundary-spanning practices, i.e. working across traditional boundaries between sectors and between groups of individuals who may not normally engage with each other (Bacq and Eddleston, 2018; Brehmer et al, 2018).

Pache and Santos (2013), for instance, suggest that the sustainability of SEs hinges on their ability to balance value creation and value capture. Attempting to create financial and social value simultaneously poses significant challenges in terms of organizational culture and personnel recruitment and development (Battilana *et al*, 2012). As we have seen in Chapters 1 and 6, this tension between social and economic missions can lead to 'mission drift', where social entrepreneurs may prioritize profit over social impact (Cornforth, 2014; Munoz and Kimmitt, 2019). To mitigate this drift, social entrepreneurs often engage stakeholders and adopt strategies that align economic success with social objectives (Ramus and Vaccaro, 2017).

Doherty et al (2014) have argued that the concept of hybrid SEs emerges from the blurring of traditional boundaries between the private (i.e. 'profit-for-shareholder organizations'), public and 'not-for-profit' sectors. They point out that in the past, organizations have been 'neatly' put into one category or another based on their aspirations and structures (Greenwood and Suddaby, 2006; Romanelli, 1991). However, as has been discussed, many organizations within the profit-for-shareholder sector are attempting to become more socially and environmentally sustainable through corporate social responsibility (CSR) (see Chapter 5); conversely, elements of the not-for-profit sector are moving to become more financially sustainable. This means that as the two sectors become closer, a number of authors have identified the emergence of 'hybrid' organizations (Brandsen and Karré, 2011; D'Aunno et al, 2000; Nee, 1992; Powell, 1987; Ruef, 2000; Tracey *et al*, 2011).

What makes hybrid organizations fascinating to researchers is that they traverse institutional boundaries and operate across multiple functional domains (Brandsen and Karré, 2011; Jay, 2013; Pache and Santos, 2013; Ruef, 2000). SEs, with their dual pursuit of financial and social aims, exemplify hybrid organizations, combining attributes associated with profit-for-shareholder organizations, public and not-for-profit sectors (Billis, 2010; Dees and Elias, 1998; Defourny and Nyssens, 2006; Evers, 2005; Liu and Ko, 2012; Murphy and Coombes, 2009; Pache and Santos, 2013; Young, 2003).

Here then lies the root of the hybrid nature of SEs, where organizations demonstrating hybridity are those with several distinct and sometimes competing logics of governance within one organization or one organizational field (Billis, 2010; Evers et al, 2002; Evers, 2005). Pache and Santos (2013) have explained how SEs exemplify such organizations by stressing how they aim to fulfil a social mission through business activities but face a dilemma between the demands of market logic and social welfare logic. They must decide whether to register as for-profit or non-profit organizations, whether to allocate profits to owners or reinvest them in their mission, and whether to employ paid professionals for efficiency or rely on volunteers for their dedication to the cause.

This utilization of hybrid logics means that SEs cannot be defined by organizational structures. Rather, it is the rationale behind the actions of individuals which defines 'social entrepreneurship' (Billis, 2010). Grohs et al (2015) have argued that the presence of social entrepreneurial organizations shows that defining the third sector as comprising entities that are neither market-based nor state-run is outdated. This view allows for a wide variety of organizations to be categorized within the 'new' intermediary social entrepreneurship sector. These can range from large foundations with millions in capital and corporate-style teams to individual initiatives focused on specific issues and often motivated by personal passion. (Grohs et al, 2015).

What makes the discourse about hybridity so important to scholars is not simply the findings – that different organizations reflect different operational logics over time and that these transcend traditional definitions of what a business 'is' – but also the fact that the discussion about hybridity moves us beyond a discussion of definitions and into one of how SEs operate: how they navigate the issues they face and attempt to maintain both their operational efficiency and their social purpose. This involves a multidisciplinary approach and reflects the growing maturity of the discussion. The remainder of this chapter attempts to explore how some of these theories have been applied to SE.

## Social innovation

Social innovation focuses on the processes of generating, diffusing and scaling innovative solutions to address social challenges (Choi and Majumdar, 2015; Bitencourt et al, 2016; Edwards-Schachter and Wallace, 2017). Unlike traditional innovation, which focuses primarily on economic value creation emerging from new inventions (see, amongst many, Drucker, 1998; see more in Chapter 9), social innovation prioritizes generating positive societal outcomes. It involves developing new solutions or adapting existing ones to meet the needs of marginalized or underserved communities (Mulgan et al, 2007). It highlights the role of creativity, collaboration and systemic change in driving social impact and draws upon insights from sociology (the study of group dynamics and social systems), economics (exploration of resource allocation), political science (the study of power relationships and advocacy) and psychology (the study of behaviour change), as well as other disciplines such as anthropology, public health management and education (Mulgan, 2012).

While social innovation has gained prominence in recent decades (Midgley, 2017; Mulgan et al, 2007; Roose, 2016; Westley and Antadze, 2010), as discussed in Chapter 1, its roots can be traced back to historical movements and initiatives aimed at social reform, such as the cooperative movement, civil rights activism and community organizing efforts. Scholars like Joseph Schumpeter (1942) and Peter Drucker (1954) laid the groundwork for understanding innovation beyond technological advancements, emphasizing its role in driving social progress. In his seminal work *Capitalism, Socialism, and Democracy*, published in 1942, Schumpeter challenged the prevailing economic theories of his time through his theory of 'creative destruction'. Schumpeter argued that innovation is the primary driver of economic growth and development in capitalist economies. He emphasized the role of entrepreneurs in introducing new products, technologies and business models that disrupt existing markets and create new ones. This process of innovation, discussed at length in Chapter 1, is, according to Schumpeter, not gradual or incremental but rather characterized by radical changes that he termed 'creative destruction'.

Schumpeter's theory challenged the traditional view of equilibrium in economic theory, which assumed a state of stability and balance. Instead, he portrayed the capitalist economy as a dynamic and evolutionary system, driven by the constant churn of innovation and entrepreneurial activity. Creative destruction is a dynamic process by which new innovations replace outdated technologies and business practices, leading to the obsolescence of existing firms and industries. Schumpeter highlighted the central role of entrepreneurs in driving innovation and economic development. He emphasized that entrepreneurs are not merely passive agents but rather visionary individuals who disrupt the status quo through their willingness to take risks and pursue new opportunities.

Not the least of Schumpeter's contributions was the role he played in influencing Peter Drucker. At the time labelled 'the father of management', Drucker was a family friend of Schumpeter (who had been a colleague of his father). Drucker's work on innovation emphasized the importance of innovation for organizational success and societal progress. He agreed with Schumpeter that entrepreneurship is a driving force for economic growth through innovation. He argued that entrepreneurs are the agents of change who identify and exploit new opportunities, whether through the introduction of new products and processes or business models. He introduced the concept of 'knowledge work' to describe work that is primarily based on the application of knowledge rather than manual labour. Central to this was the creation of a culture of innovation within organizations to unleash the creative potential of knowledge workers. He emphasized the need for leadership to create a supportive environment for innovation, encourage risk-taking, and foster collaboration and learning among employees through processes of 'planned abandonment' and 'continuous improvement'.

These two giants of innovation theory are still hugely relevant today, and their influence can be seen in the work of influential academics and thinkers such as Clayton Christensen's (2013) theories of disruptive innovation; Gary Hamel's (2008) 'Future of Management'; Henry Chesbrough's (2003) ideas around 'open innovation'; Eric von Hippel's (2013) focus on user innovation; and Tim Brown's (2008) development of Design Thinking. While there is not enough space here to explore all of these ideas in depth, you are heavily encouraged to do your own reading around all of these subjects.

**KEY THINKERS ON INNOVATION IN ONE SENTENCE**

- Joseph Schumpeter (1883–1950): Invented the concept of 'creative destruction', by which new innovations continually revolutionize and transform the economic structure, leading to the obsolescence of existing products, services and business models.
- Peter Drucker (1909–2005): A prolific author who defined innovation as an invention desired by the market and stressed that all innovators should prepare to abandon their ideas eventually.
- Clayton Christensen (1952–2020): Famously coined the phrase 'disruptive innovation', which refers to the process by which simpler, more accessible technologies or services initially target under-served markets, gradually improving to compete against established incumbents, and ultimately reshaping entire industries.
- Henry Chesbrough (1956–): A pioneer of the idea of 'open innovation', which emphasises collaboration between organizations rather than competition that enables organizations to build their competitive advantage.

## Drivers of social innovation

Just as is the case with traditional concepts of innovation, social innovation is driven by a number of societal factors. For example, economic crises, market failures and resource constraints often catalyse social innovation by highlighting the limitations of existing systems and prompting the search for alternative approaches (Mulgan et al, 2007). Social entrepreneurs may respond to these pressures by developing innovative business models, products or services that address unmet needs or create new opportunities for economic empowerment (Phillips et al, 2015). Similarly, technological advancements have significantly influenced the landscape of social innovation. The links between technological advancements and economic change, both positive and negative, have been clear since the development of the Spinning Jenny, which hugely increased production in the cotton industry, including the creation of the Luddite Movement, which emerged in response as skilled workers protested what they saw as a threat to their jobs, livelihoods and traditional ways of working.

Another example of the way in which all innovations are, in essence, 'social' is the bicycle. A study by Stephen Stearns using the parish records of births, deaths and marriages in the UK showed that until the late 19th century, the average distance between the birthplaces of two people getting married was approximately one mile. This makes sense, of course, because people meet prospective partners within a radius of an easily travelled distance. However, following the invention (and perhaps more importantly, the popularization) of the bicycle, that distance increased to 30 miles. A huge social shift with myriad implications emerged from the popularization of an innovation (Mackintosh and Norcliffe, 2016).

**STOP AND THINK**

Look around you right now. What innovations have affected the social landscape that you may now be taking for granted? The electricity that powers your light, perhaps? How would you find reading this textbook by candlelight? Think about the building you are in. Would a leaking roof or a lack of heating make studying harder? Indeed, it is a much harder task to try and think of an innovation which **does not** have a social impact than it is to think of all the ways our lives are impacted by them.

Since the early 2000s, the focus has been on advancements in digital technologies and communication tools, but we should not ignore the huge social impact created by the technological improvements, which have allowed for global supply chains and thus significant shifts in the geographic locations of key industries. Malcolm McLean (1913–2001) is often cited as the inventor of the intermodal shipping container, which cut down on the time ships spent in port and made loading them much more cost-efficient. However, technical and political shifts, which have allowed for the outsourcing of supply chains all over the world, have radically altered the global economy over the last few decades, and all of these factors create environments rich for social innovation. Indeed, changing demographics are often cited as a huge influence on the growth of social innovation. Spreading urbanization, ageing populations and cultural diversity create new challenges and opportunities for social innovation. Innovations in healthcare, housing, transportation and social services are often driven by the changing needs and preferences of diverse populations, requiring adaptive and inclusive approaches to problem-solving.

## Social enterprise as social innovation

A key point to note here is that for many practitioners, SE itself IS a social innovation. In this sense, social innovation is not something that SEs do (although they may), but rather something that they ARE. Their very existence is an example of new business models emerging from societal needs. Social entrepreneurs have seen themselves as civic entrepreneurs striving to enhance the resilience of specific communities through collaborative efforts aimed at systemic change (Adderley, 2019; Hulgard, 2010). Examples may include:

- **Microfinance initiatives**, such as Grameen Bank and Kiva, which provide small loans and financial services to low-income entrepreneurs, enabling them to start or expand businesses, build assets and improve their livelihoods. These initiatives have demonstrated the power of inclusive finance in promoting economic empowerment and poverty alleviation.
- **Civic tech platforms**, such as Ushahidi, ClickFix and FixMyStreet, which aim to facilitate citizen engagement, transparency and accountability in governance. These platforms enable individuals and communities to report issues, share information and collaborate with governments and civil society organizations to address local challenges.
- **Infrastructure organizations**, such as the Ashoka Foundation, a global organization that identifies and supports social entrepreneurs who are dedicated to solving some of the world's most pressing social, environmental and economic challenges under the slogan 'Everyone a Changemaker'.
- **Social enterprises** themselves (in all their many forms), such as TOMS shoes, Divine Chocolate or even investment funds such as Acumen.

However, increasing numbers of scholars have shown that the boundaries between innovation and social innovation are blurred at best (Del Giudice, 2019; Grimm et al, 2013; Howaldt et al, 2015). In terms of outcomes, it is rare to find a form of innovation that has no social impact, and even if one only explores the motivation of the innovator, it remains just as elusive to discover an innovation that was not in any way motivated by improving someone's quality of life. As a result, the question of how to define social innovation remains a subjective one.

In this section, we have seen that social innovation focuses on creating, spreading and expanding innovative solutions to tackle social challenges and prioritizing societal outcomes over economic value creation. Unlike traditional innovation, which centres on new inventions for economic gain, social innovation aims to meet the needs of marginalized communities through creative, collaborative and systemic approaches. It draws insights from various disciplines, including sociology, economics, political science and psychology. It is driven by societal factors such as economic crises, technological advancements and changing demographics, which create opportunities for new business models and SEs. SEs themselves are seen as a form of social innovation, addressing unmet needs through innovative approaches like microfinance. Yet, the boundaries between innovation and social innovation are often blurred, as most innovations have some social impact and aim to improve quality of life.

## Resource-based view

The next key theory we discuss is the resource-based view (RBV) of business. This is a management theory that suggests a firm's competitive advantage is primarily determined by its internal resources and capabilities rather than external factors such as market conditions or industry dynamics. Although the roots of RBV can be traced back to the work of Edith Penrose (Rugman and Verbeke, 2002), who argued that firms develop unique capabilities over time through a process of organizational learning and adaptation, it was not until the 1980s and 1990s that scholars such as Birger Wernerfelt (1984) and Jay Barney (1991) popularized the RBV as a distinct theory of competitive advantage, as noted in the following Key Research box.

### KEY RESEARCH

RBV focuses on internal organizational factors that contribute to competitive advantage and performance. Three principles underpin the RBV approach:

- **Dynamic capabilities:** This refers to a firm's ability to adapt, innovate and reconfigure its resources and capabilities in response to changing market conditions, technological advancements or competitive threats. Dynamic capabilities enable firms to seize new opportunities, overcome challenges and sustain competitive advantage over time by continuously renewing and recombining their resource base (Eisenhardt and Martin, 2000).
- **Resource immobility:** This refers to the difficulty of transferring or replicating firm-specific resources across firms or industries. Resources that are highly mobile or easily replicable are less likely to confer a sustained competitive advantage, as competitors can quickly imitate or acquire similar resources (Andersén et al, 2016).
- **Resource heterogeneity:** This is the concept that not all resources are equally valuable, rare or difficult to imitate. Firms can gain a competitive advantage by possessing resources that are valuable, rare, inimitable, and for which they are organized to capture value (VRIO), as these characteristics enable them to differentiate themselves from competitors and capture economic rents (Barney, 1991; Hoopes et al, 2003).

In traditional strategic management analysis, RBV therefore provides a framework for analysing a firm's internal strengths and weaknesses, identifying its core competencies and distinctive capabilities, and formulating strategies to leverage these resources for competitive advantage (Barney, 1991). Managers can use RBV principles to prioritize resource investments, allocate resources effectively and align organizational capabilities with strategic objectives. In doing so, they can gain insights into the sources of competitive advantage within industries and markets, and by assessing the resource endowments and strategic positions of rival firms, they can identify potential sources of sustainable competitive advantage and predict the likelihood of competitive convergence or divergence over time (Madhani, 2010).

However, RBV is not without its criticisms. For example, there is no definitive way of measuring the importance of resources in a way that allows easy comparisons. Unlike financial metrics, which are relatively straightforward to measure, resources such as knowledge, brand reputation or organizational culture can be ambiguous and challenging to quantify. This ambiguity can lead to difficulties in applying the theory in practice (Kraaijenbrink, 2010). A connected criticism is that resources are valued based on their previous value to an already existing success story. One can identify a resource, which has been valuable, rare or inimitable *after the fact* much more easily than one can predict one. Thus, resources are only seen as valuable in retrospect. For innovation, this is an important criticism, as it means that RBV tends to adopt a relatively static perspective, focusing on the current resources and capabilities of the firm rather than considering how these may evolve over time. In dynamic environments where technological, market and competitive landscapes are constantly evolving, this static perspective may limit the theory's relevance in explaining sustained competitive advantage (Kaufman, 2016).

## Social enterprise and RBV

Just as in the non-social enterprise sector, SEs face significant resource constraints as they manage their operations. Arguably, however, this issue is heightened because of the hybrid nature of their activities. SEs leverage a combination of tangible and intangible assets, including financial capital, human capital, social networks and organizational culture, to create value for stakeholders. Understanding the strategic management of resources enables researchers to assess the strengths and weaknesses of SEs and identify avenues for enhancing their effectiveness and scalability.

Research has shown that SEs focused on a social mission often prioritize social outputs over operational efficiency (Desa and Basu, 2013). Moreover, they frequently operate in environments where acquiring resources at reasonable costs is done in competition with organizations that do not have to factor in a social purpose (Zahra et al, 2014). Consequently, many SEs struggle to address large-scale problems, limiting the magnitude of their social impact (Renko, 2013; Smith et al, 2016; Sud et al, 2009; Zahra et al, 2009). Indeed, an SE's capacity to expand its social impact through scaling its operations often hinges on 'cooperative capabilities' (for more on this see the sections below on stakeholder and network theory) in addition to the traditional three capabilities highlighted by RBV (Alvord et al, 2004; Bloom and Smith, 2010; Desa and Koch, 2014; Smith and McColl, 2016).

Bell and Dyck (2011) have expanded this concept to emphasize an SE's ability to achieve social impact through capabilities that foster collaboration. This has been supported by Bacq and Eddleston (2018), who have introduced the concept of a 'stewardship culture' within SEs, which can 'either compensate for a lack of capabilities or enhance the effectiveness of existing capabilities in fostering social impact'. They argue that SEs with limited resources have to develop 'compensatory capabilities'. This includes focusing on the intrinsic motivation and commitment of volunteers and employees within the SE and thus developing a stewardship culture, which emphasizes cooperation and collective dedication to the mission.

**KEY RESEARCH**

Bloom and Chatterji (2009) delineated seven organizational capabilities vital for SEs to pursue their social missions:

- Staffing (to meet labour needs)
- Communicating (to gain public support)
- Alliance Building (to secure potential allies)
- Lobbying (to ensure supportive public policy)
- Earning Generation (to secure capital)
- Replicating (to maximize the dispersion of beneficiaries)
- Stimulating Market Forces (to enhance the availability of economic incentives)

While more research is needed to explore the comprehensiveness of this list and the relationships between the various factors identified, it is clear that the mechanisms by which SEs utilize their resources are just as complicated and, in some ways, even more nuanced than those of the profit-for-shareholder sector.

This section has made it clear that the RBV posits that a firm's competitive advantage is primarily determined by its unique internal resources and capabilities rather than external market conditions. It highlights three key principles: dynamic capabilities (the ability to adapt and innovate), resource immobility (difficulty in replicating firm-specific resources), and resource heterogeneity (the value of unique resources). While RBV aids in analysing a firm's internal strengths and strategic positioning, it faces criticisms for its static perspective and difficulty in quantifying intangible resources. In the context of SEs, RBV underscores the importance of leveraging unique resources to achieve social impact. Though SEs often face heightened resource constraints and operational challenges due to their social missions, developing collaborative and stewardship cultures can enhance their capabilities and effectiveness in creating social value, as identified through various organizational capabilities vital for pursuing their missions.

## Stakeholder theory

The next key theoretical concept to be discussed here is stakeholder theory. Stakeholder theory (discussed in Chapters 1 and 5) emerged in the mid-1980s (Freeman, 1984) and was developed in the 1990s as a widespread critique of the theory of the firm (Brenner and Cochran, 1991; Donaldson and Preston, 1995; Hosseini and Brenner, 1992; Jones, 1995; Wood, 1991). While some academics have argued that it does not actually constitute a theory in itself (Key, 1999), the concept is widely understood to argue that the success of a business is not solely measured by its financial performance but also by its ability to manage and satisfy the needs and interests of various stakeholders involved in or affected by the operations of the business. As outlined in Figure 2.1, these stakeholders may include employees, customers, suppliers, communities, government entities and shareholders.

At the core of stakeholder theory is the recognition that businesses exist within a broader societal context and thus have responsibilities beyond solely maximizing profits for shareholders. Instead, businesses should consider the impact of their decisions and actions on all stakeholders and strive to balance their conflicting interests in a manner that promotes long-term sustainability and mutual benefit (Stieb, 2009). One fundamental aspect of stakeholder theory is identifying and categorizing stakeholders. Stakeholders can be classified into various groups based on their level of involvement, influence and dependence on the organization. Internal stakeholders, such as employees and managers, have a direct relationship with the company, while external stakeholders, including customers, suppliers, local communities and regulatory bodies, are affected by the company's operations but are not directly involved in its management (see Chapter 5).

**Figure 2.1** Some examples of stakeholders

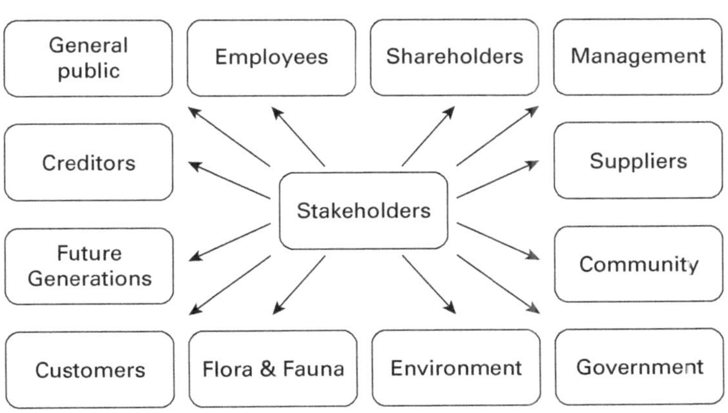

Understanding the diverse interests and concerns of different stakeholders is crucial for effective stakeholder management. This involves engaging with stakeholders through dialogue, consultation and participation to understand their needs and expectations (Agle et al, 2008). By actively involving stakeholders in decision-making processes, businesses can build trust, mitigate conflicts and create value for all parties involved (De Bussy, 2010). Moreover, stakeholder theory emphasizes the interconnectedness of stakeholders and the interdependence between the success of a business and the well-being of its stakeholders. For instance, satisfied and motivated employees are more productive, leading to better customer service and increased profitability (Wicks and Harrison, 2017). Similarly, maintaining positive relationships with suppliers and the local community can enhance the company's reputation and access to resources (O'Riordan and Fairbrass, 2008).

A further key concept in stakeholder theory is the idea of the stakeholder value proposition, which suggests that businesses should strive to create value not only for shareholders but for all stakeholders. This involves adopting a long-term perspective that goes beyond short-term profit maximization and considers the broader social, environmental and ethical implications of business decisions (Freeman, 2023). Proponents of stakeholder theory argue that adopting a stakeholder-centric approach can lead to various benefits for businesses, including improved reputation, enhanced employee morale and loyalty, reduced regulatory scrutiny and increased innovation. By aligning the interests of stakeholders with those of the company, businesses can create a sustainable competitive advantage and contribute to the overall well-being of society (Kujala et al, 2022).

However, implementing stakeholder theory in practice can present challenges for businesses, particularly in balancing the conflicting interests of different stakeholders and prioritizing their needs. Moreover, measuring and evaluating the impact of stakeholder engagement initiatives can be complex, making it difficult to demonstrate tangible outcomes in the short term (Kujala et al, 2022).

## Social enterprise and stakeholder theory

As we have seen in the previous section, stakeholder theory emphasizes the interconnected relationships between organizations and their various stakeholders, including customers, employees, investors, communities and governments (Agle et al, 2008). In the context of SE, this framework underscores the importance of balancing the interests and needs of multiple stakeholders while pursuing social and financial objectives. SEs must navigate complex stakeholder dynamics, manage competing expectations and foster meaningful engagement to build trust and legitimacy. By adopting a stakeholder perspective, researchers can analyse how SEs interact with and impact different stakeholder groups, thereby shaping organizational strategies and outcomes.

SEs utilize stakeholder theory in a number of ways. For example, they often recognize a wide range of stakeholders beyond just shareholders. In doing so they, by necessity, categorize stakeholders based on their involvement, influence and dependence on the organization. (Huybrechts et al, 2014). Because such stakeholder groups include local communities and beneficiaries as well as potential partners, they regularly develop enhanced communication tools with stakeholders to understand their needs, preferences and concerns. Many use various communication channels, such as customer feedback surveys, focus groups, town hall meetings and online platforms (Sarman et al, 2015) to solicit feedback and input from stakeholders. By involving stakeholders in decision-making processes, SEs can build trust, foster collaboration and ensure that their actions align with stakeholder interests (Durkin and Gunn, 2016).

Furthermore, SEs strive to balance the conflicting interests of different stakeholders while pursuing their social mission. Often, the concept of focusing on one group alone is anathema to SEs, and it is not unusual for them to adopt a stakeholder-centric approach that considers the needs of all stakeholders and seeks to create value for multiple stakeholders simultaneously (Imperatori and Ruta, 2015). For example, a fair trade organization may prioritize the interests of farmers, workers and consumers to ensure equitable wages, safe working conditions and high-quality products (Huybrechts and Nicholls, 2013). Similarly, SEs often collaborate with stakeholders to co-create solutions to complex social and environmental challenges. They form partnerships with government agencies, non-profit organizations, academia and other businesses to leverage resources, expertise and networks. By pooling their collective knowledge and resources, SEs can address systemic issues more effectively and create sustainable change. Colette Henry (2015), for example, has detailed the complex and interconnected networks from a series of different social and institutional backgrounds that a Social Enterprise Partnership in Northern Ireland had to effectively manage in order to recognize, develop and support opportunities for new projects.

Finally, many support structures, which may include local or national government funding streams, encourage SEs to develop inclusive governance structures that give stakeholders a voice in decision-making processes. It is not unusual for SEs to have stakeholder representatives on their boards of directors or advisory councils, ensuring that diverse perspectives are considered in strategic planning and policy development. Inclusive governance enhances accountability, legitimacy and stakeholder buy-in (Iannaci, 2020; Marcon and Dorigo, 2012).

In summary, stakeholder theory posits that a business's success is not solely measured by financial performance but also by its ability to manage and satisfy the needs of various stakeholders, including employees, customers, suppliers, communities and shareholders. This theory emphasizes that businesses exist within a broader societal context and have responsibilities beyond profit maximization, advocating for balancing the conflicting interests of stakeholders to promote long-term sustainability and mutual benefit. Effective stakeholder management involves identifying and categorizing stakeholders, engaging them through dialogue and participation, and fostering interconnected relationships to create value for all parties. While beneficial, implementing stakeholder theory presents challenges in balancing diverse interests and measuring engagement impact. In SEs, stakeholder theory is crucial, as they must navigate complex stakeholder dynamics to achieve social and financial objectives, often involving stakeholders in decision-making and forming partnerships to address social challenges. SEs also adopt inclusive governance structures to enhance accountability and stakeholder buy-in, ensuring diverse perspectives are considered in strategic planning.

## Network theory

Network theory, like stakeholder theory, focuses on multiple actors within the ecosystem within which an organization exists (Purbasari et al, 2020). However, network theory places a greater emphasis on the interconnections and interactions between those actors, and in doing so, it takes a more mathematical perspective (Möller et al, 2020). It revolves around the study of interconnected systems, where elements interact with each other to form complex structures and patterns. These elements, often referred to as 'nodes', are conceptually derived from the idea of computers in a communication network but here represent individuals in a social network. The connections between nodes, known as edges or links, carry information, resources or interactions. Nodes represent entities within a system, while edges denote the relationships or connections between them. Nodes and edges can possess various attributes, depending on the context of the network. For instance, in a social network, nodes could represent individuals, while edges could represent friendships or interactions between them. Network analysis explores relationships between individuals or groups, studying phenomena such as information diffusion, opinion formation, influence dynamics and community detection. Social network analysis tools help uncover patterns of communication, identify key influencers and understand social structures (Wasserman and Faust, 1994).

Within the study of business and management, network theory provides insights into the structure, dynamics and behaviour of various organizational systems. For example, it is often used to analyse the structure of organizations by mapping out formal and informal relationships among individuals, departments and teams. This helps managers visualize communication patterns, information flows and collaboration dynamics within the organization. Similarly, Social Network Analysis focuses on studying interpersonal relationships within organizations. Managers can identify influential individuals, assess the strength of connections between employees and uncover hidden communication channels. This can also enhance a company's ability to map innovation channels within organizations.

Another use of network analysis is to explore the relationship between the suppliers, manufacturers, distributors and customers that constitute supply chains. By modelling supply chain networks, businesses can identify critical nodes, assess vulnerability to disruptions and optimize their logistical operations. It can also help organizations determine the nature of their relationships with other organizations within their supply chain (Harland, 1996).

## Social enterprise and network theory

SEs can harness the power of network theory to strengthen their operations, maximize their impact and drive positive social change. By understanding and leveraging social networks, collaborative partnerships and community ecosystems, they can create sustainable solutions to complex social and environmental challenges (Bacq et al, 2022). Indeed, as we have seen, SEs can particularly struggle to scale up their operations. Often, social entrepreneurs will argue that rather than grow one large organization, it is more socially effective to encourage a number of smaller SEs to collaborate with each other.

Within this framework, SEs are seen as nodes within a broader network of relationships, exchanging resources, information and social capital with other actors (Granados and Rivera, 2018). Networks play a critical role in shaping the strategic choices, opportunities and constraints faced by SEs, influencing their ability to access funding, expertise and markets. By studying network structures and dynamics, researchers can uncover the mechanisms that facilitate collaboration, knowledge sharing and collective action within the SEs' ecosystems. For example, researchers have shown how SEs often collaborate with other organizations, including non-profits, government agencies, businesses and academic institutions, to achieve shared social objectives (Ebnmhana, 2018; Park and Wilding, 2014). Network theory therefore helps in identifying potential partners, assessing the compatibility of goals and values and understanding the dynamics of collaborative networks. By forming strategic partnerships and alliances, SEs can leverage complementary strengths, share resources and scale impact (Hazenberg et al, 2016). Network-based partnership strategies foster innovation, resource mobilization and collective problem-solving. Moreover, network theory helps in mapping out the diverse stakeholders discussed above, including beneficiaries, donors, volunteers, partners and community organizations (Granados and Rivera, 2018). By systematically analysing stakeholder networks, SEs can prioritize engagement efforts, build strategic partnerships and mobilize collective action to address social challenges effectively (Nielsen and Carranza, 2012).

In addition, SEs can use network theory to better understand the communities within which they work. It can provide insights into community structures, social ties and communication networks within target populations, and by understanding the social networks and influential actors within communities, SEs can design community-based interventions, leverage social capital and mobilize grassroots movements for social impact. Network-based community-building strategies enhance participation, ownership and sustainability of social initiatives (Campbell and Sacchetti, 2014; Joshi and Khare, 2024). Finally, SEs often operate within a complex ecosystem of funders and partner organizations. In such a system, the importance of informal relationships remains high, and as SEs seek to influence local and national policies, network theory can help in analysing power dynamics, policy networks and advocacy coalitions within political systems (Hazenberg et al, 2016).

In summary, network theory focuses on the interconnections and interactions between multiple actors within an ecosystem. It explores various phenomena, including information diffusion, opinion formation and community detection, providing valuable insights into organizational structures, communication patterns and supply chain dynamics. For SEs, network theory is instrumental in enhancing operations and social impact by fostering collaborative partnerships, optimizing resource exchange and understanding community structures. By leveraging social networks and strategic alliances, SEs can address social and environmental challenges more effectively, mobilize resources and scale their impact. Besides, network theory aids in mapping diverse stakeholders and analysing informal relationships, which are crucial for influencing policies and sustaining social initiatives.

## Institutional theory

Institutional theory provides a framework for analysing the external environment in which organizations operate. It emphasizes the influence of formal and informal institutions, such as laws, regulations, norms and values, on organizational behaviour and outcomes. This theory is most often associated with the sociologist W. Richard Scott (1995), who aimed to explore how organizations operate within and are influenced by their broader social, cultural and institutional environments. The theory posits that organizations are not just economic entities driven solely by efficiency and profit motives but are deeply embedded in social structures and norms. Scott's institutional theory emphasizes the importance of institutions in shaping the behaviour, structure and strategies of organizations, as pointed out in the Key Research box below.

**KEY RESEARCH**

Scott (1995) maintained that organizations are built upon three pillars, as pointed out below: the regulatory pillar, the normative pillar and the cognitive-cultural pillar:

- **Regulatory pillar:** refers to regulations, laws and governmental policies and programmes that offer support to entrepreneurs and address social problems (Busenitz et al, 2000; Stephan et al, 2014). The stronger a country's regulatory institutions in terms of laws, regulations, policies and programmes that facilitate new venture creation, the more likely it is that new start-ups will succeed (Stephan et al, 2014). Conversely, the lack of limited support from the government and weak regulatory framework create institutional voids that hinder any form of entrepreneurship.
- **Normative pillar:** focuses on the degree to which a given society accepts and encourages certain behaviour(s). In other words, it focuses on standards, moral values and codes of conduct set by professional bodies that become part of the societal moral values and conventions (Garud et al, 2002).
- **Cognitive-cultural pillar:** refers to shared values, meanings and symbols underlying predominant practices within a society (Scott, 1995; Casson and Yeung, 2006). These values, traditions and practices are institutionalized through socialization and adaptation processes. Moreover, these values frame the individuals' thoughts, information base and motivations (Krueger et al, 2000; Peng et al, 2001). Although culture is often viewed as a societal phenomenon, it can be argued that these societal values and meanings determine the motivations, cognitive logics and actions of entrepreneurs.

These three institutional pillars are interrelated and influence one another (Scott, 1995). The regulatory and normative pillars serve as key antecedents of the cognitive-cultural pillar. In other words, the stronger the country's regulatory and normative institutions, the higher the likelihood that individuals are motivated to become entrepreneurs. A large number of studies have highlighted the importance of institutional and cultural contexts in shaping and determining the level of entrepreneurship within different countries (Busenitz et al, 2000; Bowen and DeClercq, 2008). A country's institutional context determines the rules of the game and shapes individual and organizational behaviour (North, 1990; Scott, 1995).

## *Social enterprise and institutional theory*

Research has shown that SEs are hugely influenced by the context in which they emerge. Institutions constitute the broader framework within which individual social entrepreneurs operate, influencing their values and beliefs at a societal/national level (Busenitz et al, 2000; Casson and Yeung, 2006). The more a country's institutional context encourages and fosters social entrepreneurship, the more likely it is that individuals will be motivated to become one compared to countries with contrasting contexts (Casson and Yeung, 2006). In other words, formal and informal institutions influence how individuals perceive social entrepreneurship and the likelihood of becoming a social entrepreneur (Stephan et al, 2014). Defourny and Nyssens (2010) and Kerlin (2012) have revealed the institutional embeddedness of social entrepreneurial action. They have differentiated the various traditions of welfare provision within different nation-states, which have in turn led to specific 'ensembles' of institutions. Put simply, if a society encourages and values social entrepreneurship and innovation, it is more likely that individuals within that society will pursue such a path (Busenitz et al, 2000).

However, what a 'social enterprise' is may also differ from ecosystem to ecosystem. An increasing number of studies have shown that, in fact, there is no single definition but rather individual SEs reflect, and emerge from, specific socio-economic backgrounds (Kerlin, 2009; Nicholls, 2006; Nyssens, 2006; Salamon et al, 2000). In many ways, this mirrors similar findings regarding 'profit-for-shareholder' enterprise (Baumol, 1990). However, while these authors have demonstrated the broad connections between civil structures, local economies and welfare structures, and SEs, the majority of such literature has tended to concentrate on individual countries or case studies rather than developing a comparative analysis (Bagnoli and Megali, 2011; Borzaga and Defourny, 2001; Cooney, 2006; Dacanay, 2004; Les and Jeliazkova, 2005; Liu and Ko, 2012; Mulgan, 2006; Nyssens, 2006; Squazzoni, 2009; Young, 2003).

For any emerging comparative analysis to be effective, it must initially, as described earlier, explore the organizational and legal characteristics of SEs and, using Scott's regulatory pillar, describe the differences between the specific legal structures of SEs within different ecosystems. See, for example, the CIC structure within England and Wales compared to that of Scotland for only one example of the way differences can manifest themselves due to regulatory systems (for others, revisit Chapter 1 and read Evers and Laville, 2004; Defourny and Nyssens, 2010; Kerlin, 2009, 2012). Furthermore, different ecosystems lead to different types of 'social innovation' itself (Dees and Anderson, 2006; Defourny and Nyssens, 2010; Nicholls, 2006; Squazzoni, 2009). Therefore, any comparisons must focus on the activities and actions of individuals rather than the detailed structure of organizations.

As Grohs et al, (2015) have argued this conceptual gap has caused some confusion in the literature, as the definitions of the fundamental terms 'social' and 'entrepreneurship' can vary. Interpretations of social entrepreneurship terminology differ depending on the institutional context, as well as the disciplinary background, motivations, and normative perspectives of the authors.

**ACTIVITY**

Visit the European Commission's Social Affairs and Inclusion website, https://op.europa.eu/en/search-results?p_p_id=eu_europa_publications_portlet_search_executor_SearchExecutorPortlet_INSTANCE_q8EzsBteHybf&p_p_lifecycle=1&p_p_state=normal&facet.collection=EULex%2CEUPub%2CEUDir%2CEUWebPage%2CEUSummariesOfLegislation%2CPublicProcurement&language=en&startRow=1&resultsPerPage=10&SEARCH_TYPE=SIMILAR_DOCUMENTS&ORIGINAL_DOCUMENT_ID=4f68de3c-73ec-11ea-a07e-01aa75ed71a1.0001 and look at the various Member States reports of SEs within their countries. Take some time to read the reports and note the way in which different countries' ecosystems inform the developments of SEs within that country

For example, social entrepreneurship can either occur within existing non-profit organizations (social intrapreneurship) or in the form of new start-ups. Whichever one of these forms it manifests as, it will contain a number of differences from the other (DiMaggio, 1988; Kistruck and Beamish 2010; Morris et al, 2007; Smith et al, 2010). The former is more likely to reflect the internal tensions of a hybrid organization operating across, and shifting between, social and commercial activities (Cooney, 2006; Di Domenico et al, 2010). As Newth and Woods (2014) state, the 'shape' of any social innovation is based upon the expectations and demands of the stakeholders involved in its implementation. Thus, within established organizations, there will be an inherent cultural inertia of established norms and routines, which will inhibit the endogenous development of innovations that are seen to endanger the status quo or seem to violate established understandings of how the organization should achieve its mission. This reflects the findings of a more traditional literature on corporate cultures (Deal and Kennedy, 2000; Johnson, 1992; Schein, 1985, 1990).

Within SE organizations, this places a particularly large amount of stress on innovators to convince colleagues of the benefits of moving toward an SE model. Indeed, the very notion of moving towards an 'enterprise' model may be anathema to many within the 'not-for-profit' sector, embodying as it does notions of 'business' and 'profit', which may feel distinctly inappropriate (Tracey et al, 2011). Moreover, for Newth and Woods (2014), social entrepreneurs who take an offering into a competitive market face the same barriers to winning customers as their commercial counterparts in that they need an attractive value proposition, which a customer is prepared to buy.

As a result, just as the utilization of CSR initiatives by the profit-for-shareholder sector can be used to develop the value proposition of a business (Marshall, 2011;

see Chapter 5), SEs use their social aim as a way to create value for customers (see Chapter 8). For this to be effective, customers must clearly perceive and believe in the authenticity of the social aspects of the offering. The perception of authenticity is a construction of the offering's fit with the customer's beliefs about the SE's social cause (Lumpkin et al, 2011) and the method of social change being employed. This authenticity imperative is bound to the pragmatic and moral legitimacy of the social venture (Dart, 2004; Nicholls and Pharoah, 2007). A key element linked to the authenticity imperative is the social norms, or beliefs and values, which define social acceptability. In this sense, they form and inform a series of informal institutions, which have a large degree of influence over the level of community support social innovation initiatives will receive (Kistruck and Beamish, 2010). If these are supportive, it can lead to increased legitimacy for an organization (Dart, 2004; Nicholls and Pharoah, 2007; Nicholls, 2006) and obviously, because of the strong espoused social purpose within SE, this has significant benefits in terms of promoting the value proposition of the business.

Lastly, as discussed previously, social entrepreneurship does not fit with dominant organizational logics in that it attempts to use a hybrid blend of both commercial and social logics. While politicians and practitioners often laud this hybridity, many formal institutions, which traditionally imbue formal recognition on businesses (for example, tax mechanisms, banks and investors) or third-sector organizations (for example, charity regulators, funders or donors), struggle to build this into their operational models. The issue is that the very fact of the hybridity does not fit with either of the accepted organizational logics – it is not purely commercial and profit-maximizing, nor is it solely non-profit and charity oriented because it may seek profits for financial self-sufficiency or increased scale. At the very least, it brings a market orientation and a degree of innovativeness to the pursuit of social value creation (Nicholls and Pharoah, 2007). The primary implication for entrepreneurs operating without legitimacy is in resource acquisition, because it is legitimacy that enables the flow of resources to the venture (Dart, 2004; Nicholls and Pharoah, 2007).

This is apparent for social entrepreneurs, as operating in this 'institutional gap/void' means they often lack the ability to access venture capital markets to the extent that profit-maximizing businesses can (see Chapter 12). Although collective social values are arguably shifting to be more aware and accepting of social entrepreneurial approaches to social change, the development of appropriate financial institutions still lags behind. Leading practitioners advocate for funding models that enable investments to be returned to investors (Yunus et al, 2010), and thought leaders advocate for business models and investment mechanisms that enable returns to be generated for social investors (Emerson, 2003; Nicholls and Pharoah, 2007). However, such practices are still rare and still conflict with normative understandings of organizational funding and business models. The other implication of operating in this institutional gap is that social entrepreneurs may not be able to secure the same donated funds as traditional non-profits, as they lack the same perceived purity of a business model and therefore, legitimacy, to elicit donations. Similarly, the availability of appropriate legal organizational forms for SEs also constrains them in terms of the business and investment models they can employ and the types of capital they can attract.

In summary, institutional theory analyses how formal and informal institutions, such as laws, regulations, norms and values, affect organizational behaviour and outcomes. It emphasizes that organizations are not solely driven by efficiency and profit but are deeply embedded in social structures and norms, influenced by regulatory, normative and cognitive-cultural pillars. These pillars shape entrepreneurship by affecting governmental support, societal acceptance of certain behaviours, and shared values. For SEs, institutional contexts significantly influence their emergence, values and operational strategies, determining the level of social entrepreneurship within different countries. However, definitions and manifestations of SEs vary across different ecosystems due to differing socio-economic backgrounds. This variability necessitates comparative analyses to understand the legal and organizational characteristics of SEs in different contexts. SEs often face challenges due to their hybrid nature, which doesn't fit neatly into traditional commercial or non-profit categories, affecting their ability to secure funding and legitimacy. Despite increasing social acceptance of social entrepreneurship, appropriate financial institutions and legal structures lag behind, complicating resource acquisition and operational sustainability for social entrepreneurs.

## Summary and key learning points

This chapter aimed to provide an overview of the major research strands and theoretical debates within social entrepreneurship, ranging from social innovation views focused on social value creation to hybrid views balancing profit and social motives. We have shown that theoretical frameworks play a crucial role in shaping research agendas, informing empirical studies and advancing theoretical debates in the field of social entrepreneurship. Many of the theories used to explore SEs are simply (well, maybe not simply) developments of those used to explore traditional profit for shareholder enterprise. However, their application to SEs and social entrepreneurs creates a diverse and engaging research agenda, which is not only interesting to academics and practitioners but also influences the key debates discussed in later chapters of this textbook.

The key takeaways are the following:

- We have seen that the key characteristics of SEs include mission-driven orientation, innovative business models, stakeholder engagement and collaboration, impact measurement and evaluation, ethical leadership and governance, flexibility, and adaptability.

- The hybrid nature of SE reflects the blurring boundaries between private (profit-for-shareholder), public, and not-for-profit sectors and thus challenges traditional theoretical models.
- Hybrid SEs navigate tensions between economic sustainability and social impact, balancing competing priorities and maintaining organizational identity.
- SEs traverse institutional boundaries and operate across multiple functional domains, exemplifying the dual pursuit of financial and social aims.
- Theory then involves a multidisciplinary approach, reflecting a growing maturity in the discourse on SEs.

It is for the academics of the future to continue to develop such complex and multi-disciplinary theory as this exciting research agenda develops.

## CALLS TO ACTION

None of the questions below have a 'right' answer. They are deliberately written to be conceptual so that you can decide your own answers based on what you have just read and additional learning elsewhere. These prompts will help structure the response and encourage critical thinking when comparing the frameworks.

1 How do the different theoretical frameworks discussed in this chapter help us understand the concept of social enterprise? Which framework(s) do you find most convincing, and why?

**Indicative answer:** Begin by defining what a social enterprise is. How does it differ from traditional businesses or charities? Non-profits? Briefly introduce the theoretical frameworks discussed in the chapter that aim to explain or analyse SEs. Try to explain the role of SEs in addressing societal challenges. What are the strengths and limitations of these frameworks in understanding the purpose and operation of SEs? Compare the different frameworks. Try to discuss which ones focus more on the social mission versus the economic aspects of SEs. Explain whether there are any commonalities or significant differences between the frameworks in terms of how they explain the goals and impact of SEs.

2 Can the various frameworks be seen in isolation, or are they mutually supportive? Or even mutually exclusive?

**Indicative answer:** To answer this question, you could begin by summarizing the key theoretical frameworks discussed in the chapter. What are their main features and aims when applied to social enterprise? You should then consider whether each framework can stand alone in explaining SEs or whether they have limitations that require supplementation from other frameworks. Choose one or two frameworks (e.g. social innovation theory, stakeholder theory). How well do they explain SEs without reference to other perspectives? Are there areas where the frameworks complement each other? For example, can a resource-based view help explain challenges that stakeholder theory overlooks? Explore how combining multiple frameworks might provide a more complete picture of the complexities within SEs. How do they fill in gaps for one another?

3 If you were to create your own social enterprise, which theoretical model would guide your approach, and how would you implement it in practice?

**Indicative answer:** In order to answer this question, you could begin by explaining what kind of social enterprise you would create. What is the mission or primary social issue it seeks to address? Provide a brief overview of the theoretical models discussed in the chapter. Which models seem most applicable to your idea? Why does this particular framework align with your vision? Consider its strengths in terms of structure, mission, sustainability and impact. In practice, how would you foster innovation within your organization to create scalable solutions and ensure long-term impact? You could explain how the chosen theoretical framework would influence your enterprise's daily operations, decision-making processes and long-term strategy. Try to provide specific examples of how this framework would manifest in practical actions, such as organizational structure, hiring practices, partnerships or community engagement.

4 How can the theories discussed inform policy-making, funding and support for social enterprises in the future?

**Indicative answer:** One way to approach this question may be to explore how social innovation theory can help policymakers understand the potential of SEs to address societal challenges through innovative solutions. What types of policies could governments implement to foster a culture of innovation and experimentation in SEs? Think about grants, tax incentives or innovation hubs. What types of funding mechanisms could be designed to ensure social enterprises balance financial sustainability with social impact? Consider socially responsible investing or community-backed funding models. How can these theories guide the creation of regulatory frameworks that encourage the growth of SEs while maintaining accountability for their social mission? Lastly, try to consider how a combination of these theoretical frameworks (e.g. using both stakeholder theory and resource-based theory) could lead to more effective policies for supporting SEs.

## REAL-WORLD EXAMPLE INDICATIVE ANSWERS

1 How did the Big Issue's business model allow it to address the societal issues of rough sleeping and unemployment differently compared to traditional charitable efforts?

**Indicative answer:** The Big Issue is a quintessential example of a hybrid organization, blending commercial and social missions. As a social enterprise, it generates revenue by selling magazines, allowing vendors – often rough sleepers or marginally housed – to keep a portion of the profits. This model achieves dual goals: vendors earn an income while the organization sustains itself financially without relying solely on donations or grants. What distinguishes the Big Issue from traditional charities is its self-sustaining nature. By operating in the market economy, it provides a product (the magazine) that consumers willingly purchase while delivering tangible social outcomes. The ability to operate both as a business and a force for social change is the hallmark of a hybrid organization, where economic activity directly supports a social mission (Bird, 2011). This structure allows the Big Issue to adapt and evolve, such as during the Covid-19 pandemic when it shifted from street sales to digital platforms (Wood, 2020).

2 Discuss the challenges the Big Issue faced during its inception phase and how it managed to overcome them. What lessons can be drawn from these experiences for future social entrepreneurs?

**Indicative answer:** The Big Issue revolutionized the traditional model of support for rough sleepers through charity by introducing a socially innovative approach to addressing rough sleeping. Instead of providing direct financial aid, the organization empowers individuals to earn their own income. This is a form of social innovation – finding new, sustainable ways to address deep-seated social problems. By repositioning rough sleepers as vendors and entrepreneurs, the Big Issue challenges societal perceptions of rough sleeping. The innovation lies not only in the business model but in its rethinking of rough sleeping as an issue of economic participation rather than merely one of social welfare. This shift allows individuals to regain dignity, purpose and agency in their lives while addressing unemployment and rough sleeping in a more sustainable manner (Nieuwenhuis et al, 2018).

3 Evaluate the impact of Big Issue Invest on the broader social enterprise sector. How did it extend the Big Issue's influence beyond individual vendors?

**Indicative answer:** Several factors drove the social innovation behind the Big Issue:

- *Pressing social need:* During the early 1990s, rough sleeping in the UK had reached critical levels, and unemployment exacerbated the issue. Traditional welfare systems and charities struggled to meet the demand, creating the need for a new approach.

- *Economic inequality:* Growing economic disparities left a significant portion of the population marginalized, with limited access to jobs or resources. This situation catalysed the need for innovative solutions that could address both financial exclusion and rough sleeping.
- *Visionary leadership:* Founders John Bird and Gordon Roddick saw an opportunity to create a new model that gave rough sleepers the tools to help themselves, rather than relying on external aid. Their entrepreneurial vision was instrumental in making the Big Issue a successful social innovation (Bird, 2011).

These drivers collectively pushed the Big Issue to the forefront of social enterprise, addressing both immediate social needs and long-term systemic issues.

4 Critically analyse the social impact of the Big Issue based on the figures provided by the University of Northampton study. How does the organization's success underline the scale and persistence of the rough sleeping and unemployment problem?

**Indicative answer:** The Big Issue demonstrates how social enterprise can serve as a vehicle for social innovation. By adopting a market-based approach to a social problem, the organization merges profit generation with social good. The core of the Big Issue's business model is the empowerment of vendors. Vendors purchase the magazine at a reduced price and sell it for a profit, earning an income that helps them transition away from rough sleeping. This approach integrates entrepreneurial principles into social welfare, allowing individuals to take control over their economic future. In 2005, the Big Issue further expanded its impact through the launch of Big Issue Invest, a social investment arm. This innovation extended the organization's influence beyond individual vendors to other SEs, supporting them with financial resources and mentorship to scale their social impact (Paton, 2014). Through the Big Issue Invest, the organization became a catalyst for broader social change, proving the scalability and adaptability of SEs as a solution to systemic problems.

5 How can you apply the key theoretical frameworks discussed in this chapter to the Big Issue?

*Resource-based view (RBV):* From a resource-based perspective, the Big Issue relies on unique intangible assets such as its strong brand identity, social mission and dedicated vendor network. These resources are rare and difficult to imitate, providing the organization with a sustained competitive advantage in the social enterprise sector. The organization's reputation as an empathetic and effective solution to homelessness gives it leverage in attracting partnerships, donations and customers. Additionally, its vendors are a valuable resource in themselves, as they represent the mission and help maintain its grassroots connection with communities (Bird, 2011).

*Stakeholder theory:* Stakeholder theory is key to understanding the Big Issue's operational model. The enterprise carefully balances the needs of various stakeholders: the rough sleeper vendors, customers who buy the magazine, the government (which provides some regulatory oversight), and its investors and donors (especially those involved in Big Issue Invest). Each group plays a vital role in the organization's ecosystem, and the Big Issue thrives by addressing their needs and concerns. For instance, vendors gain a source of income, customers feel they are supporting a good cause, and investors see a return in social impact (Wood, 2020).

*Network theory:* Network theory is central to the Big Issue's expansion and sustainability. By building networks with vendors, SEs and investors, the Big Issue creates a web of mutual support and opportunity. The launch of Big Issue Invest further illustrates how network connections can amplify social innovation, as it forges relationships with other enterprises to drive systemic change. These networks enable the organization to scale its impact and adapt to changing social and economic conditions (Paton, 2014).

*Institutional theory:* The Big Issue also operates within and challenges existing institutional frameworks. Institutional theory emphasizes the role of societal norms, values and regulations in shaping organizational behaviour. The Big Issue challenges traditional institutional views of rough sleeping by redefining homeless individuals as entrepreneurs. The organization has also influenced public policy discussions around homelessness and social welfare by offering an alternative model of social support, encouraging a shift in how society and policymakers view social entrepreneurship as a viable solution to complex problems.

The Big Issue offers an insightful example on the intersection of social innovation, hybrid organizations and business theory. By blending entrepreneurial principles with social impact, the organization demonstrates how social enterprises can address deep-rooted societal challenges in innovative and sustainable ways. As we explore in this chapter, through the application of RBV, stakeholder theory, network theory and institutional theory, we can better understand how the Big Issue continues to thrive and adapt in a complex and ever-changing environment.

# References


Adderley, S (2019) Is it a bird? The social entrepreneurial superhero: fact or fiction?, in McAdam, M and Cunningham, J, *Entrepreneurial Behaviour: Individual, contextual and micro foundational perspectives*, London: Palgrave Macmillan, pp. 283–315

Agle, B R, Donaldson, T, Freeman, R E, Jensen, M C, Mitchell, R K and Wood, D J (2008) Dialogue: Toward superior stakeholder theory, *Business Ethics Quarterly*, 18 (2): 153–90

Alter, S K (2003) Social Enterprise: A typology of the field contextualised in Latin America, Inter-American Development Bank, Washington, DC

Alvord, S H, Brown, D and Letts, C W (2004) Social entrepreneurship and societal transformation, *Journal of Applied Behavioural Science*, 40(3): 260–82

Andersén, J, Jansson, C and Ljungkvist, T (2016) Resource immobility and sustained performance: A systematic assessment of how immobility has been considered in empirical resource-based studies, *International Journal of Management Reviews*, 18 (4): 371–96

Bacq, S and Eddleston, K A (2018) A resource-based view of social entrepreneurship: How stewardship culture benefits scale of social impact, *Journal of Business Ethics*, 152: 589–611

Bacq, S, Hertel, C and Lumpkin, G T (2022) Communities at the nexus of entrepreneurship and societal impact: A cross-disciplinary literature review, *Journal of Business Venturing*, 37 (5): 1–31

Bagnoli, L and Megali, C (2011) Measuring performance in social enterprises, *Non-profit and Voluntary Sector Quarterly*, 40: 149–65

Barney, J, (1991) Firm resources and sustained competitive advantage, *Journal of Management*, 17(1): 99–120

Battilana, J, Lee, M, Walker, J and Dorsey, C (2012) In search of the hybrid ideal, *Stanford Social Innovation Review*, 10(3): 50–55

Baumol, W J (1990) Entrepreneurship: Productive, unproductive and destructive, *Journal of Political Economy*, 98: 893–921

Bell, G G and Dyck, B (2011) Conventional resource-based theory and its radical alternative: A less materialist-individualist approach to strategy, *Journal of Business Ethics*, 99: 121–30

Billis, D (Ed) (2010) *Hybrid Organizations and the Third Sector: Challenges for practice, theory and policy*, Hampshire, TX: Palgrave Macmillan

Bird, J (2011) *The Big Issue: How it all began*, The Big Issue

Bitencourt, C C, Marconatto, D A B, Cruz, L B and Raufflet, E (2016) Introduction to special edition social innovation: Researching, defining and theorizing social innovation, *RAM, Revista de Administração Mackenzie*, 17: 14–19

Bloom, P N and Chatterji, A K (2009) Scaling social entrepreneurial impact, *California Management Review*, 51(3): 114–33

Bloom, P N and Smith, B R (2010) Identifying the drivers of social entrepreneurial impact: Theoretical development and an exploratory empirical test of SCALERS, *Journal of Social Entrepreneurship*, 1(1): 126–45

Borzaga, C and Defourny, J (Eds) (2001) *The Emergence of Social Enterprise*, New York, NY: Routledge

Bowen, H P and De Clercq, D (2008) Institutional context and the allocation of entrepreneurial effort, *Journal of International Business Studies*, 39(4): 747–67

Brandsen, T and Karré, P M (2011) Hybrid organizations: No cause for concern? *International Journal of Public Administration*, 34(13): 827–36

Brehmer, M, Podoynitsyna, K and Langerak, F (2018) Sustainable business models as boundary-spanning systems of value transfers, *Journal of Cleaner Production*, 172: 4514–31

Brenner, S N and Cochran, P (1991) The stakeholder theory of the firm: Implications for business and society theory and research. In *Proceedings of the International Association for Business and Society*, 2: 897–933

Brown, T (2008) Design thinking, *Harvard Business Review*, 86(6): 84

Busenitz, L W, Gomez, C and Spencer, J W (2000) Country institutional profiles: Unlocking entrepreneurial phenomena, *Academy of Management Journal*, 43(5): 994–1003

Campbell, C and Sacchetti, S (2014) Social enterprise networks and social capital: A case study in Scotland/UK. In Christoforou, A and Davis, J (Eds) *Social Capital and Economics*, London: Routledge, pp. 215–35

Casson, M and Yeung, B (2006) *Oxford Handbook of Entrepreneurship*, Oxford: Oxford University Press

Chesbrough, H W (2003) *Open Innovation: The new imperative for creating and profiting from technology*, Harvard Business Press

Choi, N and Majumdar, S (2015) Social innovation: Towards a conceptualisation. In Majumdar, S, Guha, S and Marakkath, N (Eds) *Technology and Innovation for Social Change*, ed. 127, UK: Springer, pp. 7–34

Christensen, C, Raynor, M E and McDonald, R (2013) Disruptive Innovation, *Harvard Business Review*

Cooney, K (2006) The institutional and technical structuring of non-profit ventures: Case study of a US hybrid organization caught between two fields, *Voluntas: International Journal of Voluntary and Non-profit Organizations*, 17(2): 137–55

Cornforth, C (2014) Understanding and combating mission drift in social enterprises, *Social Enterprise Journal*, 10(1): 3–20

Dacanay, M (Ed) (2004) *Creating Space in the Market: Social enterprise stories in Asia*, Makati City, Philippines: Asian Institute of Management and Conference of Asian Foundations and Organizations

Dacin, M T, Dacin, P A and Tracey, P (2011) Social entrepreneurship: A critique and future directions, *Organization Science*, 22(5): 1203–13

Dart, R (2004) The legitimacy of social enterprise, *Non-Profit Management and Leadership*, 14(4): 411–24

D'Aunno, T, Succi, M and Alexander, J A (2000) The role of institutional and market forces in divergent organizational change, *Administrative Science Quarterly*, 45(4): 679–703

Deal, T and Kennedy, A (2000) *Corporate Cultures: The rites and rituals of corporate life*, Da Capo Press

De Bussy, NM (2010) Dialogue as a basis for stakeholder engagement, *The SAGE Handbook of Public Relations*, 2: 127–44

De Souza João-Roland, I and Granados, M L (2023) Towards social innovation strategy: An analysis of UK social enterprises, *Technological Forecasting and Social Change*, 187: 1–12

Dees, J G, and Anderson, B B (2006) Framing a theory of social entrepreneurship: Building on two schools of practice and thought, *Research on Social Entrepreneurship ARNOVA Occasional Paper Series*, 1( 3): 39–66

Dees, J G and Elias, J (1998) The challenges of combining social and commercial enterprise-university-business partnerships: An assessment, *Business Ethics Quarterly*, 8(1): 165–78

Defourny, J and Nyssens, M (2006) Defining social enterprise, in Nyssens, M (ed.) *Social Enterprise: At the crossroads of market, public policies and civil society*, London: Routledge, pp. 3–26

Defourny, J, and Nyssens, M (2010) Conceptions of social enterprise and social entrepreneurship in Europe and the United States: Convergences and divergences, *Journal of Social Entrepreneurship*, 1: 32–53

Del Giudice, M, Garcia-Perez, A, Scuotto, V and Orlando, B (2019) Are social enterprises technological innovative? A quantitative analysis on social entrepreneurs in emerging countries, *Technological Forecasting and Social Change*, 148 C: DOI: 10.1016/j.techfore.2019.07.010 (archived at https://perma.cc/97G3-XC2G)

Desa, G and Basu, S (2013) Optimization or bricolage? Overcoming resource constraints in global social entrepreneurship, *Strategic Entrepreneurship Journal*, 7(1): 26–49

Desa, G and Koch, J L (2014) Scaling social impact: Building sustainable social ventures at the base-of-the-pyramid, *Journal of Social Entrepreneurship*, 5(2): 146–74

DiMaggio, P J (1988) Interest and agency in institutional theory, in Zucker (ed) *Institutional Patterns and Organizations: Culture and environment*, Cambridge, MA: Ballinger, pp.3–21

Di Domenico, M, Haugh, H and Tracey, P (2010) Social bricolage: Theorizing social value creation in social enterprises, *Entrepreneurship Theory and Practice*, 34(4): 681–703

Doherty, B, Haugh, H and Lyon, F (2014) Social enterprises as hybrid organizations: A review and research agenda, *International Journal of Management Reviews*, 16(4): 417–36

Donaldson, T and Preston, L E (1995) The stakeholder theory of the corporation: Concepts, evidence, and implications, *Academy of Management Review*, 20(1): 65–91

Drucker, P F (1954) *The Practice of Management*, New York: Harper & Brothers

Drucker, P F (1998) The discipline of innovation, *Harvard Business Review*, 76(6): 149–57

Durkin, C and Gunn, R (2016) Stakeholder participation and involvement in social enterprises, in Durkin, C and Gunn, R (eds) *Social Entrepreneurship*, UK: Policy Press, pp. 51-64

Ebnmhana, J (2018) Corporate social responsibility in a Saudi Arabian context: Social development centres as a bridge between the private sector and community needs, Unpublished PhD Thesis, University of Salford (United Kingdom)

Edwards-Schachter, M and Wallace, M L (2017) Shaken, but not stirred: Sixty years of defining social innovation, *Technological Forecasting and Social Change*, 119: 64–79

Eisenhardt, K M and Martin, J A (2000) Dynamic capabilities: what are they? *Strategic Management Journal*, 21(10–11): 1105–21

Emerson, J (2003) The blended value proposition: Integrating social and financial returns, *California Management Review*, 45(4): 35–51

Evers, A (2005) Mixed welfare systems and hybrid organizations: Changes in the governance and provision of social services, *International Journal of Public Administration*, 28: 736–48

Evers, A, and Laville, J L (2004) Defining the third sector in Europe, in A Evers and J L Laville (eds.) *The Third Sector in Europe*, Cheltenham, UK: Edward Elgar, pp. 11–42

Evers, A, Rauch, U and Stitz, U (2002) *Von öffentlichen Einrichtungen zu sozialen Unternehmen* [From public services to social enterprises], Berlin, Germany, Sigma

Freeman, R E (1984) *Strategic Management: A stakeholder approach*, Massachusetts: Pitman

Freeman, R E (2023) The politics of stakeholder theory: Some future directions, in *R. Edward Freeman's Selected Works on Stakeholder Theory and Business Ethics*, Cham: Springer International Publishing, pp. 119–32

Garud, R, Jain, S and Kumaraswamy, A (2002) Institutional entrepreneurship in the sponsorship of common technological standards: The case of Sun Microsystems and Java, *Academy of Management Journal*, 45(1): 196–214

Granados, M L and Rivera, A M (2018) Assessing the value dimensions of social enterprise networks, *International Journal of Entrepreneurial Behavior & Research*, 24(3): 734–54

Greenwood, R and Suddaby, R (2006) Institutional entrepreneurship in mature fields: The big five accounting firms, *Academy of Management Journal*, 49(1): 27–48

Grohs, S, Schneiders, K and Heinze, R G (2015) Social entrepreneurship versus intrapreneurship in the German social welfare state: A study of old-age care and youth welfare services, *Nonprofit and Voluntary Sector Quarterly*, 44(1): 163–80

Grimm, R, Fox, C, Baines, S and Albertson, K (2013) Social innovation, an answer to contemporary societal challenges? Locating the concept in theory and practice, *Innovation: The European Journal of Social Science Research*, 26(4): 436–55

Hamel, G (2008) *The Future of Management*, Boston, Mass: Harvard Business School Press

Harland, CM (1996) Supply chain management: Relationships, chains and networks, *British Journal of Management*, 7: 63–80

Haugh, H (2005) A research agenda for social entrepreneurship, *Social Enterprise Journal*, 1 (1): 1–12

Hazenberg, R, Bajwa-Patel, M, Mazzei, M, Roy, M J and Baglioni, S (2016) The role of institutional and stakeholder networks in shaping social enterprise ecosystems in Europe, *Social Enterprise Journal*, 12(3): 302–21

Henry, C (2015) Doing well by doing good: Opportunity recognition and the social enterprise partnership, *Journal of Social Entrepreneurship*, 6(2): 137–60

Hockerts, K (2006) Entrepreneurial opportunity in social purpose business ventures, in

Mair, J, Robertson, J and Hockerts, K (eds) *Social Entrepreneurship*, New York: Palgrave Macmillan, pp. 142–54

Hoopes, D G, Madsen, T L and Walker, G (2003) Guest editors' introduction to the special issue: why is there a resource-based view? Toward a theory of competitive heterogeneity, *Strategic Management Journal*, 24(10): 889–902

Hosseini, J C and Brenner, S N (1992) The stakeholder theory of the firm: A methodology to generate value matrix weights, *Business Ethics Quarterly*: 99–119

Howaldt, J, Kopp, R and Schwarz, M (2015) *Social Innovations as Drivers of Social Change: Exploring Tarde's contribution to social innovation theory building*, UK: Palgrave Macmillan

Hulgard, L (2010) Discourses of social entrepreneurship – Variations of the same theme, EMES European Research Network, 10(1): 2–21

Huybrechts, B and Nicholls, A (2013) The role of legitimacy in social enterprise-corporate collaboration, *Social Enterprise Journal*, 9(2): 130–46

Huybrechts, B, Mertens, S and Rijpens, J (2014) Explaining stakeholder involvement in social enterprise governance through resources and legitimacy, in Huybrechts, B, Mertens, S and Rijpens, J (eds) *Social Enterprise and the Third Sector*, UK: Routledge, pp. 173–91

Iannaci, D (2020) Reporting tools for social enterprises: Between impact measurement and stakeholder needs, *European Journal of Social Impact and Circular Economy*, 1(1b): 1–18

Imperatori, B and Ruta, D C (2015) Designing a social enterprise: Organization configuration and social stakeholders' work involvement, *Social Enterprise Journal*, 11(3): 321–46

Iskandar, Y, Joeliaty, J, Kaltum, U and Yudomartono, H (2023) Key factors affecting social enterprise performance: A literature review, *Journal of Developmental Entrepreneurship*, 28(02): 1–23

Jay, J (2013) Navigating paradox as a mechanism of change and innovation in hybrid organizations, *Academy of Management Journal*, 56(1): 137–59

Johnson, G (1992) Managing strategic change – strategy, culture and action, *Long Range Planning*, 25(1): 28–36

Jones, TM (1995) Instrumental stakeholder theory: A synthesis of ethics and economics, *Academy of Management Review*, 20(2): 404–37

Joshi, K and Khare, P (2024) The role of local connections in network configuration: A case of social enterprise in India, *Journal of Social Entrepreneurship*, 15(1): 50–76

Kah, S and Akenroye, T (2020) Evaluation of social impact measurement tools and techniques: a systematic review of the literature, *Social Enterprise Journal*, 16(4): 381–402

Kaufman, B E (2016) Will the real RBV please stand up? *Human Resource Management Journal*, 26(4): 379–89

Kerlin, J (2009) A comparison of social enterprise and its contexts, in Kerlin, J (ed.), *Social Enterprise, A Global Comparison*, Lebanon: Tufts University Press, pp. 184–200

Kerlin, J A (2012) Defining social enterprise across different contexts: A conceptual framework based on institutional factors, *Non-profit and Voluntary Sector Quarterly*, 42: 84–108

Key, S (1999) Toward a new theory of the firm: a critique of stakeholder theory, *Management Decision*, 37(4): 317–28

Kistruck, G M and Beamish, P (2010) The interplay of form, structure, and embeddedness in social intrapreneurship, *Entrepreneurship Theory and Practice*, 34(4): 735–61

Komatsu Cipriani, T, Deserti, A, Kleverbeck, M, Rizzo, F and Terstriep, J (2020) Business models & social innovation: Mission-driven versus profit-driven organizations, *International Review of Applied Economics*, 34(5): 541–66

Kraaijenbrink, J, Spender, J C and Groen, A J (2010) The resource-based view: A review and assessment of its critiques, *Journal of Management*, 36(1): 349–72

Krueger, N F, Reilly, M D and Carsrud, A L (2000) Competing models of entrepreneurial Intentions, *Journal of Business Venturing*, 15(5): 411–32

Kujala, J, Sachs, S, Leinonen, H, Heikkinen, A and Laude, D (2022) Stakeholder engagement: Past, present, and future, *Business & Society*, 61(5): 1136–96

Kulshrestha, R, Sahay, A and Sengupta, S (2022) Constituents and drivers of mission engagement for social enterprise sustainability: A systematic review, *The Journal of Entrepreneurship*, 31(1): 90–120

Les, E and Jeliazkova, M (2005) The social economy in Central, East and South East Europe, in OECD (ed.) *The Social Economy as a Tool of Social Innovation and Local Development (Background Report)*, Trento, Italy: OECD

Liu, G and Ko, W W (2012) Organizational learning and marketing capability development: A study of the charity retailing operations of British social enterprise, *Non-profit and Voluntary Sector Quarterly*, 41: 580–608

Lumpkin, G, Moss, T, Gras, D, Kato, S and Amezcua, A (2011) Entrepreneurial processes in social contexts: How are they different, if at all? *Small Business Economics*, 40(3): 761–83

Mackintosh, P G and Norcliffe, G (2016) Men, women and the bicycle: Gender and social geography of cycling in the late nineteenth-century, in Mackintosh, P G and Norcliffe, G (eds) *Cycling and Society*, UK: Routledge, pp 153–77

Madhani, P M (2010) The resource-based view (RBV): Issues and perspectives, *PACE, A Journal of Research of Prestige Institute of Management*, 1(1): 43–55

Mair, J and Martí, I (2009) Social entrepreneurship as institution building, in Robinson, J, Mair, J and Hockerts, K (eds), *International Perspective on Social Entrepreneurship*, London: Palgrave Macmillan, pp. 148–60

Marcon, G and Dorigo, L (2012) Stakeholder theory and care management: An inquiry into social enterprises, *Department of Management, Università Ca'Foscari Venezia Working Paper*, (21)

Marshall, R (2011) Conceptualizing the international for-profit social entrepreneur, *Journal of Business Ethics*, 98(2): 183–98

Martin, R L and Osberg, S (2007) Social entrepreneurship: The case for definition, *Stanford Social Innovation Review*, 5(2): 29–39

Midgley, J (2017) Social investment: Concepts, uses and theoretical perspectives, in Midgley, J, Dahl, E and Conley, A (ed) *Social Investment and Social Welfare*, UK: Edward Elgar Publishing, pp 13–32

Möller, K, Nenonen, S and Storbacka, K (2020) Networks, ecosystems, fields, market systems? Making sense of the business environment, *Industrial Marketing Management*, 90: 380–99

Morris, M H, Coombes, S M T, Schindehutte, M and Allen, J (2007) Antecedents and outcomes of entrepreneurial and market orientations in a non-profit context: Theoretical and empirical insights, *Journal of Leadership & Organizational Studies*, 13(4): 12–39

Mulgan, G (2006) Cultivating the other invisible hand of social entrepreneurship: Comparative advantage, public policy, and future research priorities, in A Nicholls (ed), *Social Entrepreneurship: New models of sustainable change*, Oxford, UK: Oxford University Press, pp. 74–95

Mulgan, G (2012) The theoretical foundations of social innovation, in Nicholls, A and Murdock, A (eds) *Social Innovation*, London: Palgrave Macmillan, pp. 33-65

Mulgan, G, Tucker, S, Ali, R and Sanders, B (2007) *Social Innovation: What it is, why it matters and how it can be accelerated*, Young Foundation

Muñoz, P and Kimmitt, J (2019) Social mission as competitive advantage: A configurational analysis of the strategic conditions of social entrepreneurship, *Journal of Business Research*, 101: 854–61

Murphy, P J and Coombes, S (2009) A model of social entrepreneurial discovery, *Journal of Business Ethics*, 87 ( 3): 325–36

Nee, V (1992) Organizational dynamics of market transition: Hybrid forms, property rights, and mixed economy in China, *Administrative Science Quarterly*, 37 (1): 1–27

Newth, J and Woods, C (2014) Resistance to social entrepreneurship: How context shapes innovation, *Journal of Social Entrepreneurship*, 5(2): 192–213

Nicholls, A (2006) *Social Entrepreneurship: New models of sustainable social change*, New York, NY: Oxford University Press

Nicholls, A and C Pharoah (2007) *The Landscape of Social Investment: A holistic topology of opportunities and challenges*, Oxford: Skoll Centre for Social Entrepreneurship

Nielsen, C and Carranza, D (2012) Networks for social enterprise: Applying a systems perspective to case studies in Latin America, *International Journal of Business and Social Research*, 2(6): 1–17

Nieuwenhuis, J, Hooimeijer, P, Meeus, W and van Ham, M (2018) Being poor in a rich society: A double deviation from the mean, *The Annals of the American Academy of Political and Social Science*, 680(1): 246–66

North, D C (1990) *Institutions, Institutional Change and Economic Performance*, Cambridge: Cambridge University Press

Nyssens, M (Ed) (2006) *Social Enterprise: At the crossroads of market, public policies and civil society*, New York, NY: Routledge

Office for Civil Society and Innovation, (2016) *In Pursuit of Impact: Mission led businesses*, HMSO, London

O'Riordan, L and Fairbrass, J (2008) Corporate social responsibility (CSR): Models and theories in stakeholder dialogue, *Journal of Business Ethics*, 83: 745–58

Pache, A and Santos, F (2013) Inside the hybrid organization: Selective coupling as a response to conflicting institutional logics, *Academy of Management Journal*, 56: 972–1001

Park, C and Wilding, M (2014) An exploratory study on the potential of social enterprise to act as the institutional glue of network governance, *The Social Science Journal*, 51(1): 120–29

Paton, R (2014) Reluctant entrepreneurs: Musicians and entrepreneurship in the 'new' music industry, *British Journal of Management*, 25(2): 320–36

Peattie, K and Morley, A (2008) Eight paradoxes of the social enterprise research agenda, *Social Enterprise Journal*, 4 ( 2): 91–107

Peng, K, Ames, D R and Knowles, E (2001) Culture and human inference, *Handbook of Culture and Psychology*, Oxford, NY: Oxford University Press

Peredo, A M and McLean, M (2006) Social entrepreneurship: A critical review of the concept, *Journal of World Business*, 41(1): 56–65

Phillips, W, Lee, H, Ghobadian, A, O'Regan, N and James, P (2015), Social innovation and social entrepreneurship: A systematic review, *Group & Organization Management*, 40(3): 428–61

Powell, W W (1987) Hybrid organizational arrangements: New form or transitional development? *California Management Review*, 30(1): 67–87

Purbasari, R, Wijaya, C and Rahayu, N (2020) Most roles actors play in entrepreneurial ecosystem: A network theory perspective, *Journal of Entrepreneurship Education*, 23(2): 1–16

Ramus, T and Vaccaro, A (2017) Stakeholders matter: How social enterprises address mission drift, *Journal of Business Ethics*, 143: 307–22

Renko, M (2013) Early challenges of nascent social entrepreneurs, *Entrepreneurship Theory and Practice*, 37(5): 1045–69

Robinson, J, Mair, J and Hockerts, K (eds) (2009) *International Perspective on Social Entrepreneurship*, London: Palgrave Macmillan

Romanelli, E (1991) The evolution of new organizational forms, *Annual Review of Sociology*, 17(1): 79–103

Roose, J (2016) Paths of innovation in social movement research theory. In Roose, J and Dietz, H (eds), *Social Theory and Social Movements*, Springer Fachmedien Wiesbaden, pp 1–12

Ruef, M (2000) The emergence of organizational forms: A community ecology approach, *American Journal of Sociology*, 106(3): 658–714

Rugman, A M and Verbeke, A (2002) Edith Penrose's contribution to the resource-based view of strategic management, *Strategic Management Journal*, 23(8):769–80

Salamon, L, Sokolowski, S W and Anheier, H K (2000) Social origins of civil society: An overview, *Working Paper of the Johns Hopkins Comparative Nonprofit Sector Project, No. 38.)*, Baltimore, MD: The Johns Hopkins Center for Civil Society Studies

Sarman, S R, Zainon, S, Atan, R, Bakar, Z A, Yoke, S K, Ahmad, S A and Shaari, N H M (2015) The web-based accountability practices in social enterprises: Validating the stakeholder theory, *Procedia Economics and Finance*, 31: 243–50

Schein, E (1985) Organizational Culture and Leadership: A dynamic view, San Francisco: Jossey Bass

Schein, E (1990) Organizational culture, *American Psychologist*, 45(2): 109–19

Schumpeter, J A (1942) *Capitalism, Socialism and Democracy*, New York: Harper & Brothers

Scott, W (1995) *Institutions and Organizations*, Thousand Oaks, CA: Sage

Smith, A M and McColl, J (2016) Contextual influences on social enterprise management in rural and urban communities, *Local Economy*, 31(5): 572–88

Smith, B R, J Knapp, T F Barr and B L Cannatelli (2010) Social enterprises and the timing of conception: Organizational identity tension, management, and marketing, *Journal of Nonprofit & Public Sector Marketing*, 22(2): 108–34

Spear, R (2006) Social entrepreneurship: A different model? *International Journal of Social Economics*, 33( 5/6): 399–410

Squazzoni, F (2009) Social entrepreneurship and economic development in Silicon Valley, *Non-profit and Voluntary Sector Quarterly*, 38: 869–83

Stieb, J A (2009) Assessing Freeman's stakeholder theory, *Journal of Business Ethics*, 87: 401–14

Stephan, U, Uhlaner, L M and Stride, C (2014) Institutions and social entrepreneurship: The role of institutional voids, institutional support, and institutional configurations, *Journal of International Business Studies*, 46(3): 308–31

Sud, M, VanSandt, C V and Baugous, A M (2009) Social entrepreneurship: The role of institutions, *Journal of Business Ethics*, 85: 201–16

Thompson, J (2008) Social enterprise and social entrepreneurship: Where have we reached?. *Social Enterprise Journal*, 4(2): 149–61

Tracey, P, Phillips, N and Jarvis, O (2011) Bridging institutional entrepreneurship and the creation of organizational forms, *Organization Science*, 22 (1): 60–80

University of Northampton (2022) The Big Issue: Social return on investment report. https://pure.northampton.ac.uk/en/publications/the-big-issue-social-return-on-investment-report (archived at https://perma.cc/576M-JR2U)

Von Hippel, E and Euchner, J (2013) User innovation, *Research-Technology Management*, 56(3): 15–20

Wasserman, S and Faust, K (1994) *Social Network Analysis: Methods and applications*, Cambridge: Cambridge University Press

Wernerfelt, B (1984) A resource-based view of the firm, *Strategic Management Journal*, 5(2): 171–80

Westley, F and Antadze, N (2010) Making a difference: Strategies for scaling social innovation for greater impact, *The Innovation Journal: The Public Sector Innovation Journal*, 15(2): 1–19

Wicks, A C, and Harrison, J S (2017) Toward a more productive dialogue between stakeholder theory and strategic management, *Stakeholder Management (Business and Society 360, Vol. 1)*, Emerald Publishing Limited, Leeds, pp. 249–73

Wood, D J (1991) Corporate social performance revisited, *Academy of Management Review*, 16(4): 691–718

Wood, V (2020) The Big Issue pivots the business model due to coronavirus, *The Guardian*

Young, D (2003) New trends in the U.S. non-profit sector: Towards market integration?, in OECD (ed), *The Non-profit Sector in a Changing Economy*, Paris, France: OECD: pp. 61–77

Yunus, M, Moingeon, B and Lehmann-Ortega, L (2010) Building social business models: Lessons from the Grameen experience, *Long Range Planning*, 43: 308–25

Zaharia, R M and Zaharia, R (2021) Triple bottom line, in *The Palgrave Handbook of Corporate Social Responsibility*, London: Palgrave, pp. 75–101

Zahra, S A, Gedajlovic, E, Neubaum, D O and Shulman, J M (2009) A typology of social entrepreneurs: Motives, search processes and ethical challenges, *Journal of Business Venturing*, 24 ( 5): 519–32

Zahra, S A, Wright, M and Abdelgawad, S G (2014) Contextualization and the advancement of entrepreneurship research, *International Small Business Journal*, 32(5): 479–500

Zaremohzzabieh, Z, Ahrari, S, Krauss, S E, Samah, A A, Meng, L K and Ariffin, Z (2019) Predicting social entrepreneurial intention: A meta-analytic path analysis based on the theory of planned behaviour, *Journal of Business Research*, 96: 264–76

# 03 Intention formation in social entrepreneurship

**PETER MCLUSKIE**

## LEARNING OUTCOMES

After reading this chapter, you should be able to:

- Understand the antecedents of social entrepreneurial behaviour.
- Explain the key characteristics and drivers of the social entrepreneur.
- Explain the social context enabling social entrepreneurial behaviour.
- Identify the theoretical frameworks that explain opportunity recognition and development.

## REAL-WORLD EXAMPLE TOMS shoes – one-for-one business model

Several of the themes and issues covered in this chapter are exemplified and illustrated by our example, TOMS shoes. TOMS was founded by Blake Mycoskie in 2006 and is a renowned social enterprise that has transformed the footwear industry through its 'One-for-One' business model. Known for his innovative approach to social entrepreneurship, Mycoskie's vision and passion have driven the success of TOMS. During a visit to Argentina, Mycoskie noticed that many children lacked proper shoes, exposing them to health risks and impeding their ability to attend school. This observation became the driving force behind TOMS' mission to provide shoes to those in need. He recognized the need for proper footwear among underprivileged children and acted. His entrepreneurial spirit led him to create the One-for-One model, a groundbreaking concept that combines business and social impact.

TOMS' approach to social entrepreneurship entails balancing profitability with a deep commitment to social impact. While the One-for-One model initially faced criticism for potentially perpetuating dependency, TOMS has evolved its strategies. The social enterprise has shifted from traditional donations to community-based initiatives that empower local economies and promote self-sufficiency. By partnering with local artisans and manufacturers, TOMS has created sustainable jobs and encouraged economic development within recipient communities (Fichter, 2014). This adaptability and willingness to learn from feedback exemplify TOMS' ethical considerations in the realm of social entrepreneurship.

Further references to TOMS shoes and its founder will be made later on in the chapter. There are also links to internet sources, which you are encouraged to explore. As you explore these resources and read this chapter, please consider the following questions related to TOMS shoes and their founder, Blake Mycoskie.

1 To what extent does the founder of TOMS shoes, Blake Mycoskie, fit the characteristics of a social entrepreneur?
2 Is there any evidence of characteristics and traits that overlap with the commercial entrepreneur?
3 How would you describe Mycoskie's leadership style?

---

## Introduction

This chapter is concerned with the antecedents of social entrepreneurship (SE). By this, we mean the things that come before, that determine and are the conditions upon which social entrepreneurship comes into being. The antecedents of social entrepreneurship are numerous and diverse (Ruskin et al, 2016). The aim of this chapter is to explore the many factors that drive individuals towards becoming social entrepreneurs. Some of these factors are common to all types of entrepreneurship, and these will be noted. However, there are distinct features that appear to lead individuals towards the path of social entrepreneurship. These will be contrasted with commercial entrepreneurship, where appropriate. The path towards social entrepreneurship is diverse, and there are many examples showing unique circumstances and individual stories. Nevertheless, it is possible to synthesize these unique stories and begin to identify common threads and recurrent tropes that appear to precede social entrepreneurship intentions and actions.

This chapter is organized around three areas of inquiry that help us understand the antecedents of social entrepreneurship and the process of setting up an SE. Firstly, personal characteristics, such as passion, education and family background, might help drive individuals towards social entrepreneurship. Yet, there are social factors that help enable social entrepreneurs to thrive. Social policy, political context, intermediaries, such as funding bodies, as well as a positive cultural attitude towards social entrepreneurship, should be present alongside personal drivers. Finally, we consider the process of starting up a social enterprise (SE) and what behaviours, actions and patterns precede this phase. Here, we can draw on theories of entrepreneurial actions, including effectuation, strategy and bricolage.

We begin by examining the personal antecedents of social entrepreneurship, then explore the social conditions that enable personal ambitions and attributes to thrive. The chapter concludes with an examination of the theories that help explain social entrepreneurial opportunity identification and start-ups. As well as TOMS' real-world example, this chapter includes an Expert View from a social entrepreneur, Mike Astbury, CEO of Mondrem Group, who provides a personal account of his journey towards social entrepreneurship.

## Personal drivers

The question of whether entrepreneurs are born or made is a recurrent one. It raises the question of whether entrepreneurs are a result of genetics and early life experiences as opposed to later events and influences, such as education and personal incidents that may trigger a desire or impulse to take entrepreneurial actions. The same question applies to the practice of social entrepreneurship: can we identify some of the personal characteristics that might be considered inherent to this identity, as well as some of the external influences that create social entrepreneurs?

### *Traits perspective*

The traits theory proposes that human personality is made up of stable and repeatable characteristics unique to the individual (Allport, 1936). Research in this area suggests that individuals are made up of five to ten personality traits that are significant predictors of subsequent actions (Novikova, 2013a). A good deal of this research has focused on what has become known as the Big Five, or the Five Factor Model, which identifies the most basic and common personality traits that make up human behaviour. These traits are openness to experience, conscientiousness, extraversion, agreeableness and neuroticism (Novikova, 2013b). In order to understand entrepreneurs, researchers have attempted to identify and explore the unique traits that predict entrepreneurial behaviour and actions. While there have been wide and diverse responses to this question, many scholars recognize that entrepreneurs tend to possess attributes consisting of the following characteristics: need for achievement, internal locus of control, creativity, risk-taking propensity and need for autonomy (Caird, 1991; McClelland, 1968). There are variations on this; for example,

Paul Burns (2016) adds 'drive and determination' to these five traits. Nevertheless, there are limitations to the trait theory. For example, do these traits necessarily lead to entrepreneurship? Might they lead to other occupations where these traits are relevant – in sports, for example? Also, do all entrepreneurs have these traits, and do they possess them with the same intensity? Furthermore, are traits fixed, or do they vary over time and through different life stages (Chell et al, 1991)?

In spite of these queries, researchers have applied the traits theory to social entrepreneurs in order to identify their particular attributes. Some research claims that the traits of social entrepreneurs are similar to those of commercial entrepreneurs – i.e. risk-taking propensity, creativity and resilience (Ernst, 2012; Santos et al, 2021; Tiwari et al, 2020). However, others dispute this. For example, Smith et al (2016) conducted research comparing commercial and social entrepreneurs. The researchers demonstrate that while they do indeed share similar traits, social entrepreneurs score significantly higher on 'creativity and innovativeness', 'moderate/calculated risk-taking' and 'need for autonomy/independence'. This can be explained given the different demands of SE vs. commercial enterprise business models. SEs are often not driven by clear market demand and typically operate in areas deemed unprofitable by the private sector (Di Domenico et al, 2010). They therefore require a good deal of creativity and innovation to make their business models viable. In addition, it could be argued that SEs are riskier (due to the lack of clear market demand). Hence, taking on an SE might require an autonomous and robust entrepreneurial mindset (Smith et al, 2016).

## Compassion

Entrepreneurial motivation is typically understood in terms of self-interest and commercial gain, whether that be financial gains or gaining a sense of achievement. However, a key determinant of the social entrepreneur has been the trait of compassion, along with a more emotional engagement driving the enterprise (Bacq and Alt, 2018; Douglas and Prentice, 2019; Douglas et al, 2021; Ip et al, 2021; Mair and Noboa, 2006). Studies show that social entrepreneurs tend to rate higher on altruism, humility, empathy, trust and integrity as compared to commercial entrepreneurs (Tiwari et al, 2020). Compassion can be characterized as an orientation towards others with a desire and compulsion to treat their discomfort and injustice. For some, this can be regarded as a defining feature of social entrepreneurship, which drives all the dimensions of the enterprise itself. Miller et al (2012: 617) argue that compassion 'plays a cognitive and affective role, influencing the way entrepreneurs think, calculate and analyse personal costs, and commit to organizing for a cause'. Compassion in the individual must be powerful enough to trigger actions and ongoing commitments, enabling entrepreneurs to take on risks and challenges in the pursuit of their goal.

As well as sparking a desire to alleviate the suffering of others, the process of identifying and feeling this suffering can bring a stronger sense of significance and authenticity to the social entrepreneur's mission (Miller et al, 2012). Nevertheless, the strength of compassion can trigger actions and attitudes that may even be detrimental to the social entrepreneur (Batson and Shaw, 1991). For example, it could mean a reckless attitude towards risk that is not so evident in a commercial entrepreneur. Because compassion is formed from emotional responses to the subject and the object of compassion, decision-making can also be prompt and perhaps lacking in robust analysis (Shiv et al, 2005). Again, care should be taken here to acknowledge the positive and negative effects of certain personality traits.

Finally, a great deal of research shows that social entrepreneurs not only empathize with their subjects but typically have experienced the suffering or trauma they wish to alleviate or else have experienced a critical incident that has spun them in a different direction with a new sense of purpose (Dickel et al, 2020; Hockerts, 2017). What this demonstrates is that the social entrepreneur feels very connected to the problem, either through compassion and empathy or through personal experiences. Indeed, this leads to the idea that social entrepreneurs are 'embedded agents' in the communities they serve.

## *Need for achievement, autonomy and influence*

It is worth noting that the drivers of commercial and social entrepreneurship often overlap and that they are close cousins. While 'other'-centred motivations and emotions such as empathy and compassion are key drivers of social entrepreneurial actions, there are also 'self'-oriented drivers that may be essential elements of effective entrepreneurship. Studies have shown that 'need for achievement' and 'autonomy' – that is the desire to be in control of one's destiny – are important elements of social entrepreneurs (Ruskin et al, 2016). Indeed, the desire to exercise influence and power, to change the minds and behaviours of others towards the social entrepreneur's own value systems, is also evident (Ruskin et al, 2016). Furthermore, when examining the antecedents and key competences driving social entrepreneurs, the motive of compassion and social justice is not always of key importance or an exclusive pathway into social entrepreneurship. In their study of antecedents, Chandra and Shang (2017) establish two typologies of social entrepreneurs. Firstly, there are those social entrepreneurs who are driven by 'other'-oriented factors, such as altruism and compassion. Secondly, there are those who possess 'economic skills' – prior business or work experience and prior financial resources – who follow a different route into social entrepreneurship. This is yet another reminder of the dual role of the social entrepreneur – the pursuit of a social mission and profit, which lends itself to different pathways, different individual characteristics and therefore different antecedents.

## Embedded agency

One of the common features of social entrepreneurs is their apparent embeddedness in the communities in which they serve (Grimes et al, 2013). Whether they were born into a particular community or if the embeddedness results from the networks they build, it is from here that they are able to identify social issues and begin developing their social entrepreneurial intentions. Shaw and Carter (2007), who surveyed social entrepreneurs, found that 84 per cent of respondents lived in the same geographical area where they had identified an opportunity and where they subsequently located their SE. It is clear that being a part of a community will very likely provide you with insight and knowledge to respond quicker and more accurately to an opportunity than those outside of the community. However, this factor also provides the social entrepreneur with credibility and social capital (see below), which enable the enterprise to thrive (Shaw and Carter, 2007). This embeddedness also has implications for how we understand the personal leadership style of the social entrepreneur. While commercial entrepreneurs are typically characterized as lone individuals who compete within a market space and are driven by an individual vision, social entrepreneurs can be viewed more as facilitators enabling others to take control, something Agnieszka Żur (2015) describes as 'empowering leadership', which helps release the potential of the community members who are served. Rather than thinking of social entrepreneurs as strong leaders, they are often seen as excellent networkers and partnership builders who can operate across diverse communities and social hierarchies, are able to empower those who are in need, and appeal to and influence those agencies and funders who can support them (Prabhu, 1999). The skills of diplomacy, empathy and emotional intelligence are therefore key to the capacities of the social entrepreneur.

## Education

The question of education and social entrepreneurship intentions is an important topic to consider. This includes further considerations: what kind of education? What topics should be taught? In terms of commercial entrepreneurship, there is evidence to suggest that higher education support is an important element of the start-up process. For example, if we take venture capital investments as an indicator, recent reports demonstrate that out of those who successfully attracted investment, 93 per cent had a university degree (Lewin, 2021). According to a study by Trivedi (2017), the general educational support offered by universities is conducive to producing entrepreneurial intentions.

With the development of entrepreneurship education over the past 20 years, we can see that training and educating students in enterprise and entrepreneurship skills and competencies can be a driver of entrepreneurial intent (Zhang et al, 2014). Key antecedents driving start-ups are self-efficacy and a sense of possessing the skills, knowledge and competencies to take on the challenge (Burns, 2016). A key goal and outcome of entrepreneurship education is the building of these skills and competencies to facilitate venture creation (QAA, 2018). Furthermore, studies have shown that a focus on social entrepreneurship education can also increase students' intentions to start an SE (Hockerts, 2018).

However, while there is compelling evidence to suggest that universities can be strong drivers of entrepreneurial intentions, it might not simply be the formal education elements that have the most impact. Instead, it is the university ecosystem that appears to play a part in supporting intentions and actions (Bazan et al, 2020). To begin with, universities themselves encourage and support social entrepreneurship as part of their social impact and citizenship agendas (Hockerts, 2015). In addition, they are a rich source of new knowledge and innovation, which can spill over into forming and driving entrepreneurial actions. This is combined with the supply of office and commercial spaces in the form of science parks and incubators as a viable ecosystem for the support of social entrepreneurs (Kim et al, 2020).

## *Critical incidents*

Many social entrepreneurs have stories to tell about critical moments that were transformative in terms of their thinking and their outlook, moving them into a mode of altruistic behaviour and activism (Mair and Noboa, 2003). A study of social founders by Barendsen and Gardner (2004) showed that half had experienced trauma in their early lives, which impacted significantly on their social entrepreneurship intentions. For example, John Bird, founder of the *Big Issue* magazine, was brought up in a poor community and experienced several periods of rough sleeping during his youth (see Chapter 2). It was this early experience that helped develop his empathy for rough sleepers and drove his commitment to setting up the *Big Issue*.

**STOP AND THINK**

Do the personal qualities and traits described in this section mean that people who possess them are likely to be social entrepreneurs? What other professions seem to possess these qualities and traits? What other elements are needed to set a person on a social entrepreneurial mission?

**KEY RESEARCH**

Theory of Planned Behaviour and further reading

In the broader field of entrepreneurship studies, researchers have drawn on the Theory of Planned Behaviour (TPB) to understand entrepreneurial intentions. This theory, as developed by Ajzen (1991), has provided an effective model for exploring entrepreneurial intentions by evaluating potential entrepreneurs from three angles:

- **subjective norms** (that is, the extent to which it is perceived to be an appropriate and acceptable option within a particular culture or society)
- **attitude towards entrepreneurship** (whether the individual is favourable towards entrepreneurship)
- **perceived behavioural control** (the extent to which a person feels able to carry out the role of entrepreneurship)

This framework is widely adopted by researchers to measure and explain entrepreneurial intentions. However, some researchers have sought to explain the differences between commercial and social entrepreneurs by exploring additional factors that might explain social entrepreneurship intentions. Mair and Noboa (2006), for instance, were some of the first to explore factors leading to social entrepreneurial intentions. They identified a number of factors that are specific to social entrepreneurs. The authors identified a direct relationship between the variables of empathy, moral obligation, perceived social support, self-efficacy and social entrepreneurship intentions. Other researchers have conducted further studies that aim to validate, extend or refine this model. For example, Hockerts (2017) added the variables of prior experience with social problems to refine the predictive power of TPB and further identified entrepreneurial self-efficacy as having the largest impact on social entrepreneurial intentions.

## Social drivers

Having considered the personal factors that inform social entrepreneurial intentions, this section will focus on the social context that impacts upon decisions to start an SE.

### *Gender*

One area worthy of consideration is the category of gender. We may feel that this is a personal attribute, which, to some extent, it is. Nevertheless, society shapes and, to some extent, determines attitudes and actions. Therefore, gender is addressed here to demonstrate that 'choice' and 'action' are socially constructed. The first point to make is that entrepreneurship in general is very much a male pursuit. This can be clearly seen in the figures published in the Alison Rose (2019) study, where only one in three UK entrepreneurs is female. This pattern of male dominance is common across the world, although some countries are exceptions. For example, according to the Global Entrepreneurship Monitor (GEM, 2022) report, the country with the highest start-up rates for women was found to be the Dominican Republic, with 43.7 per cent of women reporting start-up activity compared to 40.1 per cent of men. However, in the context of social entrepreneurship, we can find higher proportions of female founders than in commercial entrepreneurship. According to a report by Social Enterprise UK in 2021, 47 per cent of social enterprises were led by women, compared to just 16 per cent of commercial businesses (Hochlaf et al, 2023). This might not be surprising if we see that social entrepreneurship is associated with care, compassion and altruism, which are stereotypically feminine characteristics (Hechavarría et al, 2017). Indeed, there is a great deal of evidence to demonstrate that women are more interested in social value creation than men (Brieger et al, 2019). The growth of social entrepreneurship is therefore connected to increasing engagement from women and their particular skill sets and competencies around emotional intelligence, empathy and compassion (Stahl et al, 2023).

**KEY RESEARCH**

Entrepreneurship and feminist theory

Feminist theory recognizes that social and professional identities are constructed via discourse, which generates narratives and representations, impacting our understanding of ourselves and others. As we discussed, discourses around entrepreneurship tend to focus on the 'masculine' dimensions of entrepreneurial identity: competition, risk and individualism (Bruni et al, 2004). According to feminist theory, women, in their social conditioning, may not recognize themselves in these discourses and will therefore be unlikely to take on the role of entrepreneur (Marlow, 2019). This can also impact the ways in which women may be treated and addressed by other people and institutions that will have a bias towards men in their support and in their assumptions about who can be an entrepreneur (Basiglio et al, 2019). This can then be a self-fulfilling prophecy where women rate themselves poorly based on the expectations of others.

## Age and generation

The age at which entrepreneurship occurs appears to be different for social and commercial entrepreneurs. Studies demonstrate that SEs are linked to youth and younger demographics. Between the ages of 18 and 25, people are more likely to start an SE than a commercial enterprise (Bosma et al, 2016). The reasons for this trend are multiple. Younger people tend to be more concerned with social value and social justice and are likely to engage in socially and politically progressive causes (Hoogendoorn et al, 2022). As consumers and employees, Generation Z are more likely to seek out products, services and employers that have a positive impact on society and the environment (Schroth, 2019; Saarelainen, 2021). The current Millennial and Z Generations are also well connected to technology, which has helped generate global knowledge, understanding and collaborative communities, helping to share and drive social value initiatives and innovations (Chandna, 2022; Tkacz, 2016). Young people have therefore acquired the values, skills and access to technologies that have placed them at the forefront of the SE movement.

## Networks and social capital

A key factor enabling social entrepreneurial action is the possession of adequate networks and social capital. Social capital has been widely discussed, with a variety of definitions and perspectives. However, broadly, it can be defined as the goodwill that is generated by the nurturing of social relationships that can be leveraged to facilitate value (Cope et al, 2007). It has been noted that entrepreneurs in general are reliant on this notion of social capital. Rather than the traditional view of the 'lone entrepreneur', we understand the entrepreneurial identity and subsequent activities as socially embedded and reliant on other network actors (Aldrich and Zimmer, 1986). However, social capital has been understood to be particularly important in the context of social entrepreneurship in comparison with commercial entrepreneurship (Dufays and Huybrechts, 2014). One of the reasons social entrepreneurs are more reliant on social capital is that they are more resource-constrained than commercial entrepreneurs (Hidalgo et al, 2024).

**STOP AND THINK**

The reason we are talking about the role of social capital and its relationship to social entrepreneurship may be due to changes in society and the emergence of the sharing economy. The sharing economy describes forms of consumption activities such as swapping, bartering, trading, renting, sharing and exchanging (Habibi et al, 2017). This mindset, facilitated by the internet and peer-to-peer platforms, suggests that people are increasingly comfortable with different, non-fiscal types of capital and may be the key to understanding social entrepreneurs and their stakeholders. What do you think?

# Start-up theory

This section explores some of the theories that can help explain the precursors to social entrepreneurial action and the kinds of competences and behaviours that are displayed by social entrepreneurs.

## *Creating opportunity*

As well as the appropriate mindset and competencies for entrepreneurial actions, one of the key ingredients in the start-up process is opportunity. Just because an individual has the appropriate personality to be an entrepreneur, this does not mean they will start an SE. How can we understand the nature of opportunity in the context of entrepreneurial action?

There are two contrasting theoretical perspectives on the nature of opportunity – that opportunities are either discovered or created by the entrepreneur. In the former view, opportunities are the result of inefficiencies or gaps and imbalances in the market, such as lack of supply, changing consumer preferences or market failures, which the alert entrepreneur can exploit by, for example, moving products into an area where there is high demand and under-supply. The key point here is that the entrepreneurial opportunity is available to anyone who has the market knowledge and alertness to exploit it (Jong and Marsili 2010). On the other hand, opportunities can be *created* by the networks, resources and purposeful actions of the entrepreneur (Sharon and Barney 2007).

How does this relate to social entrepreneurship? We can see that while social entrepreneurs might see demand for certain products, this does not necessarily translate into market opportunity as those in need will not be able to pay. For example, as we have seen in the real-world example, Blake Mycoskie, founder of TOMS, while visiting Argentina, noticed that children lacked shoes, which exposed them to health risks and meant they were unable to attend school. This led to Mycoskie committing to providing shoes for these children in need. However, while Mycoskie identified an unmet market and a social need, these children could not pay for the shoes, so the solution called for a more innovative business model. This led to the idea for the *One-for-One*, a groundbreaking business model that was able to serve both social and market needs, where customers who bought a pair of shoes triggered a donation of a pair of shoes to a child in Argentina (Fichter, 2014). This is the key challenge facing social entrepreneurs: to support an unmet need where there is no clear market opportunity. While commercial entrepreneurs work in the context of functional markets where resources enable a viable commercial exchange, social entrepreneurs seek out markets with a paucity of resources (Domenico et al, 2010). As a result, social entrepreneurs are required to be more creative and innovative than commercial entrepreneurs. Reports confirm that social entrepreneurs are far more innovative than their commercial counterparts, with 56 per cent introducing a new product or service in 2019 compared to 36 per cent of commercial small-to-medium enterprises (Mansfield and Gregory, 2020).

In summary, in terms of opportunities, for the social entrepreneur, their role is less the discovery of existing opportunities and the balancing of market demand and supply and more the role of being a creative problem-solver focused on how to create markets using innovative models and processes to solve social problems.

**STOP AND THINK**

Jeff Bezos, the famous founder of Amazon and, more recently, the space travel company Blue Origin, is also famous for his 'lucky boots'. Following the successful launch of his craft, he explained his success with a post on X: 'Careful engineering, plus of course... the lucky boots. Successful mission.' How much of what we think about entrepreneurs and opportunity involves luck, chance and being in the right place at the right time? Does it suggest the absence of strategy and process?

## *Bricolage*

One way in which we can understand this creative process is through the concept of bricolage. The word bricolage was coined by the French anthropologist Claude Lévi-Strauss (1966) to refer to the process of making do with the resources at hand. It has since come to be applied in a variety of contexts, from arts, where artists combine found materials, to organizational theory, where it can be understood as 'the invention of resources from the available materials to solve unanticipated problems' (Cunha, 2005: 6). The idea of bricolage has been used by several scholars to explain the entrepreneurial journey, seeing strong parallels between the problem-solving and opportunity-spotting characteristics of bricolage and the actions of the entrepreneur (Baker and Nelson, 2005; Garud and Karnøe, 2003). However, this concept and perhaps the mindset of making do are frequently found in the context of social entrepreneurship (Di Domenico et al, 2010). Making do informs many of the upcycling and recycling models that have been adopted by SEs. For example, the pioneering company, **Bio Bean**, which won the Virgin Media Business Voom competition in 2016, turns waste from used coffee beans into briquettes, providing fuel for log burners.

As well as making do and creativity, a key feature identified in the bricoleur is the process of adapting, improvising and combining resources into novel combinations (Weick, 1993). Indeed, improvisation, adaptation and recombination of existing capital assets are common in SEs (Di Domenico et al, 2010). For example,

Liverpool-based company **MAKE CIC** illustrated this improvisation and reuse of assets when they led a project in the city that involved transforming empty shops into artist spaces and creating an innovation hub that breathed new life into a dilapidated community space (Liverpool City Region, 2023).

The tools and processes of bricolage come to inform the creative process of the entrepreneur, yet particularly so with the social entrepreneur, who can be seen to be improvising, adapting and combining to produce innovative business models.

## *Effectuation*

Another way in which we can understand entrepreneurial actions is through the process of effectuation, which has some overlap with bricolage. This term was developed by Saras Sarasvathy (2008a; 2008b), who investigated the business start-up narratives of successful entrepreneurs covering a range of business sectors. She identified five key principles governing the strategies and decision-making of entrepreneurs:

1. Focus on the available means and resources and what the entrepreneur has to hand.
2. Affordable loss, the idea that the entrepreneur looks at the downside, making smaller, incremental financial steps, rather than the riskier upside.
3. Building strategic partnerships and networks, getting stakeholder commitments and buy-in before the launch of the business.
4. Exploiting the unexpected, the surprise occurrence, and being responsive to new avenues and opportunities rather than sticking to a rigid plan.
5. The idea that the entrepreneur's actions shape the future rather than predetermined trends, which are inherently uncertain.

Sarasvathy describes a process that is counter to our expectations of entrepreneurs, who are assumed to be comfortable with risk, have clear business plans, have a strong and fixed vision of their future, and are driven by potential upsides and profit motives.

Social entrepreneurs also appear to adopt this process of effectuation. In their case study of the social enterprise Good-Faith Learning, Weerakoon et al (2019) demonstrate that effectuation explains their social entrepreneurial actions during the pre-start-up phase, demonstrating the effectual characteristics of 'flexibility, experimentation and affordable loss'. Given the high degree of resource constraints experienced by SEs and the lack of clear market opportunities, it could be claimed that effectuation is more relevant to the social entrepreneur (Yusuf and Sloan, 2015).

**STOP AND THINK**

What are the similarities and overlaps between effectuation and bricolage?

## Strategy

The final section on theory looks at strategy to further help explain the process of SE development and start-up. Here we consider two perspectives on strategy: deliberate and emergent (Mintzberg, 1979). Deliberate strategy is characterized by planning based on a prior vision and driven by a clear intention to reach a pre-defined destination. Emergent strategy, on the other hand, is characterized by action without clear vision, or rather, the vision emerges as a result of action and is subject to change during the journey (Waddock and Steckler, 2016). We might expect entrepreneurship to be characterized by strong vision and deliberate action, and a good deal of scholarship would support this. For example, McMullan and Long (1990) characterize entrepreneurship as the previsualization of a desired outcome. Hill and Levenhagen (1995) see vision as a 'mental model' that drives the entrepreneurial journey. However, we can also understand the entrepreneurial journey as a series of steps and iterations that are not necessarily linear or driven by a clear vision or destination.

Certainly, for social entrepreneurs, while the vision might be to change society or address a social or environmental issue, the market mechanism for achieving this might be less clear to them. This might be contrasted with commercial entrepreneurs, who are generally attempting to achieve market success with a particular product or service, and therefore the strategy might be more deliberate. There is evidence to suggest that social entrepreneurship is more likely to be driven by emergent strategies than deliberate strategies. In their study of 23 social enterprises, Waddock and Steckler (2016) report that 14 discovered their vision after taking action and followed a more emergent strategy. Besides, the study found that even when social entrepreneurs took a deliberate route, their pathways were 'fundamentally iterative, interacting continuously with actions and enhanced perspective over time'.

We can see then that the start-up process, the precursor to the launch, is rarely driven by a clear intention and a fixed vision. Rather, there is an aspiration but the route to the actual business model is characterized by iteration and an emerging vision. This section has explored several perspectives, practices and theories that help understand the start-up process. Bricolage, effectuation and emergent strategy all recognize the significance of the social entrepreneur, their resources and networks that are key to entrepreneurial outcomes. These theories and practices describe the incremental and iterative nature of the social entrepreneurial journey, and they represent success as not necessarily a result of market equilibrium and consumer demand but as a result of creativity, innovation, adaption and improvisation.

## EXPERT VIEW

Interview between the author and Mike Astbury, CEO Mondrem Group, 26 April 2024

Mike Astbury could be described as a serial entrepreneur who has set up and managed several SEs. His background and the factors leading to the founding of his businesses are instructive in the context of this chapter and its focus on the precursors to social entrepreneurship.

To begin with, Mike had not planned to set up a business. In fact, it was with some haste that he founded Mondrem in 2016. Mondrem is a 'not-for-profit public service transformation company, on a mission to make public services brilliant, everywhere, all the time'. Mike's motivation to start Mondrem was mainly the result of a growing feeling of disconnect with his then-current company, where he was a co-owner and which was going through leadership changes. Mike was not comfortable with feeling disconnected and felt that the right and most practical decision was to leave and start a new business. He named this new business Mondrem, after the ancient forests of Mondrem and Mara in Cheshire, where Mike originates from. Here he could express his personal values around supporting people and valuing the kind of public services where the end result was about improving lives and making a difference. Mike does recall a life experience that drove this desire to found Mondrem and recounts the story of Katy, his sister, who suffered brain cancer – this was where he first came into contact with public services, in this case the health service. The experience inspired Mike with a passion and a purpose and has come to be the 'why' of Mondrem and features prominently on the website as an expression of the values and purpose of the company itself.

Exploring his motivations for starting his business, Mike talks frequently about empathy and sympathy, and it is clear that he connects deeply with the people he supports both inside and outside of the organization. Empathy, of course, is frequently cited as a particular feature and driver of the social entrepreneur, but interestingly, Mike says it wasn't always this way. He has developed and learned empathy, and Mondrem has enabled this to grow as a personal trait. This helps to answer that question about whether entrepreneurs are made or born and suggests that life experiences are a key motivating factor in the equation. Mike goes on to contrast his empathetic nature and consequent 'authentic' leadership style with the mainstream definitions of business and leadership, where this might be frowned upon and considered weak, naïve and inappropriate. But it is clear that Mike, while a founder and leader, is also an enabler, and his focus is very much on facilitating and empowering others. A good example is one of Mondrem's sister companies, Nurture CIC, which was set up by a talented undergraduate from Keele University with the help of Mike and his team. In other words, contrary to commercial entrepreneurship, the vision and leadership style displayed here can be described as dispersed and inclusive.

This leads on to another feature that Mike reveals as key to Mondrem's success, and that is the networks and stakeholder relationships that he has built. Mike spends a good deal of his time going to events and attending meetings, and will generally accept every invitation that comes his way. He says he has worked really hard at 'having people bat for us' and that the social capital that this has built means he has a network of people telling the Mondrem story. Again, interestingly, Mike claims he is not a great networker, yet he also acknowledges that his introverted personality makes him good at building connections, as it makes him a good listener and enables him to put himself in the shoes of others.

Mike describes personality traits at odds with those of the commercial entrepreneur, who is typically represented as extroverted and charismatic. However, Mike does reveal some key traits common amongst commercial entrepreneurs, which are the abilities to spot opportunities, pivot and improvise in new directions. Mondrem Group is a collection of four different companies, which is testimony to Mike's creative imagination and ability to identify and pursue opportunities. Near the end of the interview, we discuss the current economic situation and the stress that businesses have been under, and Mike acknowledges that his responses have included a pivot to some more commercial products and strategies. In particular, Mike has set up a software company called Open Plan Software, which, while it has uses far beyond Mondrem's remit, can nevertheless generate income to support the group and its CICs.

In summary, Mike draws upon a diverse array of competencies, traits and life experiences that have driven his social entrepreneurial journey. His profound early experiences with the public sector drove him to champion a particular kind of service delivery that was people-centred and focused on excellence. His introversion and empathetic nature also drove this commitment to improving people's lives, whether they are inside or outside of the organization, and have enabled him to generate a network of supporters who are, in his words, all batting for Mondrem. And finally, his creativity and innovation are where the social entrepreneur meets the commercial entrepreneur: the abilities to spot, create and exploit opportunities are the essential and defining competencies of the entrepreneur.

## Summary and key learning points

In this chapter, we explored the antecedents of social entrepreneurial behaviour and start-up:

- We considered the various dimensions and factors that lead to start-up actions.
- We noted that there are personal factors to consider and very specific traits and experiences that inform social entrepreneurial behaviour, including compassion and altruism, as well as the classic entrepreneurial attitudes of need for achievement, autonomy and influence.

- We also explored the social dimensions of social entrepreneurs and established that certain sociological factors inform and affect the decision to become a social entrepreneur. Age and gender, as noted, are related to the likelihood of starting a social enterprise.
- While having the attributes and the sociological profile might help determine entrepreneurial intention, the start-up process and strategy need to be in place to execute those intentions and launch a social enterprise.
- It should be clear that traits, social context and profile, along with opportunity, work together to help predict the start-up process, and that simply possessing one or two of these three dimensions might not be sufficient to lead to behaviour.
- We should not underestimate the role of education and experience in shaping and reconfiguring these three dimensions. People can learn to become compassionate; critical incidents can change people's values, and training and education can teach people how to design and execute a successful start-up strategy.

## DISCUSSION QUESTIONS AND CALLS TO ACTION

Consider these questions related to your social entrepreneurial journey. They will help you evaluate the resources that you have and enable you to think through the areas of personal professional development that will ensure your social entrepreneurial journey will have the best chance of succeeding. Ideally, you should discuss this with a mentor, collaborator or a trusted friend who can help you reflect honestly and openly:

- Do you possess the personal characteristics of a social entrepreneur? Review what these are and remember our examples. Can these characteristics be acquired or developed? How important do you think they are? If there are gaps in your personal characteristics, can you team up with others who have the required skills?
- Is commercial acumen equally important, and do you possess the creativity and innovation to develop and sustain an enterprise? Think about the journey from idea to start-up. What kinds of skills and capabilities are needed at the different stages? Can some of these be learnt and what can you do now to prepare for the future?
- Is your network rich in support or does it need developing? Who might be your stakeholders and supporters, and how are you going to get them on board with your plans and ideas? Don't leave it to luck and chance; consider the strategies and actions you can take to help you meet collaborators and supporters.

Following these prompts and calls to action, put together an action plan, make some pledges and set targets. Setting yourself milestones and short-term goals and objectives will help you generate momentum and a sense of achievement.

## REAL-WORLD EXAMPLE INDICATIVE ANSWERS

1 To what extent does the founder of TOMS shoes, Blake Mycoskie, fit the characteristics of a social entrepreneur?

**Indicative answer:** He demonstrates empathy and compassion and is driven by a social need rather than a commercial opportunity.

2 Is there any evidence of characteristics and traits that overlap with those of a commercial entrepreneur?

**Indicative answer:** He does show innovation and commercial acumen with the introduction of the one-for-one business model, which is creative and financially robust. He is also able to pivot and continue to innovate when the business is in trouble.

3 How would you describe Mycoskie's leadership style?

**Indicative answer:** There is lots of evidence to suggest he is responsive to the needs and views of the stakeholders in his network, and we might say his leadership style is enabling and people-focused rather than market-focused.

# References

Ajzen, I (1991) The theory of planned behaviour, *Organizational Behaviour and Human Decision Processes*, 50(2): 179–211

Aldrich, H E and Zimmer, C (1986) Entrepreneurship through Social Networks, in D L Sexton and R W Wilson (eds) *The Art and Science of Entrepreneurship*, Cambridge, MA: Ballinger, pp. 154–67

Allport, G W and Odbert, H S ( 1936 ) Trait names: A psycho-lexical study, *Psychological Monographs*, 47(1): i–171

Bacq, S and Alt, E (2018) Feeling capable and valued: A prosocial perspective on the link between empathy and social entrepreneurial intentions, *Journal of Business Venturing*, 33(3): 333–50

Baker, T and Nelson, R E (2005) Creating something from nothing: Resource construction through entrepreneurial bricolage, *Administrative Science Quarterly*, 50: 329–366

Barendsen, L and Gardner, H (2004) Is the social entrepreneur a new type of leader? *Leader to Leader*, (34): 43–50

Basiglio, S, P, Devincentiis, E and Rossi, M C (2019) Credit access and approval, *CeRP Working Papers 189*, Center for Research on Pensions and Welfare Policies, Turin (Italy)

Batson, C and Shaw, L (1991) Evidence for altruism: Toward a pluralism of prosocial motives, *Psychological Inquiry*, 2(2): 107–22

Bazan, C, Gaultois, H, Shaikh, A, Gillespie, K, Frederick, S, Amjad, A, Yap, S, Finn, S, Rayner, J and Belal, N (2020) A systematic literature review of the influence of the university's environment and support system on the precursors of social entrepreneurial intention of students, *Journal of Innovation and Entrepreneurship*, 9 (4): https://doi.org/10.1186/s13731-020-0116-9 (archived at https://perma.cc/546R-QFZN)

Bosma, N S, Schøtt, T, Terjesen, S A and Kew, P (2016) *Global Entrepreneurship Monitor 2015 to 2016: Special report on social entrepreneurship*, Global Entrepreneurship Research Association, https://www.gemconsortium.org (archived at https://perma.cc/5P28-Y73A)

Brieger, S A, Terjesen, S A, Hechavarría, D M and Welzel, C (2019) Prosociality in business: A human empowerment framework, *Journal of Business Ethics*, 159(2): 361–80

Bruni, A, Gherardi, S and Poggio, B (2004) Doing gender, doing entrepreneurship: An ethnographic account of intertwined practices, *Gender, Work and Organization*, 11: 406–29

Burns, P (2016) *Entrepreneurship and Small Business: Start-up, growth and maturity*, Red UK: Palgrave

Caird, S (1991) Testing enterprising tendency in occupational groups, *British Journal of Management*, 2: 177–86

Chandna, V (2022) Social entrepreneurship and digital platforms: Crowdfunding in the sharing-economy era, *Business Horizons*, 65(1): 21–31

Chandra, Y and Shang, L (2017) Unpacking the biographical antecedents of the emergence of social enterprises: A narrative perspective, *Voluntas*, 28: 2498–29

Chell, E, Haworth, J and Brearley, S (1991) *The Entrepreneurial Personality: Concepts, cases and categories*, London: Routledge

Cope, J, Sarah, J and Rose, M (2007) Social capital and entrepreneurship: An introduction, *International Small Business Journal*, 25 (3): 3–219

Cunha, Miguel Pina e (2005), Bricolage in Organizations, FEUNL Working Paper No. 474, https://ssrn.com/abstract=882784 (archived at https://perma.cc/7APR-LKAX)

Di Domenico, M, Haugh, H and Tracey, P (2010) Social bricolage: Theorizing social value creation in social enterprises, *Entrepreneurship Theory and Practice*, 34(4): 681–703

Dickel, P, Sienknecht, M and Hörisch, J (2020) The early bird catches the worm: An empirical analysis of imprinting in social entrepreneurship, *Journal of Business Economics*, 91: 127–50

Douglas, E, and Prentice, C (2019) Innovation and profit motivations for social entrepreneurship: a fuzz set analysis, *Journal of Business Research*, 99: 69–79

Douglas, E J, Shepherd, D, and Venugopal, V (2021) A multi-motivational general model of entrepreneurial intention, *Journal of Business Venturing*, 36(4): 106–07

Dufays, F, and Huybrechts, B (2014) Connecting the dots for social value: A review on social networks and social entrepreneurship, *Journal of Social Entrepreneurship*, 5(2): 214–37

Ernst, K (2012) Social entrepreneurs and their personality, in Volkmann, C, Tokarski, K and Ernst, K (eds) *Social Entrepreneurship and Social Business*, Lehrbuch: Gabler Verlag, pp. 52–62

Fichter, M (2014) TOMS Shoes: A Case Study in Social Entrepreneurship, *Journal of Critical Incidents*, 7: 19–27

Garud, R, and Karnøe, P (2003) Bricolage versus breakthrough: Distributed and embedded agency in technology entrepreneurship, *Research Policy*, 32: 277–300

GEM (2022) 2021/22 *Women's Entrepreneurship Report: From crisis to opportunity*, Global Entrepreneurship Research Association, London, p. 99

Grimes, M, McMullen, J, Vogus, T and Miller, T (2013) Studying the origins of social entrepreneurship: Compassion and the role of embedded agency, *Academy of Management Review*, 38 (3): 460–63

Habibi, M R, Davidson, A and Laroche, M (2017) What managers should know about the sharing economy, *Business Horizons*, 60: 113–21

Hechavarría, D M, Terjesen, S A, Ingram, A E, Renko, M, Justo, R and Elam, A (2017) Taking care of business: the impact of culture and gender on entrepreneurs' blended value creation goals, *Small Business Economics*, 48(1): 225–57

Hidalgo, G Monticelli, J M and Bortolaso, I V (2024) Social capital as a driver of social entrepreneurship, *Journal of Social Entrepreneurship*, 15(1): 182–205

Hill, R C, and Levenhagen, M (1995) Metaphors and mental models: Sensemaking and sensegiving in innovative and entrepreneurial activities, *Journal of Management*, 21(6): 1057–074

Hochlaf, D, Gregory, D and Darko, E (2023) State of Social Enterprise 2023. Social Enterprise UK, https://www.socialenterprise.org.uk/app/uploads/2023/12/Mission-Critical-State-of-Social-Enterprise-2023.pdf (archived at https://perma.cc/E3UK-ACTZ)

Hockerts, K (2015) The Social Entrepreneurial Antecedents Scale (SEAS): a validation study, *Social Enterprise Journal*, 11(3): 260–80

Hockerts, K (2017) Determinants of social entrepreneurial intentions, *Entrepreneurship: Theory and Practice*, 41(1): 105–30

Hockerts, K (2018) The effect of experiential social entrepreneurship education on intention formation in students, *Journal of Social Entrepreneurship*, 9(3): 234–56

Hoogendoorn, B, Uhlaner, L, van der Zwan, P and Stephan, U (2022) Entrepreneurship, age, and social value creation: A constraint-based individual perspective, *Journal of Small Business Management*, 62(3): 1286–322, https://sifted.eu/articles/uk-founders-socioeconomic-privilege (archived at https://perma.cc/8GGM-RRMM)

Ip, C Y, Liang, C, and Lai, H J (2021) Determinants of social entrepreneurial intention: an alternative model based on social cognitive career theory, *Nonprofit Management and Leadership* 31(4): 737–60

Jong, J P J and Marsili, O (2010) Schumpeter versus Kirzner: An empirical investigation of opportunity types, *EIM Business and Policy Research, Scales Research Reports*

Kim, M G, Lee, J-H, Roh, T and Son, H (2020) Social entrepreneurship education as an innovation hub for building an entrepreneurial ecosystem: The case of the KAIST Social Entrepreneurship MBA Program, *Sustainability*, 12(22): 9736 https://doi.org/10.3390/su12229736 (archived at https://perma.cc/7UQ3-VST4)

Lévi-Strauss, C (1966) *The Savage Mind*, Chicago: University of Chicago Press

Lewin, A (2021) 'Founders are a seriously privileged bunch', https://sifted.eu/articles/uk-founders-socioeconomic-privilege (archived at https://perma.cc/8GGM-RRMM)

Liverpool City Region (2023). New creative space in Huyton is final piece in £6m campaign that's seen town centres revived across the Liverpool City Region, https://www.liverpoolcityregion-ca.gov.uk/news/new-creative-space-in-huyton (archived at https://perma.cc/78AV-VS67)

Mair, J and Noboa, E (2003) Social entrepreneurship: How intentions to create a social enterprise get formed (IESE Working Paper No. 521)

Mair, J and Noboa, E (2006) Social entrepreneurship: how intentions to create a social venture are formed, in Mair, J, Robinson, J and Hockerts K (eds) *Social Entrepreneurship*, London, UK: Palgrave Macmillan, pp. 121–135

Mansfield, C and Gregory, D (2020) Capitalism in Crisis? Transforming our economy for people and planet, Social Enterprise UK, https://www.socialenterprise.org.uk/app/uploads/2022/08/Capitalism-in-Crisis-2019.pdf (archived at https://perma.cc/XR9K-XZY4)

Marlow, S (2019) Gender and entrepreneurship: Past achievements and future possibilities, *International Journal of Gender and Entrepreneurship*, 12 (1): 39–52

McClelland, D C (1968) *The Achieving Society*, 2nd edn. Van Nostrand, Princeton: MacMillan

McMullan, W E, and Long, W (1990) *Developing New Ventures: The entrepreneurial option*, San Diego, CA: Harcourt Brace Jovanovich

Miller, T Grimes, M McMullen, J and Vogus, T (2012) Venturing for others with heart and head: How compassion encourages social entrepreneurship, *Academy of Management Review*, 37(4): 616–40

Mintzberg, H (1979). Patterns in strategy formation, *International Studies of Management & Organisation*, 9(3): 67–86

Novikova, I (2013a) Traits, Trait Theory, in Kenneth, D. Keith (ed), *The Encyclopedia of Cross-Cultural Psychology*, First Edition. UK: John Wiley & Sons, pp. 1293–295

Novikova, I (2013b) Big five: The five-factor model and the five-factor theory, in Kenneth, D. Keith (Ed), *The Encyclopedia of Cross-Cultural Psychology*, First Edition. UK: John Wiley & Sons, pp.1-3

Prabhu, GN (1999) Social entrepreneurial leadership, *Career Development International*, 4(3): 140–45

QAA (2018) Entrepreneurship Education: Guidance for UK Higher Education Providers https://www.qaa.ac.uk/the-quality-code/enterprise-and-entrepreneurship-education (archived at https://perma.cc/DCZ3-ZUY4)

Rose, A (2019) The Alison Rose Review of Female Entrepreneurship, https://www.gov.uk/government/publications/the-alison-rose-review-of-female-entrepreneurship (archived at https://perma.cc/RPY9-EKUD)

Ruskin, R, Seymour, R and Webster, C (2016) Why create value for others? An exploration of social entrepreneurial motives, *Journal of Small Business Management*, 54(4): 1015–37

Saarelainen, A (2021) How do different drivers in marketing messages elicit sustainable consumer intentions for Generation Z?' A qualitative study. Master's Thesis Aino Saarelainen Aalto University School of Business Creative Sustainability Spring

Santos, S C, Nikou, S and Brännback, M (2021) Are social and traditional entrepreneurial intentions really that different? *International Journal of Entrepreneurial Behavior & Research*, 27(7): 1891–911

Sarasvathy, S (2008a) What makes entrepreneurs entrepreneurial? *SSRN Electronic Journal*, 10.2139/ssrn.909038

Sarasvathy, S (2008b) *Effectuation: Elements of entrepreneurial expertise*, Cheltenham, MA: Edward Elgar Publishing

Schroth, H (2019) Are you ready for gen Z in the workplace? *California Management Review*, 61(3): 5–18

Sharon, A and Barney, J (2007) Discovery and creation: Alternative theories of entrepreneurial action, *Strategic Entrepreneurship Journal*, 1: 11–26.

Shaw, E and Carter, S (2007) Social entrepreneurship: Theoretical antecedents and empirical analysis of entrepreneurial processes and outcomes, *Journal of Small Business and Enterprise Development*, 14(3): 418–34

Shiv, B, Loewenstein, G and Bechara, A (2005) The dark side of emotion in decision-making: When individuals with decreased emotional reactions make more advantageous decisions, *Cognitive Brain Research*, 23: 85–92

Smith, B R, Kistruck, G M and Cannatelli, B (2016) The impact of moral intensity and desire for control on scaling decisions in social entrepreneurship, *Journal of Business Ethics*, 133: 677–89

Stahl, G, Burnard, P and McDonald, S (2023) Exploring the experiences of women social entrepreneurs: Advancing understandings of 'emotional capital' in women-only networks, *Feminist Review*, 134(1): 86–103

Tiwari, P, Bhat, A K, and Tikoria, J (2020) Mediating role of prosocial motivation in predicting social entrepreneurial intentions, *Journal of Social Entrepreneurship*, 13(1): 118–41

Tkacz, M (2016) New generation of social entrepreneurs: Exploratory research and cross case study analysis of new generations of social enterprises, *Ekonomia Społeczna*, 2: 20–37

Trivedi, R (2017) Entrepreneurial-intention constraint model: A comparative analysis among post-graduate management students in India, Singapore and Malaysia, *International Entrepreneurship and Management Journal*, 13(4):1239–261

Waddock, S, and Steckler, E (2016) Visionaries and wayfinders: Deliberate and emergent pathways to vision in social entrepreneurship, *Journal of Business Ethics*, 133: 719–34

Weerakoon, C, Gales, B and McMurray, A J (2019) Embracing entrepreneurial action through effectuation in social enterprise, *Social Enterprise Journal*, 15(2): 195–214

Weick, K E (1993) The collapse of sensemaking in organizations: The Mann Gulch disaster, *Administrative Science Quarterly*, 38: 628–52

Yusuf, J-E (Wie) and Sloan, M F (2015) Effectual processes in nonprofit start-ups and social entrepreneurship: An illustrated discussion of a novel decision-making approach, *The American Review of Public Administration*, 45(4): 417–35

Zhang, Y, Duyesters, G and Cloodt, M (2014) The role of entrepreneurship education as a predictor of university students' entrepreneurial intention, *International Entrepreneurship and Management Journal*, 10(3): 623–41

Żur, A (2015) Social problems as sources of opportunity: Antecedents of social entrepreneurship opportunities, *Entrepreneurial Business and Economics Review*, 3(4): 73–87

# 04 Social or commercial business?

LUCY FINDLAY

**LEARNING OUTCOMES**

By the end of this chapter, you should be able to:

- Differentiate between social and commercially led organizations based on their social purposes and objectives.
- Identify and explain the key characteristics of social enterprises that balance mission- and market-driven strategies.
- Compare and contrast these characteristics with commercially driven organizations.
- Identify how social value is created in social versus commercially led organizations, with a focus on social impact metrics versus financial performance indicators.
- Explain and evaluate the role of the accreditation processes both at UK and international levels.
- Discuss opportunities for growth, including the challenges faced by socially led organizations.

## Introduction

Throughout this textbook, we have highlighted the confusion over the terms used in the context of social enterprise (SE). Despite this, we have argued that social enterprise is an activity that is 'spearheaded' by a social entrepreneur (or groups of social entrepreneurs) to develop a novel approach to addressing pressing social or environmental problems (Austin et al, 2006; Dees, 2001; Johnson, 2000; Mair and Martí, 2006;

Mulgan, 2012). Social enterprise is therefore distinct from corporate social responsibility (CSR), which is often led by profit-for-shareholder businesses seeking to balance shareholder interests with social impact (see Chapter 5) (Blowfield and Murray, 2011; Steurer et al, 2005). Of equal importance, it differs from not-for-profit organizations (NFPs) that rely on government subsidies and charitable donations due to its dual objectives: social value creation and economic value creation (Dees, 2001; Mair and Martí, 2006; Martin and Osberg, 2007; Peredo and McLean, 2006).

This chapter focuses on clarifying some of the terms used to describe social enterprises (SEs). It examines the practical day-to-day challenges faced by SEs and explores the differences and similarities between running a socially led entity and a shareholder profit-driven business (i.e. a commercial entity). First, the chapter delves into the common drivers of social entrepreneurship, highlighting how commercial and social entrepreneurs share common traits yet differ in their approaches to social value creation. Then, the chapter unpacks the meaning of social enterprise, focusing on its key defining characteristics. We explore the meaning of social value, including procurement and commissioning processes driven by the Social Value Act 2013, and for which SEs have been positioned as the panacea to delivering social services that have been unmet by traditional providers such as mainstream businesses and charitable actions. Next, we explore the importance of accreditation standards for SEs, including the models available in both the UK and internationally. The chapter delves into opportunities and challenges of growth for SEs.

## Common drivers for social enterprises

SEs emerge due to a number of different circumstances and stimuli, from general market failure to better public service delivery. Some key drivers are outlined here:

### *Public markets and market failure vs commercial markets*

The profit motive is different in a social enterprise. Many SEs come about because their founders want to address a social problem that a traditional market-led business will not as there is not enough profitability to make the business viable. SEs are often prepared to operate at a lower profit margin or to cross-subsidize a more profitable good or service with those with a lower margin in order to help solve the social issue identified as their main social mission.

More recently government commissioning and procurement for goods and services has recognized the special role that SEs have in delivering public services and goods. This is because shareholder profit is not the main motive – the social/environmental mission is central, meaning SEs can use profits to improve and innovate to make that service better. For example, healthcare services for rough sleepers run by a social enterprise might invest and implement solutions aimed at prevention of homelessness, rather than just delivering the healthcare service (this is added social value).

## Social issues vs commercial drivers

Commercially led businesses are driven by profit for shareholders, fast growth and exit of investors for large profit margins whereas SEs focus on profit reinvestment for social impact for the long term.

As described above, social entrepreneurs are driven by a social motive rather than making money for shareholders. Social entrepreneurs are likely to see a problem and think 'How can I solve that problem?' and 'Can I make a business viable whilst solving the problem?' Traditional entrepreneurs are more likely to think about how the business will become financially lucrative for shareholders, become attractive to investors and what the exit point is when the business can be sold.

## Investment driven vs asset locked

Most investment in business is delivered through equity (i.e. an investor owning part of the business and exiting at a point when they can sell for a profit). Equity investors are likely to be motivated by a high return on investment so that they can exit with a large profit as soon as possible. The reason SEs are 'asset locked' is to stop this type of investment. This removes the profit motive from the potential investor but can lead to challenges to find the right kind of finance for SEs to grow,

## Ethical businesses vs social enterprises

Mainstream business practice now places an emphasis on what is known as 'mission led' or 'purpose led' business practices – that is, integrating social and environmental concerns into the fabric of the business and in some cases governance. Potential investors are also increasing this trend through what is known as Environmental, Social and Governance (ESG)-led investment decisions (see Chapter 5).

Although this is sometimes 'window dressing' or 'greenwash' (Dahl, 2010; see Chapter 5) there are significant numbers of businesses that want to demonstrate true ethical credentials by setting their governance to limit shareholder-driven profiteering either through limiting profits and asset stripping by shareholders or in some cases increasing democratic and/or stakeholder-driven processes within the business.

## Who is the entrepreneur?

Although research on entrepreneurship has been ongoing since the 1960s, to date, there is no universally accepted definition. Whether a social enterprise aims to eradicate the problem of rough sleeping, support the disadvantaged or address environmental challenges, we believe that one of the key challenges for social start-ups, due to their dual logic of social and business, is to build a compelling social value proposition that serves the needs of beneficiaries (on whom the social mission is built), paying customers to ensure financial sustainability, and the overall societal impact engendered through their activities (see Chapter 8). As we have explored in Chapter 3, it is important to realize that there are many factors that may influence social entrepreneurial intentions. However, since social entrepreneurs borrow market-based practices from mainstream entrepreneurship, we explore, in the next section, what we mean by an entrepreneur and how they are different from social entrepreneurs. One of the key questions we want to explore is whether entrepreneurs are born with key characteristics or whether there are any other factors that influence entrepreneurial intentions.

Nevertheless, given that entrepreneurs play a pivotal role in the entrepreneurial process, earlier studies focused primarily on examining their psychological characteristics/personal traits (Brockhaus, 1980; Gartner, 1989; 1990; Henry et al, 2003; McClelland, 1965; Reynolds et al, 2004; Timmons, 1989). A number of personality traits have been associated with entrepreneurs, notably high need for achievement (McClelland, 1965), risk-taking (Brockhaus, 1980; Kihlstrom and Laffont, 1979), internal locus of control (Rotter, 1996), self-confidence (Lowell et al, 1997; Stevenson and Gumpert, 1985), tolerance for ambiguity (Shere, 1982) and innovation (Schumpeter, 1947). As a result, many of the earlier entrepreneurship studies have focused on the psychological characteristics of entrepreneurs that distinguish them from non-entrepreneurs.

Notwithstanding, since the 1980s, debates on the nature of entrepreneurship have proliferated, focusing not only on the characteristics of an entrepreneur but also on a range of other factors that may influence entrepreneurial intentions. As pointed out in Chapter 3, this shift suggests that entrepreneurial intentions are influenced by a variety of factors beyond individual traits. These can include personal goals and motivation, prior experience, education, gender and the overall entrepreneurial ecosystem in which an entrepreneur is embedded (Cromie, 2000; Greenberger and Sexton, 1988; Herron and Sapienza, 1992; Shane et al, 2003).

## KEY RESEARCH

In his 1989 seminal article, 'Who is an entrepreneur? is the wrong question', Gartner argues for a paradigm shift in understanding entrepreneurship. He notes that entrepreneurship is a multidimensional phenomenon and, therefore, the focus should be not just on examining the unique traits of the entrepreneur but also on a broader understanding of how organizations come into existence. This includes examining the interplay between three dimensions: the entrepreneur (that is, the individual), the process of venture creation, including the types of ventures created, and the context in which the entrepreneur is embedded. This approach not only recognizes how new ventures are created within specific cultural, economic and political contexts but also the process by which they are created, their types, as well as the role of the individual entrepreneur in the start-up process (Gartner, 1989).

Reflective question:

Gartner tends to encourage a process view of entrepreneurship, in which the focus of inquiry should be on the process of creating new ventures. How do you think entrepreneurs recognize and act on entrepreneurial opportunities in their specific environment? And is the only aim of entrepreneurship to create a new venture?

Drawing on these debates, entrepreneurship research has also explored the differences between opportunity entrepreneurs and necessity entrepreneurs (Alam et al, 2021; Reynolds et al, 2004). While opportunity entrepreneurs are pulled to entrepreneurship to satisfy a particular personal need such as self-fulfilment, independence and flexibility, necessity entrepreneurs are pushed into entrepreneurship due to a lack of alternative employment opportunities (Amorós et al, 2021; Dencker et al, 2019). Notwithstanding, despite multifaceted interpretations, there is a common understanding that entrepreneurs identify entrepreneurial opportunities at the intersections of markets, industries and technologies. They are alert to entrepreneurial opportunities in the market based on an identified customer problem and exploit these to provide a solution for which customers are willing to pay. However, how do social entrepreneurs identify a social and/or environmental need while balancing a social mission with financial sustainability?

## *Who is the social entrepreneur?*

In Chapter 3, we have already drawn attention to the antecedents that influence social entrepreneurial intentions. Social and commercial entrepreneurs share similar traits such as innovation, risk-taking, and internal locus of control (Santos et al, 2021; Tiwari et al, 2020; To et al, 2020); however, they differ in their entrepreneurial intentions. While traditional entrepreneurs are primarily motivated by the pursuit of profit, social entrepreneurs are driven by creating social value despite adopting market-based practices (Ashraf et al, 2019). As such, social entrepreneurs are often characterized by their compassion, social responsibility, moral obligation and altruism (Bacq and Alt, 2018; Douglas and Prentice, 2019; Douglas et al, 2021; Ip et al, 2021; Mair and Noboa, 2006; Tiwari et al, 2020). Further findings suggest that social and commercial entrepreneurs differ in relation to the context in which they are embedded. While commercial entrepreneurs seek profitable market conditions to generate economic value and ultimately maximize shareholder value, social entrepreneurs operate in under-resourced communities and hence contend with unfavourable market mechanisms in order to create social change (Di Domenico et al, 2010; Ashraf et al, 2019; Miller and Wesley, 2010; Peredo and McLean, 2006).

We have explored thus far how social entrepreneurs tend to have distinguishing characteristics that influence their social entrepreneurial intentions. Besides, we argue that compared to traditional entrepreneurs who pursue entrepreneurial opportunities for profit, social entrepreneurs tend to operate in unfavourable market conditions, with an emphasis on addressing a specific social and/or environmental need. This leads us to the argument that building a social business model requires a different social value proposition and a different mechanism by which the social venture is created (see Chapter 8).

## What do we mean by trading in a social vs commercial context?

Profit-for-shareholder businesses and SEs often share common objectives in addressing social and environmental challenges. They both address a wide range of social or environmental needs while contributing to economic development through job creation and innovation. As we will discuss in Chapter 5, profit-for-shareholder businesses contribute to social good through their corporate social responsibility (CSR) mission (Garriga and Melé, 2004; Porter and Kramer, 2002). However, they prioritize shareholder value over a social mission. In contrast, SEs adopt business practices in the pursuit of their social mission. They develop innovative products and/or services to solve a particular social need for their target beneficiaries on whom the social mission is built (Borgaza and Defourny, 2001; Bagnoli and Megali, 2011). Hence, what makes a good social enterprise?

### *What makes a good social enterprise?*

In the majority of cases, the term SE has no legal definition in the UK and many international contexts, as outlined in Chapter 1. However, within the UK, the SE legal structure is often built on the government's definition of a hybrid organization that balances for-profit motives with a social mission. This differentiates SEs from other types of organizations, such as profit-for-shareholder organizations (i.e. private businesses) and NFPS (i.e. charities). While profit-for-shareholder organizations address social and/or environmental challenges through their CSR activities, they primarily exist to maximize shareholders' value (see Chapter 5). Conversely, charities and NGOs, such as Oxfam, may engage in commercial activities to diversify their revenue streams, but more often they rely on government subsidies and donations to support their operation.

Although SEs blur the boundaries between the private (commercial businesses) and NFP sectors (charity model), they have the following distinct characteristics.

## Clear social/environmental mission

Compared to profit-for-shareholder organizations that often adopt a standard template for their governance structure with wider commercial purposes, focused mainly on the rights and responsibilities of shareholders, SEs are required to articulate a clear social/environmental mission in their governing documentation. While many profit-for-shareholder organizations are increasingly committed to creating a 'better world' and supporting social and/or environmental causes – evidenced, for instance, by movements such as B Corp certification, which requires the inclusion of a legal clause in the governing document that allows directors to consider the interests of all stakeholders (not just shareholders) – these efforts remain secondary to their primary goal of maximizing shareholder value. Even in cases when profit-for-shareholder businesses trade for social good, their activities must be assessed against their key drive for enhancing shareholder value, including the monetization of value when selling the business.

## Clarity of ownership

In today's corporate environment, it is sometimes hard to untangle the relationship between organizations and who owns them. This is important because ultimately, the ownership structure defines the drivers of the business. Increasingly, SEs are being bought, taken over or set up by regular profit-for-shareholder businesses, which, although this may be seen as altruistic, can also be used as a greenwash activity (see Chapter 5). Therefore, in the context of SEs and their governance, they must demonstrate through their governing document that the power of the shareholder-led parent is limited, including a limit on their control in decision-making processes. This means that even if there is a financial lock on the assets and profits, SEs, particularly when owned by a different type of business, such as a profit for shareholders, must take all the necessary steps to demonstrate they are not led by the motivation to maximize shareholder value and are not unduly influenced by the parent company. This enables SEs to create a form of 'guardian' over their interests to ensure their independence from the interests of shareholders.

## Led by trade, not donations

Within the SE literature and the social sector movement as a whole, there have been many discussions related to the role of government-led grants. While all types of start-ups, including SEs, may access grants during their early stages or during economic crises, such as Covid-19, grants should not be the main driver or the main source of income. Reliance on grants can foster a 'grant-led' mentality rather than creating financially sustainable business models, driven by a trading model. Typically, mature SEs (not start-ups) should prove their financial independence and generate more than 50 per cent of their income through trading over a sustained number of years. Trading may take various forms:

1. **Service-level agreements:** these include contracts for providing an ongoing service.
2. **Government-procured contracts:** secured through a competitive bidding process.
3. **Open market transactions:** directly selling products or services for a fee to customers, with or without a formal contract.

## Government-procured contracts

The emphasis on trading is to ensure that SEs remain commercially viable by charging fees for their services or products to cover costs and generate profit, unless there are obvious reasons to cross-subsidize the goods/service being delivered. This aligns with sustainable business practices often adopted by hybrid SEs' business models, as exemplified by the Big Issue (Chapter 2). In this example, the Big Issue addresses systemic social challenges like rough sleeping by empowering rough sleepers to earn an income through direct sales of the magazine to the public. This example underscores the importance of balancing a social mission with financial sustainability.

## Assets locked both in profit distribution and on closure/sale

Many investors in the current business environment use an 'equity' model, which means that they own a portion of the business to yield, both in the medium and longer terms, a return on their investments through financial gains. This can be achieved through shareholder dividends and also through a lump sum on sale. However, this creates a problem for SEs that are not driven by financial gains for shareholders, and instead by their social and/or environmental mission. It is particularly problematic, for instance, when an SE is tackling complex social needs such as unemployment or mental health that have been unmet by mainstream open markets and is not sufficiently profitable for shareholders. Nevertheless, SEs must operate under asset lock provisions that restrict profit distribution and ensure that any residual assets are allocated for social purposes upon dissolution. However, there is a lack of understanding of this fundamental point among many business and financial advisors, which can pose barriers to SEs when accessing finance and business support (see Chapter 11).

## Demonstrate social impact and value

Although the governance structure of SEs is important, they are still required to provide evidence of the difference they are making to the target beneficiaries they serve. Articulating how an SE is engendering social change is critical to gaining legitimacy among stakeholders, including customers and partners, who can gain an understanding of the social value created. For social start-ups or smaller SEs, this may be limited to an annual social impact statement following a stakeholder survey. However, for more mature and bigger SEs, there has been a movement to develop some frameworks that can measure social impact in financial terms. An example of this is the Social Return on Investment (SROI) framework, as we will explore in Chapters 6 and 12, which puts a quantifiable value on the impact created by an SE, alongside a report that helps it to improve its impact, which is often non-articulated in conventional accounting practices. Nevertheless, in many cases, whatever the measurement framework or tool adopted, it is often hard to capture benefits through monetization and data-driven methodologies. Hence, more often SEs are required to capture their impact through qualitative methods such as storytelling and/or case studies.

## Stakeholder involvement

SEs should consider how to involve their stakeholders, including customers and beneficiaries, in their governance structure and decision-making processes. This practice tends to be more straightforward for smaller SEs who may achieve this through Board of Directors representation or steering groups alongside regular feedback loops. However, it is important to find ways to react to stakeholder involvement and to implement recommended actions to avoid the risk of being perceived as a 'token gesture'. Cooperatives, as we have pointed out in Chapter 1, are good examples of ventures where stakeholders are put first through their ownership structure, which fosters a sense of shared ownership and directs the business in ways that advantage those who are recipients of services. Many community businesses are governed in this way.

## Effective governance

Effective governance is critical to running an effective SE. It should be fit for purpose and focused on the type of SE that is needed. The balance between practicality and representation must be considered, with stakeholders' input being found in other ways (see above).

The starting point is to ensure that effective governance is enshrined in the governing documents of the business and include a clear social and/or environmental mission – that is, how the business will make a change and a transparent ownership structure that shows who is driving the business as well as limiting potential shareholder profiteering.

For smaller SEs, a small board (max 6–8 people) comprising individuals with practical and business experience is preferable, to provide clarity about how decisions are made. A flat management structure compared to a hierarchical structure is also desirable to support fast decision-making processes and a degree of flexibility.

Larger SEs, however, are more likely to face challenges around communication and responsiveness, as well as being in touch with the communities they serve. Therefore, other community engagement techniques as well as transparent decision-making processes are essential for maintaining alignment with the SE's social mission.

All the above needs to show work in practice – i.e. not just theoretical. This is one of the biggest challenges for SEs, especially once a founder moves on. However, if practice is embedded in the governance structures from bottom to top it is more likely that no changes will occur with new leadership or ownership.

### Ethical business practices

SEs are not a cheap alternative. Hence they must reflect their social mission and values through ethical business practices. These include fair working conditions and equitable pay. Ideally, staff should be paid at least the Real Living Wage (or what might be perceived as a fair level of pay) and reasonable pay differentials should be maintained between the highest- and lowest-paid employees. Ethical practices should therefore extend both within and beyond the SE to ensure it aligns with their broader social and/or environmental mission.

We have explored how, by adhering to the above principles, SEs can demonstrate their distinctiveness as hybrid organizations that balance commercial viability with a social mission. This dual objective enables SEs to ensure their financial sustainability while addressing social and/or environmental challenges.

**STOP AND THINK**

Imagine you are the founder of a social enterprise that is aimed at reducing dental healthcare inequalities in an area that has both a rich and poor population. Using the above guidance, how would you go about pricing and contracting your services in order to enable access for all, and how would you go about setting up your social enterprise to ensure social and financial sustainability?

## Procurement, commissioning and social value

The term social value gained significant prominence in the UK following the introduction of the 'Public Services' (Social Value) Act 2012, often referred to as the

'Social Value Act', which came into effect on 31 January 2013. The Social Value Act requires public sector organizations in the UK, including local authorities and National Health Service (NHS) organizations, to consider the broader social, economic and environmental benefits – beyond purely financial factors – when commissioning or procuring public service contracts. This means that public sector organizations are required to assess how the services they commission or procure could contribute to positive societal outcomes for local communities beyond simply purchasing products or services from others (Bonwick, 2014). For instance, public sector contracts may specify the inclusion of products that promote fair trade in procurement or require suppliers and subcontractors to not only deliver the product or the service required but to generate employment opportunities for those disadvantaged. This legislative framework seeks to ensure that public sector procurement processes positively contribute to society and promote sustainable development (see more in Chapter 6).

It is worth considering the root of the Act originated through the advocacy of Chris White, a UK backbench Conservative member of parliament, who in particular recognized the potential of SEs to deliver better public services due to their unique hybrid business model that blends business practices with social objectives. Although SEs exist to make a profit like any other business, their profits are often reinvested back into the community rather than distributed to shareholders. Besides, SEs' performance is often evaluated based on the difference they make within the community rather than solely on profit maximization for private shareholders (Agafonow, 2013). However, in order to gain wider cross-party support, the Act ultimately shifted its focus to the value created by any business, including SEs, rather than the type of business itself.

Although the Social Value Act has contributed to embedding more widely social value considerations in business practices, it has also raised concerns about 'green/social washing' (see Chapter 5). These concerns are particularly salient during austerity measures, where public sector budgets are under constraints, and mainstream businesses are under increasing pressure to demonstrate their social and environmental impact. In addition, the rise of ESG legislation has amplified the need for more robust accountability measures to ensure that any claims of social or environmental impact are genuine and not merely performative (Atkins, 2020).

## Definition of social value

Although social procurement has a long history, the UK Social Value Act (2012) and new European Union public procurement directives (European Union, 2014) constitute part of a series of policy developments to broaden public procurement beyond cost. This places a duty on public service organizations and also those tendering for projects to consider the wider social, environmental and economic impact of their procurement decision-making processes and how these might improve society's well-being.

According to Social Value UK (n.d.), 'Social Value is a broader understanding of value. It moves beyond using money as the main indicator of value, instead putting the emphasis on engaging people to understand the impact of decisions on their lives.' You can see more discussion about social value in Chapter 6.

## The case for accreditations

Accreditations often serve as alternatives to formal regulations or legislations, offering a degree of flexibility, and can support SEs to achieve recognition for their broader social impact. The first accreditation scheme that emerged in the UK specifically designed for SEs was the Social Enterprise Mark CIC (SEMCIC), which operated from 2010–2024. SEMCIC was an SE in its own right and was led by the social entrepreneur Lucy Findlay MBE in partnership with stakeholders in the social enterprise sector. SEMCIC initially launched as a regional pilot project in the South West of England and then was incorporated as a national Community Interest Company (CIC) in 2010. Since its inception, its accreditation mark has expanded internationally, reaching over 10 countries, including South Africa, Spain and the United Arab Emirates (UAE). The original motivation for SEMCIC was to enhance the visibility, credibility and legitimacy of SEs, addressing critical challenges:

**a.** the overwhelming bias towards shareholder-led business models, which are seen as the main drivers of economic prosperity, often overshadowing the unique contributions of SEs

**b.** the diversity of legal structures available to SEs, which posed challenges for some social entrepreneurs in selecting the most appropriate structure for their social business model

**c.** the need to distinguish SEs from the charity and voluntary-led sectors, which are predominantly grant- and donations-led

**d.** raising the profile and awareness of the social enterprise business model

SEMCIC was originally launched with support from the UK government, with the aspiration that, in time, the government would increase the types of incentives for SEs based on their accreditation status, particularly with regard to government commissioning and procurement activities. However, with a few notable exceptions (e.g. support from some local authorities, such as Somerset County Council in the UK), these ambitions were not fully realized. SEMCIC's limited impact was largely due to the fractured nature of social commissioning and procurement processes, as well as political complexity and lack of sustained governmental support. Despite these challenges, the accreditations provided by SEMCIC played a critical role in due diligence processes for SEs and supporting their differentiation and distinctive business models.

While it did not achieve widespread adoption as a marker of social value in public sector procurement, it nonetheless raised awareness about the impact SEs create in addressing social and/or environmental challenges.

SEMCIC developed a set of criteria to define what constitutes an SE and how it differs from profit-for-shareholder businesses and not-for-profit organizations such as charities and non-governmental organizations (NGOs).

## *SEMCIC accreditation criteria*

- **Primarily trading for social purpose:** SEs must explicitly articulate their social and/or environmental purposes in their governing documents, such as Articles of Association and company rules.
- **Independently owned or managed:** SEs must demonstrate they are autonomous and able to manage their own operation, ensuring they are not subject to undue control by shareholders or members who do not share similar purposes.
- **Generate the majority of trading income through trading activities:** SEs should primarily rely on income from trading activities, including fees, contracts and grants that have been competitively tendered for or commissioned by other agencies, including the sale of goods or services.
- **Commitment to maximizing income and allocating the majority of profits to social purposes:** The SE's governing documents, including its annual financial accounts, should demonstrate clearly that 51 per cent or more of any annual profits generated are in the pursuit of their social mission or other social purposes. It is worth noting, however, that many SEs, like any other start-ups, particularly during the early stages of their life cycle, may not generate significant profits.
- **On dissolution, be committed to all assets being distributed for social purposes:** The SE's governing documents should include clauses that clearly state that in the event of dissolution, and after satisfying all debts and liabilities, any residual financial or physical assets will be dedicated to social purposes.
- **Demonstrate how social purposes are achieved:** SEs must be able to describe and/or provide evidence of how they are fulfilling their social mission and delivering tangible social benefits to their intended beneficiaries.

## *SEMCIC tiered accreditation framework*

As noted, SEMCIC developed a tiered accreditation framework tailored to the needs of SEs and their business lifecycle. These include:

1. **Aspiring Social Enterprise Mark:** This tier was designed for nascent and aspiring SEs that have not yet reached the required trading thresholds of 50 per cent of

their income. Many early-stage SEs often rely on grants and donations to kickstart their social start-up. To gain the 'Aspiring Social Enterprise Status', early social start-ups needed to demonstrate they achieve 50 per cent of their income through trading within three years of starting.

2 **Social Enterprise Mark:** This relates to the original accreditation developed by SEMCIC to support SEs in differentiating themselves and demonstrating the social value they create. The criteria to gain this status included:

   a. have formally defined social and/or environmental objectives (or dedicate at least 51 per cent of its annual profits to such objectives)

   b. be able to demonstrate that it operates as an independent business

   c. generate at least 50 per cent of its annual income from trading

   d. commit the principal proportion (51 per cent +) of annual profit to social/environmental purposes

   e. on dissolution, be committed to distributing all residual assets for social/environmental purposes

   f. be able to demonstrate that social/environmental objects are being achieved

3 **Social Enterprise Silver Mark:** This was designed for SEs aiming to demonstrate continuous improvement to their processes and operational activities. To gain this status, SEs are required to be assessed via expert assessors and include additional criteria:

   a. demonstrate effective stakeholder engagement

   b. demonstrate ethical and good business practices

   c. demonstrate financial transparency

   d. demonstrate social impact reporting

4 **Social Enterprise Gold Mark:** This was designed for SEs that can showcase excellence in their operations. It was assessed against the same criteria as the Silver Mark but with higher levels of evidence thresholds.

## SEMCIC accreditation process

In general, assessments against the above accreditation statutes were conducted through a mixture of desk-based application reviews and expert evaluations, with support from SEMCIC. For the Silver and Gold Marks, the process included a combination of existing evidence supplied by the SE, surveys and interviews with existing stakeholders (tailored to the organization's size). Annual fees were tiered based on size, organizational turnover and the complexity of the assessment. Full assessments were carried out once every three years, with 'light touch' interim reviews conducted annually.

## Governance and oversight

Accreditation assessments were overseen by an independent Certification Panel comprising a number of social sector experts, professionals (legal and financial), commissioners and academics. This allowed the decision-making process to remain impartial and transparent. The panel's decision created assessment precedents for the application of accreditation criteria that ensured consistency and 'case law' for future decisions.

### TRAILBLAZING RECOGNITION IN HIGHER EDUCATION

SEMCIC accreditation gained significant acceptance and recognition within the Higher Education sector, with many UK universities holding the SE Mark based on their social mission and impact with students and their wider community and partnerships. The University of Plymouth was the first university to hold the Social Enterprise Mark. Other examples of Social Enterprise Gold Mark Holders include the University of Salford, York St John University, University of Westminster, University of Winchester, Bath Spa University and University of Northampton. These institutions demonstrate the alignment of their educational and community-focused missions with SE principles.

## Benefits of social enterprise accreditation

Benefits of accreditation:

- **Proof of credibility:** SEs could gain more credibility through accreditation as they could demonstrate they went through rigorous external assessment processes. These evaluations serve as evidence that they operated ethically, were commercially sound, and upheld sector-agreed standards.
- **Social impact articulation:** Accreditation provided SEs with the opportunity to articulate their social impact. By responding to tailored survey questions, they could showcase how they were contributing to social value and creating meaningful change within their communities.
- **Differentiation:** Possessing the accreditation 'mark' enabled SEs to distinguish themselves from competitors that did not carry an accreditation status. This differentiation was particularly valuable in markets where consumers were actively seeking ethical products or services.
- **Approved SE status:** Accreditation granted SEs a recognized status that supports the marketing and sales of their products and/or services, particularly as customers are increasingly valuing businesses that demonstrate ethical and social accountability.
- **Demonstrate good practice and feedback:** Accredited SEs could demonstrate how their activities focus on creating social impact, ensuring that their efforts align with the needs of their beneficiaries.

**REAL-WORLD EXAMPLE OF A SOCIAL ENTERPRISE MARK HOLDER** Lendology CIC – a social lending model

Lendology CIC is a UK-based social lender that has disrupted traditional lending practices by focusing on empowering partners and people in the decision-making processes. Its social mission is to enrich lives and homes through the provision of affordable finance. Lendology believes that every homeowner deserves to live in a home where they can feel safe, warm and secure, with access to affordable lending, often perceived as a critical enabler for achieving this vision.

Lendology currently manages a portfolio of over £10 million on behalf of local councils, making a positive difference to over 1,500 households. They look beyond financial metrics; it is the social impact on clients and the tangible benefits to their lives that matter.

A quote from the CEO, Emma Lower CEO of Lendology CIC, which held the Social Enterprise Silver Mark:

> As an established social enterprise trading for over 20 years, we are always looking for ways to increase consumer awareness and trust in the industry. The silver mark accreditation gave the industry another opportunity to work together to highlight our commitment to social value. Building an ethical and inclusive economy is key to achieving sustainable growth, and the social enterprise industry already acknowledges this. Consumer and stakeholder buy-in about the ethics of every social enterprise is vital to ensuring the continued growth of the sector for a better economy for all, and the Silver Mark recognizes this commitment to shared values.

The above statement underscores the role of accreditations, such as the Social Enterprise Mark, as discussed in this chapter, in fostering consumer trust and reinforcing the blended goals of SEs: a social mission with financial sustainability. By focusing on creating social value for disenfranchised communities, Lendology demonstrates the broader social impact engendered by SEs.

For more information, please visit: www.lendology.org.uk

---

**REAL-WORLD EXAMPLE** The case of Social Traders accreditation in Australia

Building on findings and using the experiences and precedents of SEMCIC in the UK (and others), Social Traders set up a specialist SE certification in Australia in 2018. This was based on an assessment framework specifically designed for the contextual conditions of

SEs in Australia while remaining flexible to adapt to the future development of the SE sector. The criteria for accreditation set by Social Traders are slightly broader than those of SEMCIC, requiring SEs to demonstrate:

1 a defined primary social, cultural or environmental purpose consistent with a public or community benefit
2 that a substantial portion of income is derived from trade
3 a commitment to invest efforts and resources into their purpose, ensuring that public or community benefit outweighs private benefit

#### Governance and applicability

The application of these criteria is overseen by the Social Traders Certification Advisory Group, which provides an independent perspective and ensures that the framework remains adaptive and relevant. The flexibility in the governance structure allows the framework to evolve based on the changing needs of the SE sector, contributing to its credibility and applicability.

#### Policy integration and sector growth

A significant factor that contributed to the success and growth of Social Traders certification has been its integration into funding and social procurement policies by key government bodies. Both the Queensland and Victoria state governments, as well as the Australian Federal Government, have adopted the certification as a standard for funding and procurement, encouraging the existence of SEs as a business model at the policy level.

This incentive has led to a number of mainstream businesses converting to a social enterprise model, which has posed some challenges for robust decision-making processes. To distinguish between authentic SEs and those adopting the SE model solely to gain procurement advantages remains a challenge.

#### Alignment with advocacy and data

Social Traders certification is not stand-alone but embedded within the broader activities of social traders, including policy and advocacy efforts. This embeddedness ensures alignment between the certification processes and the social enterprise's broader social mission while also leveraging data generated through the certification process to inform policy advocacy and the growth of the SE sector.

In summary, the Social Traders accreditation framework has played a critical role in nurturing the growth of the SE sector in Australia due to its adaptable framework and alignment with policy advocacy to drive its success.

For more information, please visit https://www.socialtraders.com.au/

## Growth models and journey to sustainability for social enterprises

One of the challenges for SEs is what the term 'growth' means. In most commercial contexts, growth equates to a greater increase in the bottom line – overall profits. However, this is not the main driver for SEs since they are driven by their core social and/or environmental mission. This is often perceived as an inherent tension within the SE's social business model, as increasing profits needs to be aligned with social value creation as core to its main mission and objectives (Mair and Martí, 2006). This is the reason why it is important to have a board of directors who understands this tension and helps SEs to make a judgement on the balance between financial sustainability and social/environmental sustainability (Battilana and Lee, 2014). This can prove challenging to SEs that are presented with lucrative opportunities that enable them to grow financially as they mature while demonstrating the social impact they are creating. However, if this balance is not achieved, either the social mission will be degraded or the financial viability can be compromised. Teething problems are common, especially if the drive for financial growth outweighs social impact.

Nevertheless, one of the key ways for SEs to grow is to collaborate and work in partnership with others. SEs are often promoted as being more collaborative and partnership-driven in contrast with other types of businesses. However, establishing partnerships can be challenging as it may distract and dilute the core business strategy and focus of an SE. Although missions may superficially align with your own business, partnership working is not easy. It will involve some dilution or realignment of focus; therefore, it is about give and take. Costs and benefits should be evaluated up front. If it involves too much diversion from the main focus, then it should not be embarked on. 'You have to kiss a lot of frogs to find your prince'! Above all try to keep it simple.

**REAL-WORLD EXAMPLE** Social Enterprise Mark CIC's sustainability journey

Following a national consultation, viability study and pilot programme conducted with the wider social enterprise sector, SEMCIC was set up as a social enterprise in 2010. Its formation was supported by resources transferred from the Regional Infrastructure for Social Enterprise (RISE), a business support body based in the UK, and UK National Lottery funding. SEMCIC's core mission was to accredit SEs for a licence fee, enabling them to distinguish themselves through a third-party accrediting body that could independently assess and validate the transparency of their processes and operations.

During the initial stages, SEMCIC received a modest investment from the UK government, which was primarily used to support the launch and initial marketing of the accreditation service. It received support from government officials who provided strategic guidance, particularly on the assumptions behind the business model, which was built on a low-price, high-volume approach to enhance the visibility of its accreditation services. However, these assumptions were regrettably flawed.

### Challenges in the initial business model

SEMCIC's business model, which relied on a low pricing strategy to attract a high volume of SEs requiring accreditation, revealed significant flaws. The anticipated volume of accreditations did not materialize, and the organization faced challenges in marketing its services due to limited resources available. Early sales were largely reliant on word-of-mouth promotion, with some direct sales activities, which were insufficient to financially sustain the business model.

Recognizing these challenges and the lack of success of the high-volume, low-pricing model, SEMCIC pivoted its business model. It introduced a tiered-licensing fee structure based on the SE's financial turnover. This meant that larger SEs with higher turnover paid higher licensing fees. These revenues were used to offset the lower fees charged to smaller SEs with lower annual turnover. While this shift created a scalable social business model, the transition to a different pricing model proved extremely challenging. Many customers were lost during the transition phase, which lasted approximately one year.

### Repositioning and market focus

Alongside the new pricing structure, SEMCIC worked on repositioning its brand in the market. It began emphasizing its role as an accreditation service provider that validated SEs' social impact within their local communities, rather than focusing solely on legal structures or financial reporting. This shift aimed to provide SEs with a more transparent and accessible framework to showcase their social impact and demonstrate the difference they make.

To further diversify its offering and increase its revenue streams, SEMCIC introduced a multi-tiered accreditation model. This included a two-tier Mark: the Gold Social Enterprise Mark and the Silver Social Enterprise Mark. Each tier was priced differently and involved varying levels of assessments. These tiers created pathways for SEs to demonstrate continuous improvements and achieve a journey of excellence. Additionally, SEMCIC launched an 'aspiring social enterprise accreditation' mark to support early-stage SEs working towards a full Social Enterprise Mark status.

### International expansion

SEMCIC expanded its operation internationally, offering accreditation services in a number of countries through direct partnerships and social franchising arrangements. While SEMCIC's international expansion achieved some success, it faced challenges associated with differing local conditions, political landscapes, capacity constraints, as well as the varying levels of maturity within the social enterprise sector.

Despite the above obstacles and the limitations of the initial social business model, SEMCIC emerged as a pioneering accreditation provider that responded to the needs of the SEs, both within the UK and internationally.

### The role of the founder – Lucy Findlay MBE

Lucy Findlay MBE, the founder and the driving force behind SEMCIC, played an instrumental role in establishing and promoting the Social Enterprise Mark. As a prominent figure in the social enterprise sector, she led discussions with local and international partners and actively contributed to blogging and commenting on the state of the SE sector at both local and international levels. Her leadership significantly strengthened the presence of SEMCIC. However, this strong association between SEMCIC and its founder created challenges, as the organization's identity became closely tied to Findlay's personal brand, which overshadowed the range of accreditation services offered by SEMCIC.

### Closure of SEMCIC

Despite operating successfully for over 14 years, during which SEMCIC influenced accreditation standards at both the national and international levels, the organization eventually went into voluntary liquidation in April 2024. The decision to exit was primarily attributed to sustained decline in demand for its accreditation services, compounded by the challenging economic climate that threatened the survival of many SEs.

SEMCIC's closure highlights the complex interplay between the leadership role of the social entrepreneur, organizational identity and external market conditions. While the organization contributed significantly to accredit the social enterprise sector, its closure underscores the need for flexibility and resilience in navigating the complex SE landscape.

### Lesson learnt: social finance – is it relevant to my business?

At various points along their journey, SEMCIC considered social finance. This exploration helped to clear up some of the 'myths' around social financing, such as the belief that it is widely available and without risk. Any form of finance is considered a debt, which presents a challenge for most SEs, since it requires repayment within a (relatively) tight timetable with interest. In many cases, it takes up to 5–10 years for an SE to become financially sustainable. Getting into debt is an additional problem, which can be daunting, especially if you are unclear whether it would be affordable. However, social finance can be useful for addressing minor cashflow issues. Nevertheless, its suitability for expansion and growth depends on a lot of certainty and confidence in the business model as well as the externalities and the operating environment.

### Lesson learnt: for business development from start-up

- Do not let non-business considerations, such as political pressures, guide your business model.

- Always make sure that you make the most of a product launch – be prepared with examples of existing customers and how to access the product with simple calls to action and a sales journey.
- Always ensure that a product is properly priced and do not over-discount, as it will be much harder to put prices up in the longer term, and customers do not value cheap or free products.
- Do not underestimate the challenges of working internationally. It can be time-consuming and diverting. Draw up a set of criteria that you require of partners. The key to this is a shared value set and capacity to deliver. Be mindful that social entrepreneurs are likely to want to adapt the product. You also need to ensure that you have the capacity to deliver, including understanding of international contract laws and staff training.

Lessons from maturity

- Focus: maintain your credibility and integrity at all costs since this is your reputation as well as your Unique Selling Point (USP). Due to the dual logics of social and business, it may be easy for SEs to drift from the social mission, focusing on commercial opportunities. If profits overtake, then it becomes questionable whether you should be operating as a social enterprise.
- Personal branding is important, but it can limit personal exit from a business.
- Do not underestimate the amount of time that human resource management takes. Life events happen within your business – births, deaths and personal crises! These require immediate attention as they are hard to plan for and can be very resource-intensive to deal with.

Lessons from closure

- Success is not about the presence of the SE. It is about impact. Hence, SE is a journey, not just a destination. If the business model is not able to create the best impact, then the mission may need to be carried out in other ways.
- The ongoing sustainability of a business is guided by the person/people who lead it. Burnout is not sustainable. Mature business mentoring and guidance can help reduce this.
- Understand when there is no longer a market for a product and/or service. A need for a product or a service does not necessarily mean that customers will buy it. In the context of accreditation, many SEs underestimated the true costs involved, which led to the closure of SEMCIC.
- It is hard for a small-scale SE to survive as an accreditation agent since specialist infrastructure and complementary products are needed to create economies of scale and efficiency.
- Bootstrapping for growth is a difficult financial model to maintain as a small SE. It relies on the capacity of the staff/team.

- Use your board to support your decisions, as it can be a stressful time.
- Closure is not a failure; it is a recognition that impact has been created, but the model to deliver further social impact needs to change.

Discussion questions:

1. How did Lucy Findlay MBE's leadership contribute to SEMCIC's success? What are the potential drawbacks of the social enterprise being associated solely with her name?
2. What were the main flaws in SEMCIC's initial pricing and business model? How could these be identified and addressed?
3. SEMCIC discovered that the demand for its accreditation services was limited despite an identified need. How can SEs, in general, better understand and predict customer willingness to buy the product or service they have on offer?
4. SEMCIC highlighted the need to adapt to changing market conditions. How can SEs identify the right time to pivot their social business model and stay relevant?

---

## Summary and key learning points

In this chapter we began by understanding what motivates individuals and organizations to set up SEs and how they come about. We also discussed and explored the differences between the shareholder-led business approach and SEs. We then went into some detail about what makes a good SE and what the key elements are as well as the current public sector commissioning environment, a market that can potentially be exploited by SEs.

Finally, we looked into some detail around the reasoning for accrediting SEs and how the first accreditation (The Social Enterprise Mark CIC) was set up in the UK (as a social enterprise itself). We learned the lessons from the 14 years of business as well as the influence that it had in the world in improving standards. The example also provided insight into setting up and running a social enterprise, direct from its founder – its ups and downs and lessons for the future.

Key learning points:

- There are a huge number of drivers for SE establishment but what holds them together is the need to set up a business that is truly focused on making a difference to people and planet rather than being driven by profit for individual shareholders. The business needs to be commercially viable, however, to carry out its mission.
- Social entrepreneurs when compared with traditional entrepreneurs often differ in their approach to a problem by seeing the social/environmental challenge as key and making money as secondary but necessary to mission implementation.

- There are many aspects to what makes a good SE and accreditation can help to highlight ongoing good practice as well as helping potential customers understand whether a business is a true reflection of an SE approach rather than greenwashing.
- SEs do not remain static and need to change with the times. We can learn from the experiences of others, e.g. the Social Enterprise Mark CIC, as to how to change as well as when to close. Closure is not necessarily a failure, it is a learning experience.

## REAL-WORLD EXAMPLE SEMCIC, INDICATIVE ANSWERS

1 How did Lucy Findlay MBE's leadership contribute to the SEMCIC success? What are the potential drawbacks of the social enterprise being associated solely with her name?

**Indicative answer:** Lucy was a leader who drove forward the vision and was key to the success of SEMCIC. It was hard to translate that vision to others so SEMCIC became over-reliant on Lucy to drive the business forward, which is a common problem for founders. It also limited the company's expansion potential as it became too reliant on Lucy's leadership. Exit planning is key but is hard for small businesses where there is an overreliance on one individual.

2 What were the main flaws in SEMCIC's initial pricing and business model? How could these be identified and addressed?

**Indicative answer:** The initial pricing was not based on cost of delivery and the margins required to make the business financially viable. Many SEs do not consider costs such as overheads in their delivery. A clearer model of pricing and cross-subsidy would have helped. Commercial pricing skills and support would have helped as well as greater understanding of customer behaviour, e.g. understanding the emotion of buying behaviour and the type of product that was being offered. Buyers do not value something that is sold as a cheap option (see more in Chapter 9).

3 SEMCIC discovered that the demand for its accreditation services was limited despite an identified need. How can SEs in general better understand and predict customer willingness to buy the product or the service they have on offer?

**Indicative answer:** Better testing of products and feedback. Testing pricing as well as ensuring that the service can be delivered for the price that customers are willing to pay. The demand for a product such as accreditation is also dependent on the market – having incentives to accredit is vital and will help sell the service. Remember that accreditation is a 'nice to have' and not vital if there are no direct requirements for it, particularly in an economic downturn (see more in Chapter 8).

4 SEMCIC highlighted the need to adapt to changing market conditions. How can SEs identify the right time to pivot their social business model and stay relevant?

**Indicative answer:** This needs to be evaluated constantly by talking to customers and being aware of competition and opportunities. This should be done in person by regularly speaking to customers either through customer relationship calls or via customer surveys – all opportunities for feedback should be used, including online. Regular horizon scanning is also important for the Board and employees (see more in Chapter 7).

**USEFUL LINKS**

Social Enterprise UK, https://www.socialenterprise.org.uk/

Just Buy UK, www.justbuyuk.co.uk

# References


Agafonow, A (2013) Toward a positive theory of social entrepreneurship. On maximizing versus satisficing value capture, *Journal of Business Ethics*, 125(4): 709–13

Alam, M S, Biswas, K, and Sulphey, M M (2021) A Case study on the entrepreneurial process of push and pull women entrepreneurs, *South Asian Journal of Business and Management Cases*, 10(2): 207-217.

Amorós, J E, Ciravegna, L, Mandakovic, V, and Stenholm, P (2019) Necessity or opportunity? The effects of state fragility and economic development on entrepreneurial efforts, *Entrepreneurship Theory and Practice*, 43(4): 725–50

Ashraf, M, Razzaque, M A, Liaw, S, Ray, P K and Hasan, R (2019) Social business as an entrepreneurship model in emerging economy, *Management Decision*, 57(5): 1145–161

Atkins, B (2020) Demystifying ESG: Its history & current status, *Forbes*

Austin, J, Stevenson, H and Wei-Skillern, J (2006) Social and commercial entrepreneurship: same, different, or both? *Entrepreneurship Theory and Practise*, 30(1): 1–22

Bacq, S and Alt, E (2018) Feeling capable and valued: A prosocial perspective on the link between empathy and social entrepreneurial intentions, *Journal of Business Venturing*, 33(3): 333–50

Bagnoli, L and Megali, C (2011) Measuring performance in social enterprises, *Non-profit and Voluntary Sector Quarterly*, 40:149–65

Battilana, J and Lee, M (2014) Advancing research on hybrid organizing: Insights from the study of social enterprises, *Academy of Management Annals*, 8 (1): 397–441

Blowfield, M, and Murray, A (2011) *Corporate Responsibility*, Oxford, UK: Oxford University Press

Bonwick, A (2014) *Corporate Social Procurement in Australia: Business creating social value*, Social Traders, Melbourne, Australia

Borgaza, C and Defourny, J (2001) *The Emergence of Social Enterprise*, London: Routledge

Brockhaus, R H Sr (1980) Risk taking propensity of entrepreneurs, *Academy of Management*, 23(3): 509–20

Cromie, S (2000) Assessing entrepreneurial inclinations: Some approaches and empirical evidence, *European Journal of Work and Organizational Psychology*, 9(1): 7–30

Dahl, R (2010) Greenwashing: Do you know what you're buying? *Environmental Health Perspectives*, 118(6): 246–52

Dees, J G (2001) The Meaning of 'Social Entrepreneurship'. Centre for the Advancement of Social Entrepreneurship, https://web.stanford.edu/class/e145/2007_fall/materials/dees_SE.pdf (archived at https://perma.cc/E7AQ-HUHT)

Dencker, J C, Bacq, S, Gruber, M and Haas, M (2021) Reconceptualizing necessity entrepreneurship: A contextualized framework of entrepreneurial processes under the condition of basic needs, *Academy of Management Review*, 46(1): 60–79

Di Domenico, M, Haugh, H and Tracey, P (2010) Social bricolage: Theorizing social value creation in social enterprises, *Entrepreneurship Theory and Practice*, 34(4): 681–703

Douglas, E, and Prentice, C (2019) Innovation and profit motivations for social entrepreneurship: A fuzz set analysis, *Journal of Business Research*, 99: 69–79

Douglas, E J, Shepherd, D and Venugopal, V (2021) A multi-motivational general model of entrepreneurial intention, *Journal of Business Venturing*, 36(4): 106–07

European Union (2014) Directive 2014/24/EU of the European Parliament and of the Council, of 26th February on Public Procurement and repealing Directive 2004/18/EC

Garriga, E, and Melé, D (2004) Corporate social responsibility theories: Mapping the territory, *Journal of Business Ethics*, 53: 51–71

Gartner, W B (1989) Who is the entrepreneur?' is the wrong question, *American Journal of Small Business*, 12: 47–67

Gartner, W B (1990) What are we talking about when we talk about entrepreneurship?. *Journal of Business Venturing*, 5: 15–28

Greenberger, D B, and Sexton, D L (1988) An interactive model of new venture initiation, *Journal of Small Business Management*, 26(3): 1–7

Henry, C, Hill, F and Leitch, C (2003) *Entrepreneurship Education and Training*, Aldershot: Ashgate

Herron, L and Sapienza, H J (1992) The entrepreneur and the initiation of new venture launch activities, *Entrepreneurship Theory and Practice*, 17(1): 49–55

Ip, C Y, Liang, C and Lai, H J (2021) Determinants of social entrepreneurial intention: An alternative model based on social cognitive career theory, *Nonprofit Management and Leadership*, 31(4): 737–60

Johnson, S (2000) *Literature Review on Social Entrepreneurship*, Canadian Centre for Social Entrepreneurship, Edmonton

Kihlstrom, R E and Laffont, JQ (1979) A general equilibrium entrepreneurial theory of firm formation based on risk aversion, *Journal of Political Economy*, 87(4): 719–48

Lowell, W B, and Barney, B (1997) Differences between entrepreneurs and managers in large organizations: Biases and heuristics in strategic decision-making, *Journal of Business Venturing*, 12(1): 9–30

Mair, J, and Martí, I (2006) Social entrepreneurship research: A source of explanation, prediction, and delight, *Journal of World Business*, 41: 36–44

Mair, J and Noboa, E (2006) Social entrepreneurship: How intentions to create a social venture are formed, in Mair, J, Robinson, J and Hockerts, K (eds) *Social Entrepreneurship*, London, UK: Palgrave Macmillan, pp. 121–35

Martin, R L and Osberg, S (2007) Social entrepreneurship: The case for definition, *Stanford Social Innovation Review*, https://ssir.org/articles/entry/social_entrepreneurship_the_case_for_definition (archived at https://perma.cc/9EY6-GQLF)

McClelland, D C (1965) N achievement and entrepreneurship: a longitudinal study, *Journal of Personality and Social Psychology*, 1: 389–92

Miller, T L and Wesley, C L (2010) Assessing mission and resources for social change: An organizational identity perspective on social venture capitalists' decision criteria, *Entrepreneurship Theory and Practice*, 34(4): 705–33

Mulgan, G (2012) The theoretical foundations of social innovation, in Nicholls, A and Murdoch, A (eds) *Social Innovation-blurring Boundaries to Reconfigure Markets*, New York: Palgrave Macmillan, pp. 33–65

Peredo, A M and McLean, M (2006) Social entrepreneurship: A critical review of the concept, *Journal of World Business*, 41: 56–65

Porter, M E and Kramer, M R (2002) The competitive advantage of corporate philanthropy, *Harvard Business Review*, 80(12): 56–68

Reynolds, P, Bygrave, W D and Autio, E (2004) GEM 2003 Global Report, Babson College/London Business School, London

Rotter, J B (1966) Generalized expectancies for internal versus external locus of control of reinforcement, *Psychological Monographs*, 80: 1–28

Santos, S C, Nikou, S, Brännback, M et al (2021) Are social and traditional entrepreneurial intentions really that different? *International Journal of Entrepreneurial Behavior & Research*, 27(7): 1891–911

Schumpeter, J A (1947) *Capitalism, Socialism and Democracy*, 2nd ed, New York: Harper and Bros

Shane, S, Locke, E A and Collins, C J (2003) Entrepreneurial motivation, *Human Resource Management Review*, 13(2): 257–79

Shere, J (1982) Tolerance and ambiguity as a discriminating variable between entrepreneurs and managers, *Proceedings of the Academy of Management*, New York, Academy of Management (pp. 404–08)

Social Value UK (nd) What is social value? https://socialvalueuk.org/what-is-social-value/ (archived at https://perma.cc/K6R6-FPEP)

Steurer, R, Langer, M E, Konrad, A, and Martinuzzi, A (2005) Corporations, stakeholders and sustainable development: A theoretical exploration of business-society relations, *Journal of Business Ethics*, 61: 263–81

Stevenson, H H, and Gumpert, D (1985) The heart of entrepreneurship, *Harvard Business Review*, 63(2): 85–94

Timmons, J A (1989) *The Entrepreneurial Mind*, Andover: Brick House Publishing

Tiwari, P, Bhat, A K and Tikoria, J (2020) Mediating role of prosocial motivation in predicting social entrepreneurial intentions, *Journal of Social Entrepreneurship*, 13(1): 118–41

To, C K Martínez, J M G and Orero-Blat, M (2020) Predicting motivational outcomes in social entrepreneurship: Roles of entrepreneurial self-efficacy and situational fit, *Journal of Business Research*, 121: 209–22

# 05 Corporate social responsibility and social enterprise

ZEINEB DJEBALI

## LEARNING OUTCOMES

After reading this chapter, you should be able to:

- Explain the core characteristics of corporate social responsibility and social enterprise.
- Describe both of their significance in addressing social and environmental challenges.
- Evaluate the similarities and differences between corporate social responsibility and social enterprise.
- Discuss the limitations of corporate social responsibility.
- Discuss the challenges inherent in social enterprise.

## REAL-WORLD EXAMPLE Warby Parker: Revolutionizing vision care through the power of social good

Warby Parker is an American eyewear brand co-founded in 2010 by Neil Blumenthal, Andy Hunt, Dave Gilboa and Jeff Raider. The founding team's mission extended beyond profitability, believing in the power of business as a force for social good. Warby Parker sought to disrupt the traditional eyewear market, which consists of prescription lenses, frames, eye exams, contact lenses and accessories, by offering an *at-home try-on service* that enables customers to try on five samples of prescription frames from the comfort of their own homes. Meanwhile, the company has embedded a social mission by supporting those in need through their slogan of the 'Buy a Pair, Give a Pair' programme, where for each pair of glasses sold, another is distributed to someone in need.

As of 2024, the eyewear market is dominated by major players, including EssilorLuxottica (28 per cent market share), Costco Wholesale Corp. (17.9 per cent), National Vision Inc. (9.1 per cent), and Visionworks of America Inc. (7.0 per cent), with the remaining players holding a combined 37.9 per cent (IBISWorld, 2024). Despite entering a highly saturated and competitive market, Warby Parker was able to capture a significant niche by offering stylish, high-quality eyewear at affordable pricing, combined with their home-try-on service. In 2023, the company announced plans to introduce eye exam suites into over 200 stores in the United States to create a one-stop shop for consumers (IBISWorld, 2024).

While the eyewear market continues to be dominated by larger corporations (as above), price remains a primary consideration for consumers when deciding where to buy. This supported the growth of value-based eyeglasses and contact lens chains like Costco and National Vision. However, rising competition between retailers has spurred the reinvention of in-store eyeglass shopping, with many retailers increasingly integrating new digital technologies, such as virtual try-ons, in-store eye exams and artificial intelligence (AI)-enabled try-on programs to enhance customer experience and facilitate online sales. Warby Parker revolutionized the traditional brick-and-mortar retail model by adopting a multi-channel approach, including physical retail, home try-on and digital services, which changed the way customers shopped for eyeglasses and was a key value proposition for the brand.

Warby Parker was also the first in the eyewear market to integrate a social mission by adopting the 'one-for-one' donation model across all of its product lines, where for every pair of glasses sold, a pair is distributed for someone in need. According to the International Agency for the Prevention of Blindness Report (2024), approximately 1 billion people around the world lack access to glasses, with the vast majority, around 90 per cent, of them in low- and middle-income countries. Warby Parker's novel 'one-for-one' model has sought to solve this problem through market-based solutions.

**Figure 5.1** Warby Parker eyewear

**Figure 5.2** Warby Parker eyewear

**SOURCE** Credit to Warby Parker: https://www.warbyparker.com/

Warby Parker has a dual-core social mission: the first is to sell stylish, high-quality and affordable eyeglasses, and the second is to support those in need to access eyewear. Using business for social good not only translated into the 'Buy a Pair, Give a Pair' programme, it also influenced the company's growth and competitive positioning in the eyewear market. Warby Parker continued to scale by opening over 40 new locations across the United States; its net revenue increased by 16.3 per cent and gross profit by 19.7 per cent (IBISWorld, 2024; Global Data, 2024).

Discussion questions:

1 What is your view on the *one-for-one* business model adopted by Warby Parker?

2 What is Warby Parker's strategy for achieving social impact? What could be the challenges?

## Introduction

The term 'corporate social responsibility' (CSR) has become an important subject of academic enquiry and policymaking, calling for 'traditional' corporations (i.e. profit-for-shareholder organizations) to embed more sustainable and socially responsible practices that demonstrate their social and environmental responsibility (Lichtenstein et al, 2004). Similarly, SEs are being perceived as key vehicles in developing innovative approaches to social and environmental challenges through market-based mechanisms (Dees, 2001; Mair and Martí, 2006; Martin and Osberg, 2007; Peredo and McLean, 2006). Although CSR and SEs share common social goals, they differ in their approach to social value creation – defined, as discussed further in Chapter 6, as the impact of activities, policies and programmes on the well-being of individuals, communities and society at large (Tomlins, 2015).

This chapter explores the similarities and differences between CSR and SEs. First we explore the evolution of CSR and the extent to which it has evolved beyond charitable giving to include the corporations' social and environmental responsibility. Then we examine the inherent characteristics of SEs, balancing social and economic value creation. This is followed by exploring the similarities and differences between CSR and SEs. Next we evaluate the inherent limitations of CSR, with a particular focus on the issues of greenwashing. Finally we explore the challenges inherent in SEs, with a specific focus on social impact measurement.

## Corporate social responsibility

While the widespread adoption of CSR is relatively recent, the concept itself can be traced back to the English Industrial Revolution (1760–1804, see Chapter 1), a period marked by deteriorating working conditions, prompting corporate philanthropists, mainly business owners, to begin donating to social causes and improving working standards (Peattie and Morley, 2008). However, such philanthropic giving was largely discretionary, driven by the whims of executive directors rather than being embedded into the corporate strategy of the firm (Blowfield *et al,* 2011; Callado-Muñoz and Utrero-Gonzalez, 2011; Porter and Kramer, 2002).

It was not until the 1950s that the term 'CSR' was formally coined by the US economist Howard Bowen in his book titled *Social Responsibilities of the Businessman* (1953). Bowen highlighted the growing power of corporations and their significant impact on society (Latapí Agudelo et al, 2019) and believed that corporations should use this power to help better society. His work played a significant role in paving the way towards the concept of 'responsible corporations'. However, it was not until the 1960s that scholars brought a new understanding of CSR, framing it as a social contract that exists between corporations and society (Garriga and Melé, 2004; Porter and Kramer, 2002; Steiner and Steiner, 2000; World Business Council for Sustainable Development, 2000). This period saw calls for corporations to demonstrate their social responsibility, yet this was more limited towards employee satisfaction and the social welfare of local communities (Davis, 1973; Frederick, 1994).

By the 1970s, the growing concerns over the environment and human and labour rights made CSR increasingly popular, but it remained limited to voluntary philanthropic actions. It was only in the 1990s that a new, modern form of CSR began to take root: CSR as a process embedded into the corporate strategy. This was accompanied by a set of protocols and international agreements, such as the creation of the European Environmental Agency in 1990 and the United Nations (UN) Summit on Environment Development held in Rio de Janeiro, which translated into the adoption of Agenda 21 (the UN Action Plan for Sustainable Development) and the UN Framework Convention on Climate Change (UNFCCC) (1992), all of which expanded the expectations placed on corporations to be socially and environmentally responsible (Latapí Agudelo et al, 2019).

From a theoretical perspective, Carroll's (1991) pyramid provides an understanding of the economic, legal, ethical and philanthropic responsibilities of corporations. As shown in the following Key Research box, the pyramid categorizes CSR into four levels, where each level represents the corporations' responsibilities. Carroll suggests that the primary responsibility of corporations is to be profitable; crucially, however, they are required to comply with laws and regulations as part of their corporate governance, conduct their business ethically, and engage in philanthropic giving.

## KEY RESEARCH

Carroll (1991) argues that CSR is characterized by four levels: corporations are responsible for their economic profitability, must comply with the laws and regulations, demonstrate ethical conduct, and contribute to broader social and environmental needs through philanthropic giving:

- **Economic responsibilities:** Representing the foundation level of the pyramid, this is the responsibility of corporations to be profitable to ensure their long-term financial sustainability, ultimately benefiting their stakeholder groups (any group or individual who can affect or is affected by the corporation's actions and objectives) (Carroll and Shabana, 2010; Freeman, 1984). Profitability, in this context, is seen to enable corporations to sustain their business operations, optimize the efficiency of their processes and productivity, and maximize shareholder returns, as well as contribute to the broader economy by driving economic growth, job creation, tax contributions and overall innovation. Economic responsibility is therefore a basic requirement that must be met by all corporations (Cho et al, 2019).
- **Legal responsibilities:** This second level of the pyramid represents the responsibility of corporations to comply with laws and regulations in the environment in which they operate. Compliance involves conducting business in line with local, national and international laws and industry standards.

- **Ethical responsibilities:** This level of responsibility focuses on the ethical behaviour/conduct of corporations and demonstrates the extent to which they are required to go beyond mere compliance with economic and legal requirements to show their ethical responsibility. This involves corporations prioritizing the needs of their stakeholder groups and treating them all fairly, conducting their business ethically and respecting the social and cultural norms in which they operate (Carroll and Shabana, 2010; Freeman,1984; Gunningham et al, 2004).
- **Philanthropic responsibilities:** This top layer of the pyramid represents the responsibility of corporations to contribute philanthropically (often voluntarily) to social and environmental needs (Porter and Kramer, 2002). Philanthropic responsibility is defined as the 'direct' contributions made by any corporation towards a cause, a project, or an organization, which can involve financial contributions, in-kind donations and/or sponsoring a particular social project or event (Kotler and Lee, 2007). Although this layer of the pyramid is not considered a responsibility due to its voluntary nature, it represents the social contract that exists between corporations and their environment and their overall responsibility to society and the environment.

Questions to test your learning:

1. What are the four components of Carroll's Pyramid Framework? Can you note down some examples you have seen in your daily life or in business practices?
2. What do you think are the main advantages of the framework for corporations?
3. What are the main limitations of the framework?
4. How universal is the framework in considering other cultural contexts?

Carroll's CSR pyramid has provided a foundational understanding of the different levels f corporations' responsibilities; 30 years later, the scope and the expectations of CSR have expanded tremendously. Globalization, the rise of Information and Communication Technologies (ICT), and increasing public awareness of global challenges, such as pandemics (e.g. Covid-19 and Ebola), environmental disasters, pollution, global warming and social injustices, means that modern CSR now encompasses a broader range of issues related to labour rights and workforce conditions (Yu and Choi, 2014), employees' pensions systems (Husted, 2015), environmental protection, education, healthcare and human rights (Monshipouri et al, 2003), and more recently for corporations to play a relevant role in the global efforts to achieve the UN Sustainable Development Goals, comprising 17 global goals such as ending poverty (SDG1) and providing clean water and sanitation (SDG6) (Gallardo-Vazquez et al, 2021; Iazzi et al, 2022; Khalid et al, 2023; Leena et al, 2023).

Traditionally, governments and their agents were seen as the primary providers of the public good (e.g. education, healthcare, and culture). However, the liberalization of financial markets and increasing deregulation – a process of minimizing government control (Kaminsky and Schumkler, 2008) – means that the role of governments in delivering the public good is being reduced, paving the way for private corporations to engage in CSR activities and contribute to society's well-being. Matten and Crane (2005), for instance, argue that corporations have increasingly taken some of the traditional government roles and responsibilities and do so by administering the social, civil and political rights of those affected. From this perspective, corporations have become 'agents of change' in a modern globalized world (Kudłak and Low, 2015).

Scholars argue that CSR is influenced by multiple and interconnected factors. These include liberalization of international trade and the subsequent dilution of the traditionally separated public and private spheres, the rise of the knowledge economy (e.g. computerization and automation), global competition and international operating standards, including increasing stakeholder expectations (Carroll and Shabana, 2010; Nikolova and Arsić, 2017; Sweeney and Coughlan, 2008), all of which have played a critical role in shaping CSR practices. Corporations have come under extreme pressure from their stakeholder groups, including consumers, investors, employees, suppliers, civil rights activists, environmentalists, non-governmental organizations (NGOs) and civil society organizations, to engage in CSR practices and consequently align their business objectives with the broader social and environmental goals (Awa et al, 2024; Albuquerque and Cabral, 2020; Li, 2018).

Furthermore, CSR has been shaped by the evolving regulatory and policy environment. As pointed out in the box below, the growing number of regulatory measures introduced by governments and international institutions, such as mandatory CSR reporting, restrictions on certain investments, and policies for sustainable public procurement (see Chapter 6), aim to mobilize corporations to take more responsibility for their environmental and social impacts (Awa et al, 2024). For example, in 2001, the European Commission initiated a debate on how CSR could be encouraged at the European and international levels (European Commission, 2001). This was followed by the launch of the European multi-stakeholder forum in 2004 and the introduction of the European Union Directive 2014/95/EU declaring the non-financial disclosure to be a mandatory requirement (La Torre et al, 2018). The EU Directive introduced compulsory integrated reporting to be published on corporate annual reporting referring to CSR activities, such as environmental protection, social and employee welfare, respect for human rights, anti-corruption and bribery issues, and diversity in board selection (Steurer et al, 2005).

- **United Nations Global Compact (UNGC):** Established in 1999 by the former UN Secretary General Kofi Annan, the UNGC is a voluntary initiative aimed at aligning corporations' strategies and operations with 10 principles covering human rights, labour rights, environmental sustainability and anti-corruption efforts (UNGC, 2023). These principles are endorsed by private corporations and other stakeholders in collaboration with the UN to promote their active implementation (Rose, 2020; Tsalis et al, 2023). The UNGC serves therefore as a local and global network that connects a diverse set of stakeholders to foster a global economy characterized by justice and sustainability (Barrese et al, 2020; Berliner and Prakash, 2012; Martínez-Ferrero et al, 2020; Schembera, 2018).
- **The Global Reporting Initiative (GRI):** The GRI standards, which were introduced by an international independent standards organization, provide corporations with the means to understand and report on their impact on the environment, society and the economy. GRI is regarded as the most widely adopted global standard for CSR disclosure (Michelon et al, 2015; www.globalreporting.org).
- **International Integrated Reporting Framework (IIRF):** Introduced by the International Integrated Reporting Council (IIRC) in 2013 as a guide for corporations to enhance their disclosure and accountability to their stakeholder groups beyond merely financial profits. An IR report should disclose how the corporation's strategy, governance, performance and overall activities lead to the creation of value for all stakeholder groups (IIRC, 2013). The IR is a reporting structure that includes nine elements such as governance, business model and performance, alongside seven guiding principles that aim to improve the quality and comparability of reporting (Eccles et al, 2015; Eccles et al, 2019; Liu et al, 2019). It outlines six types of capital: financial, manufactured, human, social/relational, intellectual and natural (IIRC, 2013) to ensure a comprehensive assessment of the corporation's impact across these dimensions (Busco et al, 2018).

The adoption of the above sustainability reporting frameworks played a critical role in the development of sustainability reports that demonstrate corporations' social and environmental responsibility. However, findings suggest the quality of these reports varies from one organization to the other, with some only disclosing favourable 'metrics' as opposed to strictly following the guidelines of these standards (Boiral et al, 2020). The IR, for instance, despite its applicability, faced criticism due to it being perceived as a reporting framework that prioritizes investors' interests over the corporation's broader social and environmental responsibility (Flower, 2015).

In summary, CSR has come to be understood as a strategic process that demonstrates how corporations' policies, business practices and actions demonstrate their social and environmental responsibility (Davis, 1973; Kotler and Lee, 2007; Li, 2018). However, as we explore below, SEs play a key role in addressing social and environmental challenges, making them also accountable to demonstrate their social and environmental responsibility.

## Understanding social enterprise

As we have explored, corporations are increasingly mandated by their stakeholder groups to demonstrate their social and environmental responsibility beyond just making profits. How, then, do SEs differ from the concept of CSR? To what extent do SEs address social and/or environmental needs that profit-for-shareholder businesses (i.e. corporations) are unable to address?

As discussed in Chapters 1 and 2, SEs have been defined in different ways. While the Western European perspective emphasizes their dual social and business objectives, the US-based approach encompasses two variations – those that focus on the 'profit-making' activities of not-for-profit organizations (e.g. charities and NGOs) and those that focus on business-based solutions by both not-for-profit and profit-for-shareholder organizations (Nagy and Kratki, 2024). Despite variations in interpretations, social entrepreneurship research can be summarized in two strands. The first is social innovation, emphasizing the role social entrepreneurs play in developing innovative approaches to social or environmental problems (Dees, 2001; Mair and Marti, 2006; Martin and Osberg, 2007; Peredo and McLean, 2006). The other focuses on the hybridity of SEs as business organizations that balance an explicit social and/or environmental mission with for-profit motives (Santos et al, 2015). The latter defines SEs as spanning the boundaries of the private (i.e. profit-for-shareholder organizations/corporations) and NFPs such as charities, while remaining its own separate concept (Doherty et al, 2014; Haigh and Hoffman, 2011). What binds these two streams together is the role social entrepreneurs and enterprise play in developing and initiating innovative approaches to social or environmental challenges (Haigh et al, 2015).

SEs have therefore attracted the attention of policymakers as a vehicle for economic growth and sustainable development due to their blended logic. As explored in Chapter 1, policy interventions within the UK context sought to bring to the fore the role of SEs in addressing pressing social needs through market-based mechanisms. On an international level, organizations such as the World Bank, the Organization for Economic Co-operation and Development (OECD) and the European Union supported the development and the growth of the social enterprise sector due to the mounting social and environmental challenges that can only be solved through innovative and viable solutions (European Commission, 2020). Of equal importance, scholars examined the role of the social, economic, cultural and political contexts that shape the development of SEs as a vehicle for creating social value (Bahena-Alvarez et al, 2019; Naderi et al, 2019). Overall, SEs are characterized by the following principles.

Firstly, SEs are organizations that are characterized by their **innovative solutions,** often led by *change agents* (i.e. social entrepreneurs) who play a key role in driving 'social innovation' – defined, as explored in Chapter 2, as a process of generating, diffusing and scaling innovative solutions to address social challenges such as reducing economic inequality, improving social justice and environmental sustainability (Edwards-Schachter and Wallace, 2017; Fulgenico and Le Fever, 2016). According to Social Enterprise UK, there are more than 131,000 SEs in the UK that together contribute £60 billion to the UK economy and employ around 2.3 million people, with many outperforming traditional businesses in bringing innovative solutions to reduce inequality and build a more inclusive economy (Social Enterprise UK, 2025).

Secondly, SEs use **revenue-generating activities to create social value.** SEs, as hybrid organizations, follow two core institutional logics – commercial and social welfare (Pache and Santos, 2013) – blending them together to generate both economic and social value. The commercial logic means that SEs follow market-based principles, such as providing products and services for customers, to generate economic value (Thornton and Ocasio, 2008). The social welfare logic looks to solve social or environmental problems, thereby creating social value for the beneficiaries rather than maximizing private and shareholder wealth (Weerawardena et al, 2021).

Finally, SEs are characterized by their **multiagency environment.** The term 'multiagency', as explained in Chapter 1, refers to the extent to which SEs build relationships with different actors at different levels to achieve their social objectives. SEs collaborate with a wide set of stakeholders, such as private corporations, NFPs, government agencies and the local communities in which they are embedded, to develop and deliver innovative solutions that serve the needs of their beneficiaries (Clarke and Crane, 2018; Quarshie and Leuschner, 2018; Selsky and Parker, 2005; Trujillo, 2018). Research findings also indicate that, although supported by government policies, SEs continue to be under pressure to access resources and reduce their dependence on government support (Defourny and Nyssen, 2010). Due to these resource constraints, SEs tend to require the participation of multiple stakeholders, including governments, charities, volunteers and others, to access the resources they require.

Collaborations with other stakeholders also enable SEs to build the legitimacy of their organizations. Organizational legitimacy refers to the perceptions and evaluations of stakeholder groups and whether the actions of an organization conform to widely held norms, values and beliefs (Certo and Hodge, 2007). In SEs' context, legitimacy is defined as the congruence between the social enterprise's actions and stakeholders' expectations of its performance based on their own judgements (Huybrechts and Nicholls, 2013; Marshall and Macdonald, 2016; Wadham and

Warren, 2013). Hence SEs more often consider the demands of their stakeholder groups, such as donors, local governments, volunteers and communities, all of which are embedded into their social welfare logic, resulting in these stakeholders being more willing to support their social mission (Thorgren and Omerede, 2018).

**STOP AND THINK**

A report published by the United Nations Development Programme (2016) titled 'Human Development for Everyone' indicates that the world's most marginalized communities, such as ethnic minorities, women and girls, people with disabilities, migrants and refugees, elderly people, lesbian, gay, bisexual, transgender and intersex (LGBTI) communities, Indigenous people and people in vulnerable locations, still suffer from social exclusion, discrimination, social norms violence and inequality. Addressing the challenges these marginalized communities face requires novel approaches that are directed at supporting them. Can you think of a solution that can help remove some of the barriers these communities face and enable them to access the relevant support mechanisms that will improve their social integration?

Key questions and prompts:

- Revisit the key characteristics of SEs we discussed in this section. Identify the problems your beneficiaries (i.e. the marginalized community) face and provide evidence of the problem. To explore the problem, see Chapter 7, where we introduce the 'Problem Statement Canvas' as a tool that supports you to define and assess the problem and the resulting impact on those affected.
- Evaluate how your solution will solve the challenges these marginalized communities face. How will it create tangible benefits for them? Could your solution be related to providing access to housing, education, employment and upskilling opportunities, or access to green spaces?
- Evaluate the nature of the social impact you will create as a result of your solution. For further support, you may want to apply some of the theoretical frameworks we discussed in this textbook, such as the ToC (see Chapter 1), network, resource-based view and stakeholder theories (see Chapter 2).

## CSR and social enterprises – overlaps and differences

Thus far, we have demonstrated that corporations have a responsibility to demonstrate their social and environmental credentials in areas such as labour rights, workforce conditions, environmental protection, education and healthcare, and human rights issues (Monshipouri et al, 2003). Of equal importance, SEs play a key role in addressing social and environmental challenges and therefore create social value for the beneficiaries they serve as well as the broader social and environmental impact (Austin et al, 2006; Baron, 2007). Creating social value therefore demonstrates how organizations – any type, including SEs – demonstrate their social and environmental responsibility and engender positive outcomes. In this instance, as pointed out in Figure 5.3, SEs and CSR overlap in their social goals and their focus on social value creation. However, they differ significantly in the ways in which social value is created.

**Areas of overlap – social value creation:** corporations and SEs aim to improve social or environmental outcomes. While corporations integrate CSR practices to demonstrate their environmental and social responsibility, SEs create social value by employing entrepreneurial approaches in the pursuit of their social mission. In this instance, both contribute broadly to social and environmental outcomes, although to different extents.

**Areas of difference – mission centrality:** although corporations demonstrate their social or environmental responsibility through CSR practices, their primary goal is to maximize profit and shareholder value, while CSR remains secondary to their core strategy (Carroll and Shabana, 2010). In contrast, SEs, often led by social entrepreneurs who are characterized by their salient characteristics (Austin et al, 2006; Clark et al, 2017; Dickel and Eckardt, 2021; Estrin et al, 2016), such as accountability,

**Figure 5.3** CSR and SEs: areas of overlap and differences

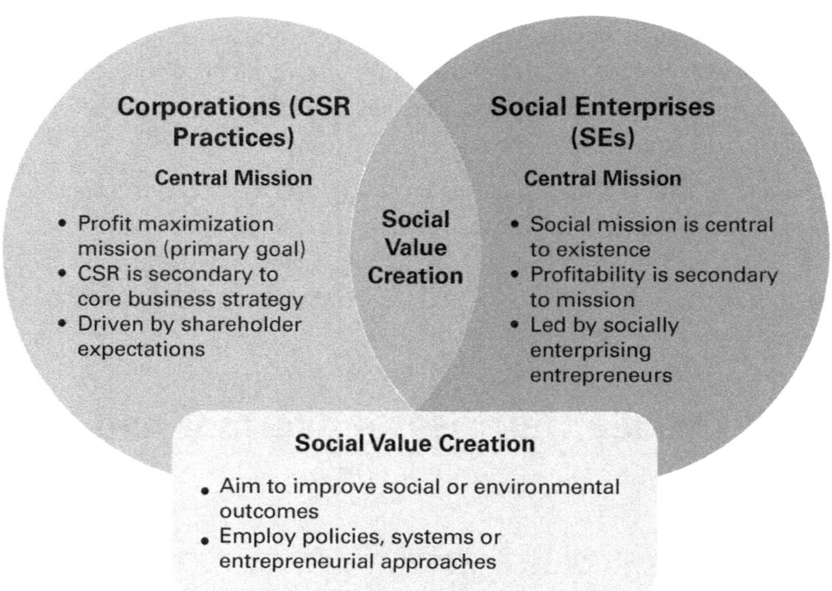

ethical behaviour, moral responsibility and empathy, altruism and compassion (see Chapter 8) (Bacq and Alt, 2018; Douglas et al, 2021; Ernst, 2011; Ip et al, 2021; Mair and Noboa, 2006; Tiwari et al, 2020), give priority to their social mission over profitability. The social mission is therefore central to SEs, and the pursuit of profit remains secondary to their overall social objectives. Although SEs employ entrepreneurial approaches to create economic value, it is often for the purpose of sustaining their social impact. As a result, the scope of social value creation can differ greatly between CSR and SEs.

In summary, CSR posits that corporations are mandated by their stakeholder groups, such as employees, customers and suppliers, as well as by international reporting standards, to demonstrate their social and environmental responsibility beyond their financial performance. CSR therefore puts emphasis on corporations that exist within the broader social and environmental context to have responsibilities beyond profit maximization. While CSR practices are beneficial, demonstrating how corporations create social value for stakeholder groups and generate broader social and environmental outcomes, they often remain secondary to the corporation's strategic objective, which is to maximize profit and enhance shareholder value. In contrast, SEs balance a social mission with financial sustainability. Although there is no single universal definition of SEs, a common thread in the literature is that they are characterized by their explicit social mission, and the use of revenue-generating activities is for the benefit of achieving their social objectives. Unlike profit-oriented corporations, SEs balance two institutional logics, social and business objectives, making generation of revenues essential to their long-term sustainability.

## CSR challenges

Findings suggest that socially responsible corporations benefit from enhanced brand loyalty, improved employee loyalty and retention, building better customer loyalty, developing more positive relationships with policymakers and the media (particularly in a rich media environment), and overall advancing their competitive positioning in the market (Bear et al, 2010; Eilert and Robinson, 2020; Mohr et al, 2001; Porter and Kramer, 2002; Turban and Greening, 1997). The case of Patagonia, in the box below, shows how corporations can contribute to social good without compromising profitability. Nevertheless, critics argue that more often corporations utilize CSR as a greenwashing activity to enhance their market reputation without any substantial social or environmental change. So how can CSR, even when embedded into the corporate strategy of corporations, be used as a greenwashing mechanism to build a competitive edge?

**REAL-WORLD EXAMPLE** The case of Patagonia – empowering sustainability

According to the World Economic Forum (2023), the apparel industry is responsible for approximately 6.7 per cent of Greenhouse Gas (GHG) emissions worldwide, with around 85 per cent of clothing ending up in landfills or being incinerated. Patagonia, the outdoor clothing company, is on a mission to not only drastically reduce its emissions but also to reshape the mindset of its business, customers and employees. In 2021, Patagonia became the first company to register as a 'benefit corporation', prioritizing environmental concerns over profits. The company produces all its clothing lines using recycled materials and donates 1 per cent of sales to environmental projects through their '1 per cent for the planet' initiative. Furthermore, its environmental internship programme allows employees to take up to two months off work to engage in a paid internship for an environmental organization. Its 'worn wear' initiative incentivizes customers to recycle clothing responsibly by providing awareness and support related to product maintenance, repair, reuse, resale and disposal.

Questions:

1 In what way has Patagonia embedded environmental sustainability in its business?
2 What is the competitive edge of Patagonia?
3 How might Patagonia ensure its long-term commitment to the environment without compromising its financial objectives?

## 'Greenwashing'

The term 'greenwashing' was first coined in the 1980s by the environmentalist Jay Westerveld, who criticized the practices of the hospitality industry and their false claims about reusing towels to save the environment. Westerveld contended that hotels in particular claim to reuse towels to save the environment, even though it was principally done to reduce laundry costs (Pizzetti et al, 2021; Williams, 2024; Zhang et al, 2018). Since then, greenwashing has become associated with the practice of using misleading communication strategies about a corporation's positive environmental performance, products and practices, whereas in reality such a corporation avoids taking substantive actions to change its business processes (Torelli et al, 2019) for fear of profit loss. For instance, the Coca-Cola Company advertises its plastic bottles as 100 per cent recyclable, while simultaneously being ranked as the top plastic polluter in the world (see Swartz v. Coca-Cola Co, No21-cv-04643, 2022 https://climatecasechart.com/case/swartz-v-coca-cola-co/). Meanwhile, Chevron (a multinational energy corporation) has committed to a low-carbon future while in reality dedicating only 1 per cent or less in sources related to low-carbon energy (Global Witness, 2021). In this context, corporations may disclose information about their commitment to environmental issues but mislead stakeholders through greenwashing, known to be an effective strategy enabling them to manage the tensions between stakeholder expectations and environmental pressures (Nemes et al, 2022; Li et al, 2022; Yu et al, 2020).

There is no single definition of greenwashing; however, among the various definitions, two research strands have been identified. The first strand states that greenwashing can be defined as corporations' attempts to disclose information only related to their *positive* environmental impact while obscuring the *negative* one to mislead their stakeholders (Lyon and Maxwell, 2011; Lyon and Montgomery, 2015). The second strand contends that greenwashing is a 'decoupling strategy' that shows a misalignment between what corporations propose to do ('green talk'), and the tangible actions they take to reduce their harmful impact on the environment ('green walk') (Li et al, 2022; Shahab et al, 2021).

Greenwashing has therefore attracted the attention of scholars and policymakers due to its effect on society as well as the corporations themselves. Corporations that get involved in greenwashing practices can benefit from improving their public image and competitive position; however, once identified, it can lead to a loss of reputation and reduced consumer trust (Jahdi and Acikdilli, 2009; Porter and Kramer, 2006; Torelli et al, 2019). Scholars argue there are many internal and external drivers for greenwashing. Internal drivers, such as the corporation's size, growth, profitability, resources and competencies, can influence the occurrence of greenwashing (Delmas and Burbano, 2011; Seele and Gatti, 2015; Testa et al, 2018; Lyon and Maxwell, 2011). For instance, it has been found that corporations with greater financial constraints tend to engage in more greenwashing than those with fewer constraints (Zhang et al, 2018). On the other hand, corporations that adhere to the GRI guidelines and disclose sustainability reports are less likely to engage in greenwashing than others (Ruiz-Blanco et al, 2021; Yu and Choi, 2014). Environmental regulations and guidelines also play a role in preventing greenwashing (whether for advertising purposes or as part of the corporate mission).

The Environmental, Social and Governance (ESG) investment framework, for instance, released in 2004 by the UN Secretary General Kofi Annan and several other institutions in a report called 'Who Cares Wins', developed a set of guidelines to integrate environmental, social, and governance concerns in financial reporting. By 2006, the UN integrated ESG criteria into their Principles for Responsible Investment (PRI) report, requiring it to be incorporated into the financial evaluation of all corporations (Atkins, 2020; Krishnamoorthy, 2021). This is to enable corporations to disclose their approach to achieving sustainability as well as provide investors with quantifiable performance indicators (Yin et al, 2025).

The ESG rating contains an evaluation of a corporation's social, environmental and governance dimensions. While the environmental dimension is related to issues such as environmental pollution, biodiversity loss, and climate change, the social dimension focuses on issues like human and labour rights and public safety (Billio et al, 2021; Tan and Zhu, 2022). The governance dimension puts emphasis on shareholders' rights, anti-competitive practices and the administrative board. Findings suggest that corporations with better ESG performance can increase shareholder value, build better reputation and brand equity among socially conscious consumers and investors, facilitate growth, minimize regulatory and legal interventions, increase employee productivity, optimize investment, contribute to the sustainable development of society, and build a strong competitive advantage (Allman and Joonsung, 2021). However, critics argue that ESG can exacerbate greenwashing due to inconsistency between a corporation's ESG claims and their actual practices, such as in the Coca-Cola example above (Ballan and Czarnezki, 2024).

In summary, we explored how CSR practices support corporations to demonstrate their social and environmental responsibility. Nevertheless, CSR remains secondary to their overall strategic objective, which is to maximize profit and shareholder value. Regulations and guidelines, such as UNGC, GRI, IIRF and ESG, as discussed throughout this chapter, enhance reporting standards and allow corporations to report on their activities that are socially, environmentally and governance friendly. However, CSR can be awash with greenwashing activities to advance the corporations' competitive positioning over their social and environmental responsibility.

## Social enterprise challenges

SEs, by blending social and business objectives, have emerged as viable solutions for bringing about social change and promoting society's well-being. Unlike traditional corporations, an SE's mission is directed at not only generating revenues but also at addressing complex social problems in response to social or environmental needs (Battilana and Lee, 2014; Doherty et al, 2014). As a result, SEs create a broader social or environmental impact (Haigh et al, 2015; Haugh and Talwar, 2016). However, they often face challenges in measuring their social impact, as we will now explore.

### *Measuring social impact*

Despite there being no single definition of what constitutes social impact, it is often defined as the result of a programme or an intervention by any individuals, community or organization with the objective of causing a positive effect on social, economic and environmental well-being (André and Pache, 2016; Perrini et al, 2021; Tello, 2020 ). Of similar importance, as explored in Chapter 1 through the Theory of Change (ToC), impact can be defined as the process of *inputs*, which represent the activities undertaken by the social enterprise, creating *outputs* for individuals or communities that are receiving the products or services from the organization, which result in long-term positive outcomes (Ragan and Gregg, 2019).

Measuring social impact is important for SEs on two levels. First, it enables SEs to demonstrate how well their explicit social mission is performing – that is, providing evidence of the tangible benefits created for individuals, communities or society at large as a result of their intervention. Second, it can support them to build the legitimacy and credibility of their social enterprise as well as attract government and impact investors' funding (Lyon and Owen 2019; Liston-Heyes and Liu, 2021). A study by Block et al (2021), for instance, found that social impact investors use three criteria when deciding on investment in SEs: the authenticity of the founding team, the significance of the social or environmental problem being addressed, and financial sustainability.

Since SEs' main focus is on their social mission, a set of measurements is therefore required to capture their social value-creation activities and their broader social impact (Westley et al, 2014). Nevertheless, as argued by Pinheiro et al (2021), economic performance is equally important to demonstrate, as it is the primary mechanism for SEs to sustain their social mission and provide the services or products for their beneficiaries. Some scholars argue that social impact can be measured in relation to the number of individuals/communities supported and for which tangible benefits have been noticed (Ragan and Gregg, 2019). Others, however, argue that impact can be measured based on how the social enterprise sustains social value over time (Jayawardhana et al, 2022).

There are a wide range of methods to measure social impact. These include, for instance, the GRI, Social Accounting (see Chapter 12) and Social Return on Investment (SROI), which is regarded as one of the most common evaluation techniques used to measure the value of social impact achieved through an intervention (Cerioni and Marasca, 2021; more will be discussed in Chapter 6). However, compared to financial measures that can be used to measure economic value, attempting to do so within the context of SEs is challenging (Perrini et al, 2021). This is particularly due to the complexities of the social problems being addressed, such as poverty, unequal access to education or mental health (André and Pache, 2016; Smith et al, 2013). To which level, for instance, should someone be schooled for them to be considered 'educated'? How is it possible to measure when someone is no longer in poverty, and for how long must they be above the poverty line? And how is it possible to quantifiably measure the improvement in mental health for those affected?

Further studies found that some of the common challenges in using measurement tools include insufficient technical expertise, time and commitment requirements, insufficient financial and human resources, and the need for longitudinal data that demonstrates a long-term impact (Hadad and Gauca, 2014; Corvo et al, 2021; Lombardo et al, 2019). Findings also suggest that not all SEs would like to measure their social impact due to it being costly and time-consuming and may distract them from their core activities – supporting their beneficiaries (Perrini et al, 2021).

In summary, we explored how SEs blend social and business objectives to address social and environmental challenges and create social value for the beneficiaries they serve and society at large. Compared to corporations that use CSR practices to demonstrate their social and environmental responsibility, SEs are built, at their core, with an explicit social mission directed at creating social impact. Despite there being a number of measurement tools (e.g. SROI or ESG), SEs face challenges in tangibly demonstrating their social or environmental impact. Findings suggest that the complexities of social problems SEs often address make it challenging to demonstrate real quantifiable impact. Besides, adopting social impact measurement tools requires technical expertise, a large amount of data and resources (time, technical and human) to be effective. More importantly, for some SEs, measurement tools are costly and can distract them from their core mission, which is to directly serve their beneficiaries.

## Summary and key learning points

In this chapter, we began by tracing the evolution of CSR and the extent to which it has become a strategic approach used by corporations to demonstrate their social and environmental responsibility. We also examined the policy and regulatory landscape, including various reporting measures, such as UNGC, GRI, IIRF and ESG, that guide corporations to report on their social, economic and environmental performance. We also discussed the role SEs play in tackling social and environmental challenges. SEs blend business and social objectives to create social value for the beneficiaries they serve as well as create broader social and environmental impact. In this regard, corporations that are often shareholder-led and SEs that focus primarily on their social mission share common social goals.

However, we also established that they both differ in the way social value is created. For corporations, CSR remains secondary to their overall objectives, which is to maximize value for shareholders. In contrast, SEs prioritize their social mission over profit, and in the case of adopting revenue-generating activities, it is to meet their social objectives. Finally, we explored the challenges with CSR, particularly the issue of greenwashing, where corporations may exaggerate their social or environmental claims to gain a competitive edge. While both are required to demonstrate their social impact, SEs often face challenges due to the complexity of social problems they address, which may not be easily quantified.

The key takeaways are the following:

- CSR practices adopted by corporations aim to demonstrate their environmental and social responsibility.
- Carroll's CSR Pyramid provides a foundational understanding of the four levels of corporations' responsibilities: economic, legal, ethical and philanthropic.
- Due to globalization, ICT, global challenges, environmental pollution and social challenges, CSR has come to be understood as a strategic process by which corporations demonstrate their responsibility.
- The regulatory environment, with the introduction of some reporting tools as GRI, UNGC and IIRF, has also contributed to enhancing the level of reporting corporations are required to make to demonstrate their social and environmental responsibility.
- CSR practices remain secondary to corporations' profit-oriented mission directed at maximizing shareholder value.
- Compared to CSR, SEs are characterized by their explicit social mission, directed at creating social value for the beneficiaries they serve and society at large.
- Due to their blended objectives, SEs use market-based mechanisms to generate revenue; however, this is for the benefit of serving their social mission rather than maximizing shareholder value.
- CSR can be used as a 'greenwashing' activity by corporations to boost their competitive positioning in the market over their social and environmental responsibility.
- SEs more often face challenges in measuring their social impact due to various factors, such as the complexity of the social problem they address, resource constraints and expertise, as well as the risk of being distracted from their core mission, which is to serve their beneficiaries.

## REAL-WORLD EXAMPLE WARBY PARKER, INDICATIVE ANSWERS

1 What is your view on the *one-for-one* business model adopted by Warby Parker?

**Indicative answer:** Initially, you may want to watch this short video from Warby Parker's website that illustrates key aspects about their brand: https://www.youtube.com/watch?v=TuJao1sbrMQ (archived at https://perma.cc/FP6R-QYNK)

Warby Parker's dual mission is based on not only making stylish, high-quality, and affordable glasses accessible but also promoting social good. Their innovative 'at-home try-on service' together with their multi-channel retail strategy, including physical retail and digital services, allowed them to disrupt a market traditionally dominated by global players, such as EssilorLuxottica, Costco, National Vision and Visionworks.

However, Warby Parker was able to differentiate itself in the market through their 'Buy a Pair, Give a Pair' programme, which is a form of one-for-one business model, where for each pair of glasses sold, another is distributed to someone in need. This market-based solution not only enables customers to contribute to social good but also for Warby Parker to develop a sustainable solution to the problem of lack of access to eyewear in impoverished communities.

Nevertheless, while the one-for-one business model has attracted widespread attention, it is not without criticism – we recommend you read Marquis and Park (2014), 'Inside the Buy-One Give-One Model', where they argue that this approach may not bring about economic prosperity for those in need or systemic social change. Furthermore, giving away a product for free with every purchase can create dependency and pose risks to the long-term viability of the social business model.

2 What is Warby Parker's strategy for achieving social impact? What could be the challenges?

**Indicative answer:** Drawing on the content of this chapter, first, pay attention to how Warby Parker is driving social change through their slogan for the 'Buy a Pair, Give a Pair' programme, where for each pair of glasses sold, another is distributed to someone in need. Warby Parker's core social mission is to directly address the global issue of lack of access to affordable eyewear – an issue affecting approximately a billion people worldwide, especially in low- and middle-income economies, as indicated by the International Agency for the Prevention of Blindness.

However, there are potential challenges that can threaten Warby Parker's social impact. For example, the company has scaled significantly, indicated by the 40 new locations opened in 2023 in the United States, as well as an increase in net revenue and gross profits. Is there a likelihood that they might drift from their core social mission, prioritizing profit over social objectives? Do they have the correct frameworks in place to prevent mission drift from occurring? Furthermore, the simplicity of the one-for-one model (see Marquis and Park, 2014) could be replicated by competitors with more resources, wider distribution channels and a better customer base, which may threaten the long-term viability of the organization.

**CALLS TO ACTION**

In groups of two to three, critically evaluate the key differences between the LEGO Group as a privately held construction toy production corporation (ranked first place in 2025 by the Reputation Institute for their effective CSR practices) and a social enterprise of your choice:

1. Using LEGO Group as an example, revisit Figure 5.3 and identify the key distinctions between LEGO's Group CSR mission and the social mission of a social enterprise of your choice.
2. Evaluate the mechanisms that the LEGO Group uses to implement its CSR strategy. Compare these to those used by the social enterprise you have chosen to fulfil its social objectives.
3. Evaluate the nature of social impact created by the LEGO Group. In what way does this differ from the impact generated by the social enterprise you have chosen?
4. Outline your argument for discussing both the overlaps and differences between CSR and SEs, particularly as they both contribute to social good alongside financial sustainability.

**USEFUL LINKS**

United Nations Global Compact: https://unglobalcompact.org/ (archived at https://perma.cc/HGY8-VB6P)

European Commission – Social Enterprises: https://single-market-economy.ec.europa.eu/sectors/proximity-and-social-economy/social-economy-eu/social-enterprises_en (archived at https://perma.cc/X74R-CAVL)

The 17 Sustainable Development Goals: https://sdgs.un.org/goals (archived at https://perma.cc/D7EM-NQ6J)

# References


Albuquerque, R and Cabral, L M B (2020) Strategic Leadership in Corporate Social Responsibility. Discussion Paper DP16564, Centre for Economic Policy Research. London

Allman, E and Joonsung (Francis), W (2021) Can ESG Disclosure Improve Investment Efficiency?, World Bank: World Bank Blog (Sept 20)

André, K and Pache, A C (2016) From caring entrepreneur to caring enterprise: Addressing the ethical challenges of scaling up social enterprises, *Journal of Business Ethics*, 133: 659–75

Atkins, B (2020) Demystifying ESG: Its history & current status, Forbes (June 8)

Austin, J, Stevenson, H and Wei-Skillern, J (2006) Social and commercial entrepreneurship: Same, different, or both? *Entrepreneurship, Theory and Practice*, 30: 1–22

Awa, H O, Etim, W and Ogbonda, E (2024) Stakeholders, stakeholder theory and corporate social responsibility, *International Journal of Corporate Social Responsibility*, 9(11): 1–14

Bacq, S and Alt, E (2018) Feeling capable and valued: a prosocial perspective on the link between empathy and social entrepreneurial intentions, *Journal of Business Venturing*, 33(3): 333–50

Bahena-Álvarez, IL, Cordón-Pozo, E and Delgado-Cruz, A (2019) Social entrepreneurship in the conduct of responsible innovation: Analysis cluster in Mexican SMEs, *Sustainability* 11: 3714

Ballan, B and Czarnezki, J J (2024) Disclosure, greenwashing, and the future of ESG litigation, *Washington and Lee Literature Review*, 545: 588

Baron, D P (2007) Corporate social responsibility and social entrepreneurship, *Journal of Economic Management Strategy*, 16: 683–717

Barrese, J, Phillips, C and Shoaf, V (2020) Why do U.S. public companies continue to join the UN Global Compact: Ethics or economics? *International Studies of Management and Organization*, 50(3), 209–31

Battilana, J and Lee, M (2014)Advancing research on hybrid organizing – insights from the study of social enterprises, *Academy of Management Annals*, 8 (1): 397–441

Bear, S, Rahman, N and Post, C (2010) The impact of board diversity and gender composition on corporate social responsibility and firm reputation, *Journal of Business Ethics*, 97(2): 207–21

Berliner, D and Prakash, A (2012) From norms to programs: The United Nations global compact and global governance, *Regulation & Governance*, 6(2): 149–66

Billio, M, Costola, M, Hristova, I, Latino, C and Pelizzon, L (2021) Inside the ESG ratings: (Dis) agreement and performance, *Corporate Social Responsibility and Environmental Management*, 28(5): 1426–445

Block, J H, Hirschmann, M and Fisch, C (2021) Which criteria matter when impact investors screen social enterprises? *Journal of Corporate Finance*, 66(2020): 101–813

Blowfield, M and Murray, A (2011) *Corporate Responsibility*, Oxford University Press: Oxford, UK

Boiral, O, Talbot, D and Brotherton, M C (2020) Measuring sustainability risks: A rational myth? *Business Strategy and the Environment*, 29: 10.1002/bse.2520

Busco, C, E Giovannoni, F G, and Izzo, M F (2018) Making sustainability meaningful: Aspirations, discourses and reporting practices, *Accounting, Auditing & Accountability Journal*, 31(8): 2218–246

Callado-Muñoz, F J and Utrero-González, N (2011) Does it pay to be socially responsible? Evidence from Spain's retail banking sector, *European Financial Management*, 17: 755–87

Carroll, A B (1991) The pyramid of corporate social responsibility: Toward the moral management of organizational stakeholders, *Business Horizons*, 34(4): 39–48

Carroll, A B and Shabana, K M (2010) The business case for corporate social responsibility: A review of concepts, research and practice, *International Journal of Management Reviews*, 12(1): 85–105

Cerioni, E and Marasca, S (2021) The methods of social impact assessment: The state of the art and limits of application, *Calitatea*, 22: 29–36

Certo, S T, and Hodge, F (2007) Top management team prestige and organizational legitimacy: An examination of investor perceptions, *Journal of Managerial Issues*, 19(4): 461–77

Cho, J S, Chung, Y C and Young, J (2019)Study on the relationship between CSR and financial performance, *Sustainability*, 11(2): 1–26

Clark, K D, Newbert, S and Quigley, N (2017) The motivational drivers underlying for-profit venture creation: Comparing social and commercial entrepreneurs, *International Small Business Journal*, 36(4): 220–41

Clarke, A and Crane, A (2018) Cross-sector partnerships for systemic change: Systematized literature review and agenda for further research, *Journal of Business Ethics*, 150(2): 303–13

Corvo, L, Pastore, L, Manti, A and Iannaci, D (2021) Mapping social impact assessment models: A literature overview for a future research agenda, *Sustainability*, 13, 4750

Davis, K (1973) The case for and against business assumption of social responsibilities, *Academy of Management Journal*, 16: 312–23

Dees, J G (2001) The Meaning of 'Social Entrepreneurship', Centre for the Advancement of Social Entrepreneurship, https://web.stanford.edu/class/e145/2007_fall/materials/dees_SE.pdf (archived at https://perma.cc/E4XC-XG7S)

Defourny, J and Nyssens, M (2010) Conceptions of social enterprise and social entrepreneurship in Europe and the United States: Convergences and divergences. *Journal of Social Entrepreneurship*, 1(1): 32–53

Delmas, M A and Burbano, V C (2011) The drivers of greenwashing, *California Management Review*, 54(1): 64–87

Dickel, P and Eckardt, G (2021) Who wants to be a social entrepreneur? The role of gender and sustainability orientation, *Journal of Small Business Management*, 59(1): 196–218

Doherty, B, Haugh, H and Lyon, F (2014) Social enterprises as hybrid organizations: A review and research agenda, *International Journal Management Review*, 16(4): 17–436

Douglas, E J, Shepherd, D and Venugopal, V (2021) A multi-motivational general model of entrepreneurial intention, *Journal of Business Venturing*, 36(4): 106–07

Eccles, R G, Krzus, M P and Ribot, S (2015) Meaning and momentum in the integrated reporting movement. *Journal of Applied Corporate Finance*, 27(2): 8–17

Eccles, R G, Krzus, M P and Solano, C (2019) A comparative analysis of integrated reporting in ten countries, https://papers.ssrn.com/sol3/papers.cfm?abstract_id=3345590 (archived at https://perma.cc/F37N-RFZV)

Edwards-Schachter, M and Wallace, M L (2017) 'Shaken, but not stirred': Sixty years of defining social innovation, *Technological Forecasting and Social Change*, 119: 64–79

Eilert, M and Robinson, S (2020) The impact of cause portfolio focus and contribution amount on stakeholder evaluations, *Business & Society*, 59(7): 1483–514

Ernst, DK (2011) *Heart Over Mind: An empirical analysis of social entrepreneurial intention formation on the basis of the theory of planned behaviour*, Doctoral Dissertation. Wuppertal, Germany: University of Wuppertal

Estrin, S, Mickiewicz, T and Ute, S (2016) Human capital in social and commercial entrepreneurship, *Journal of Business Venturing*, 31(4): 449–67

European Commission (2001) Promoting a European Framework for Corporate Social Responsibility, Green Paper 366, Brussels

European Commission (2020) Social enterprises and their ecosystems in Europe: Updated country report: Italy. Author: Carlo Borzaga. Luxembourg: Publications Office of the European Union, https://base.socioeco.org/docs/social_enterprises_and_their_ecosystems_in_europe._comparative_synthesis_report.pdf (archived at https://perma.cc/4JTS-DK9Z)

Flower, J (2015) The International Integrated Reporting Council: A story of failure, *Critical Perspectives on Accounting*, 27(1): 1–10

Frederick, W C (1994) From CSR1 to CSR2: The maturing of business-and-society thought, *Business & Society*, 33(2), 150–64

Freeman, R E (1984) *Strategic Management: A stakeholder approach*, Boston: Pitman

Fulgencio, F and Le Fever, H (2016)What is the social innovation system? A state-of-the-art review,*International Journal of Business Innovation and Research*, 10(2/3): 434–52

Gallardo-Vazquez, D, Hourneaux, F, Gabriel, M and Valdez-Juarez, L E (2021) On earth as it is in heaven: Proxy measurements to assess sustainable development goals at the company level through CSR indicators, *Sustainability*, 13(2): 1–20

Garriga, E and Melé, D (2004) Corporate social responsibility theories: Mapping the territory, *Journal of Business Ethics*, 53: 51–71

Global Data (2024) Warby Parker Inc – Company Profile – Market Research, https://www.globaldata.com/store/report/warby-parker-inc-company-profile/ (archived at https://perma.cc/Z8KF-9H6K)

Global Reporting Initiative (2024) https://www.globalreporting.org/ (archived at https://perma.cc/5K36-HKL2)

Global Witness (2021). Accountability groups file first of its kind FTC complaint against Chevron for misleading consumers on climate action, https://globalwitness.org/en/press-releases/accountability-groups-file-first-of-its-kind-ftc-complaint-against-chevron-for-misleading-consumers-on-climate-action/ (archived at https://perma.cc/N7M5-JG6H)

Gunningham, N, Kagan, R A and Thornton, D (2004)Social license and environmental protection: Why businesses go beyond compliance, *Law & Social Inquiry*, 29 (2): 307–41, https://onlinelibrary.wiley.com/doi/abs/10.1111/j.1747-4469.2004.tb00338.x (archived at https://perma.cc/G7L3-5SGD)

Hadad, S and Gauca, O (Drumea) (2014) Social impact measurement in social entrepreneurial organizations, *Management and Marketing*, 9: 119–36

Haigh, N and Hoffman, A J (2011) Hybrid organizations: The next chapter in sustainable business, *Organizational Dynamics*, 41(2): 1–27

Haigh, N, Walker, J, Bacq, S and Kickul, J (2015) Hybrid organizations: Origins, strategies, impacts and implications, *California Management Review*, 57(3): 5–12

Haugh, H M and Talwar, A (2016) Linking social entrepreneurship and social change: The mediating role of empowerment, *Journal of Business Ethics*, 133: 643–58

Husted, B W (2015) Corporate social responsibility practice from 1800-1914: Past initiatives and current debates, *Business Ethics Quarterly*, 25(1): 125–41

Huybrechts, B, and Nicholls, A (2013) The role of legitimacy in social enterprise-corporate collaboration, *Social Enterprise Journal*, 9(2): 130–46

Iazzi, A, Ligorio, L, Vrontis, D and Trio, O (2022) Sustainable development goals and healthy foods: Perspective from the food system, *British Food Journal*, 124(4): 1031–102

IBISWorld (2024) Eyeglasses and contact lens stores in the US, https://my-ibisworld-com.liverpool.idm.oclc.org/us/en/industry/44613/at-a-glance (archived at https://perma.cc/7U9N-Q8T3)

International Agency for the Prevention of Blindness (2024) https://www.iapb.org/ (archived at https://perma.cc/GUH2-CT34)

International Integrated Reporting Council (IIRC) (2013) The International IR Framework, https://integratedreporting.ifrs.org/the-iirc-2/council/ (archived at https://perma.cc/RY3A-EAC6)

Ip, C Y, Liang C and Lai, H J (2021) Determinants of social entrepreneurial intention: An alternative model based on social cognitive career theory, *Nonprofit Management and Leadership*, 31(4): 737–60

Jahdi, K S and Acikdilli, G (2009) Marketing communications and corporate social responsibility (CSR): Marriage of convenience or shotgun wedding? *Journal of Business Ethics*, 88 (1): 103–13

Jayawardhana, K, Fernando, I and Siyambalapitiya, J (2022) Sustainability in social enterprise research: A systematic literature review, *Sage Open*, 12(3)

Kaminsky, G L and Schumkler, S L (2008) Short-run pain, long-run gain: Financial liberalization and stock market cycles, *Review of Finance*, 12: 253–92

Khalid, F, Kefu, Y, Akram, R and Batool, K (2023) Linking corporate social responsibility and energy poverty: An environmental sustainability paradigm, *Energy and Environment*, 0(0): 1–21

Kotler, P and Lee, N (2007) *Corporate Social Responsibility. Doing the most good for your company and your cause,* Hoboken, NJ, USA: John Wiley & Sons

Krishnamoorthy, R (2021) Environmental, social, and governance (ESG) investing: Doing good to do well, *Open Journal of Social Sciences*, 9, 189–91

Kudłak, R and Low, K Y (2015) Special issues dedicated to CSR and corporate sustainability: A review and commentary, *Long Range Planning*, 48(3): 215–27

Latapí Agudelo, M A, Jóhannsdóttir, L and Davídsdóttir, B A (2019) Literature review of the history and evolution of corporate social responsibility, *International Journal of Corporate Social Responsibility*, 4 (1): 1–23

La Torre, M, Sabelfeld, S, Blomkvist, M, Tarquinio, L and Dumay, J (2018) Harmonising non-financial reporting regulation in Europe: Practical forces and projections for future research, *Meditari Accountancy Research*, 26(4), 598–621

Leena, S, Balaji, K R A, Ganesh, K R, Prathima, K B and Satya, N A (2023) Corporate social responsibility and sustainable development goals, *Journal of Global Responsibility*, 1–27

Li, F A (2018) Survey of corporate social responsibility and corporate governance. In Boubaker, S, Cumming, D and Nguyen, D K (eds) *Research Handbook of Finance and Sustainability*, Cheltenham: Edward Elgar, pp. 126–38

Li, W, Li, W, Seppänen, V and Koivumäki, T (2022) Effects of greenwashing on financial performance: Moderation through local environmental regulation and media coverage, *Business Strategy and the Environment*, 32(1): 820–41

Lichtenstein, D R, Drumwright, M E and Braig, B M (2004) The effect of corporate social responsibility on customer donations to corporate-supported nonprofits, *Journal of Marketing*, 68(4): 16–32

Liston-Heyes, C, and Liu, G (2021) To measure or not to measure? An empirical investigation of social impact measurement in UK social enterprises, *Public Management Review*, 23(5): 687–709

Liu, Z, Jubb, C and Abhayawansa, S (2019) Analysing and evaluating integrated reporting: Insights from applying a normative benchmark, *Journal of Intellectual Capital*, 20(2): 235–63

Lombardo, G, Mazzocchetti, A, Rapallo, I, Tayser, N and Cincotti, S (2019) Assessment of the economic and social impact Using SROI: An application to sport companies, *Sustainability*, 11, 3612

Lyon, F, and Owen, R (2019) Financing social enterprises and the demand for social investment, *Strategic Change*, 28(1): 47–57

Lyon, T P, and Maxwell, J W (2011) Greenwash: Corporate environmental disclosure under threat of audit. *Journal of Economics &Management Strategy*, 20(1): 3–41

Lyon, T P and Montgomery, A W (2013) Tweetjacked: The impact of social media on corporate greenwash, *Journal of Business Ethics*, 118(4): 747–57

Mair, J and Noboa, E (2006) Social entrepreneurship: how intentions to create a social venture are formed. In Mair, J, Robinson, J and Hockerts K (eds) *Social Entrepreneurship*, London, UK: Palgrave Macmillan, pp. 121–135

Mair, J and Martí, I (2006) Social entrepreneurship research: A source of explanation, prediction, and delight, *Journal of World Business*, 41: 36–44

Marquis, C and Park, A (2014) Inside the buy-one give-one model, *Stanford Social Innovation Review*, Winter

Marshall, S and Macdonald, K (2016) What gives fair trade its right to operate? In *Organizational Legitimacy and Strategic Management Fair Trade: Corporate accountability and beyond* (pp. 113–140) Routledge

Martin, R L and Osberg, S (2007) Social entrepreneurship: The case for definition, *Stanford Social Innovation Review*, https://ssir.org/articles/entry/social_entrepreneurship_the_case_for_definition (archived at https://perma.cc/44YM-U4TK)

Martínez-Ferrero, J, Eryilmaz, M, & Colakoglu, N (2020) How does board gender diversity influence the likelihood of becoming a UN Global Compact signatory? The mediating effect of the CSR committee. Sustainability (Switzerland), 12(10), 4329

Matten, D and Crane, A (2005) Corporate citizenship: Toward an extended theoretical conceptualization, *Academy of Management Review*, 30(1): 166–79

Michelon, G, Pilonato, S and Ricceri, F (2015) CSR reporting practices and the quality of disclosure: An empirical analysis, *Critical Perspectives on Accounting*, 33, 59–78

Mohr, L A, Webb, D J and Harris, K E (2001) Do consumers expect companies to be socially responsible? The impact of corporate social responsibility on buying behaviour, *Journal of Consumer Affairs*, 35(1): 45–72

Monshipouri, M, Welch, C E and Kennedy, E T (2003) Multinational corporations and the ethics of global responsibility: Problems and possibilities, *Human Rights Quarterly*, 25 (4): 965–89

Naderi, A, Nasrolahi Vosta, L, Ebrahimi, A and Jalilvand, M R (2019) The contributions of social entrepreneurship and transformational leadership to performance: Insights from rural tourism in Iran, *International Journal of Sociology and Social Policy*, 39: 719–37

Nagy, Á and Krátki, N (2024) Open value creation for the common good: A comprehensive exploration of social innovation in the context of social enterprises, *Social Enterprise Journal*, 20(3), 318–38

Nemes, N, Scanlan, S J, Smith, P, Smith, T, Aronczyk, M, Hill, S, Lewis, S L, Montgomery, A W, Tubiello, F N and Stabinsky, D (2022) An integrated framework to assess greenwashing, *Sustainability*, 14(8): 4431

Nikolova, V and Arsić, S (2017) The stakeholder approach in corporate social responsibility, *Engineering Management*, 3(1): 24–55

Pache, A C, and Santos, F (2013) Inside the hybrid organization: Selective coupling as a response to competing institutional logics, *Academy of Management Journal*, 56(4), 972–1001

Peattie, K and Morley, A (2008) Eight paradoxes of the social enterprise research agenda, *Social Enterprise Journal*, 4(2): 91–107

Peredo, A M and McLean, M (2006) Social entrepreneurship: a critical review of the concept, *Journal of World Business*, 41: 56–65

Perrini, F, Costanzo, L A and Karatas-Ozkan, M (2021) Measuring impact and creating change: A comparison of the main methods for social enterprises, *Corporate Governance (Bingley)*, 21(2): 237–51

Pinheiro, P, Daniel, A and Moreira, A (2021) Social enterprise performance: The role of market and social entrepreneurship orientations, *VOLUNTAS: International Journal of Voluntary and Non-profit Organizations*, 32(1): 45–60

Pizzetti, M, Gatti, L and Seele, P (2021)Firms talk, suppliers walk: Analyzing the locus of greenwashing in the blame game and introducing 'vicarious greenwashing' *Journal of Business Ethics*, 170 (1): 21–38.

Porter, M E and Kramer, M R (2002) The competitive advantage of corporate philanthropy. *Harvard Business Review*, 80(12): 56–68

Quarshie, A M and Leuschner, R (2018) Cross-sector social interactions and systemic change in disaster response: A qualitative study, *Journal of Business Ethics*, 150(2): 357–84

Ragan, V K, and Gregg, T (2019) How social entrepreneurs zig-zag their way to impact at scale, *California Management Review*, 62(1): 53–76

Rose, K J (2020) Introducing the missing 11th principle of the United Nations Global Compact to reach sustainability – Follow the money, *Journal of Money Laundering Control*, 23(2), 355–67

Ruiz-Blanco, S, Romero, S and Fernandez-Feijoo, B (2021) Green, blue or black, but washing – what company characteristics determine greenwashing? *Environment, Development and Sustainability*, 24(3): 4024–45

Santos, F, Pache, A C and Birkholz, C (2015) Making hybrids work: Aligning business models and organizational design for social enterprises, *California Management Review*, 57(3): 36–58

Schembera, S (2018) Implementing corporate social responsibility: Empirical insights on the impact of the UN global compact on its business participants, *Business & Society*, 57(5): 783–825

Seele, P and Gatti, L (2015) Greenwashing revisited: In search of a typology and accusation-based definition incorporating legitimacy strategies, *Business Strategy and the Environment*, 26 (2): 239–52

Selsky, J W and Parker, B (2005) Cross-sector partnerships to address social issues: Challenges to theory and practice, *Journal of Management*, 31(6): 849–73

Shahab, Y, Gull, A A, Ahsan, T and Mushtaq, R (2021) CEO power and corporate social responsibility decoupling, *Applied Economics Letters*, 29(21): 1965–69

Smith, W K, Gonin, M and Besharov, M L (2013) Managing social-business tensions: A review and research agenda for social enterprise, *Business Ethics Quarterly*, 23(3): 407–42

Social Enterprise UK (2025) The national voice for social enterprise, https://www.socialenterprise.org.uk/ (archived at https://perma.cc/9HV6-MPK5)

Steiner, G A and Steiner, J F (2000) *Business, Government and Society: A managerial perspective*, UK: McGraw Hill

Steurer, R, Langer, M E, Konrad, A and Martinuzzi, A (2005) Corporations, stakeholders and sustainable development: A theoretical exploration of business-society relations, *Journal of Business Ethics*, 61: 263–81

Swartz v Coca-Cola Co (2021) https://climatecasechart.com/case/swartz-v-coca-cola-co/ (archived at https://perma.cc/5DFZ-WTJJ)

Sweeney, L and Koughlan, J (2008) Do different industries report corporate social responsibility differently? An investigation through the lens of Stakeholder Theory, *Journal of Marketing Communications*, 14(2): 113–24

Tan, Y and Zhu, Z (2022) The effect of ESG rating events on corporate green innovation in China: The mediating role of financial constraints and managers' environmental awareness, *Technology in Society*, 68: 1–13

Tello, M A (2020) Conceptualizing social impact: A geographic perspective, *Journal of Business Research*, 119: 562–71

Testa, F, Miroshnychenko, I, Barontini, R and Frey, M (2018) Does it pay to be a greenwasher or a brownwasher? *Business Strategy and the Environment*, 27(7): 1104–16

Thorgren, S and Omorede, A (2018) Passionate leaders in social entrepreneurship: Exploring an African context, *Business & Society*, 57(3): 481–524

Thornton, P H, and Ocasio, W (2008) Institutional logics, *The Sage Handbook of Organizational Institutionalism*, 840: 99–128

Tiwari, P, Bhat, A K and Tikoria, J (2020) Mediating role of prosocial motivation in predicting social entrepreneurial intentions, *Journal of Social Entrepreneurship*, 13(1): 118–41

Tomlins, R (2015) *Social Value Today: Current public and private thinking on social value*, Coventry: HouseMark

Torelli, R, Balluchi, F and Lazzini, A (2019) Greenwashing and environmental communication: Effects on stakeholders' perceptions, *Business Strategy and the Environment*, 29 (2): 407–21

Trujillo, D (2018) Multiparty alliances and systemic change: The role of beneficiaries and their capacity for collective action, *Journal of Business Ethics*, 150(2): 425–49

Tsalis, T A, Terzaki, M, Koulouriotis, D, Tsagarakis, K P and Nikolaou, I E (2023) The nexus of United Nations' 2030 agenda and corporate sustainability reports, *Sustainable Development*, 31(2), 784–96

Turban, D B and Greening, D W (1996) Corporate social performance and organizational attractiveness to prospective employees, *Academy of Management Journal*, 40(3): 658–72

UNGC (2023) The ten principles of the UN global compact, https://unglobalcompact.org/what-is-gc/mission/principles (archived at https://perma.cc/98L8-XW53)

United Nations Development Programme (2016). Human Development for Everyone, https://hdr.undp.org/content/worlds-most-marginalized-still-left-behind-global-development-priorities-undp-report (archived at https://perma.cc/25FE-544S)

Wadham, H and Warren, R (2013) Inspiring action, building understanding: How cross-sector partnership engages business in addressing global challenges, *Business Ethics, the Environment and Responsibility*, 22 (1): 47–63

Weerawardena, J, Salunke, S, Haigh, N and Sullivan Mort, G (2021) Business model innovation in social purpose organizations: Conceptualizing dual social-economic value creation, *Journal of Business Research*, 125: 762–71

Westley, F, Antadze, N, Riddell, D J, Robinson, K and Geobey, S (2014) Five configurations for scaling up social innovation: Case examples of nonprofit organizations from Canada, *The Journal of Applied Behavioral Science*, 50(3), 234–60

Williams, J (2024) Greenwashing: Appearance, illusion and the future of 'green' capitalism. *Geography Compass*, 8 (1): 1–13, https://compass.onlinelibrary.wiley.com/doi/10.1111/gec3.12736 (archived at https://perma.cc/BAS4-9HDP)

World Business Council for Sustainable Development (2000) *Corporate Social Responsibility: Making good business sense*, Geneve, Switzerland

World Economic Forum (2023) Patagonia sparking the sustainability cultural shift at every level, https://initiatives.weforum.org/industry-net-zero-accelerator/case-study-details/patagonia---sparking-the-sustainability-cultural-shift-at-every-level/aJYTG00C00001H34AI (archived at https://perma.cc/G77A-9MH9)

Yin, H, Tang, Y, and Jin, H (2025) Sustainability in the supply chain, environmental, social and corporate governance performance, and corporate value, *Finance Research Letters*, 77, 107061, https://doi.org/10.1016/j.frl.2025.107061 (archived at https://perma.cc/PEM3-N78M)

Yu, E P, Luu, B V and Chen, C H (2020) Greenwashing in environmental, social and governance disclosures, *Research in International Business and Finance*, 52, 101192

Yu, Y and Choi, Y (2014) Corporate social responsibility and firm performance through the mediating effect of organizational trust in Chinese firms, *Chinese Management Studies*, 8 (4): 577–92, https://www.emerald.com/insight/publication/issn/1750-614x (archived at https://perma.cc/AW2G-2TVQ)

Zhang, L, Li, D, Cao, C and Huang, S (2018) The influence of greenwashing perception on green purchasing intentions: The mediating role of green word-of-mouth and moderating role of green concern, *Journal of Cleaner Production*, 187: 740–50

# 06 Social innovation and social value creation

DR RICHARD TOMLINS

## LEARNING OUTCOMES

By the end of this chapter, you should be able to:

- Identify the importance of social innovation for social enterprises.
- Identify the different measures of social value so that you can measure impact made by social enterprises.
- Explore the scope for social value to be a driver of change for social enterprises as well as a measurement of change.

## REAL-WORLD EXAMPLE Zipline: A model of technological innovation for societal impact

Zipline, a US medical product delivery service, demonstrates how innovative technology and entrepreneurial tenacity can transform healthcare delivery. Born from the vision of its founders, Keller Rinaudo, William Hetzler and Keenan Wyrobek, Zipline employs drone technology to deliver critical medical supplies to remote areas (Zipline, 2021).

The genesis of Zipline was a reflection on the dearth of timely access to critical medical supplies in remote, infrastructure-limited regions. The co-founders' background in robotics and drones offered a glimpse into the technology's latent potential to bridge this chasm (Rinaudo, 2017). Technological hurdles included optimizing drone reliability, endurance and payload capacity. Regulatory obstacles involved securing government permissions, implementing rigorous safety protocols and substantiating the system's efficacy. Zipline embraced the technological challenges as opportunities for **innovation**, persistently enhancing drone capabilities. Similarly, it engaged proactively with governments, exhibiting the system's safety and reliability (Kell, 2021).

Zipline epitomizes the principle of 'technology for good'. Its autonomous drone delivery system has reshaped the healthcare logistics landscape, particularly where conventional supply chains falter due to geographical constraints. Each of Zipline's distribution centres, part of an intricate network, can cater to numerous healthcare facilities within an 80 km radius, delivering crucial medical supplies like vaccines, emergency medication and blood products (Zipline, 2021). The **social impact** has been profound and lifesaving. By slashing delivery times of critical supplies from hours to minutes, they have saved countless lives, especially in dire emergencies. In Rwanda, for example, the drone service has reportedly trimmed the delivery time of blood products from four hours to a mere 15 minutes (Wakabayashi, 2020).

This remarkable ability to swiftly deliver medical supplies to remote locations, previously deemed unreachable, underscores the potential of innovative technology when applied with an entrepreneurial mindset. In doing so, Zipline has addressed a significant societal issue, manifesting the essence of **social entrepreneurship**. Zipline's business model stands as an exemplar of social entrepreneurship. By transforming obstacles into opportunities, they have generated tremendous social value while also establishing a commercially viable enterprise. It has reimagined and revolutionized healthcare delivery in regions where conventional logistics are ineffective, thereby converting a significant societal challenge into a unique market opportunity. Zipline's narrative presents a compelling fusion of technology and entrepreneurship working in tandem to serve societal good. Their ability to identify an unmet need, harness technology, overcome daunting challenges and build a sustainable and impactful business showcases the incredible power of innovation and persistence.

In essence, Zipline's story provides invaluable insights into the role technology can play in addressing societal needs and the potential for businesses to be agents of significant social change. With an innovative approach, entrepreneurial spirit and a focus on social impact, Zipline has painted a vivid picture of how enterprises can build transformative business models that not only thrive commercially but also make a substantial societal difference.

## Introduction

Throughout this textbook, the authors have argued that **social enterprises** (SEs) are organizations that balance profit with a social mission. This chapter suggests that a focus on **social innovation** and **social value** creation are key drivers if SEs are to fulfil their **social mission** through creating **social impact**. Indeed, as the OECD (2010) notes, this is part of a wider societal shift whereby government and stakeholders note that innovation, economics and societal health impact are not simply through science and research and development. They are also through actors who 'put the social first'. We can see social innovation as those progressive activities and services that are motivated by the goal of meeting a social need (Mulgan, 2006).

Social innovation is the process of creating and implementing new ideas to address social issues and improve the lives of people and communities. Social value approaches then become the measurement of how effectively social innovation is being deployed and whether SEs are establishing the best balance between the financial profit (or loss) they make and their social impact. It provides a guide as to how far SEs are best placed to achieve this outcome compared with other socially oriented businesses such as B Corporations but also with not-for-profit organizations (NFPs).

In the first section, we delve deeper into the concept of social innovation, what it means and how it is perceived as a key driver for financial sustainability, including potential barriers. Then we explore the concept of social value and its application in legislation, policy and practice. Following this, the chapter provides our deep dive into the measurement opportunities of social innovation and social value before a summary is presented and key learning points identified.

## Social enterprises and social innovation

As we have illustrated, Zipline is an example of social innovation; however, we can see this as a more widespread process whereby social motivation, cooperative collective action and the relative diversity of stakeholder interactions come together to drive social innovation (Tortia et al, 2020). Social challenges are often complex and multifaceted, making traditional or linear approaches insufficient to address these complexities. Social innovation is the means for SEs to develop creative and context-specific solutions that are best suited to the complexities of the challenges they seek to address.

In the context of SEs, social innovation therefore offers the promise of new ideas that meet social needs by addressing **societal** challenges. It brings an opportunity to enhance well-being in contrast to a sole organizational focus on profit. It is about transforming challenges into opportunities, as we will explain later with examples of **Design Thinking** and **Design Sprints**. Consequently, this chapter focuses on the role of **social innovation** in SEs as a driver of **social impact** and therefore the 'turbo-charger' behind the creation of **social value**. By adding a mindset of design thinking and iteration, social entrepreneurs are enabled to step into the '**opportunity space**' (Tomlins, 1999) and break from the idea of the public servant being a purely constrained officer (Lipsky, 1980; Pahl, 1975), rather focusing on what creativity might be possible to be new, inventive and socially impactful. Social entrepreneurs might be seen as opportunity space driven (Guclu et al, 2002).

**Social innovation** therefore should provide the tools and mindset necessary for SEs to remain relevant and effective in a changing environment through design thinking. By continuously innovating, SEs can anticipate emerging trends, respond to shifts in demand and adapt their strategies accordingly. For example, during the Covid-19 pandemic, many SEs had to innovate rapidly to continue delivering services, shifting from in-person services to online delivery models (Wells et al, 2020).

## *Social innovation as a key driver for financial sustainability*

The Social Enterprise World Forum (n.d.) identifies the six primary key characteristics of a social enterprise as:

- being mission-focused
- investing surplus in its mission
- having ownership tied to mission
- ethically transparent and accountable
- trade-generated income
- mission locked

While **social innovation** is not amongst the six primary key characteristics of SEs, these six might be seen as focused primarily on **processes** and **outputs** rather than on **outcomes,** which demonstrate fulfilment of **social mission**. The OECD (2024) argues that **social innovation** refers to the design and implementation of conceptual, process, product or organizational change to benefit the welfare and well-being of individuals and communities. Therefore, social impact through social innovation might be seen as a facilitating and overarching outcomes-focused theme (The Melting Pot, 2023).

Whilst SEs prioritize social impact, they must also ensure financial sustainability to continue their operations (Spreckley, 2022). **Social innovation** is a key driver of financial sustainability (Harsanto et al, 2022) as it can lead to the development of new products, services or business models that generate additional revenues. By diversifying revenue streams, SEs can reduce their dependence on traditional funding sources such as grants or donations and ensure long-term financial sustainability (Wells et al, 2020).

SEs that demonstrate a commitment to innovation are also more likely to be more attractive to investors (Miller and Bowcock, 2020). Investors are increasingly seeking organizations that are not only socially responsible but also capable of adapting to changing market conditions and driving growth. Social innovation signals to investors that the enterprise is forward-thinking, resilient and capable of scaling its impact. For example, SEs that leverage technology to solve social problems may attract impact investors who are interested in supporting technology-driven solutions.

Social innovation can lead to cost-effective methods of delivering products or services, reducing operational expenses and improving the financial 'bottom line' (van Niekerk et al, 2021). For example, a social enterprise providing healthcare services in underserved areas might innovate by adopting virtual solutions, which can reduce the cost of service delivery while expanding access to care. These cost savings can be reinvested in the enterprise's social mission, further enhancing its social impact.

Nevertheless, social innovation often involves collaboration with various stakeholders, including businesses, government agencies and NFPs (Zakaras, 2021). These partnerships can lead to new opportunities for funding, resource sharing and joint ventures. For example, a social enterprise focused on renewable energy might partner with a technology company to develop innovative solar energy solutions, gaining access to expertise and resources that enhance both social impact and financial sustainability.

For social innovation to thrive, SEs must foster a culture of innovation within their organizations (Social Enterprise World Forum, n.d.). This involves creating an environment that encourages experimentation, learning and collaboration, as outlined in the next 'Stop and Think' box.

**STOP AND THINK**

How would you rank in importance the different ways in which social innovation is a key driver of financial sustainability from the information in the paragraphs above?

Fostering a culture of innovation and experimentation supports SEs to drive innovation and create solutions for addressing societal and/or environmental challenges, and as we have noted above, supports financial sustainability. The key elements of such a culture include encouraging creativity and experimentation: SEs should actively encourage their teams to think creatively and experiment with new ideas (Hillman et al, 2018). This can involve setting aside time and resources for innovation as well as nurturing an organizational culture that values risk-taking and learning from failure. For example, a social enterprise might establish an 'innovation lab' or designate a portion of its budget for pilot projects that explore new approaches to social challenges. An 'innovation lab' might be formal and costly but can be simply an informal space for creating.

Fostering a culture of innovation and experimentation includes promoting collaboration and knowledge sharing and, in particular, the exchange of ideas. SEs should promote collaboration both within the organization and with external partners. This chimes with the 'opportunity space' idea identified above. This can involve creating cross-functional teams, engaging with communities to understand their needs and participating in networks or ecosystems that support social innovation (Rihter and Mešl, 2024).

Investing in capacity building can also drive social innovation. SEs must invest in building the capacity of their teams, including providing training and development opportunities that equip staff with the skills and knowledge required to innovate (Osorio et al, 2024). For example, a social enterprise might offer training in areas such as design thinking, data analysis or impact measurement, enabling employees to develop and implement innovative solutions more effectively.

The ability to adapt quickly to changing circumstances is critical in this context for social innovation. SEs should adopt an agile mindset, embracing flexibility, rapid iteration and continuous improvement (Joffre, 2020). This can involve using methodologies, such as design thinking, lean start-up or agile project management, all of which emphasize iterative development, testing and learning. For example, a social enterprise might adopt a lean start-up approach to develop a new service, design sprinting, rapidly prototyping and refining the offering based on user feedback.

**STOP AND THINK**

A social entrepreneur will typically start a social enterprise because of the desire to create a positive change in the community as well as in their own lives (Penroe, 2023). Please carry out a web search to identify how a social entrepreneur might distribute business leadership amongst their organization to achieve the culture of innovation and experimentation identified above. That is, what are the most effective leadership models for a social enterprise?

## *Barriers to social innovation*

While social innovation is critical to SEs' success, they often face barriers.. These include resource constraints given that, more often, they typically operate with limited financial and human resources, hindering their ability to invest in innovation. Without adequate funding or skilled personnel, developing and implementing new ideas can be challenging. SEs may therefore need to seek external support through grants, impact investment or partnerships to overcome these resource constraints. This is why the author of this chapter supports play and playfulness as frugal and impactful approaches for innovation (Jayawardhana et al, 2022).

In some cases, regulatory or institutional barriers can stifle social innovation. For example, SEs operating in highly regulated industries, such as healthcare or education, may face challenges in introducing new products or services due to compliance requirements. Navigating these barriers necessitates engaging with policymakers and advocating for regulatory frameworks that support innovation (Davies et al, 2019).

SEs, like any other organization, may be risk-averse, especially when their financial sustainability is at stake or perhaps wedded to the original organizational approach. This aversion to risk can lead to a reluctance in experimenting with new ideas or approaches. To overcome this challenge, SEs must create a culture that values learning from failure and encourages calculated risk-taking. Besides, identifying and measuring social value as part of the implementation process may provide an alternative and more positive narrative (Choi et al, 2018).

Additionally, SEs often struggle with effectively measuring the impact of their innovations. Without clear metrics or evaluation methods, it can be difficult to assess whether a new approach is achieving the desired social outcomes. Developing robust **impact measurement** frameworks is essential for SEs to demonstrate the effectiveness of their innovations and secure ongoing support (MacColl, 2022). Notwithstanding, as SEs innovate and explore new business models, there might be a risk of mission drift (Kulshrestha et al, 2022) where the pursuit of financial sustainability overshadows the social mission. SEs therefore must remain vigilant in ensuring their innovations align with their core values and social objectives.

**STOP AND THINK**

- What social enterprise might you develop?
- What might the mission for your social enterprise be or involve?
- How might you ensure that your social enterprise remains true to its core values and social objectives?

## *Design thinking to tackle barriers to social innovation*

Design thinking incorporates play and playfulness, which can be seen as a critical tool to achieve a cycle of continuous innovation and breaking down the barriers to social innovation (Tomlins, 2024). **Design thinking** is a systemic, though not systematic, intuitive, customer-focused problem-solving approach that organizations can use to respond to rapidly changing environments and to create maximum impact. It also offers the opportunity to engage with communities to enable a more equitable and resilient future (Malynka and Tomlins, 2021). As such, design thinking is an insightful approach (Razzouk and Shute, 2012) that supports SEs to develop play and playful approaches for innovation.

Imagine diving into a **transformative** journey where insights become the catalyst for innovation, where every problem presents an opportunity, and every solution is a breakthrough. The rise of global challenges has seen a rise in complicated and **wicked** problems. Design thinking can be an antidote to a world that can be characterized as VUCAH (volatile, uncertain, complex, ambiguous and hyperconnected) or more widely brittle, anxious, nonlinear and incomprehensible (BANI) (Tomlins, 2024).

Design thinking offers several advantages for social innovation through a human-centred approach emphasizing the importance of understanding the needs and experiences of the people affected by social issues, ensuring that solutions are relevant and impactful (Brown and Wyatt, 2009). Powering social innovation design thinking involves an **iterative process**, promoting prototyping and testing ideas quickly, allowing for rapid feedback and refinement. This adaptability can lead to more effective social innovation and therefore solutions, although control of the process is important in ensuring the speed of innovation (Wynn and Eckert, 2017). It fosters collaboration among diverse stakeholders, including community members, which can generate a wider range of ideas and insights whilst also being a strong driver for equity, equality and diversity (Wingfield et al, 2024).

By focusing on empathy, design thinking helps innovators connect with communities on a deeper level, which can lead to more meaningful and sustainable changes (Peng, 2022). Empathy in turn can support creative problem-solving. It encourages out-of-the-box thinking, enabling teams to tackle complex social issues from new angles; this includes being flexible with the methodology for maximum impact. Hence, think of design thinking as a philosophy that brings in elements as required to enable social innovation (Bender-Salazar, 2023). This highlights the way that design thinking promotes cross-disciplinary insights to bring together professionals from various fields and promote interdisciplinary solutions that can address social challenges more holistically, including in quite specific disciplines (Hsieh et al, 2023).

The interdisciplinary focus of design thinking encompasses a focus on feasibility. It considers not just what is desirable but also what is feasible and viable, helping to ensure that solutions are practical and can be implemented effectively. Visualization and moving outside of comfort zones to gather contrasting views are seen as effective catalysts for successful social innovation (Carella et al, 2023):

- By involving communities in the design process, it empowers them to take ownership of solutions, fostering resilience and self-efficacy (Barile and Kelestyn, 2023).
- The emphasis on understanding root causes might lead to solutions that address systemic issues rather than simply treating symptoms, resulting in more sustainable social change and long-term impact. There has been a lack of empirical studies to evidence long-term impact, though it is persuasive that design thinking affects project performance through psychological empowerment – that is, design thinking can facilitate a different way of 'doing', which can in turn unlock resources for more positive social innovation outcomes.

In summary, design thinking enhances social innovation by creating a more empathetic, inclusive and effective approach to problem-solving.

## Social value

The OECD sees social value measurement as a means of adopting rational and objective value measurements, enabling accountability whilst stimulating discussions on change. However, it cautions against measurement that is not related to decision-making or is disproportionately large and resource-intensive compared to the area of potential change.

'Social value' can be seen as the currency of social impact, enabling SEs to account for the difference they make, including against competitors. Social value refers to the impact of activities, policies and programmes on the well-being of individuals, communities and society at large. It extends beyond financial or economic metrics, although, as we will see below with SROIs and the Triple Bottom Line (Elkington,1994), these still remain important. However, accounting is extended to include social, environmental and cultural benefits, which can be more challenging to quantify yet are equally crucial in assessing the effectiveness and sustainability of various initiatives (Tomlins, 2015). It becomes a measure of the social impact of social innovation.

The concept of social value has gained increasing attention in various sectors, including public services, business and community development, and not least government, as stakeholders are increasingly asked to demonstrate how their actions contribute to society, the environment and the economy. Investors have also become interested in these issues both through philanthropy and also through **ESG** (Environmental, Social and Governance) as a set of criteria (below) used to evaluate a company's performance and impact in three key areas (Bell, 2021):

1. **Environmental:** This looks at how a company performs as a steward of nature. It includes factors like climate change, greenhouse gas emissions, waste management and resource conservation.
2. **Social:** This focuses on the company's relationships with employees, suppliers, customers and the communities where it operates. It includes issues like labour practices and human rights along with diversity and inclusion.
3. **Governance:** This examines the company's internal practices and policies, such as executive compensation, audits, internal controls and shareholder rights.

**STOP AND THINK**

Revisiting the Zipline example at the start of this chapter, how would you find out what you need to measure to keep attracting private investment?

## Identifying social value

The idea of social value has its roots in the broader discourse on **'value theory'** (Pirgmaier, 2021) and the debate on 'what' constitutes value and 'how' it should be measured. Traditionally, value was equated with economic value – essentially the market price of goods and services; however, this narrow view has been increasingly challenged by the recognition that the most important aspects of life, for example, clean air, education, public health and community well-being, cannot be adequately captured by market transactions. This perspective aligns with the broader trend toward **'triple bottom line accounting'**, which considers social, environmental and financial performance (Elkington, 1994). Conventional financial accounting methods in this context are insufficient for capturing the full range of impacts that activities have on society.

In an era marked by heightened awareness of societal challenges, ranging from environmental degradation to social inequality, the concept of 'social value' is a pivotal framework for understanding and enhancing the broader impacts of organizational activities, which include public policies; however, it goes beyond these to the sphere of the private sector (Tomlins, 2015). Social value is the net positive impact of activities on society, encompassing a range of dimensions, including social, environmental and economic outcomes. This includes the importance of considering the long-term and initially intangible benefits that activities can generate, as opposed to merely focusing on short-term financial gains (Tomlins, 2015).

**Stakeholder engagement** is crucial in determining social value. Elkington (1994) argues that this area of focus is inherently subjective, as different stakeholders may have different views on what constitutes value. For example, a community might prioritize environmental sustainability, while a business might focus on economic returns. To reconcile these differing perspectives, organizations need to actively engage with their stakeholders to understand their priorities and incorporate these insights into their value assessments (Tomlins, 2015). Stakeholder involvement needs to be paramount in decision-making, as we shall explore below in the context of the danger of average values trumping specific individual and community experiences.

## The role of social value in public policy and practice

SEs will need to be aware that governments in Europe increasingly legislate for consideration of social value as part of the public contracting process. In essence, the concept of social value has increasingly been integrated into policy and practice through legislation. In the UK public sector, for instance, social value has become a key consideration in procurement processes. This is particularly where the **Public Services (Social Value) Act 2012** requires public authorities and providers of public services to consider social value when awarding contracts, i.e. there is the option to not award a contract to the lowest tender price (see Chapter 4).

The Act has led to a growing emphasis on generating social value through public spending, with many public bodies adopting social value frameworks to guide their procurement decisions. To that effect, in June 2018, the UK Government (Cabinet Office, 2018) announced it would go further and explicitly evaluate social value when awarding most major contracts in England and Wales. Since 2021, government departments are expected to report on the social impact of their major contracts. In this context, the UK Cabinet Office developed a 'Social Value Model' to provide a consistent approach for departments and suppliers. This model outlines priority themes and policy outcomes that are important to deliver through government contracts. A minimum weighting of 10 per cent is applied to social value in the evaluation of bids, and the government has trained thousands of commercial buyers to take account of social value in procurement processes to ensure consistent and effective integration of measures.

### STOP AND THINK

Can you access the UK Cabinet Office 'Social Value Model'?

- What measures do you think that the government should prioritize within the model?
- How would you decide what to prioritize at a local authority or municipality level?

In this context, social value might be seen as a transformative lens through which to assess and guide public policy and organizational activity. By prioritizing outcomes that enhance societal well-being, environmental sustainability and economic inclusivity, social value offers a pathway towards more equitable and resilient communities. As societies navigate complex challenges, the integration of social value into decision-making processes emerges as both an ethical imperative and a strategic advantage for businesses and specifically for SEs' competitive advantage, given their mission in this context.

The Social Value Model probes outcome-related qualitative issues, such as the tenderer's existing or planned understanding of employment and skills issues and the education and training issues relating to the contract being tendered in that instance. Illustrative examples include demographics, skills shortages, new opportunities in high-growth sectors, under-represented groups in the workforce (e.g., prison leavers, disabled people), geographic/local communities and skills/employment challenges' (Government Commercial Function, 2020). However, the reporting metrics remain predominantly output rather than outcome-related. For example, those suggested in the Social Value Model include the number of full-time-equivalent (FTE) employment opportunities created under the contract, by UK region (output), rather than the social impact and social innovation that has occurred (outcome).

**STOP AND THINK**

You are the manager of a large London local authority Parks and Cemeteries Department. You are about to re-tender its grounds maintenance contract, including grass cutting and more general grounds maintenance. You have a meeting with the Chief Executive of the local authority and her commissioning and procurement department.

Given the material that you have read in this chapter, what are you going to recommend?

1. 'Budgets are tight; we simply need to get the lowest possible price for the grass to be cut and the grounds to be kept to a particular standard.'
2. 'Even though budgets are tight, I'm sure that we can get a little more value from the contract through...'
3. 'Budgets are tight; however, let's see how creative we can be with the bidding contractors. If they're cutting the grass anyway, we could even have a walk in the cut grass day if we programme it for the benefit of local residents' mental health.'

How would you seek to persuade the Chief Executive of your preference in comparison to the other options?

## *The case of Scotland and Northern Ireland – social value and public procurement*

In Scotland, social value is a key consideration in public procurement and has been guided by several legislations and policies, including the Procurement Reform (Scotland) Act 2014. This requires public sector bodies to consider how their procurement activities can improve the economic, social and environmental well-being of the area. The Community Empowerment (Scotland) Act 2015 also includes provisions for asset transfers, allowing community bodies to request the transfer of public sector assets. The guidance for this Act highlights the importance of social value in decision-making processes. In this context, the Scottish Futures Trust (SFT) TOMs (Themes, Outcomes and Measures) framework provides guidance for measuring social value in construction projects. It includes various measures related to social, economic and environmental factors. This includes some of the very output-based criteria rather than outcomes-based criteria: 'The number of employees (FTE) taken who are long-term unemployed (for a year or longer)' (SFT, 2020: 12); similarly, 'Equality, diversity and inclusion training provided both for staff and supply chain staff' (SFT, 2020: 25) rather than the difference the training has made.

In Northern Ireland, Procurement Policy Note (PPN) 01/21 mandates that tenders for government contracts must allocate a minimum of 10 per cent of the total award criteria to social value. The policy encourages companies to think innovatively for the common good, promoting well-being, ethical supply chains and environmental sustainability. Social value in Northern Ireland focuses on four key themes:

- increasing secure employment and skills
- building ethical and resilient supply chains
- delivering zero carbon
- promoting well-being

The policy also mandates that staff working on government contracts must be paid at least as set by the Living Wage Foundation. The reference to 'well-being' might seem to promise an outcome-based approach; however, the sample metrics are less stretching and output-based. For example, the 'environmental' points are awarded on the basis that the strategy will be submitted in relation to work carried out on this contract (Social Value Unit, 2021) rather than something that socially innovates.

**STOP AND THINK**

Can you suggest, on the basis of the information that we have shared so far, some outcomes rather than output-based measures for the government to take forward?

The 2023 Procurement Act came into force in England, Northern Ireland and Wales, and is, in part, a response to the implications of Brexit, as the UK is no longer bound by European Union (EU) Public Procurement Directives, which require member states to incorporate social considerations into their national procurement laws and practices. Those directives include that public authorities across the EU must consider social value aspects, such as promoting employment opportunities, social inclusion and ensuring fair working conditions when awarding contracts. These directives provide a flexible legal framework that allows public buyers to pursue various social objectives, including job creation, fair treatment of workers and facilitating access for social businesses. While Scotland has opted out of this new procurement regime, there are arrangements for joint and cross-border procurement with Scottish contracting authorities. The Act includes a focus on removing barriers for businesses to contract with the public sector, including those previously facing new entrants, including SEs. There is also greater emphasis on procurement as an enabler to deliver wider benefits for the public good and a shift to a duty to award to the most advantageous tender rather than purely the most economically advantageous.

Key to realizing social value benefits of the 2023 Procurement Act will be the monitoring of post-award implementation of the organization's tender commitments. It is relatively easy to commit to outputs rather than their realization. This is, of course, where the virtuous mission of SEs will be important. In turn, this is where the government and society might benefit from the socially innovative approaches that are often the core mission of SEs.

The EU's Single Market Act 2011 shapes much of its approach to social value, emphasizing the crucial role of the social economy and SEs in driving social innovation, inclusiveness and trust. These are imperatives for which SEs should engage with social innovation and social value. In addition, the European Commission's Directive on Non-financial Reporting, adopted in April 2014, requires nearly 6,000 public bodies to report on environmental, social, employee and human rights issues. This Directive applies to large public-interest companies with more than 500 employees. These include both listed companies and some unlisted organizations, such as banks, insurance companies and other companies designated by member states based on their activities, size or number of employees. Companies are required to disclose in their management reports relevant and material information on policies, outcomes and risks, including due diligence of their implementation. It also requires the identification of key non-financial performance indicators concerning environmental aspects, social and employee-related matters, respect for human rights, anti-corruption and bribery issues, and diversity within the boards of directors. Alongside this, in 2019, the European Commission published guidelines to help companies report climate-related information, integrating recommendations from the Financial Stability Board's Task Force on Climate-related Financial Disclosures (TCFD). This was part of the broader action plan on financing sustainable growth.

**STOP AND THINK**

What reporting metrics would you design for an outcomes-based social value approach for the award of contracts? How might that encourage social innovation?

## Measurement challenges and methodologies

So far, the importance of social innovation to society has been outlined, and SEs' pivotal role in creating social value has been discussed, which has become a measure of societal progress and the SEs' currency. However, one of the key challenges in demonstrating the impact of social innovation through social value is its measurement, and the value for the commissioning and procurement process is moving beyond the short-term impact measure of outputs through to the depth and long-term perspective of outcomes as discussed below.

As the concept of social value continues to gain traction across sectors, the **challenges of measurement, subjectivity**, and **long-term impact assessment** must be addressed to fully realize the potential of social value in contributing to a more equitable and sustainable society. This includes developing a shared understanding of outcomes-based and qualitative social value and an understanding of how to promote its integration into decision-making processes in addition to being a monitoring tool. Therefore, in this section we 'deep-dive' into measurement challenges and methodologies. We will look at ways of providing more understanding of change beyond simple output metrics to identify behavioural change.

Financial profit at its most basic might be seen as occurring where revenue is greater than costs. Let's call this notion of profit the '**bottom line**'. SEs replace this single bottom line with a '**triple bottom line**' (Elkington,1994).

**STOP AND THINK**

The 'triple bottom line' suggests retaining the importance of profit, but regarding it as of equal standing with the impact on people and planet. It is up to you, as a social entrepreneur, to determine the balance between the three in practice; one is not automatically more important than the others.

If you think of a social enterprise that you would like to develop, what would be your balance between the three? People, planet or profit?

Unlike discrete financial metrics, which are concrete and standardized, social impacts might be seen as new and qualitative, subjective and diffuse. This in turn has spurred the development of various methodologies, such as Social Return on Investment (SROI), well-being indices, and impact assessments to establish clear methodologies for the social value elements of the triple bottom line.

We identify three broad ways of measuring social value:

1 storytelling
2 data bank monetary proxies
3 co-created monetary proxies

## Storytelling

This vision of focusing on key value changes is seen at a micro level by the Citizen Housing Social Return on Investment (SROI) analysis of a community-developed chicken run in Coventry using the SROI data bank managed by Social Value UK. While the SROI indicated a positive return on the funder's investment, more profound questions were raised regarding how to quantify the term 'good'. What represents a good return on investment? Is it two pounds of social value returned for every £1 of financial investment, or five or ten (Tomlins, 2015)?

The story of the 'chicken run' is of a residents' initiative on a working-class estate where the local residents' association identified themselves as animal lovers who wanted to establish both outputs and outcomes for chickens rescued from 'battery farming'. This included:

- Three elderly widowed gentlemen visited daily, seeking company and a sense of community belonging.
- The youth club became involved in cleaning the chicken sheds, challenging the pejorative view that the youth club was too close to the run and might be a source of vandalism to the project.
- The primary school on site has benefitted as the chickens became part of a science project exploring the source of food.
- One teacher reported on one conversation, which reflected the need for a science project as she asked, 'Where do eggs come from? Class?' and noting a hand going up. 'Jonny, your hand is up,' she said, 'The supermarket, Miss!' came the reply, with the result that a couple of chickens would be plucked up each term and taken into school for the social value of better demonstrating the source of the food that we eat.
- People began discussing the project at the local bus stop, beginning conversations and consequently adding social value to the community.
- The local knitting club started knitting sweaters for the chickens. In part, this was to keep them warm, as they arrived short of feathers from being kept as battery hens; however, as importantly, it was to prevent the redness from loss of feathers being seen as a trigger to peck at another bird.
- The café at the community centre started using the local eggs produced by the chickens. One of the local young people who was characterized as a 'tearaway' started volunteering at the chicken run and eventually secured an apprenticeship at the café.

While these stories may well be a coincidence, the power of the story effectively captured the essence of change and inspired others far more than the ratios of value invested to value produced.

**STOP AND THINK**

Did the researchers simply get lucky by discovering a social value narrative with 'Hollywood' story qualities? Perhaps all SEs have a rich story to tell.

With this example, are you persuaded that storytelling can be impactful in identifying the social value of social impact initiatives? Which social enterprise that you know of has a story that can be amplified in the way we have outlined?

## Monetary proxies

There is no single accepted measure of social value. According to the Social Value Portal (2015), almost 10 years ago there were over 1,150 social and environmental impact metrics in use across the world. Subjective measures include the 'happiness index' and 'sentiment analysis' (Helliwell et al, 2019). Equally, PWC (Ménard, 2013), one of the biggest accounting firms in the UK, has highlighted that all credit rating agencies factor 'non-financial' metrics into their models for assessing business performance. This underscores the importance of articulating social and environmental metrics in the social investment market. Amongst this diversity, the 'Gold Standard' (Tomlins, 2015) approach to measuring social value has been seen as Social Return on Investment (SROI). This method seeks to quantify social value in monetary terms and compare the costs of an activity to its social benefits.

### Social return on investment (SROI)

By monetizing social impacts, SROI provides a framework for quantifying the value generated for society, helping organizations, investors and stakeholders to understand the broader effects of their work. SROI is expressed as a ratio of benefits to costs, where a ratio greater than 1:1 indicates that the social benefits exceed the costs involved. For example, an SROI ratio of 3:1 (Salverda, 2024) suggests that for every pound invested, three pounds of social value are generated. This value can include factors like improved health, increased educational attainment or reduced environmental degradation. SROI is built around seven key principles:

1. Involve stakeholders
2. Understand what changes
3. Value the things that matter
4. Only include what is material
5. Do not over-claim
6. Be transparent
7. Verify the result

**Figure 6.1** Identifying SROI

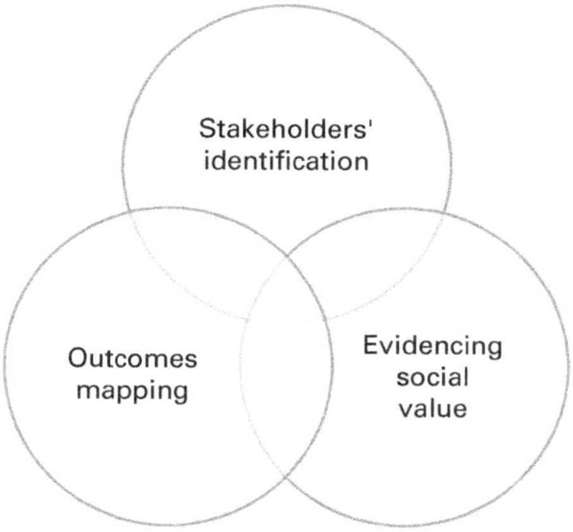


Social Value UK, the custodian of SROI, believes that the lack of a standard measurement approach is in itself not important; rather, the key to being able to compare different values is consistency in applying these principles around three core features (Figure 6.1).

The process of calculating SROI can be seen through six steps, each designed to ensure a comprehensive and accurate assessment of an organization's impact:

1. **Establishing scope and identifying stakeholders:** The first step involves defining the scope of SROI analysis. This includes identifying the project, programme or organization to be evaluated, as well as determining the timeframe over which SROI will be calculated. It is also crucial to identify stakeholders – those affected by the project or organization's activities. Stakeholders can include beneficiaries, employees, investors, community members and more. However, transparently focusing on key stakeholders might be necessary to ensure that the SROI does not lose time, resources and focus.
2. **Mapping outcomes:** In this step, the relationship between inputs (the resources used), outputs (the tangible products or services delivered) and outcomes (the changes experienced by stakeholders) is mapped out. For example, a programme aimed at reducing unemployment might have outcomes like increased income for participants (outputs) and also improved self-esteem (outcomes).
3. **Evidencing outcomes and giving them a value:** The next step is to collect data to demonstrate that these outcomes have occurred. This could involve surveys, interviews or reviewing existing data. After evidencing the outcomes, the next challenge is assigning a monetary value to them. This is often the most complex aspect of SROI, as it requires converting qualitative outcomes into quantitative financial terms.

4 **Establishing impact:** To ensure the accuracy of the SROI ratio, it is important to isolate the impact of the organization's activities from other external factors. This step involves considering factors such as deadweight (what would have happened anyway), displacement (how much of the outcome simply displaced other outcomes so there is no net gain), attribution (how much of the outcome can be attributed to the organization's activities) and drop-off (how outcomes diminish over time).

5 **Calculating the SROI:** With all necessary data in place, SROI is calculated by comparing the total value of benefits (outcomes) to the total value of investments (inputs). The result is a ratio indicating the social return on every pound invested (see the references above). Whereas in traditional cost-benefit analyses, the ratios would be used to compare different projects, the SROI ratio is much more seen as one element in explaining and communicating the general progress of certain developments. The number itself is not the end goal; rather, it is aiding the particular initiative narrative.

6 **Reporting, using and embedding:** The final step involves reporting the findings to stakeholders and using the insights to inform decision-making. This could mean refining programmes to enhance positive outcomes, adjusting strategies to mitigate negative impacts, or improving stakeholder engagement. Embedding SROI in an organization's practices can lead to a culture of continuous improvements and a stronger focus on creating social value.

## The benefits of SROI

The importance of SROI lies in its ability to **enhance accountability**. It should allow organizations to be transparent about their impacts, helping to build trust with stakeholders. This is particularly important for NFPs, SEs and public sector organizations. It should also **improve organizational decision-making** by allowing the full range of impacts to be understood. Thereby, SROI enables organizations to make better-informed decisions about where to allocate resources. It helps them to focus on the activities that generate the most significant social value, although, as we note, it should not outweigh the customer's voice. Investors are increasingly looking for opportunities that offer both financial returns and positive social or environmental impacts. SROI offers a clear and quantifiable method to demonstrate this, making it easier to attract impact investors or grant funding. It can also support **advocacy**, as organizations can use SROI data to advocate for policy changes or increased funding. By highlighting the broader societal benefits of their work, they can make a stronger case to policymakers or funders.

## Challenges with SROI

Despite its benefits, SROI is not without its challenges and criticisms. These include **complexity and cost**. Conducting an SROI analysis can be resource-intensive, requiring significant time, expertise and money. Smaller organizations, in particular, may find it challenging to undertake a comprehensive SROI analysis without external support. Assigning monetary values to social outcomes is also subjective and can vary depending on the methods used. This subjectivity can lead to questions about the accuracy and comparability of SROI ratios across different organizations or projects.

There is also a danger that SROI might focus on outcomes that can be easily quantified and monetized. This can lead to the undervaluation of important but less tangible outcomes, such as cultural impacts or long-term social changes. Like any metric, SROI can be misused or misinterpreted. Organizations might be tempted to inflate their SROI ratio by selecting only the most favourable outcomes or by using optimistic assumptions in their calculations.

There has also been the use of large proxy banks, the most expansive and eclectic being the SROI data bank, containing tens of thousands of financial products from different studies, times and countries. The SROI data bank was community-produced and 'owned' by SROI practitioners. Practitioners conducted their studies, contributed their data and sought the best matching proxy, including trying to match the qualitative comments of the chicken run practitioners with the SROI data bank.

If we take the example we discussed of the 'Chicken Run' project, the neighbours were talking about the chicken run whilst they were at the bus stop: 'It's the best feeling ever; it feels like shopping at Harrods.' To complete SROI, this then meant diving into the data bank and looking for the best fit amongst the proxies available. Was there an immediate read across which states the value of shopping at Harrods? No! What was the next best fit? The financial value of luxury shopping, maybe? Nothing in the database again. Hmmm....

On reflection the community member said that it 'feels' like shopping at Harrods, so maybe the search for proxies was too literal, so the iteration of the conversation was, 'So you said it feels like shopping at Harrods; tell me a bit more about what that feels like?' 'It feels like being at the top of the world.' And hence, by iteration, the process of identification continued until the best-fit proxy was found.

The demise of the SROI data bank has created momentum for co-created monetary proxies (below), and in that context the exploration of the best financial proxies for the chicken run provides useful learning. It reflects the subjectivity of social value, as different stakeholders have different views on what constitutes value. It means that the diversity of experiences can be captured and reflected in social value measures. However, it also moves away from developing standardized measures of social value that are widely accepted and applicable across different contexts. There is a barrier to showing simple (or maybe oversimplified) 'better' and 'worse' social value between different case studies.

Arguably the search for a standard is beyond simple and over-simplistic. For example, it can lead to a belief in the importance of average data banks, which can overrule the specificity of social, spatial and ultimately community experience. This is not necessarily problematic, as social value frameworks, which focus on more easily definable and generalizable outputs where spatial and socio-economic start points are less important, can lead to unintended impacts. This is most problematic where the nuances of the specificity of social value are ignored.

## Well-being indices

Another data bank approach is through the use of **well-being indices**, which measure social value in terms of improvements in individual and community well-being. These indices often include a range of indicators, such as health, education, employment and environmental quality, which are aggregated to provide an overall measure of well-being. This approach aligns with the emphasis on the holistic nature of social value (above), as it considers multiple dimensions of well-being rather than focusing solely on economic outcomes. It is also an approach recognized by His Majesty's (HM) Treasury Green Book. In this context, the Housing Association Charitable Trust (HACT) Social Value Bank is one useful tool and source of financial proxies for qualitative data, since it adopts the well-being valuation approach.

The 133 financial proxies in the HACT Social Value Bank set offer a less exact match with qualitative outcomes, leading to some awkwardness of fit compared with the wider, albeit more eclectic, SROI data bank (above). The challenge in one social value study was to identify, at individual, organizational and societal levels, the social impact of an organization's business support work. The prime impacts were supporting creative economy business skills development, organizational income resilience, and societal sector growth and resilience.

The very best fits were for individual business skills development – government training scheme at £9,447 per beneficiary; for the organization's better income resilience – relief from being heavily burdened by debt at £10,836 per beneficiary; and for society – financial comfort at £8,917 per beneficiary.

The World Health Organization-Five Well-Being Index (WHO-5) (2024) is a short, self-reported questionnaire designed to measure subjective psychological well-being. It was originally developed by the WHO in 1998 as a screening tool for depression, but over time, it has been used widely for measuring general emotional well-being in both clinical settings and research. The WHO-5 focuses on positive aspects of emotions and well-being, potentially overlooking negative emotional experiences that can influence overall well-being. While the WHO-5 measures the frequency of emotions, it lacks measurement of intensity and duration, which are also important aspects of emotional experience.

**STOP AND THINK**

Do you think these proxies are close enough to generate organizational and wider discussion of social value, or are they too removed from organizational delivery to add organizational and societal 'value'?

### Action Funder framework

Other perspectives that you might consider are from Action Funder, which match-makes businesses with non-profits and then tracks impact. It offers to identify the best fit of impact framework for each business from a menu of four approaches. These are:

- **The National TOMs** (Themes, Outcomes and Measures): The National Social Value Task Force developed the National TOMs framework (Social Value Portal, 2024), which is now operated by the Social Value Portal specifically in response to the Social Value Act 2012. TOMS helps organizations measure, report and amplify their social value, albeit its focus on outputs makes it challenging to capture long-term social impact through outcomes.
- The **17 UN Sustainable Development Goals (SDGs)**, which result from the work of the Inter-Agency and Expert Group on SDG Indicators (IAEG-SDGs, 2024) – a global framework with 231 indicators to measure social value in the context of SDGs. These indicators remain largely output-focused; however, they are useful if you are engaging with a global sustainability audience (UN, 2024).
- **Business for Societal Impact (B4SI, 2024)** – the framework provides one further global standard for businesses to manage and measure corporate social impact. It organizes social activities under three pillars – inputs, outputs and impacts – with the tagline 'You decide what's relevant to your business'. There is a flexible approach around community investment, business innovation for social impact and procurement for social impact. The focus on outcomes and depth of impact is useful and important in identifying the extent and depth of the social impact.
- **B Impact Assessment** (BIA) (SEISMIC 2024) – B Lab developed the BIA as a means to certify companies as B Corporations. Businesses can apply this framework to evaluate how their operations impact employees, communities, environments and customers. It uses 250 questions to examine a company's policies, practices, outputs, business models and positive outcomes. It is a digital and interactive tool that enables organizations to work at their own pace; however, its limitation for measuring social impact is that it focuses on outputs rather than outcomes, similar to other approaches.

## *Co-created monetary proxies*

Co-created monetary proxies provide participatory approaches to measuring social value and might therefore be seen as particularly suited to the community focus of SEs. The approach involves engaging stakeholders in the evaluation process to ensure that measures used reflect their values and priorities. The social value is not drawn from a large database; it is rather generated locally. Participatory approaches can help to address some of the challenges associated with measuring social value, such as the subjectivity of value and the difficulty of capturing qualitative outcomes. In this respect, community-focused businesses might want to look at co-created social value monetary proxies.

**Design thinking** can enable working with communities in this context through using play to achieve engagement with the process of monetization of social outcomes for social value measurement. One approach that has become published in this context is The Values Game (Gerrickens, 2024). For example, a project with young people might involve asking them to draw and then price the dozen things that they 'most need' with the first caveat from the facilitator – 'Do you really need that?' – and then a discussion on the specificity of the product, 'so what type of trainers?' or 'what model of phone?'. This enables a monetary proxy and ranking of the things that they have drawn. A discussion on the social outcomes from the project is then facilitated, with participants requested to insert a social outcomes card into the priced deck of 'things that they really need' as an indicator of its financial worth, thereby achieving an approximate monetary value for the social outcome. The monetary proxy can then be refined through discussion or simply as the average of the two adjacent priced cards.

You would move from individual ranking of value with the cards to a group discussion and thereby group conclusion regarding the proxy value. The benefits from this process are that you get a very specific value and monetary proxy, which is meaningful to that particular group of stakeholders, rather than a downloaded value that someone else experienced in a different place at another time. This is very different from the generalized experience discussed previously. The design thinking process is highly participatory, which is also important in moving the social value process from measurement to a driver of change.

In contrast to this iterative approach, Glasgow's Regeneration Agency (GRA) used the Value Game, simply displaying cards for participants represented by images without reference to price and then ranking. It argues that stakeholders are therefore forced to apply a more intuitive assessment of value, leading to a more realistic ranking. GRA addresses challenges to the relevance of the published cards by providing stakeholders with a number of blank cards to create their own.

## Difficulty of capturing long-term and intangible outcomes

Many of the benefits associated with social value, such as improved community cohesion or environmental sustainability, may not be immediately apparent and can take years to materialize. This can make it challenging in demonstrating the impact of activities on social value, particularly in contexts where short-term results are prioritized.

## KEY RESEARCH

Indarti et al (2024), in 'Breaking barriers! Social entrepreneurship in empowering people with disabilities', engage with critical debates on social enterprise, social innovation and social value. The work bridges theory and practice by employing **Identity Theory** (IT) and **Social Role Valorization** (SRV) to unpack the motivations and characteristics of social entrepreneurs in Indonesia, focusing on empowering disabled people whilst noting that there was an active debate about the medical and social models of disability and the naming of 'people with disabilities' and 'disabled people'. The study's innovative approach offers both theoretical contributions and actionable insights:

1. **Social entrepreneurship and social innovation:** The paper engages with foundational theories on **social entrepreneurship**, particularly in terms of how SEs address systemic inequalities and empower marginalized communities through social innovation and resultant social value. It extends previous work on the role of entrepreneurship in social change by focusing specifically on the empowerment of disabled people, an often-under-represented group in social entrepreneurship literature. It challenges conventional definitions of **social innovation**, emphasizing the adaptability and creativity of social entrepreneurs in overcoming barriers that prevent inclusivity. This builds on earlier studies; however, it offers new insights by positioning disability as central to the innovation process.
2. **Social value and impact:** The paper argues for a **social value** approach, where societal well-being is prioritized over economic returns. It further adds to the discussion of **value creation** in SEs by examining the role of entrepreneurship in transforming societal perceptions of disabled people, which is less explored in earlier works.
3. **Inclusive social enterprise models:** The paper engages with the growing body of research on **inclusive business models** by offering case studies of SEs in Indonesia that blend economic activities with cultural and spiritual values. This approach challenges the more traditional models of SEs that are often based on Western frameworks, offering a more contextualized understanding of how, inclusively, they can operate within different cultural contexts.
4. **Engagement with theoretical frameworks:** By utilizing Identity Theory (IT) and Social Role Valorization (SRV) in the context of social entrepreneurship, the paper challenges and builds on these theories. These frameworks are commonly used in studies on social roles and stigma but are less frequently applied in the realm of social entrepreneurship. The study expands their use to explore how social entrepreneurs navigate personal and societal identities while creating social change.

Critically, the paper tackles the growing body of research on inclusive business models by offering case studies of SEs in Indonesia that blend economic activities with cultural and spiritual values. This approach challenges the more traditional models of SEs that are often based on Western frameworks, offering a more contextualized understanding of how, inclusively, they can operate within different cultural and spiritual contexts. The paper engages with and challenges existing scholarly arguments as well as contributing new ideas, positioning itself within ongoing discussions in social entrepreneurship, social innovation and disability studies.

**STOP AND THINK**

What reporting metrics would you design for an outcomes-based social value approach for the award of contracts?

## Summary and key learning points

This chapter argues that the central question should be 'how' to measure social value, not 'whether' to measure social value as a tool of social innovation. By linking social innovation and social value, there is the potential of identifying a strategic tool for societal betterment. In this context, social value becomes both a measurement of impact and a driver of change for SEs. As a measurement of impact, it provides a framework for assessing the effectiveness of SEs in achieving their goals, including their social innovation. By focusing on social value, SEs can differentiate themselves in the marketplace and play a critical role in driving systemic change towards a more equitable and sustainable world. SEs' work enables us to see social value as not only a definition but also an action, a judgement and a driver of change. Social value should shape the mission, strategy and operations of SEs, ensuring that their activities contribute to positive social and environmental outcomes.

The key learning points are:

- The importance of Elkington's triple bottom line approach, which emphasizes the balance of people, planet and profit. However, the concern is that it has increasingly become an accounting tool rather than a true driver for social change.
- Despite the growing importance of social value, including in legislation, the concept is not without criticisms, including that its subjective nature complicates

its measurement and integration into decision-making frameworks. This chapter argues that subjectivity should be embraced, providing a locally nuanced map and demand for services.

- Despite challenges of measurement and reporting, this chapter emphasizes the importance of authenticity and transparency. In the pursuit of social value, SEs must commit to genuine engagement, rigorous measurement and continuous improvement to realize the full potential of social innovation.
- Global challenges, such as climate change, social inequality and economic volatility, necessitate holistic approaches that transcend traditional silos. This chapter proposes a future where social value becomes a cornerstone of strategic decision-making. It advocates for a 'values-driven' paradigm wherein organizations align their missions and operations with broader societal objectives, fostering societal well-being and enhancing organizational resilience and legitimacy.
- The pursuit of social value often requires SEs to innovate and adapt to changing social and environmental conditions. This drive for innovation not only helps SEs stay relevant but also contributes to broader systemic change.
- Social innovation is a key driver of financial sustainability for several reasons:
    - creating new revenue streams by leading to the development of new products, services or business models that generate additional revenue
    - SEs that demonstrate a commitment to innovation are more likely to be more attractive to investors
    - improving cost-effectiveness – methods of delivering products or services, reducing operational expenses and improving the financial 'bottom line'
    - building stronger partnerships and collaboration with various stakeholders, including businesses, government agencies and NFPs
    - fostering a culture of innovation within SEs involves creating an environment that encourages experimentation, learning and collaboration

## SELF-CHECK QUESTIONS

1 How far do you feel that the six primary key characteristics of SEs identified by the Social Enterprise World Forum (n.d.) are the focal point for SEs?

- mission-focused
- surplus invested in the mission
- ownership tied to the mission
- ethically transparent and accountable
- trade-generated income
- mission locked

2. What are the opportunities for social enterprises to socially innovate?
3. What are the barriers for social enterprises to socially innovate?
4. How do you think design thinking can unlock social innovation?
5. What role can social value play for SEs?

## DISCUSSION QUESTIONS AND CALLS TO ACTION

1. What issues do you feel most strongly about?
2. Using this tool, how can these issues be addressed by a new social enterprise? https://miro.com/miroverse/corporate-social-entrepreneurship-canvas/
3. How would you negotiate the barriers to innovation that you have identified?
4. What are the opportunities for your social enterprise?
5. How will you measure your success?
6. What tools will you have to engage with public procurement in the UK and win contracts?

## USEFUL WEBLINKS

Harvard Business School: https://online.hbs.edu/

Miro: https://miro.com/miroverse/corporate-social-entrepreneurship-canvas/

Social Enterprise UK: https://www.socialenterprise.org.uk/all-about-social-enterprise/

Social Enterprise World Forum: https://sewfonline.com

Social Value Portal: https://www.socialvalueportal.com/

The Stanford Social Innovation Review: https://ssir.org/

World Economic Forum: https://www.weforum.org/

## REAL-WORLD EXAMPLE INDICATIVE ANSWERS

1. How did Zipline identify and address the gap in the market for timely medical supply delivery in remote areas? Discuss the role of the founders' backgrounds and experiences in this process.

**Indicative answer**: The genesis of Zipline was a reflection on the dearth of timely access to critical medical supplies in remote, infrastructure-limited regions. The co-founders' background in robotics and drones offered a glimpse into the technology's latent potential to bridge this chasm.

2 What challenges did Zipline face in the initial stages of developing their drone technology and healthcare logistics model? How did they overcome these obstacles to create a sustainable and commercially viable business?

**Indicative answer:** Technological hurdles included optimizing drone reliability, endurance and payload capacity. Regulatory obstacles involved securing government permissions, implementing rigorous safety protocols and substantiating the system's efficacy. Zipline embraced the technological challenges as opportunities for **innovation**, persistently enhancing drone capabilities. Similarly, it engaged proactively with governments, exhibiting the system's safety and reliability.

3 Analyse the impact of Zipline's drone delivery system on healthcare delivery in infrastructure-limited regions. How has their innovative approach to 'healthcare logistics' helped save lives and improve healthcare outcomes?

**Indicative answer:** Its autonomous drone delivery system has reshaped the healthcare logistics landscape, particularly where conventional supply chains falter due to geographical constraints. Each of Zipline's distribution centres, part of an intricate network, can cater to numerous healthcare facilities within an 80 km radius, delivering crucial medical supplies like vaccines, emergency medication and blood products. The **social impact** has been profound and lifesaving. By slashing delivery times of critical supplies from hours to minutes, they have saved countless lives, especially in dire emergencies. In Rwanda, for example, the drone service has reportedly trimmed the delivery time of blood products from four hours to a mere 15 minutes).

4 Discuss Zipline as an example of 'technology for good'. How does its model of business demonstrate the potential of technology to address significant societal challenges?

**Indicative answer:** This remarkable ability to swiftly deliver medical supplies to remote locations, previously deemed unreachable, underscores the potential of innovative technology when applied with an entrepreneurial mindset. Its ability to identify an unmet need, harness technology, overcome daunting challenges and build a sustainable and impactful business showcases the incredible power of innovation and persistence.

5 How does Zipline's journey exemplify the principles of social entrepreneurship? Discuss its approach to turning societal challenges into unique market opportunities.

**Indicative answer:** Zipline has addressed a significant societal issue, manifesting the essence of social entrepreneurship. Zipline's business model stands as an exemplar of social entrepreneurship. By transforming obstacles into opportunities, it has generated tremendous social value while also establishing a commercially viable enterprise. It has reimagined and revolutionized healthcare delivery in regions where conventional logistics are ineffective, thereby converting a significant societal challenge into a unique market opportunity. Zipline's narrative presents a compelling fusion of technology and entrepreneurship working in tandem to serve societal good.

6 In what ways has Zipline set precedents in healthcare delivery? Discuss the potential for other businesses to apply similar approaches to societal issues in their industries.

**Indicative answer:** In essence, Zipline's story provides invaluable insights into the role technology can play in addressing societal needs and the potential for businesses to be agents of significant social change. With an innovative approach, entrepreneurial spirit and a focus on social impact, Zipline has painted a vivid picture of how enterprises can build transformative business models that not only thrive commercially but also make a substantial societal difference.

## References

B Lab (2024) B Lab is the nonprofit network transforming the global economy to benefit all people, communities, and the planet, https://www.bcorporation.net/en-us/movement/about-b-lab/ (archived at https://perma.cc/D6CL-DTC3)

Barile, L and Kelestyn, B (2023) Using design thinking to create sustainable communities, *International Journal of Management and Applied Research*, 10 (2)

Bell, M (2021) Why ESG performance is growing in importance for investors, https://www.ey.com/en_gl/insights/assurance/why-esg-performance-is-growing-in-importance-for-investors (archived at https://perma.cc/SLC9-SKND)

Bender-Salazar, R (2023) Design thinking as an effective method for problem-setting and need finding for entrepreneurial teams addressing wicked problems, *Journal of Innovation and Entrepreneurship*, 12, 24

Brown, T and Wyatt, J (2009) Design thinking for social innovation, *Stanford Social Innovation Review*, 8(1): 31–35

Business for Societal Impact (2024) Manage your social impact, engage your stakeholders, tell your story, https://b4si.net/ (archived at https://perma.cc/XX4H-KFFZ)

Cabinet Office (2024) Social Value Act: information and resources, https://www.gov.uk/government/publications/social-value-act-information-and-resources/social-value-act-information-and-resources (archived at https://perma.cc/LZY2-6TRF)

Carella, G, Cautela, C, Melazzini, M, Pei, X and Schmittinger, F (2022) Design thinking for entrepreneurship: An explorative inquiry into its practical contributions, *The Design Journal*, 26(1): 7–31

Choi, S, Kim, N and Kim, W (2018) Are social entrepreneurs more risk-averse? *Applied Economics Letters*, 26(11): 933–37

Davies, I, Haugh, H and Chambers, L (2019) Barriers to social enterprise growth, *Journal of Small Business Management,* 57 (4): 1616–636

Elkington, J (1994) Towards the sustainable corporation: Win-win-win business strategies for sustainable development, *California Management Review*, 36: 90–100

Gerrickens (2024) The Values Game, https://www.kwaliteitenspel.nl/en/card-games/the-values-game (archived at https://perma.cc/9BP8-CDTD)

Government Commercial Function (2020) The Social Value Model, https://assets.publishing.service.gov.uk/media/5fc8b7ede90e0762a0d71365/Social-Value-Model-Edn-1.1-3-Dec-20.pdf (archived at https://perma.cc/MK95-7UGF)

Guclu, A J, Dees, G and Battle Anderson, B (nd) The process of social entrepreneurship: Creating opportunities worthy of serious pursuit, https://centers.fuqua.duke.edu/case/knowledge_items/the-process-of-social-entrepreneurship-creating-opportunities-worthy-of-serious-pursuit/#:~:text=For%20social%20entrepreneurs%2C%20an%20%E2%80%9Cattractive,required%20to%20pursue%20it%20seriously (archived at https://perma.cc/J3HL-JLQ2)

Harsanto, B, Mulyana, A, Ahmad Faisal, Y and Mellandhia Shandy, V (2022) Open innovation for sustainability in the social enterprises: An empirical evidence, *Journal of Open Innovation: Technology, Market, and Complexity*, 8(3): 160

Helliwell, J, Layard, R and Sachs, J (2019) *World Happiness Report 2019*, New York: Sustainable Development Solutions

Hillman, J, Axon, S and Morrissey, J (2018) Social enterprise as a potential niche innovation breakout for low carbon transition, *Energy Policy*, 117: 445–56

Hsieh, M C, Kuo, Y M and Kuo, Y L (2023) *Utilizing Design Thinking for Effective Multidisciplinary Diabetes Management*, Basel: Healthcare

IAEG-SDGs (2024), SDG Indicators, https://unstats.un.org/sdgs/indicators/indicators-list/ (archived at https://perma.cc/RN64-A97H)

Indarti, N, Anggadwita, G, Purnomo, R A and Tomlins, R (2024) Breaking barriers! Social entrepreneurship in empowering people with disabilities, *Journal of Social Entrepreneurship*, pp 1–35

Jayawardhana, K, Fernando, I and Siyambalapitiya, J (2022) Sustainability in social enterprise research: A systematic literature review, *Sage Open*, 12(3)

Joffre, L (2020) Innovative, agile and resilient: social enterprises worldwide have adapted to survive pandemic, reveals new report, https://www.pioneerspost.com/news-views/20201214/innovative-agile-and-resilient-social-enterprises-worldwide-have-adapted-survive (archived at https://perma.cc/462P-YLPR)

Kell, J (2021) The drones that deliver blood, *Fast Company,* https://www.fastcompany.com/91328059/how-ziplines-keller-cliffton-built-the-worlds-largest-drone-delivery-network (archived at https://perma.cc/2SWM-FWQ5)

Kulshrestha, R, Sahay, A and Sengupta, S (2022) Constituents and drivers of mission engagement for social enterprise sustainability: A systematic review, *The Journal of Entrepreneurship*, 31(1): 90–120

Lipsky, M (1980) *Street-level Bureaucracy: Dilemmas of the individual in public services*, New York, NY: Russell Sage Foundation

MacColl, S (2022) Why social enterprises struggle to measure impact – and what impact investors can do about it, https://nextbillion.net/social-enterprises-measure-impact-investors/ (archived at https://perma.cc/M7S4-6JVB)

Malynka, O and Tomlins, R (2021) LEGO Serious Play and LEGO-A-GO-GO – innovative training methods for strategic and ecosystem development: features of application, *Actual Problems in the System of Education: General Secondary Education Institution – Pre-University Training – Higher Education Institution*, 1(1): 181–84

Ménard, D (2013) Business is developing real social values – passing trends, protective instinct or what? https://www.pwc.com/gx/en/corporate-reporting/assets/pwc-creating-social-values.pdf (archived at https://perma.cc/8UG7-5MVV)

Miller, T and Bowcock, M (2020). Why is social innovation needed for the recovery? https://bettersocietycapital.com/latest/why-social-innovation-needed-recovery/ (archived at https://perma.cc/X7CS-8KX6)

Mulgan, G (2006) The process of social innovation, *Innovations: Technology, Governance, Globalization*, 1 (2): 145–62

OECD (2010) SMEs, Entrepreneurship and Innovation, https://www.oecd.org/content/dam/oecd/en/publications/reports/2010/05/smes-entrepreneurship-and-innovation_g1ghc219/9789264080355-en.pdf (archived at https://perma.cc/MJ7C-7FP2)

OECD (2024) Social economy and social innovation, https://www.oecd.org/en/topics/sub-issues/social-economy-and-social-innovation.html#:~:text=Social%20innovation%20involves%20creating%20and,being%20of%20individuals%20and%20communities (archived at https://perma.cc/FX6T-25B3)

Osorio, F, Cruz, F, Camargo, M, Dupont, L and Ismael Peña, J (2024) Exploring team roles for social innovation labs: Toward a competence-based role self-assessment approach, *Journal of Engineering and Technology Management*, 71

Pahl, R E (1975) *Whose City? And further essays on urban society,* Harmondsworth: Penguin

Peng, F (2022) Design thinking: From empathy to evaluation, in Herath, D and St-Onge, D (eds) *Foundations of Robotics*, Springer: Singapore

Penroe, J (2023) Why do people become social entrepreneurs and what is their role in our globalised world? https://businessschool.blogs.bristol.ac.uk/2023/11/27/why-do-people-become-social-entrepreneurs-and-what-is-their-role-in-our-globalised-world/ (archived at https://perma.cc/XE3L-HV2W)

Pirgmaier, E (2021) The value of value theory for ecological economics, *Ecological Economics*, 179

Razzouk, R and Shute, V (2012) What is design thinking and why is it important? *Review of Educational Research,* 82(3): 330–48

Rihter, L and Mešl, N (2024) Innovative approaches to social activation using collaborative social work concepts: The case of social enterprise in working with the vulnerable long-term unemployed, *Human Service Organizations: Management, Leadership and Governance*, 1–18

Rinaudo, K (2017) How we're using drones to deliver blood and save lives, https://www.ted.com/talks/keller_rinaudo_how_we_re_using_drones_to_deliver_blood_and_save_lives (archived at https://perma.cc/PKY6-9M3U)

Salverda, M (2024) Social return on investment, https://www.betterevaluation.org/methods-approaches/approaches/social-return-investment (archived at https://perma.cc/K2EG-AS55)

Scottish Futures Trust (2020) Guidance: Measuring social value using the SFT TOMs developed in conjunction with the social value portal, https://www.scottishfuturestrust.org.uk/publications/documents/guidance-measuring-social-value-using-the-sft-toms (archived at https://perma.cc/FG5M-G7P3)

Scottish Government (2015) Community Empowerment (Scotland) Act 2015 – asset transfers: social value guidance, https://www.gov.scot/publications/community-empowerment-scotland-act-2015-asset-transfer-guidance-considering-social-value/pages/3/ (archived at https://perma.cc/DZ9M-QSLX)

SEISMIC (2024) Are you ready to B Corp? https://www.seismic-change.com/services/b-corp/ (archived at https://perma.cc/R7S4-JS3W)

Social Enterprise World Forum (n.d.) About SEWF, https://sewfonline.com/about-sewf/ (archived at https://perma.cc/5JP9-RW2N)

Social Enterprise World Forum (n.d.) Latest research shows £1bn impact of UK social enterprises, https://sewfonline.com/about/about-social-enterprise/ (archived at https://perma.cc/YAK3-USVM)

Social Value Portal (2024) Social Value Measurement, https://www.socialvalueportal.com/measurement (archived at https://perma.cc/24JZ-MYMU)

Social Value Unit (2021) Scoring Social Value for public bodies is a mandatory part of the public procurement landscape in Northern Ireland, https://socialvalueni.org/ (archived at https://perma.cc/VFU2-LL9W)

Spreckley, F (2022) Six social enterprise essentials: Why financial viability aligns perfectly with the triple bottom line, https://www.pioneerspost.com/business-school/20220311/six-social-enterprise-essentials-why-financial-viability-aligns-perfectly#:~:text=So%20financial%20viability%20%E2%80%93%20making%20a,apportioned%20from%20year%20to%20year (archived at https://perma.cc/7NPP-JETC)

The Melting Pot (2023) The importance and meaning of social enterprises: Creating positive change, https://www.themeltingpotedinburgh.org.uk/resources/the-importance-and-meaning-of-social-enterprises-creating-positive-change/ (archived at https://perma.cc/EZ8U-WDN9)

Tomlins, R (1999) Race equality initiatives in housing provision: Organizational change and the role of gatekeepers, *Journal of Ethnic and Migration Studies*, 25:1: 113–32

Tomlins, R (2015a) *Social Value Today: Current public and private thinking on Social Value*, Coventry: HouseMark

Tomlins, R (2015b) 'Uncaging Social Value': Workshop presentation for the Homes and Communities Agency Investment Team, London

Tomlins, R (2024) Can we play at a time of war? The innovation potential of design thinking for medical students and other innovators, *Conference presentation for Poltava State Medical University Conference*, November

Tortia, E C, Degavre, F and Poledrini, S (2020) Why are social enterprises good candidates for social innovation? Looking for personal and institutional drivers of innovation, *Annals of and Public Cooperative Economics*, 91(3): 459–77

UN (2024) The 17 Goals, https://www.globalgoals.org/take-action/ (archived at https://perma.cc/6W7W-2Z99)

van Niekerk, L, Manderson, L and Balabanova, D (2021) The application of social innovation in healthcare: a scoping review, *Infectious Diseases of Poverty*, 10, 26

Wakabayashi, D (2020) California today: Delivering blood by drone, *New York Times*, https://www.nytimes.com/2022/06/16/technology/delivery-drones.html (archived at https://perma.cc/WXR7-KG7S)

Wells, D, Gipp, D, Schwab, H and Billimoria, J (2020) Social entrepreneurs are first responders to the COVID-19 crisis. This is why they need support, World Economic Forum, https://www.weforum.org/stories/2020/09/social-entrepreneurs-are-first-responders-to-the-covid-19-crisis/ (archived at https://perma.cc/QK3W-G8PG)

Wingfield, M, Carson, J, Mujulizi, M, Von Lieres, B, Adamovic, M, Piper, L and Lundqvist-Westin, W (2024) International collaboration and connections through design thinking: A case study of the Global Classroom for Democracy Innovation (GCDI), https://www.researchgate.net/publication/380221468_International_collaboration_and_connections_through_design_thinking_A_case_study_of_the_Global_Classroom_for_Democracy_Innovation_GCDI#fullTextFileContent (archived at https://perma.cc/6KP8-R2CB)

World Health Organization (2024) WHO-5, https://www.who.int/publications/m/item/WHO-UCN-MSD-MHE-2024.01#:~:text=The%20WHO-5%20is%20a%20self-report%20instrument%20measuring%20mental,instrument%20has%20been%20translated%20into%20over%2030%20languages (archived at https://perma.cc/J3QB-Q98N)

Wynn, D C and Eckert, C M (2017) Perspectives on iteration in design and development, *Research In Engineering Design*, 28: 153–84

Zakaras, T (2021) Why companies partner with social enterprises, Resonance, https://www.resonanceglobal.com/blog/why-companies-partner-with-social-enterprises (archived at https://perma.cc/5Q6C-ZSFX)

Zipline (2021) About Us, https://www.flyzipline.com/about (archived at https://perma.cc/T3SV-CD4C)

# 07 Starting a social enterprise

**LUNA DOU**

**LEARNING OUTCOMES**

After reading this chapter, you should be able to:

- Understand the process of starting a social enterprise.
- Utilize the 'Problem Statement Canvas' to identify a genuine social problem.
- Evaluate the process of turning a problem into a social entrepreneurial opportunity.
- Conduct primary and secondary research to evaluate and exploit the identified social opportunity.
- Recognize the pivotal role of community engagement in problem identification and opportunity exploitation.
- Implement various engagement tools when starting a social enterprise.

**REAL-WORLD EXAMPLE** Adventure Alternative and Moving Mountains Trust: A hybrid social enterprise in tourism

Adventure Alternative (AA) is a British social enterprise (SE) specializing in adventurous tours. Its primary income source is tour operations, with profits reinvested through its charity, Moving Mountains (MM), to support disadvantaged communities in Eastern Africa and Far East Asia where the tours take place. Senior management, including founder Gavin Bate, spends significant time in these communities, helping to develop and implement projects that improve living conditions and enhance employability skills. This hands-on approach strengthens ties with local stakeholders and ensures projects align with community needs.

Originally, AA sought to help street children in Nairobi, Kenya, by providing opportunities to study and improve their circumstances. Over time, this effort expanded significantly, transforming AA into a global SE operating in multiple countries and impacting countless children and families. MM has funded initiatives such as schools, clinics and vocational training, directly improving local lives. Many beneficiaries later joined AA/MM's workforce, demonstrating the transformative power of combining social and economic missions. The synergy between AA and MM exemplifies how a hybrid model can balance business sustainability with social impact. Through its operations, AA not only creates revenue streams but also promotes education and economic empowerment, addressing root causes of poverty. Its tours often include visits to MM-supported projects, providing clients with a personal connection to the impact of their contributions, fostering loyalty and additional donations.

AA's commitment to community engagement has been instrumental in its success. By investing in long-term relationships, the enterprise has cultivated trust, enabling effective problem identification and opportunity exploitation. These efforts have earned AA and MM multiple awards and international recognition for their social impact, solidifying their reputation as leaders in responsible tourism.

Discussion questions:

1 How do you think Gavin truly understood the needs of the local people in Kenya? What challenges might he have faced in this process?

2 How did AA turn the identified social problem into an entrepreneurial opportunity? What steps would you take to evaluate whether this opportunity is viable?

3 Since community engagement is so important, AA's case provides valuable insights into the tools entrepreneurs can use to strengthen engagement during the start-up phase. What could some of these tools be, and how can they be effectively implemented?

See indicative answers at the end of the chapter.

---

## Introduction

Having gained an understanding of the concepts and principles of SE, this chapter primarily guides you through the process of starting a successful SE in uncertain markets. You will be introduced to the fundamental stages involved in setting up an SE, recognizing the importance of identifying social issues in the initial stages, and how to transform these identified social issues into entrepreneurial opportunities. This process is crucial – arguably the most critical phase in establishing an SE – yet it is often overlooked. Many rush to find solutions, believing this to be the path to entrepreneurial opportunities. However, this approach can lead to failure if there is a lack of comprehensive understanding of the social issues at hand. Social problems are inherently complex, often more so than they appear on the surface, leading to multifaceted and diverse solutions. Identifying the optimal or practical solution requires a thorough understanding of the problem's complexity. This is why many scholars have emphasized that understanding the problem is a more time-consuming task than finding the solution (e.g. Osterwalder and Pigneur, 2010).

In this chapter, we review the practical steps needed to start an SE, including the range of methods required for a social start-up. This can involve three start-up stages: the identification of the social entrepreneurial opportunity, the establishment of the SE, and scaling up. Or it can involve a five-stage model that encompasses 'opportunity identification', 'opportunity evaluation', 'opportunity formalization', 'opportunity exploitation' and 'opportunity scaling up'. Next, we explore the concept of problem identification and the definition of a social problem. This section looks at the motivational drivers to problem identification, ranging from antecedents influencing social entrepreneurial intentions to pull and push factors that may influence why certain individuals wish to start an SE. This is followed by considering the Problem Statement Canvas as a strategic tool that enables social entrepreneurs to develop a solution to the needs of those being affected. We will explore the steps to be followed for identifying a problem worth solving by understanding the needs of beneficiaries, the context in which the problem occurs, the impact this is having on those affected, and the shortcomings of alternative solutions. We look at opportunity recognition and the key steps involved, from data collection and a collective approach to social problems to the role of lived experiences and community engagement. In this section, we look at engagement principles and tools such as cultural sensitivity, long-term orientation, reciprocity and trust. Finally, the last section outlines the key learning points of this chapter.

**STOP AND THINK**

Before we continue with the next parts of this chapter, you could think about these questions: Since SEs are different from 'profit-for-shareholder' organizations, do social entrepreneurs need different skills than commercial entrepreneurs? Starting any project has its own difficulties, so how do you start an SE from the outset? Besides, how do you spot a social issue and turn it into a business opportunity for an SE?

## Social start-up skills

Starting from this point, you will learn more about the practical aspects needed to start an SE. This part includes a range of stages and methods, discussed in terms of the practical skills needed by social entrepreneurs. Firstly, we explore the key steps to starting an SE. Then, we explore how to effectively carry out the initial stages of setting up an SE, which involve identifying relevant social issues and establishing the core focus of the enterprise.

## Process of starting a social enterprise

SEs do not suddenly appear; they are carefully created and nurtured over time via a complex process by the founder (i.e. often the social entrepreneur and a core team) (Guclu et al, 2002). Various studies have explored how SEs are started, and they generally produce two types of conclusions. The first type is a traditional three-stage approach, and the second type breaks the process down into more detailed steps:

- **Three-stage process:** On the 'simpler' side, the works of Chell (2007), Bhatt and Altinay (2013) and Guo and Bielefeld (2014) consistently recommended a three-stage process. This involves the 'identification of the social entrepreneurial opportunity', the 'establishment of the social enterprise' and the 'scaling up of the social impact'.
- On the more 'complex' side, some **process models** consist of more than three stages. A notable work that formed the basis for many other studies (e.g. Lanteri, 2015; Salamzadeh et al, 2017) is that of Perrini et al (2010). Drawing on multiple data sources from a single case study on an SE in Italy, the authors proposed a five-stage model of the social entrepreneurial process: 'opportunity identification', 'opportunity evaluation', 'opportunity formalization', 'opportunity exploitation' and 'opportunity scaling up'. The model also identifies the interplay between the individual social entrepreneur (e.g. ability to articulate a clear vision, commitment, ability to network) and contextual factors (e.g. resource availability, institutional voids) that may intervene in the process. Although not explicitly stated, the model covers the entire process of social entrepreneurship, including both the pre- and post-start-up process.

These different process models teach us a couple of important things:

- First, the initial stage in social entrepreneurship involves the identification of a problem/opportunity. Subsequent steps involve researching this problem to devise a solution, which then forms the basis for starting an SE.
- Second, more complex models for starting an SE tend to break down the first stage of problem and opportunity identification into several more detailed steps, thereby underscoring the significance of this process. Social entrepreneurs need the skills to identify a social problem that is worth solving. Given its paramount importance, let us now turn our attention to exploring how to identify a problem.

## Problem identification

In our world, myriad issues await resolution. We can find many social problems through the media, the websites of international humanitarian organizations, friends and our own experiences. Hence, deciding which problem to solve becomes a crucial question for all social entrepreneurs. It is important not to try to solve too many problems at once. Instead, we need to focus on understanding and thoroughly researching one problem. Doing this well is enough to create social value.

### *Definition of the social problem*

By 'social problem', we mean anything in the world that negatively affects others, whether humans, animals or plants, and which you wish to change. Defining a social problem can equally stem from your personal experiences. In Chapter 5, we have already spoken about how SEs are different from profit-for-shareholder businesses. Social entrepreneurs are more focused on their social mission than just making money. They enjoy the process of solving social problems, and as long as they find meaning in their work, they will go to great lengths to continue, despite various setbacks and challenges.

> **STOP AND THINK**
>
> Your personal inventory
>
> What is the problem that you feel strongly about and want to solve? Why would you never give up on this project? Understanding yourself and what matters to you is often key to finding the right social problem to tackle. Ask yourself, why should I solve this problem instead of someone else? If your motivation and passion align with the social problem, you will be more driven to keep looking for the best solutions and eventually succeed.

### *From motivation to problem identification*

Researchers have dedicated significant efforts to exploring the critical role of problem identification in the process of starting an SE. For instance, through in-depth interviewing of 30 Israeli social entrepreneurs, Yitshaki and Kropp (2016) developed a model explaining the dynamics leading to the identification of unmet social needs (social problems). The authors offered insights into the motivational drivers of social entrepreneurs. They argued that social entrepreneurs' life experiences help them become aware of unmet social needs. This ultimately leads to opportunity recognition and the formation of the SE. A growing number of studies have also identified the antecedents that influence social entrepreneurial intentions (Dickel and Eckardt, 2021; Douglas et al, 2021; Santos et al, 2021). Mair and Noboa (2006), for example, argue that perceived desirability, mediated by emotional and cognitive constructs such as empathy and moral responsibility towards helping those in need, influences social entrepreneurial intentions. Hockerts (2017) identified that prior experience with social problems is a key influencing factor that shapes social entrepreneurial intentions. Bacq and Alt (2018) note that empathy, self-efficacy and social worth are key antecedents to social entrepreneurial intentions. Other research findings demonstrate that social entrepreneurs may be motivated by pull factors, like a desire to contribute positively to society, often influenced by their own past experiences or current life situations. Others were driven by push factors, such as dissatisfaction with their jobs and a quest to find more meaningful work.

## Problem Statement Canvas

Once you understand the problem that interests you the most, the next step is to see how to better understand the essence of the problem to find more reliable and feasible solutions. Every problem has multiple aspects, and to fully grasp all aspects of an issue, we will use the Problem Statement Canvas (Figure 7.1), which is a visual and intuitive analytical tool that supports you in gradually conducting your research on the problem. While it is not perfect, it provides a systematic approach to analysing a problem. It has six main aspects, and its logic is based on the following:

> When *context* occurs, *problem owners* who have specific traits encounter a *problem*. This issue leads to an *emotional* response and results in a measurable *impact*. Currently, these individuals resort to *alternatives*, even though these solutions have their own *shortcomings*.

To better illustrate how to use this tool, let us consider an example, mentioned at the beginning of this chapter. In the early stages of AA, the social entrepreneur Gavin Bate identified a problem: the presence of many street children in the streets and alleys of Kenya. If we do not carefully study the key aspects of this problem and jump to conclusions, we might say:

> *'Kenyan children have nothing to do but wander on the streets. We can provide parents with education on safety to better supervise and care for their children.'*
>
> Or
>
> *'Kenyan children have nothing to do but wander on the streets; this is due to a shortage of spaces in local orphanages. We can find ways to provide more places for these orphans.'*

**Figure 7.1** The Problem Statement Canvas

| CONTEXT<br><br>When does the problem occur? | PROBLEM<br><br>What is the root cause of the problem? | ALTERNATIVES<br><br>What do problem owners do now to fix the problem? |
|---|---|---|
| PROBLEM OWNERS<br><br>Who has the problem most often? | EMOTIONAL IMPACT<br><br>How does the problem owner feel? | ALTERNATIVE SHORTCOMINGS<br><br>What are the disadvantages of the alternatives? |

Adapted from Ursache (2019)

These guesses are a good starting point. However, we need to do more research to fully understand all aspects of the problem before finding effective solutions. Let us go through each area of the canvas.

## Problem owners – who has the problem most often?

You want to find the real owners of the problem – not those who are indifferent to it, but those who are very eager to solve it. Who are they? Where are they? What is their background? What do their daily activities look like? The more you understand the life situations of these people, the more accurate your research on the problem will be. (How to better access this useful information will be discussed later in this chapter.) After some investigation, the problem owners for the example could be:

> *'Kenyan children' have been redefined as 'School-aged children who live in the slums in Kenya'.*

## Context – when does the problem occur?

Most problems are not permanent; they usually have a peak period of occurrence or activation. Researching the context in which a problem appears, including the time-frame and any potential triggers that preceded it, can greatly aid in analysing the root cause and devising strategies to address it. Some problems, if their triggers are controlled, might be resolved. For example, consider a person who wants to go running but always loses motivation before leaving the house, overwhelmed by the choice of shoes and socks among several pairs. When they recognize this trigger and separate the preparation of shoes and socks from the act of going out to run – meaning they prepare what to wear in advance – they no longer abandon the idea of running at the last minute.

For the AA example, through observation and information integration, the context then became:

*Each weekday afternoon, following the end of school, for approximately two to three hours daily.*

## Problem – what is the root cause of the problem?

The true owners of the problem and the context in which it arises can help in analysing the problem itself. However, we must be cautious, as sometimes what we see are merely symptoms, not the root cause. Take our example with AA. We might initially think that the core issue is the lack of safety awareness among Kenyan parents, who let their children wander the streets unsupervised. Alternatively, we might assume that most of these children are orphans without guardians, and the solution would be to find suitable orphanages for them, allowing professionals to handle the situation.

However, after deeper investigation, social entrepreneur Gavin discovered that most of these children do have families and attend school. While the aforementioned issues do exist, they are not the primary reasons for the problem. The fundamental issue is that these children have nothing to do after school, leading them to wander the streets and sometimes engage in illegal activities. It is essential to dig into the root cause of the problem rather than just addressing the superficial symptoms. This step requires critical thinking and often involves a combination of investigation and data analysis to ensure that the identified cause is directly related to the problem. Here, we can use the 'Five Whys' technique, repeatedly asking 'why' to uncover the core reason. Therefore, we can define the problem in our example as follows:

*They could be doing more meaningful things in safer places instead of wandering on the streets.*

## Emotional impact – how does the problem owner feel?

Merely understanding a problem as a phenomenon or event is not enough; you also need to consider its emotional impact. This helps you think from the perspective of the problem owners and understand their behaviours. Every problem elicits an emotional response (joy, sadness, anger, fear, surprise and anticipation), and the intensity of these emotions is directly related to people's interest in using your solution. Fully grasping these emotions is crucial for identifying windows of opportunity and triggers that will prompt the problem owners to adopt your solution. In the case we discussed, if children often wander the streets after school, their emotions might include:

*Loneliness, boredom, and even anxiety or fear.*

## *Alternatives – what do problem owners do now to fix the problem?*

Before jumping directly to a solution, should you first observe how the problem owners are currently coping with their pain or symptoms? If what you have identified is indeed a problem, these individuals are likely using various tools and actions, or a combination of them, to alleviate or manage their pain. Sometimes, they might cleverly improvise to meet their needs. Observing these alternative solutions and analysing the pros and cons of each will greatly help in identifying opportunities for solutions that address the pain points. Many successful innovations are developed from existing products or services. For example, the smartphones we use today integrate the functions of computers and cameras into one portable device, allowing people to handle various tasks conveniently anytime and anywhere. Similarly, those children wandering the streets often:

> *Choose to make friends with older children and learn from them how to have fun on the streets.*

## *Alternative shortcomings – what are the disadvantages of the alternatives?*

Competition is a good thing; it proves that the problem truly exists. But what if you can't outcompete your rivals, which is often the case in many mature markets? This

**Figure 7.2** The Problem Statement Canvas for AA

| CONTEXT | PROBLEM | ALTERNATIVES |
|---|---|---|
| When does the problem occur?<br><br>Each weekday afternoon, following the end of school, for approximately 2–3 hours daily | What is the root cause of the problem?<br><br>Could be doing more meaningful things in safer places instead of wandering on the streets | What do problem owners do now to fix the problem?<br><br>Choose to make friends with older children and learn from them how to have fun on the streets |
| **PROBLEM OWNERS** | **EMOTIONAL IMPACT** | **ALTERNATIVE SHORTCOMINGS** |
| Who has the problem most often?<br><br>School-aged children who live in the slums in Kenya | How does the problem owner feel?<br><br>Loneliness, boredom, anxiety and fear | What are the disadvantages of the alternatives?<br><br>Being with older children sometimes leads to being bullied, and they may also be forced to engage in illegal activities, which makes them feel very uneasy |

is why identifying the shortcomings or limitations of alternative solutions will help you understand the core of your solution – your unfair advantage. In the case of our AA example, the situation is clear:

> *Being with older children sometimes leads to being bullied, and they may also be forced to engage in illegal activities, which makes them feel very uneasy.*

In this way, our Problem Statement Canvas can present the details as in Figure 7.2.

By using the Problem Statement Canvas, we can gain an understanding of the background of a social problem, who is impacted and to what extent, how they are affected, the root of the problem, existing solutions and their drawbacks. Based on this information, we can further consider how to better resolve a social problem and transform it into an entrepreneurial opportunity.

**STOP AND THINK**

Have you ever experienced this? While discussing a problem with a colleague, you find that your understanding of the issue is very different from theirs. Who is right and who is wrong? It is often difficult to convince the other person, and they find it equally hard to persuade you. Why does this happen? The answer is quite simple: due to our different backgrounds and life experiences, each of us has unique perceptions and understandings of things. Even when dealing with the same issue, different people will have varied interpretations and approaches.

In a team setting, this necessitates a lot of communication to understand each other and reach a consensus. At this point, using a Problem Statement Canvas to clearly articulate a problem and identify its root cause can make your thinking more rigorous and your logic clearer, making it easier for others to understand. Why not try it out and see how effective it can be?

## Opportunity recognition

In starting an SE, we define 'opportunity recognition' as the process of identifying and acting on new or improved ways of solving a social problem to create social value. Clearly identifying a social problem, as we previously discussed, is the foundation of opportunity recognition. In fact, the journey from identifying a problem to seizing an opportunity and taking action often spans a considerable length of time. As Yitshaki and Kropp (2016) noted, it is a process of transitioning from intention to action, influenced by various factors. These factors might stem from the social entrepreneur's own motives and experiences, the resources available to them, and external influences such as government policies and other relevant entities.

The process of turning a social problem into a social entrepreneurial opportunity echoes Guclu and colleagues' (2002) earlier work, in which two broad stages of developing an SE were identified:

1 **Generating promising ideas,** which refers to identifying a problem and a potentially viable social enterprise idea.
2 **Developing promising ideas into attractive opportunities,** which is about analysing the idea and developing it into a formal business opportunity for positive and sustainable social impact. This process needs social entrepreneurs to have a combination of cognitive skills, like pattern recognition, and social skills, such as engaging with others to refine ideas. This process is fundamentally about learning along the way. The topic of social entrepreneurial learning will be further explored in Chapter 10. We first look at the importance of conducting primary and secondary research in opportunity recognition.

## *Data is power*

For social entrepreneurs eager to take action, spending time on research may seem like a challenge. However, gathering extensive data can guide the direction of their action, making it easier to achieve the intended outcomes and increasing the chances of creating social value. This aligns with the Chinese proverb: 'Sharpening your axe will not delay your job of cutting wood'. Proper preparation makes tasks more efficient and effective. To understand a problem's root causes and potential solutions, you could start with secondary research, followed by primary research.

Secondary research involves analysing existing data that has been collected by others. This includes reviewing published research, data reports, case studies and other relevant materials. Such pre-existing information is readily available and can be easily gathered for thorough analysis and study. By learning from the experiences of others, you can achieve more with less effort and avoid unnecessary mistakes. Additionally, trying out the effective and convenient methods used by others might yield excellent results.

Once you have thoroughly reviewed the existing relevant materials and gained a detailed understanding of the field, you can begin primary research. This involves gathering new data that has not been collected before. This data comes directly from the source and is specific to your needs. In other words, there are specific questions and situations that previous research may not address or explain. You can design a fieldwork project to collect first-hand data and analyse it systematically to investigate and answer your questions.

In the field of social entrepreneurship, common methods for collecting primary data include observation, interviews and surveys. The choice of data-collection method will depend on the questions you want to answer and the nature of those questions. This chapter will not go into the specifics of these methods. For more detailed information, please refer to relevant business research methods books, such as *Research Methods for Business Students* (Saunders et al, 2023).

After gathering data, synthesize the information to form a comprehensive view of the social problem. Identify common themes, contradictions and gaps in knowledge. By thoroughly conducting both primary and secondary research, social entrepreneurs can ensure that their initiatives are well-informed, targeted and capable of making a sustainable impact.

Wait a moment: is there still something important we have not covered? When conducting primary research, who would be a reliable data source? Do not worry; let us explore this topic in the next section.

## A collective approach

There is a consensus in the academic world that many SE start-ups take a collective approach. The process of creating an SE is a collaborative effort, especially during the initial stages of understanding and researching the problem. Social entrepreneurs should mobilize all resources to connect with both problem owners and pioneers in solving similar issues, as their insights are crucial. Those who are knowledgeable and eager to offer advice can be termed co-creators of the social venture. Later in this chapter, we will explore how to reach potential co-creators.

## Lived experience

Your unique life experiences, influenced by the context in which you are embedded alongside your background, can shape your understanding of social challenges. Engaging closely with a social problem, either personally or through connections, positions you better to address it effectively. In choosing a social challenge to tackle, prioritize those who have first-hand experience with the problem. Alternatively, you can collaborate with those who do, focusing on empowering them. This approach, rooted in direct experience, is common in successful entrepreneurship, where understanding the problem deeply is key. The first questions you will get from investors are: Whose problem are you trying to solve? Why are you the right person for us to support you?

Even for someone with first-hand experience, individual understanding of a social problem can be limited. To gain a comprehensive view, it is important to connect with more people who have experienced the issue directly. This is particularly true for problems within a specific community, where diverse perspectives and insights can be gathered from various community members. Thus, the importance of community engagement in understanding and addressing social problems becomes evident.

### Community engagement

A community is a social group in which individuals have one or more things in common. The work of Heinze et al (2016) highlighted the critical role of community engagement in a four-stage social enterprise development process:

1. defining the social problem in reference to local needs and interests
2. building social capital by forming strong relations with communities via formal and informal interactions
3. educating potential partners to develop their capacity
4. convening partners with complementary competencies to develop innovative solutions

Compared to the work of Guclu et al (2002), Heinze et al (2016) offer more insights into how social entrepreneurial opportunity is exploited after initial identification.

Community engagement provides the SE with opportunities to identify real social needs (Ishigaki and Sashida, 2013), acquire and mobilize critical resources (Aquino et al, 2018; Civera et al, 2019), and overcome cultural and institutional barriers (Altinay et al, 2016). Indeed, without actively engaging members of the local community, the development of innovative solutions to social problems may not materialize (Tobias et al, 2013), or the solutions may not truly address the needs of the community, thus leading to a lack of acceptance (Aquino, 2022).

Nonetheless, community engagement can be a major challenge for SEs. Not only because community engagement involves multiple activities (Satar, 2019), but also because local communities may not even have an interest in or a willingness to engage with the SE (Dhanesh, 2017; Yudarwati, 2019). In fact, residents' desire to change is a critical factor in facilitating engagement. Yet, some policymakers or business leaders just assume that communities (particularly those in poorer and underdeveloped areas) are just keen to be involved with whatever engagement activities are on offer (Dahles et al, 2020), which was not the case in many studies (e.g. Bunyan, 2013; Dhanesh, 2017; Stott, 2011). Among many reasons, the organization's approach, or orientation, to community engagement impairs the community's willingness to be engaged. For example, a top-down or ethnocentric approach, where community members are involved but have little or no say in decision-making, is a notable barrier to effective engagement (Jelen-Sanchez, 2017).

## Engagement principles and tools

This section focuses on enhancing the effectiveness of community engagement. It covers the application of various principles and tools designed to improve how we engage with communities in addressing social problems.

## Cultural sensitivity

Cultural sensitivity is an engagement principle that plays an instrumental role in SE start-ups. Cultural sensitivity refers to the awareness of, acceptance of and sensible treatment of cultural similarities and differences among people (Glover and Friedman, 2015; Harrison and Huntington, 1991). It is 'a state of mind' that underpins and drives the thoughts and actions of a social entrepreneur. It requires a social entrepreneur to be open-minded, humble and empathetic towards others, no matter how similar or different their behaviour may seem. It has been found that being culturally sensitive enables the social entrepreneur to have meaningful interactions with the local community and gain an in-depth understanding of the local context that gives rise to social problems.

It is important to note that cultural sensitivity is not pre-dispositional and needs to be developed/demonstrated. Respecting the local community and embracing their culture is critical to developing cultural sensitivity. Not only does this mean that the social entrepreneur needs to appreciate local cultural norms and values while making no judgement on their merits, but it also involves recognizing, acknowledging and accepting the wide range of tacit knowledge and know-how held by local community members. Otherwise, community members might feel disrespected and thus display unwillingness towards further collaboration (Voorberg et al, 2014).

## Long-term orientation

'Long-term orientation', in this textbook, refers to the mindset of the social entrepreneur, which involves persistent actions for a prolonged period before any desired outcomes may materialize. It is about taking time to understand local communities in terms of their ways of thinking, talking and doing things, and adapting one's own approach as needed in order to work together efficiently. A long-term orientation, therefore, prepares the social entrepreneur for being immersed in the local environment, which facilitates a more comprehensive and in-depth understanding of the problems and challenges experienced by local communities (Scheiber, 2014; Weerawardena and Mort, 2006). As an engagement principle, long-term orientation underpins everything the SE does, especially when the aim is to develop a disadvantaged community into a sustainable one.

Long-term orientation is crucial for developing meaningful and beneficial social entrepreneurial projects. This corresponds to the views of Martin and Novicevic (2010) in their case study of social entrepreneurship among Kenyan farmers, where social entrepreneurs attributed their success primarily to their long-term commitment to cultural learning. This helped them gain a deep understanding of unique cultural norms of wealth creation and institutional idiosyncrasies. However, a long-term-oriented approach to social entrepreneurship seems to be in contrast with several SE studies (Haugh, 2007; Henry, 2015), where the identification of international social entrepreneurial opportunities appears to be a 'quick and simple' process and often takes place without a deep understanding of the local context. Given that people from different cultural contexts respond to the same problems in different ways (Glover and Friedman, 2015), the resulting social entrepreneurial outcome (e.g. project) may, therefore, fail to create meaningful value for the local community and can even damage its status quo (Andersson and Ford, 2015). As argued by Bhawuk et al (2009), it is those social entrepreneurs who dedicate their time and live with the local people who are more successful than those who simply 'come and go'.

## Reciprocity and trust

The relationship between social entrepreneurs and the community ideally aims to be mutually beneficial and built on trust. Previously, we mentioned that many people believe social entrepreneurs engage with communities with the intention of helping others, so it seems natural that they should be trusted. However, due to past negative experiences and inherent misunderstandings between different cultures, this is not always the case. Reciprocity and trust between the SE and the local community are not readily available or accessible. This aligns with Seanor and Meaton's (2008) finding that mistrust is a significant challenge in a social enterprise's network, and it takes time and effort to earn the locals' trust to achieve better community engagement.

According to social exchange theory (Blau, 1964), simple reciprocal activities are the foundation for building trust. Sahlins' (1972) typology of reciprocal relationships suggests three types of reciprocity:

- **'Generalized'** is the most altruistic, where people with very close relationships give each other 'pure gifts'. While the giver may expect a return, the counter is not stipulated by time, quantity or quality; the expectation of reciprocity is indefinite (Sahlins, 1972).
- **'Balanced':** Balanced reciprocity, according to Pesämaa et al (2013), involves a more or less immediate exchange of equally valuable goods or services and occurs among more distant relationships, such as with acquaintances in the same community. It is characterized by social norms of even-handedness and honesty and serves as a vehicle for alliance contracts and the transformation from separate to harmonious interests (Sahlins, 1972).
- **'Negative' reciprocity:** Negative reciprocity is practised with 'other people' and is an impersonal mode of exchange where, through 'self-interested seizure' (Sahlins, 1972), both parties seek to maximize their own gains.

Our goal should be to achieve the first two types of reciprocity, enabling community members to better understand our motivations and goodwill, thereby establishing closer relationships and laying the foundation for building trust.

Trust is one of the strongest drivers of interpersonal and group behaviour (Golembiewski and McConkie, 1975; Kouzes and Posner, 2002) and it can vary in degrees (weak, moderate and strong) (Fulmer and Gelfand, 2012). Interpersonal trust is conceptualized as trust between two individuals. In the context of a SE start-up, it denotes the trust between the social entrepreneur and a local community member (e.g. a beneficiary or an individual partner). This type of trust typically develops through the trustor's (i.e. community member's) assessment of the trustee's (i.e., social entrepreneur's) trustworthiness, which includes three main dimensions: benevolence, capability and integrity (Mayer et al, 1995). By consistently demonstrating these three qualities in interactions, it is highly likely to earn the other person's trust. The reciprocal behaviours mentioned earlier provide an excellent opportunity to showcase all three qualities. Additionally, it is important to understand specific practical methods, especially in communication. How can we converse in a way that better captures the other person's interest, holds their attention and effectively presents our qualities? Keep reading.

## *Engaging communication*

Given that communities may not always be eager to engage, SEs must consider this when planning their engagement activities. It is often easier for organizations to label local people as 'consumers' and create structured mechanisms for discussion about defined services than to adopt participatory approaches to engagement. This is because the participatory approach to engagement requires a higher level of commitment from organizations. In a similar fashion to White's (1996) 'transformative' engagement, a participatory approach is expected to create a process that allows local people to take ownership in decision-making and ultimately lead to community-wide benefits.

Similarly, Yudarwati (2019) criticized existing community engagement strategies as predominantly organization-centric and devised from evidence in Western, developed-country contexts, thus calling for more community-centric and non-Western-oriented suggestions on community engagement. Yudarwati found that 'appreciative inquiry' (Cooperrider et al, 2008) as a communication technique was essential to foster community engagement. The application of appreciative inquiry particularly highlights its potential to build and engage community groups by focusing on their strengths and positive attributes. This approach is fundamentally different from traditional problem-solving techniques that often focus on identifying and rectifying problems. Instead, appreciative inquiry aims to discover and build upon what communities are doing right, fostering a more positive and supportive environment for change.

Specifically, the humour and storytelling are excellent approaches for facilitating engaging conversations. Humour, involving amusing verbal and/or nonverbal communications (Romero and Cruthirds, 2006), has been documented as a valuable tool in various contexts such as the 'salesperson-customer relationship' (Lussier et al, 2017), 'leader-subordinate relationship' (Tremblay, 2017), 'online community building' (Marone, 2015), and more recently, entrepreneurship (Lin et al, 2018). For a SE, during the stage of identifying a social problem and mobilizing useful resources, the social entrepreneur needs to interact with unfamiliar local people to gather information and resources. Humour can help establish initial connections. The active use of humour (e.g. a joke, funny story, funny face, sound, or gesture to elicit laughter) helps de-emphasize social hierarchy (Kurtzberg et al, 2009) and alleviates any stress or anxiety locals may have about their interaction (Greatbatch and Clark, 2003). Laughing together helps the social entrepreneur and community members perceive commonalities in their worldview or identity (Hall et al, 1993; Smith et al, 2000) and fosters a sense of connection (Suttie, 2017), making the social entrepreneur more approachable and welcomed by the local community.

While humour brings interest, storytelling helps the social entrepreneur bond with local people. Storytelling, like humour, is a key ingredient in bringing together various groups within the local community. In this context, storytelling refers to communication through compelling narratives, which are temporally sequenced accounts of interrelated events or actions undertaken by individuals and/or groups (Barry and Elmes, 1997; Gabriel, 2004). It has long been recognized as an effective means for humans to make sense of their environment, organize experiences and ideas, and communicate with others to create shared understanding (Robinson, 1981; Sundin et al, 2018). Notably, storytelling also plays a significant role in the SE's resource mobilization efforts. Powerful stories about the social entrepreneur and the beneficiaries can convince local community members and investors/donors that the SE is genuinely interested in addressing unmet social needs. This, in turn, motivates community members to engage with the SE's operations. For more on resource mobilization, refer to Chapters 3 and 12.

## Summary and key learning points

In this chapter, we started by considering various social start-up skills and the key steps and processes involved in starting an SE. We further delved into the concept of problem identification and how social entrepreneurs identify a social problem and develop innovative approaches or solutions to these problems. We explored the factors and antecedents that influence social entrepreneurial intentions. These can include perceived desirability, social norms, empathy, moral responsibility, self-efficacy and prior experience with social problems. We have also explored the Problem Statement Canvas as a systematic approach to evaluating and analysing a problem worth solving. The chapter concluded with considerations related to opportunity recognition, the role of data, community engagement, collective approaches and cultural sensitivity in ensuring the SE solves problems for those in need as well as creating social value.

The key takeaways are the following:

- The specific nature of the SE, having to balance social mission with for-profit activity, determines the approaches adopted by the social entrepreneur in identifying an unmet social need and developing a solution to this need.
- Problem identification and problem evaluation are instrumental in designing a solution to a specific problem that is connected to local community needs and for those disadvantaged.
- Apart from the factors that may influence social entrepreneurial intentions, social entrepreneurs need to adopt a systematic approach to solving acute problems to ensure long-term orientation.
- The Problem Statement Canvas is a strategic tool that supports entrepreneurs in understanding who is impacted by the problem, the context in which the problem occurs, the root cause of the problem, the disadvantages of alternative solutions and how the solution identified by the social entrepreneur meets the needs of those affected.
- Community engagement, collective approaches and cultural sensitivity are of paramount importance to social entrepreneurs, given that they are focused on their social mission and social value creation.

## CALLS TO ACTION / DISCUSSION QUESTIONS

We have established in this chapter that starting a social enterprise requires a unique combination of skills, processes and approaches. Unlike traditional entrepreneurship, social enterprises are driven by a dual mission: creating social value while achieving financial sustainability. This balance requires social entrepreneurs to identify unmet social needs, systematically evaluate problems and design solutions that align with the needs of disadvantaged communities. Additionally, factors such as cultural sensitivity and community engagement play a pivotal role in ensuring the long-term success of a social enterprise.

The following prompts will help you explore these concepts further, encouraging you to reflect on problem identification, opportunity recognition and the role of collective and systematic approaches in creating impactful social solutions:

1 In small groups, identify a real-world social enterprise and analyse how it identified the social problem it addresses. What tools or frameworks, such as the Problem Statement Canvas, might the enterprise have used to evaluate the problem? Discuss whether their solution aligns with the needs of the community they serve.

2 Think of a social or environmental issue you are passionate about. Using the Problem Statement Canvas, outline the root cause of the problem, who is impacted and the potential solutions. How will your solution create social value and balance a for-profit model with a social mission? Present your idea to your peers for feedback.

3 Reflect on the factors that influence social entrepreneurial intentions, such as empathy, moral responsibility and self-efficacy. How do these factors apply to your own motivations or experiences? Share an example from your life or studies where these factors shaped your understanding of a social issue.

4 Reflect on the skills outlined in this chapter – problem identification, opportunity recognition and community engagement. What skills do you currently have, and which do you need to develop further to succeed as a social entrepreneur? How can you build these skills? Share your thoughts with a peer or mentor to create a personal development plan.

## REAL-WORLD EXAMPLE INDICATIVE ANSWERS

1 How do you think Gavin truly understood the needs of the local people in Kenya? What challenges might he have faced in this process?

**Indicative answer:** Gavin immersed himself in the community, living and interacting directly with residents to understand their challenges, such as poverty and lack of educational resources. Challenges he might have faced include cultural differences, language barriers and the time required to build trust with the community. Additionally, he may have encountered scepticism or misunderstandings about his intentions, requiring persistent and transparent engagement to overcome them.

2 How did AA turn the identified social problem into an entrepreneurial opportunity? What steps would you take to evaluate whether this opportunity is viable?

**Indicative answer:** AA transformed the social problem of poverty and lack of opportunities into an entrepreneurial opportunity by using adventure tourism to generate income for community development projects. Gavin Bate identified how tourism could address local issues while providing travellers with meaningful, ethical experiences. By employing and training locals – often former beneficiaries of Moving Mountains (MM) – AA created a sustainable model where business success directly supported social impact. This integration made the enterprise financially viable and socially impactful.

To evaluate whether this opportunity is viable, key steps include:

- Conducting primary research: Engaging with community members to understand needs and interviewing potential clients to gauge interest in socially responsible tourism.
- Secondary research: Analysing tourism trends and competitors to confirm demand for ethical travel.
- Assessing feasibility: Reviewing start-up costs, potential revenues and the ability of tourism profits to sustain community projects.
- Piloting: Testing the model with a smaller-scale tour to gather feedback and refine the approach before expanding.

**3** Since community engagement is so important, AA's case provides valuable insights into the tools entrepreneurs can use to strengthen engagement during the start-up phase. What could some of these tools be, and how can they be effectively implemented?

**Indicative answer:** To strengthen community engagement during the start-up phase, entrepreneurs can adopt these tools, as demonstrated by Gavin Bate in the case of AA:

- Cultural sensitivity:
  Understanding and respecting local traditions is essential. Entrepreneurs should adapt their approaches to fit the community's context. Gavin achieved this by living within the community, participating in daily activities and learning local customs. This helped him build trust and ensured his initiatives respected cultural norms, avoiding resistance or misalignment.
- Long-term orientation:
  Lasting relationships require sustained commitment. Gavin invested years in building schools and clinics, integrating them into the community's development plans. His continued presence reassured locals of his dedication, fostering trust and loyalty, which ensured the enterprise's efforts were seen as genuine and beneficial.
- Reciprocity and trust:
  Mutual benefit strengthens relationships. Gavin employed locals, including former beneficiaries, in AA, giving them ownership of the enterprise while providing skills and income. This reciprocal approach embedded trust and ensured projects were co-created with community input.

- Engaging communication:
  Transparent, ongoing dialogue ensures alignment. Gavin engaged in direct conversations, community meetings and local events, listening to needs and co-designing solutions. This inclusive communication created shared goals and strengthened collaboration.

## References


Altinay, L, Sigala, M and Waligo, V (2016) Social value creation through tourism enterprise, *Tourism Management*, 54: 404–17

Andersson, F O and Ford, M (2015) Reframing social entrepreneurship impact: Productive, unproductive and destructive outputs and outcomes of the Milwaukee school voucher programme, *Journal of Social Entrepreneurship*, 6(3): 299–319

Aquino, R S (2022) Community change through tourism social entrepreneurship, *Annals of Tourism Research*, 95: 103–442

Aquino, R S, Lück, M and Schänzel, H A (2018) A conceptual framework of tourism social entrepreneurship for sustainable community development, *Journal of Hospitality and Tourism Management,* 37: 23–32

Bacq, S and Alt, E (2018) Feeling capable and valued: a prosocial perspective on the link between empathy and social entrepreneurial intentions, *Journal of Business Venturing,* 33(3): 333–50

Barry, D and Elmes, M (1997) Strategy retold, *Academy of Management Review,* 2: 429–52

Bhatt, P and Altinay, L (2013) How social capital is leveraged in social innovations under resource constraints? *Management Decision*, 51(9): 1772–792

Bhawuk, D, Mrazek, S and Munusamy, V P (2009) From social engineering to community transformation: Amul, Grameen Bank, and Mondragon as exemplar organizations, *Peace and Policy,* 14, Ethical Transformations for a Sustainable Future

Blau, P M (1964) *Exchange and Power In Social Life,* New York: John Wiley

Bunyan, P (2013) Partnership, the Big Society and community organizing: Between romanticizing, problematizing and politicizing community, *Community Development Journal*, 48(1): 119–33

Chell, E (2007) Social enterprise and entrepreneurship: Towards a convergent theory of the entrepreneurial process, *International Small Business Journal*, 25(1): 5–26

Civera, C, De Colle, S and Casalegno, C (2019) Stakeholder engagement through empowerment: The case of coffee farmers, *Business Ethics: A European Review*, 28(2): 156–74

Cooperrider, D, Whitney, D and Stavros, J (2008) *The Appreciative Inquiry Handbook: For leaders of change*, Berrett-Koehler Publishers

Dahles, H, Khieng, S, Verver, M and Manders, I (2020) Social entrepreneurship and tourism in Cambodia: advancing community engagement, *Journal of Sustainable Tourism*, 28(6): 816–33

Dhanesh, G S (2017) Putting engagement in its PRoper place: State of the field, definition and model of engagement in public relations, *Public Relations Review*, 43(5): 925-933

Dickel, P and Eckardt, G (2021) Who wants to be a social entrepreneur? The role of gender and sustainability orientation, *Journal of Small Business Management*, 59(1): 196–218

Douglas, E J, Shepherd, D and Venugopal, V (2021) A multi-motivational general model of entrepreneurial intention, *Journal of Business Venturing*, 36(4): 106–07

Fulmer, C A and Gelfand, M J (2012) At what level (and in whom) we trust: Trust across multiple organizational levels, *Journal of Management*, 38(4): 1167–230

Gabriel, Y (2004) Narratives, stories, texts. In: Grant, D, Hardy, C, Oswick, C and Putnam, L (eds) *The Sage Handbook of Organizational Discourse*, London: Sage, pp. 61–79

Glover, J and Friedman, H L (2015) *Transcultural Competence: Navigating cultural differences in the global community*, American Psychological Association.

Golembiewski, R T and McConkie, M (1975) The centrality of interpersonal trust in group processes, *Theories of Group Processes*, 131(1): 131–85

Greatbatch, D and Clark, T (2003) Displaying group cohesiveness: Humour and laughter in the public lectures of management gurus, *Human Relations*, 56(12): 1515-1544.

Guclu, A, Dees, J G, and Anderson, B B (2002) *The Process of Social Entrepreneurship: Creating opportunities worthy of serious pursuit,* Centre for the advancement of Social Entrepreneurship, Duke University

Guo, C and Bielefeld, W (2014) *Social Entrepreneurship: An evidence-based approach to creating social value*, San Francisco: John Wiley and Sons

Hall, S, Keeter, L and Williamson, J (1993) Toward an understanding of humour as popular culture in American society, *Journal of American Culture*, 16(2): 1–6

Harrison, L and Huntington, S (1991) *Culture Matters*, New York: Basic Books

Haugh, H (2007) Community-led social venture creation, *Entrepreneurship Theory and Practice*, 31(2): 161-182

Heinze, K, Banaszak-Holl, J and Babiak, K (2016) Social entrepreneurship in communities: Examining the collaborative processes of health conversion foundations, *Nonprofit Management and Leadership*, 26(3): 313–30

Henry, C (2015) Doing well by doing good: Opportunity recognition and the social enterprise partnership, *Journal of Social Entrepreneurship*, 6(2): 137–60

Hockerts, K (2017) Determinants of social entrepreneurial intentions, *Entrepreneurship Theory and Practice*, 1: 105–30

Ishigaki, K and Sashida, N (2013) Use of social innovation to solve problems at the community level and create new businesses in the social domain, *FUJITSU Science and Technology Journal*, 49(4): 430–39

Jelen-Sanchez, A (2017) Engagement in public relations discipline: Themes, theoretical perspectives and methodological approaches, *Public Relations Review*, 43(5): 934–44

Kouzes, J M and Posner, B Z (2002) *The Leadership Challenge*, San Francisco: Jossey- Bass

Kurtzberg, T R, Naquin, C E and Belkin, L Y (2009) Humour as a relationship-building tool in online negotiations, *International Journal of Conflict Management*, 20(4): 377–97

Lanteri, A (2015) The creation of social enterprises: Some lessons from Lebanon, *Journal of Social Entrepreneurship*, 6(1): 42–69

Lin, S, Li, J and Han, R (2018) Coping humour of entrepreneurs: Interaction between social culture and entrepreneurial experience, *Frontiers in Psychology*, 9: 1449

Lussier, B, Grégoire, Y and Vachon, M A (2017) The role of humour usage on creativity, trust and performance in business relationships: An analysis of the salesperson-customer dyad, *Industrial Marketing Management*, 65: 168–81

Mair, J and Noboa, E (2006) Social entrepreneurship: how intentions to create a social venture are formed. In: Mair, J, Robinson, J and Hockerts, K (eds) *Social Entrepreneurship*, London, UK: Palgrave Macmillan, pp.121–135

Marone, V (2015) Online humour as a community-building cushioning glue, *The European Journal of Humour Research*, 3(1): 61–83

Martin, J S and Novicevic, M (2010) Social entrepreneurship among Kenyan farmers: A case example of acculturation challenges and programme success, *International Journal of Intercultural Relations*, 34: 482–92

Mayer, R, Davis, J and Schoorman, F (1995) An integrative model of organizational trust, *Academy of Management Review*, 20(3): 709–34

Osterwalder, A and Pigneur, Y (2010) *Business Model Generation: A handbook for visionaries, game-changers, and challengers,* San Francisco: John Wiley and Sons

Perrini, F, Vurro, C and Costanzo, L A (2010) A process-based view of social entrepreneurship: From opportunity identification to scaling-up social change in the case of San Patrignano, *Entrepreneurship and Regional Development*, 22(6): 515–34

Pesämaa, O, Pieper, T, Da Silva, R V, Black, W C and Hair Jr, J F (2013) Trust and reciprocity in building inter-personal and inter-organizational commitment in small business co-operatives, *Journal of Co-operative Organization and Management*, 1(2): 81–92

Robinson, J A (1981) Personal narratives reconsidered, *Journal of American Folklore*, 94: 58–85

Romero, E J and Cruthirds, K W (2006) The use of humour in the workplace, *Academy of Management Perspectives*, 20(2): 58–69

Sahlins, M D (1972) *Stone Age Economies*, Chicago, IL: Aldine Atherton

Salamzadeh, A, Arasti, Z and Elyasi, G M (2017) Creation of ICT-based social start-ups in Iran: A multiple case study, *Journal of Enterprising Culture*, 25(1): 97–122

Santos, S C, Nikou, S, Brännback, M and Liguori, E W (2021) Are social and traditional entrepreneurial intentions really that different? *International Journal of Entrepreneurial Behaviour & Research*, 27(7): 1891–911

Satar, M (2019) Towards developing a comprehensive model for describing the phenomenon of community engagement in social enterprises, *Journal of Enterprising Communities*, 13(4): 472–88

Saunders, M N K, Lewis, P and Thornhill, A (2023) *Research Methods for Business Students,* 9th edition, Harlow, UK: Pearson

Scheiber, L A (2014) Social capital and the target population, *Social Enterprise Journal*, 10(2): 121–34

Seanor, P and Meaton, J (2008) Learning from failure, ambiguity and trust in social enterprise, *Social Enterprise Journal,* 4(1): 24–40

Smith, W J, Harrington, K V and Neck, C P (2000) Resolving conflict with humor in a diversity context, *Journal of Managerial Psychology,* 15(6): 606–25

Stott, M (2011) *The Big Society Challenge*, Thetford: Keystone Development Trust Publications

Sundin, A, Andersson, K and Watt, R (2018) Rethinking communication: Integrating storytelling for increased stakeholder engagement in environmental evidence synthesis, *Environmental Evidence*, 7(1): 1–6

Suttie, J (2017) *How Laughter Brings Us Together*, Greater Good Magazine

Tobias, M J, Mair, J and Barbosa-Leiker, C (2013). Toward a theory of transformative entrepreneuring: Poverty reduction and conflict resolution in Rwanda's entrepreneurial coffee sector, *Journal of Business Venturing*, 28: 728–42

Tremblay, M (2017) Humour in teams: Multilevel relationships between humour climate, inclusion, trust, and citizenship behaviours, *Journal of Business and Psychology*, 32(4): 363–78

Ursache, M (2019) The problem statement canvas for startups and innovation teams, https://medium.com/disciplined-entrepreneurship/the-problem-statement-canvas-for-startups-and-innovation-teams-663364c1a951 (archived at https://perma.cc/L4HY-R3GB)

Voorberg, W, Bekkers, V and Tummers, L (2014) The key to successful co-creation: an explanation of causal processing, presented at EGPA conference 10-12 September, Speyer (Germany)

Weerawardena, J and Mort, G S (2006) Investigating social entrepreneurship: A multidimensional model, *Journal of World Business*, 41(1): 21–35

White, S C (1996) Depoliticising development: The uses and abuses of participation, *Development in Practice*, 6(1): 6–15

Yitshaki, R and Kropp, F (2016) Motivations and opportunity recognition of social entrepreneurs, *Journal of Small Business Management*, 54(2): 546–65

Yudarwati, G A (2019) Appreciative inquiry for community engagement in Indonesia rural communities, *Public Relations Review*, 45(4): 101833

# 08 Social value proposition

**ZEINEB DJEBALI**

## LEARNING OUTCOMES

After reading this chapter, you will be able to:

- Understand key concepts relating to social entrepreneurship.
- Recognize the role social entrepreneurs play in the social entrepreneurial process.
- Recognize the need to reconcile a social mission with business objectives to avoid mission drift in social value creation.
- Understand how social entrepreneurial opportunities are formed and the processes involved, from ideation and experimentation to refinement.
- Be able to assess the design of a social value proposition that aligns the needs of beneficiaries, customers and the broader social outcomes.

## REAL-WORLD EXAMPLE Oakleaf Enterprise: Making a difference for those with mental health conditions

Oakleaf Enterprise was founded as a charity organization dedicated to improving the lives of those with mental health conditions through the power of well-being activities, work-related training, employment support and counselling services in the local area of Surrey, UK. Clive Stone, who soon joined the charity as a Chief Executive Director (CED), understood the challenges of mental health conditions through his own professional background as an accredited member of the British Association of Counselling & Psychotherapy. Clive continues to run a private counselling and supervision practice to this day.

Oakleaf Enterprise was founded following the Care in the Community Act 1990, where an occupational therapy unit at the Old Victorian mental health hospital at Brookwood (UK) closed and relocated to Guildford in Surrey. In 1997, it registered as a charity, which was essentially a not-for-profit organization with a mandate to provide support for those with mental health conditions (referred to as 'clients'). Stone played a pivotal role in broadening the charity's ambition in tackling a problem as significant as mental health. His vision was something much greater than traditional government support – it was to support clients to transform their lives.

Social entrepreneurship is often perceived as a novel approach to addressing social and environmental challenges. As such, Oakleaf Enterprise exemplifies this by fulfilling a real social need – offering clients access to support activities, empowering them to become active members of society, and creating a positive change in their lives. The charity offers a range of services, including:

- **Well-being activities:** In-person and online sessions such as art, fitness, cookery, football, yoga and upholstery, aimed at improving clients' confidence, physical and mental well-being, and reducing isolation and loneliness.
- **'Pathways to Work' employment project:** Funded by the National Lottery Community Fund, this programme delivers tailored employment guidance and support.
- **Information Technology (IT) and gardening courses** to help clients gain new skills, qualifications and work experience.
- **Counselling services:** Offering clients a safe and confidential space to speak with professional counsellors.
- **Guildford Safe Haven:** In partnership with Catalyst (a charity based in the local area of Surrey that promotes mental health and well-being) and Surrey and Borders Partnerships National Health Services (NHS) Trust, a drop-in and out-of-hours service to support those experiencing mental health crises.

To financially sustain its interventions, Oakleaf Enterprise relies on a variety of voluntary donation funding sources including trusts and foundations, individuals, businesses, community groups and events. In addition to donations and grants, Oakleaf Enterprise has embedded a social enterprise model to diversify its revenue streams. This includes gardening services, where clients perform paid gardening work for individuals and businesses as part of their training.

Oakleaf Enterprise's impact report highlights its steadfast commitment to enhancing the lives of their clients. As of 2022/2023, they saw 1,874 attendances at the Safe Haven, there were 1,374 attendances at their training courses in IT and gardening, and 194 people were supported by the 'Pathway to Work' employment project. They also delivered approximately 950 well-being activity sessions (both online and in person) and 2,037 counselling sessions with 192 clients. Overall, Oakleaf Enterprise reported that approximately 96 per cent of their clients felt more confident, with 98 per cent feeling their mental well-being had improved, and a large number of their clients resumed volunteering roles, gained qualifications and found full- or part-time employment.

Over the years, Oakleaf Enterprise has clearly made a positive impact on its clients' lives by helping them regain their lives and reintegrate into society. Find out more on their website: https://www.oakleaf-enterprise.org/

Discussion questions (see indicative answers at the end of the chapter):

1. Which specific social problems did Oakleaf Enterprise identify in the local community, leading to its foundation?
2. How does Oakleaf Enterprise's social business model differ from charitable business models, and what are the advantages of embedding a social enterprise?
3. Using the Social Value Proposition Canvas presented in this chapter, who are the key beneficiaries of Oakleaf Enterprise? And how are their needs balanced with customers and the broader social outcomes?

**Figure 8.1-8.4** Oakleaf Enterprise

**SOURCE** Credit to Oakleaf Enterprise, https://www.oakleaf-enterprise.org/

# Introduction

Although there is no universal single definition of social entrepreneurship (Weerawardena and Sullivan Mort, 2006), it is widely recognized as a process that involves solving social or environmental problems to create social value (Cagarman et al, 2020). Social entrepreneurship therefore has the power to alleviate the mounting social or environmental challenges facing modern societies, such as from climate change, poverty, hunger, gender inequality, unequal access to equitable education and health, among many others (Battilana and Lee, 2014). However, engaging in social entrepreneurial actions requires a social entrepreneur who identifies an unmet social need and develops an innovative approach to solve this. Social entrepreneurs therefore play a key role in the social entrepreneurial process, driven by their social mission over profits (Dees, 2001).

Amidst the multiple definitions of social entrepreneurship, social enterprises (SEs) have emerged as a distinct organizational structure that balances a social mission with financial sustainability. SEs therefore exist at the intersection of social and business logics – that is, they draw from for-profit business models that are driven by economic value creation, as well as from not-for-profit organizations (NFPs) that are driven by their social mission (Defourny and Nyssens, 2006; Dacin et al, 2010; Nicholls and Cho, 2006). Nevertheless, SEs often face tensions in balancing their social mission and financial sustainability. While many social entrepreneurs are passionate about addressing social or environmental needs, without a good understanding of their Social Value Proposition (SVP) – specifically, what they aim to address and how they intend to achieve broader outcomes – their attempts can often lead to failure. Hence, this chapter goes into the practical process of building an SVP that aligns the needs of three intersecting but distinct groups: beneficiaries, customers and broader social outcomes.

First, we revisit the definitional debates related to social entrepreneurship, identifying similarities and differences among these. Then we explore the role social entrepreneurs play in the social entrepreneurial process, including the antecedents that inform their social entrepreneurial intentions (SEIs) and how they act upon social entrepreneurial opportunities (SEOs). We revisit the concept of 'social value' and examine how SEs can face challenges in balancing social and business objectives, potentially leading to mission drift. Next, we explore the concept of SEOs and their relevance to the social entrepreneurial process. This involves exploration, experimentation and refinement to create meaningful social value. Finally, we look at the key components of an SVP that meets the needs of three interrelated but distinct groups – beneficiaries, customers and social outcomes – followed by a summary of the key learning points of this chapter.

## Conceptual definitions of social enterprise

Social entrepreneurship continues to be a relevant scholarly field in academic literature in conjunction with its increasing role in developing innovative solutions to social problems (Cagarman et al, 2020; Schaltegger et al, 2018). Despite this attention, however, the concept still lacks a collective definition (Peredo and McLean, 2006; Weerawardena and Sullivan Mort, 2006). As demonstrated in this textbook (e.g. Chapters 1, 2 and 5), social entrepreneurship emerged from the intersection of two conceptual traditions: profit-driven business models, which primarily focus on economic objectives, and not-for-profit (NFP) models, characterized by their charitable actions and which prioritize serving the public interest (Defourny and Nyssens, 2006; Dacin et al, 2010; Nicholls and Cho, 2006). This conceptual intersection has developed into innovative hybrid business models that combine social objectives alongside financial sustainability, eschewing the reliance of NFPs on government subsidies/grants and philanthropic donations to instead generate revenue to better serve their social missions (Armstrong and Grobbelaar, 2023; Kamaludin, 2023).

However, it is important to note that their objectives extend beyond financial sustainability. SEs seek to build the 'social capital' of individuals and communities, broadly understood as enhancing the well-being of others through feelings of inclusiveness, belonging and trust (Calò et al, 2018; Farmer et al, 2016). Social capital also refers to resources embedded within an individual's or a community's social networks, helping to strengthen and expand social and supportive networks and promoting cooperation for mutual benefits (Awaworyi and Mishra, 2017; Helliwell and Putnam, 2004; Szreter and Woolcock, 2004). So too do SEs focus on creating social value by selling or offering services, programmes or interventions that respond to beneficiaries' needs (Mair and Schoen, 2007; Roger and Osberg, 2015), and thus operate like commercial businesses, with a defined business model, a clear customer base and strategies for revenue generation, to ensure long-term financial sustainability.

Due to this relative economic independence, SEs have therefore been seen as a vehicle for meeting social needs and supporting economic activities in areas neglected by both the market and the state (see Chapter 1; Battilana and Lee, 2014; Battilana and Dorado, 2010). The continued retraction of governments from public service provision has resulted in the subsequently larger involvement of non-state players, such as charities and SEs, in addressing community needs and advancing the well-being of those affected (Munoz et al, 2015; Scarlato, 2013; Weaver, 2018). In this instance, at the policy level, SEs have been actively promoted by governments as a cost-effective and innovative mechanism for tackling social challenges and delivering public services (Farmer et al, 2016), and a study by Di Domenico et al, (2010) found that, more often, SEs operate in under-resourced communities with significant welfare problems.

Against this backdrop, a number of studies have examined the role social entrepreneurs play in identifying unmet social needs, as explored below.

## Social entrepreneurs

Mainstream entrepreneurship research has been broadly conceptualized from a profit-oriented perspective, where business ventures are created to maximize profits and shareholder value (Cunningham and Lischeron, 1991; Low and MacMillan, 1988). As explored in Chapters 1 and 2, Schumpeter (1947) argues that entrepreneurs are innovators who exploit entrepreneurial opportunities and introduce new methods of production, new sources of supply and new markets to disrupt the existing economic equilibrium and create financial value (Hagedoorn, 1996). Research has also explored the entrepreneurship 'traits' view, which perceives entrepreneurs to have 'unique' inherent traits that enable them to discover and exploit entrepreneurial opportunities (Chell, 2010; Gartner, 1990; Shane and Venkataraman, 2000). Among the many traits attributed to them are risk-taking (Brockhaus, 1980), alertness (Kirzner, 1979), self-efficacy (Bandura, 2000; 2006), internal locus of control and tolerance for ambiguity (Begley and Boyd, 1987), and high need for achievement (McClelland, 1965).

The economic and traits perspectives of entrepreneurship have significantly advanced our understanding of the entrepreneur's role in the entrepreneurial process by which business ventures are created. However, research also foregrounds the role of the historical, institutional, social and cultural contexts in which entrepreneurs operate, all of which deeply affect the shape of entrepreneurial actions and determine the values and strategies undertaken. As explored in Chapter 2, institutions, for example, constitute the broader framework within which individual entrepreneurs operate, influencing their values and beliefs at a societal/national level (Busenitz et al, 2000; Casson and Yeung, 2006). As such, individuals are more likely to become entrepreneurs in contexts that foster and motivate entrepreneurship, compared to those embedded in less favourable contexts (Casson and Yeung, 2006). Scott's (1995) Institutional Theory provides further clarification, differentiating between the 'regulatory' (regulations, laws, and governmental policies and programmes), 'normative' (standards, moral values and codes of conduct) and 'cognitive-cultural' (shared values, meanings and symbols, institutionalized through various processes) that influence entrepreneurial action.

Entrepreneurship, then, cannot be simply reduced to the entrepreneur and their traits, nor purely to the context; rather, it involves complex interactions between them (Jack and Anderson, 2002; Zahra et al, 2014). Sarason et al, (2006, 2010) argue that entrepreneurs are active agents who spot, interpret and act on entrepreneurial opportunities while simultaneously embedded within networks of social ties and institutional frameworks that both constrain and enable entrepreneurial action. Both the entrepreneur and the context determine entrepreneurial opportunities, but it is only with an entrepreneur's action as an 'agent of change' (Sarason et al, 2010; Chell, 2010) that these opportunities can be realized, structured or maintained to create a desired outcome. Opportunities are not simply discovered, but co-created through a dynamic interplay of individual and context.

Building on the above theories, social entrepreneurs are also 'agents of change' who realize social entrepreneurial opportunities (SEOs) through their embedded context and antecedents that influence their social entrepreneurial intentions (SEIs). Antecedents are 'what comes before' an action and more often determine the likelihood of an individual to become a social entrepreneur. Findings demonstrate that antecedents such as ethical fibre and virtuous behaviour, compassion, coherent unity of purpose, integrity, honesty, empathy and an innate capacity to contribute meaningfully to social and economic development, all of which contribute to SEIs (Bacq and Alt, 2018; Douglas and Prentice, 2019; Douglas et al, 2021; Ip et al, 2021). Mair and Noboa (2006) argue that the desirability to act on SEOs is shaped by emotional and cognitive constructs such as empathy and moral responsibility to help those in need, self-efficacy and perceived social support. Hockerts (2017) further extends this by considering prior experience with social problems as antecedents to empathy and moral obligations towards supporting those affected. Further findings (e.g. Bacq and Alt, 2018; Ernst, 2011) show that empathy, self-efficacy, social worth, social norms and personal values influence SEIs.

Where social entrepreneurs differ from traditional profit-oriented entrepreneurs, however, is in the nature of the 'mission' they choose and how their motivations determine the concept and scale of their mission (Weerawardena et al, 2003). Although both seek financial sustainability and make changes in the marketplace, profit-oriented entrepreneurs focus on their market-oriented mission, while social entrepreneurs identify entrepreneurial opportunities to solve social problems (Austin et al, 2006; Dees, 2001). A study by Massetti (2008) offers a practical way to conceptualize this distinction. Massetti argues that entrepreneurs exist in a continuum, depending on how they define their mission. 'Socially based mission' entrepreneurs prioritize a social mission over profit, 'balanced-mission' entrepreneurs combine a social mission with market-based mechanisms, and 'market-based' entrepreneurs pursue primarily commercial goals but may engage in social causes when aligned with market opportunities.

Massetti posits that this continuum is useful in understanding social entrepreneurship for three reasons. First, it allows an understanding of *what* social entrepreneurs do rather than who they *are*. One of the challenges with the concept of antecedents is that it overlooks the range of other determinants that influence SEIs, and does not consider how social entrepreneurs act on opportunities as well as the tangible outcomes resulting from their actions. Second, it introduces a 'degree' of distinctiveness so that social ventures can be realistically assessed by investors or other stakeholders. Third, it accounts for the possibility of 'mission transformation' over time – that is, social entrepreneurs who start with a 'social mission' may change over time to a more 'market-driven' one, while those with a 'market-driven mission' may develop social practices depending on market demands (Tiku, 2008). Massetti further conceptualizes social entrepreneurship through the 'Social Entrepreneurship Matrix', where social entrepreneurs can exist within four quadrants depending on how they define and pursue their social mission:

- *The traditional business quadrant* represents 'market-driven' organizations that make a profit to maximize shareholder value. Social entrepreneurs within this quadrant support socially responsible activities when they align with profitability (see CSR in Chapter 5).
- *The transient organization quadrant* represents organizations that respond to market needs but are not driven by making a profit. Social entrepreneurs within this quadrant tend to depend heavily on government subsidy and private donations to support their social mission. However, since their only means of survival is the continuous flow of external support, they may cease to exist if market demands change or their offering is no longer interesting.
- *The traditional not-for-profit quadrant* represents organizations that are driven by a social mission but do not make a profit, such as charities, foundations and public museums. More often they rely on donations, grants and members' fees to support their operation. Social entrepreneurs within this quadrant use surpluses to drive efficiency and grow their operations.
- *The tipping point quadrant* represents organizations that are not only driven by their social mission but also make a profit to achieve social objectives. Social entrepreneurs within this quadrant build hybrid SEs to address social problems sustainably and have the promise of creating systemic social change – defined as the process of altering existing structures, policies, mindsets and behaviours within a particular system that can lead to revolutionary change (Zhao, 2020).

Massetti's study thus highlights the diverse range of social entrepreneurs and how they differ depending on whether they focus on a more market- or socially driven mission.

A further study by Zahra et al, (2009) found that social entrepreneurs have different motivations, which influence the type of venture created and the nature of activities to create social value. While some may be 'grand visionaries' who address large-scale or even worldwide social problems, others may focus on solving local and community challenges. To reflect this diversity, the authors identified three categories of social entrepreneurs. *Social bricoleurs* act on locally discovered opportunities with locally available resources. As discussed in Chapter 3, the term 'bricolage' was first coined by

Claude Lévi-Strauss (1966), referring to the process of 'making do' with the resources at hand. These social entrepreneurs therefore tend to rely on their local tacit knowledge of social needs and leverage their expertise, motivation and personal resources to create local social value. In contrast, *social constructionists* address social needs that are often unmet by traditional providers such as charities, seeking to implement scalable solutions to create broader social impact. Finally, *social engineers* resemble the Schumpeterian entrepreneur in that they seek to engender revolutionary change by replacing existing, often ineffective social structures with new methods and 'sources of supply' of social value. Social engineers often address national, transnational or global issues to achieve systemic social change.

In summary, we have demonstrated that social entrepreneurship is perceived as a novel approach to solving social problems despite the lack of a universally accepted definition. SEs emerged from the intersection of profit-for-shareholder organizations driven by financial goals and NFPs that pursue a social mission to generate public good and therefore combine and differ from both by generating revenue to achieve their social mission. Building on this, we also examined the antecedents that shape SEIs. Antecedents, such as empathy, moral obligations, ethical fibre, personal values and prior experience with the social problem, all influence SEIs and determine how a social entrepreneur defines their social mission. Massetti (2008) argues that entrepreneurs can exist in a continuum: *socially-based mission* entrepreneurs prioritize a social mission over profit, *balanced-mission* ones balance a social mission with profit, and *market-based* ones focus on financial goals but may act on social causes through CSR. Zahra et al, (2009) extend this through three categories of social entrepreneurs. While *social bricoleurs* use their tacit knowledge and leverage their own resources, expertise and motivation to solve local problems, *social constructionists* focus on solving broader social problems that are unmet by traditional providers such as charities. Finally, *social engineers* are Schumpeterian in that they focus on transforming social systems and replacing them with newer ones to create systemic social change. Nevertheless, social entrepreneurs may face tensions in combining social and business logics, as we explore below.

## Social value creation and its tensions

As explored in Chapter 6, social value refers to the creation of value for others in a way that positively impacts their lives and leads to broader social changes (Lackéus, 2018; Raiden et al, 2019). Social value can therefore be understood as a set of interventions, products or services that SEs provide to meet social needs (Tomlins, 2015), such as promoting community empowerment, advocating for more inclusive and fairer policies or addressing a wide range of social and environmental problems. These services seek to build the social capital of communities or individuals or remove barriers to social inclusion for a particular group or a community (Pansera and Sarkar, 2016; Wry and Haugh, 2018).

As hybrid organizations that utilize and combine not-for-profit (i.e. mission-driven) and commercial for-profit (i.e. market-driven) elements within a single organizational structure (Battilana and Dorado, 2010), SEs can often face tensions in balancing these two competing institutional logics and are thus susceptible to 'mission drift' (Battilana and Lee, 2014). Mission drift has been defined as a situation where a social enterprise may lose sight of its social mission in favour of revenue generation, or vice versa when the social mission dominates at the expense of commercial viability, potentially weakening the social business model (SBM) and leading to organizational failure (Cornforth, 2014; Kraatz and Block, 2008; Wry and Zhao, 2018). For instance, institutions such as the Grameen Bank have the social mission of alleviating poverty through microloans – small loans which do not require collateral. These microloans in theory enable people to purchase resources such as seeds or plants to generate income, or empower women in rural areas to achieve financial independence. While this has been effective in many cases, there has also been criticism that microloan institutions tend to pressure borrowers into repaying their loans as soon as possible, in some cases pushing them to sell some of their belongings or sentimental items. The social mission in this case is negatively affected by the pursuit of revenue generation, resulting in mission drift (Augsburg and Fouillet, 2010; Mader, 2013).

Scholars suggest that potential causes of mission drift can be attributed to pressures from donors for SEs to become more financially sustainable, volatility of subsidies, or external demands to prioritize one of the institutional logics over the other (D'Espallier et al, 2016; Battilana and Dorado, 2010; Ebrahim et al, 2014). As discussed in Chapter 1, one way of combating mission drift is through legal structures that ensure restrictions on the transfer of assets as well as capped dividends (Cornforth, 2014; Wolf and Mair, 2019). However, in this chapter, we shift the focus to the role of the SVP to explore how SEs can balance social and commercial objectives by aligning the interests of three key stakeholder groups: beneficiaries, customers and the broader social outcomes. To develop an SVP, social entrepreneurs must first identify an SEO in response to an unmet social need, as explored below.

## Social entrepreneurial opportunity

Social entrepreneurs often identify an unmet social need to solve through entrepreneurial actions (Di Domenico et al, 2010). The social entrepreneurial process therefore involves two critical aspects: entrepreneurial actions and social value creation (Di Domenico et al, 2010). As explored earlier, a key distinction between social and profit-oriented entrepreneurs lies in 'for whom the value is created'. While profit-oriented entrepreneurs identify opportunities to create value for shareholders, social entrepreneurs identify SEOs to solve a social problem and create value for others – that is, those underserved.

Many factors may influence how social entrepreneurs identify and exploit SEOs. While some are primarily driven by a social mission that they deem important (Dees, 2001), others are influenced by prior experience with the social problem, significantly shaping the type of opportunity they identify and choose to act upon (Mair and Noboa, 2006). Further research has identified the role of antecedents such as integrity, compassion, altruism, ethical fibre and virtuous behaviour (Bacq and Alt, 2018; Douglas and Prentice, 2019; Douglas et al, 2021; Ip et al, 2021) in shaping how social entrepreneurs act on SEOs. The specific process, however, by which social entrepreneurs identify an SEO, most often involves three key stages: (1) idea generation, (2) experimentation to explore how the idea might be implemented, and (3) refinement to create meaningful social value (Corner and Marcus, 2010).

## *Idea generation*

Entrepreneurs often respond to market gaps through an ideation process aimed at bringing novel solutions to the market (Schultz, 1975). Idea generation is influenced by many interrelated factors, and much of the research distinguishes between internally or externally driven ideas. Internally generated ideas include ideas which arise from an entrepreneur's knowledge base – often cultivated through education and entrepreneurial learning – that equips them with the right knowledge, skills and mindsets to turn creative ideas into actions (Hafeez et al, 2018; Sevak and Baker, 2014). Ideas can also stem from prior knowledge gained through lived experiences, enhancing an entrepreneur's ability to identify entrepreneurial opportunities. They may also emerge from cognitive abilities, such as alertness to overlooked possibilities. Research has shown that entrepreneurs have unique mental alertness enabling them to recognize new patterns, analyse changes in the macro environment and identify opportunities better than those with lesser alertness (Baron, 2006; Busenitz and Lau, 1996; Kirzner, 1979; Machlup, 1980). Externally generated ideas, on the other hand, tend to result from a process of information search and processing, whereby entrepreneurs utilize the information at hand to create a solution (Ibrahim et al, 2022). As such, technology – in particular, information technology – has been seen to play a key role in the development of entrepreneurial ideas (Fisher and Julien, 2009; Nambisan, 2017).

As explored in Chapter 6, design thinking – a human-centred approach that emphasizes observation, collaboration, iterative learning, visualization, rapid concept development and business analysis (IDEO, 2016; Lockwood, 2010) – has emerged as a key approach in generating ideas for social impact. Brown (2016), for instance, argues that design thinking involves three interrelated spaces: *inspiration*, which catalyses the search for novel solutions; *ideation*, which involves identifying ideas and testing these through experimentation; and *implementation*, which is about realizing the social project. It is important to note, however, that these spaces are iterative, and social entrepreneurs often move back and forth between these as ideas are refined and new directions emerge. Building on Brown's work, we propose the following process when generating ideas for social impact:

1 **Identifying the social problem:** As discussed, social entrepreneurs are moved by their social mission and seek to develop novel solutions to social problems (Dees, 2001). Hence, this process will involve coming up with ideas that relate to a specific social or environmental problem you aim to address. The key question here, as indicated by Brown (2016), is: 'What problem am I trying to solve?' This can include supporting those with mental health conditions to gain access to support services, helping disabled people access the workplace, building the infrastructure of impoverished communities that lack access to clean water or, more broadly, saving food waste from going to landfill.

2 **Brainstorm for ideas:** As discussed in Chapter 2, social entrepreneurships often involve a variety of stakeholders, such as profit-for-shareholder organizations, communities, volunteers, charities and public sector agencies. Hence, this process will involve brainstorming for ideas and sharing insights with your stakeholders to gain fresh perspectives, which will lead to a focus on one specific idea you would like to experiment with and implement.

3 **Make sketches and scenarios:** Try to visualize what the idea will look like in practice. This can be sketching a new digital application, upskilling interventions for refugees, or an online social marketplace for underserved artisans to sell their products.

4 **Put beneficiaries at the heart of your idea:** Describe their pains, the challenges and barriers they face, and what can be done to alleviate these.

## *Experimentation*

The experimentation stage involves seeking feedback from the external environment relative to existing solutions, where a social entrepreneur may adapt or explore alternative approaches to address the identified social problem. During this stage, social entrepreneurs draw on their existing means to see how the SEO might work in practice. Like their profit-oriented counterparts, social entrepreneurs often compete for limited resources; therefore, collaboration provides access to resources they would have otherwise been unable to have or would be costly to develop themselves (Bacq and Eddleston, 2018; Chell, 2007; Haugh, 2007). As discussed in Chapter 2, this includes leveraging the participation of their social networks and involving stakeholders such as individuals, organizations, committees and volunteers (Shaw and Carter, 2007) to access resources (financial or human), gain valuable insights or establish partnerships that facilitate opportunity development (Ozgen and Baron, 2007).

One of the common approaches adopted by social entrepreneurs to mobilize resources is *social appeal*, which involves appealing to stakeholders' sense of altruism and social responsibility to persuade them to contribute with goods and services that the social entrepreneur may otherwise lack (Jayawarna et al, 2020). This bricolage technique, as explored in Chapter 3, fosters resource sharing and collective commitment to the social enterprise's social mission (Jayawarna et al, 2020). Oakleaf Enterprise (see the beginning of this chapter) is a good example. The charity, which has embedded a social enterprise model within its structure, delivers a range of targeted interventions for individuals with mental health conditions (referred to as 'clients'). However, these interventions are embedded within its broader social mission by collaborating with local businesses, charitable organizations and volunteers to access resources and build the necessary support networks to deliver its services.

The experimentation stage also involves assessing how the SEO will address the biggest problem beneficiaries face. As explored in Chapter 7, understanding the root cause of the problem requires conducting in-depth research, whether that be *primary* research, conducted by directly engaging with beneficiaries, communities or stakeholders affected by the problem, or *secondary* research, done by analysing data that has already been collected by others (e.g. industry reports) to assess the broader social or environmental implications of the problem (Saunders et al, 2023). The aim of this research is to understand the beneficiaries' needs, evaluate the effectiveness of existing solutions, and validate the need for the proposed solution and how well it will create value for the beneficiaries by answering the following questions:

- Who are the targeted beneficiaries (e.g. disadvantaged youth, disabled individuals, rough sleepers or groups affected by climate change)?
- What impact does the problem have on them? This could be *emotional* (e.g. feeling isolated), *functional* (e.g. inability to do an activity or access to resources), *psychological* (e.g. affecting their mental well-being) or a mix of all three.

We recommend revisiting the 'Problem Statement Canvas' (Ursache, 2019) in Chapter 7 to explore how to assess the problem and develop a solution that meets beneficiaries' needs.

## Refinement

The final stage is refinement, which involves enhancing the proposed solution to effectively address the social problem and create meaningful social value. The term 'refinement', often referred to as pivoting, is broadly associated with the lean start-up

**Figure 8.5** Social entrepreneurial opportunity

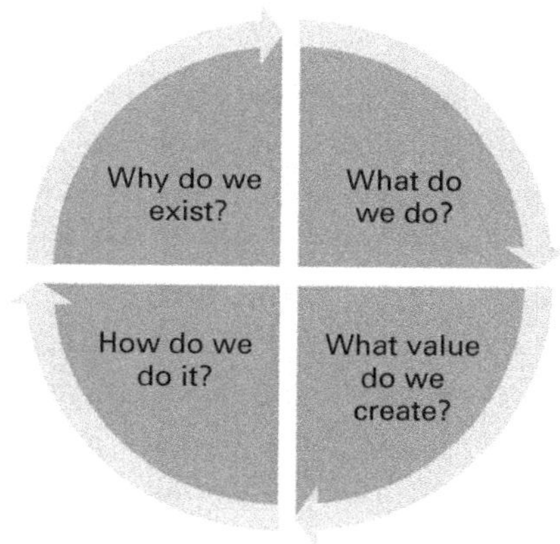


approach (Ries, 2011), where entrepreneurs build a minimal viable product (MVP) to test the quality of their business idea. This includes conducting a market test to gather data, learning and then iteratively refining the concept. At the end of this process, an entrepreneur makes the 'pivot decision' whether to persevere with the idea or develop a new one (McDonald and Eisenhardt, 2020). While profit-driven entrepreneurs typically pivot to ensure they can capture a bigger market share or improve profitability, social entrepreneurs not only have their 'market mission' but also their 'social mission' (Ebrahim et al, 2014). Therefore, refinement within a social entrepreneurial context is not only related to financial growth but also about ensuring that the solution addresses the identified social problem and creates meaningful impact.

As pointed out in Figure 8.5, during the refinement process, the SEO identified should clearly articulate the objectives of the social mission (*why do we exist?*), the specific interventions to address the social problem (*what do we do?*), how to balance social and commercial objectives (*how do we do it?*) and the overall social value created – both at targeted beneficiaries and broader social outcomes (*what value do we create?*)

- **Why do we exist?** This identifies the SEO's core social objectives and the social or environmental problem it aims to address. This component must have a clearly defined idea of whether it is targeting broader social or environmental challenges (e.g. climate change) and/or a defined beneficiary. In the case of a beneficiary, it must be specified who the beneficiaries are (e.g. underprivileged youth, individuals with disabilities or rough sleepers), their psychographic (e.g. attitudes, beliefs, values, interests and lifestyle choices) and demographic (e.g. age, gender, ethnicity, income, education and occupation) characteristics, and the challenges they face. As we explored in Chapter 5, the outdoor clothing company **Patagonia** demonstrates this by having a clear environmental mission, which is to reduce greenhouse gas emissions. Patagonia produces all of its clothing lines using recycled materials and stimulates awareness among customers relating to product maintenance, repair, reuse, resale and disposal.

- **What do we do?** This describes the specific interventions the SEO is intending to implement to address the identified social problem. The interventions must be clearly defined to ensure that the intention to create social value is translated into tangible, specific actions. For example, **d.light**, a social enterprise that offers solar panels and solar-powered lighting systems to off-the-grid rural communities in Africa, demonstrates not only a profound understanding of its beneficiaries – those who live in rural communities and lack access to reliable and affordable electricity – but translates the intention to create social value into the specific tangible actions of enabling underserved communities to attend school, facilitate their learning and communication, and provide them with devices that open up access to the digital world.
- **How do we do it?** Here the focus is on explaining how the SEO balances the creation of social value with commercial value. It should communicate how the products and services generate financial sustainability to then create value for beneficiaries (Dacin et al, 2010; Mair and Martí, 2006). The **Aravind Eye Hospital** in India, for example, provides free eyecare and surgery to 50 per cent of its patients using their *free* hospital while generating revenues from the *main* hospital that operates like a standard hospital with paying patients. The cross-subsidization approach ensures the hospital remains financially sustainable while making eyecare accessible to those in need.
- **What value do we create?** The final component outlines the social value created resulting from the proposed solution. While commercial activities are important, the SEO must demonstrate the positive benefits (both tangible and intangible) for beneficiaries as well as the broader social or environmental outcomes. For instance, **Divine Chocolate**, a Fairtrade chocolate brand which is co-owned by cocoa farmers in Ghana, creates social value for farmers by empowering them through fair prices, better trading terms, and sustainable practices. On the broader level, Divine Chocolate addresses the underlying issues of low income and poor working conditions in the chocolate industry.

In the following box, we provide further guidance on how to assess the identified SEO.

## SOCIAL OPPORTUNITY IDENTIFICATION

When identifying an SEO, it is important to evaluate how well it will address the identified problem for the target beneficiaries. Hence, this process is not just about the opportunity but also about ensuring that the solution is both needed and impactful. In the context of addressing a particular unmet social or environmental need you have identified, review the following reflective prompts:

- **Revisit the earlier section** and reflect on what drives your SEIs. Do they stem from feelings of empathy, altruism, compassion, personal values or others?
- **Identify** whether you prefer addressing a social or an environmental problem you have personally experienced, a local need in the community in which you are embedded, or whether you are motivated by broader social challenges you see in your everyday life.
- **Define your goals:** Begin by clearly stating the goals of the SEO you have identified and what you aim to address. This will help you clarify your vision and set clear impact objectives.
- **Broaden your horizons:** To fully understand the broader outcomes of your SEO, look beyond your immediate beneficiaries – that is, explore who else is offering a similar solution to yours, i.e. your competitors. Identify what their strengths and weaknesses are and how your solution differs.
- **Revisit the earlier section** and consider which social networks you can draw upon to support the development of the identified opportunity; assess their relevance to your social mission and how they can contribute.
- Finally, **identify how you will refine your proposed solution** to effectively create social value – both for the identified beneficiaries and the broader social or environmental outcomes.

In summary, the identification of an SEO is shaped by a range of factors. While some social entrepreneurs identify a SEO within the community in which they are embedded, others may be driven by a social problem they have personally experienced or by antecedents such as ethical fibre and moral judgement that inform their SEIs. Regardless of these motivations, identifying an SEO is an iterative and a dynamic process. It starts with *ideation*, where social entrepreneurs identify a range of social problems they aim to address. This is followed by *experimentation* where they engage with their stakeholder groups to seek feedback and assess the feasibility of the SEO. Finally, *refinement* involves social entrepreneurs clearly defining their social objectives (*why do we exist?*), the specific intervention they intend to implement (*what do we do?*), how they will balance social and commercial objectives (*how do we do it?*) and the overall social value they aim to create (*what value do we create?*). The next step involves developing the SVP, which needs to align the needs of three interrelated but distinct groups: beneficiaries, customers and the broader social outcomes.

# Social value proposition

The concept of value proposition (VP) has attracted significant attention in entrepreneurship literature, perceived as one of the core pillars in defining a business model and a key element for value creation (Budler et al, 2021; Zott et al, 2011; Wirtz et al, 2016). The VP often has dual roles: 1) it communicates the value created to customers and 2) articulates how the products or services offered to customers generate better value than those of competitors. This can be achieved through a range of attributes such as quality, convenience, reliability, usability, design or simply exceptional customer service (Mousavi and Aghdaie, 2021).

Osterwalder et al, (2014) introduced the Value Proposition Canvas as a practical tool to identify the 'jobs, pains, and gains' of potential customers. According to this tool, a well-designed VP should demonstrate an understanding of customers' needs, identify their pain points and the jobs to be done (i.e. what tasks they want to achieve in their daily lives), and clearly articulate the benefits of the proposed solution. Hence, the VP should explicitly address the following: *who* is the target customer? *What* is being offered? *How* is the value delivered? And *why* is a value proposition sustainable in terms of revenue generation? (Gassmann et al, 2020).

While most of the literature recognizes the central role of designing a VP that creates value for customers (Baldassarre et al, 2017), the majority of this research has centred on for-profit business models, where value is often assessed in financial terms. In SEs' context, however, value creation comprises not just the financial – customers – but also the social – beneficiaries – as well as broader social or environmental outcomes (Austin et al, 2006; Perrini et al, 2010). Thus, an SVP seeks not only to communicate the value of the product to customers but also to communicate the value of the social mission, the way in which the SE provides value for the beneficiaries, and the broader societal impact it aims to make while differentiating from 'competitors'.

## *Components of the social value proposition*

As noted in Table 8.1, an SVP should answer the following key questions: *who* the beneficiaries are and what value it offers them – that is, the types of interventions (the social side); *who* the customers are to generate value (the trading side); and *what* broader social or environmental outcomes are created.

## *Defining the social value proposition*

Just as Osterwalder et al, (2014) introduced the VP Canvas for for-profit enterprises, we propose the SVP Canvas for SEs. This canvas should not only focus on the needs

**Table 8.1** Components of the social value proposition

| Descriptions | Questions to ask |
|---|---|
| **Beneficiaries** | • To which beneficiaries (demographic/geographic/psychographic) is the social enterprise offering this value?<br>• What set of interventions is the social enterprise performing to offer this value? |
| **Customers** | • To which customers (demographics/geographic/psychographic) is the social enterprise offering this value?<br>• What are the products and services offered? |
| **Social outcomes** | • How does social enterprise create broader social or environmental outcomes?<br>• How does it sustain social impact? |

of customers and the ways in which the proposed solution can best generate revenue but should also modify and extend the proposition to include all three quadrants relevant to a social enterprise:

1 **beneficiaries** and how they intersect with the customers and the broader social outcomes generated
2 **customers** engaged in commercial transactions with the social enterprise and how they intersect with the beneficiaries and broader social outcomes
3 the **broader social outcomes** and how they align with the beneficiaries and customers

## *Interplay between beneficiaries and social outcomes*

We define beneficiaries as those targeted individuals, groups or communities whom the social mission of the social enterprise is supporting and for whom social value is created (Ebrahim et al, 2014). Social entrepreneurship literature has distinguished between social entrepreneurs who focus on addressing small-scale local needs and those who focus on the broader social systems (Zahra et al, 2009). This distinction demonstrates the decision social entrepreneurs need to make within their SVP since they need to choose whether to create social value at large or focus on a defined and specific group of beneficiaries (Battilana and Lee, 2014).

In this quadrant of the SVP, we propose that social entrepreneurs identify who they aim to generate value for (e.g. disabled individuals, impoverished communities, refugees or women in indigenous communities) and the types of interventions they offer to address the needs of their beneficiaries (access to healthcare, education and support networks). Meanwhile, they need to identify how the social value created for the targeted beneficiaries overlaps with the broader social outcomes created. For

**Figure 8.6** Social Value Proposition Canvas

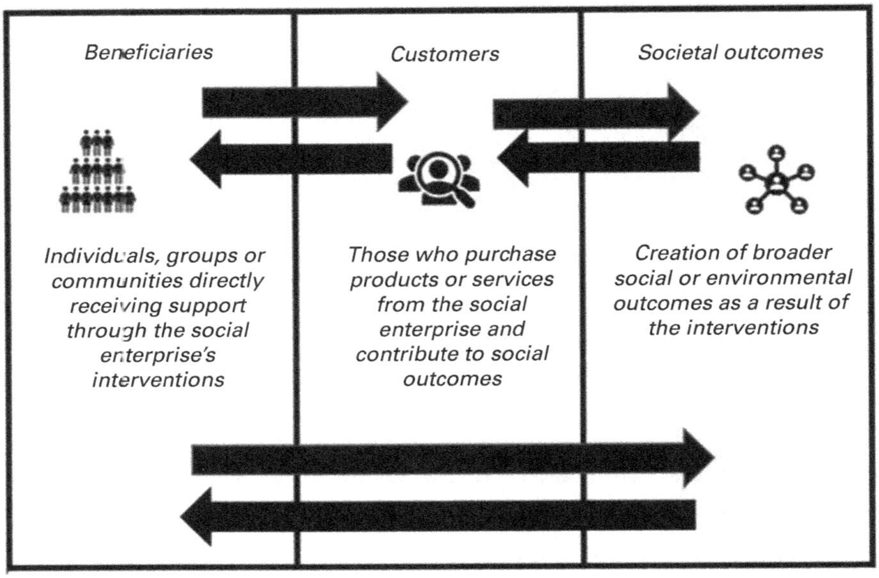


instance, **Evenbreak**, a UK-based social enterprise, supports disabled individuals to find work with inclusive employers through an online jobs board and career support services. Evenbreak creates direct social value for disabled individuals by integrating them in the workplace. However, their social value extends beyond the immediate beneficiaries to the broader social outcomes, which include raising awareness of inclusive practices in the workplace, reducing workplace discrimination and closing the disability employment gap.

## *Interplay between customers and social outcomes*

In this quadrant, SEs' commercial activities serve a dual purpose: to generate revenue and achieve the social mission. We define customers as those engaged in the commercial activity (i.e. the trading side) of the social enterprise by purchasing products and services, and thus this quadrant represents customers who are not only essential to generate revenue but also contribute to the achievement of the social enterprise's social mission, both towards the beneficiaries and its broader societal impact (Seelos and Mair, 2005). As will be explored in Chapter 9, in the SE context, customers may overlap with beneficiaries or may be a separate group whose purchases support a social enterprise's social mission. Research shows that commercial and social value are often created simultaneously in SEs' context (Mair and Schoen, 2007), but that SEs prioritize their social or environmental mission over profits. Take for instance **TOMS** shoes (see Chapter 3), a US-based social enterprise, known for their *one-for-one* business model. TOMS' social mission is to lift children in need out of poverty by donating a shoe to a poor child for free for every shoe they sell. Customers contribute to TOMS' social mission, as for every shoe they buy, they create social value for a child in need, thereby contributing to broader social outcomes such as improving children's health and access to education.

## *Interplay between beneficiaries, customers and social outcomes*

We define social outcomes as the broader social or environmental impacts created by SEs. As discussed in Chapter 6, social impact is often viewed as a process of generating positive change by addressing social or environmental challenges. SEs address unmet social needs and play a pivotal role in driving economic growth, alleviating poverty and creating sustainable development (Battilana and Lee, 2014). In this instance, this quadrant represents the ideal scenario where the needs of three interrelated but distinct groups are met: **beneficiaries**, **customers** and **society** at large. SEs meet their social mission by directly addressing beneficiaries' needs. To do so, they generate revenues by selling products or services to customers whose purchasing decisions support their social mission. By balancing social and commercial objectives, SEs create broader social outcomes, such as alleviating poverty, reducing economic inequality, improving social justice and contributing to environmental sustainability.

In the next box, we demonstrate how the **Big Issue** manages this balance by creating value for those experiencing rough sleeping, customers through ethical and social trading, and the broader social outcomes.

### A WORKED EXAMPLE: THE BIG ISSUE

The Big Issue is a social enterprise founded in 1991 by John Bird and Gordon Roddick in response to the systemic problem of rough sleeping that is impacting human populations worldwide. According to the United Nations (2025), approximately 1.6 billion people globally in 2020 lived in inadequate housing, and more than 100 million people had no housing at all. Rough sleeping is widely recognized as a complex issue to solve because the root cause of the problem is interconnected with multiple social inequalities such as unemployment, lack of affordable housing, lack of mental health and addiction services, racial inequality, domestic violence and systemic policy failures (Human Rights Careers, 2021). Rough sleeping therefore poses an ongoing public health threat affecting the global population.

As explored in this chapter, an SVP is built on creating social value for three interconnected but distinct groups: beneficiaries, customers and the broader social outcomes. The founders of the Big Issue responded to the systemic issue of rough sleeping by developing a novel approach aimed at empowering those affected, structuring their social business model around the three pillars of an SVP (Figure 8.7):

- **Beneficiaries:** According to the United Nations (2025), rough sleeping contributes to a variety of complex social issues, such as poor health, premature and preventable deaths, criminalization and violence, and discrimination on the basis of lack of official address, affecting the political, economic and social rights of rough sleepers in aspects such as voting rights, access to employment and certain social benefits. The Big Issue aims to solve these problems by offering rough sleepers (i.e. beneficiaries) the opportunity to earn a legitimate income. Rough sleepers can purchase copies of the *Big Issue* magazine at a discounted price (£2) and sell them to the public for £4, keeping the profit for themselves. This 'help people help themselves model' fosters financial independence and self-reliance among rough sleepers. As reported in their Impact Report (2022), the Big Issue supported 3,637 vendors in that year, who collectively earned £3.67 million in income. The money from the discounted magazine sales was reinvested back into providing additional support services such as digital inclusion, cashless payment solutions, skills training, employment support and the production and distribution of the magazine across the UK and worldwide.

**Figure 8.7** The Big Issue Social Value Proposition Canvas

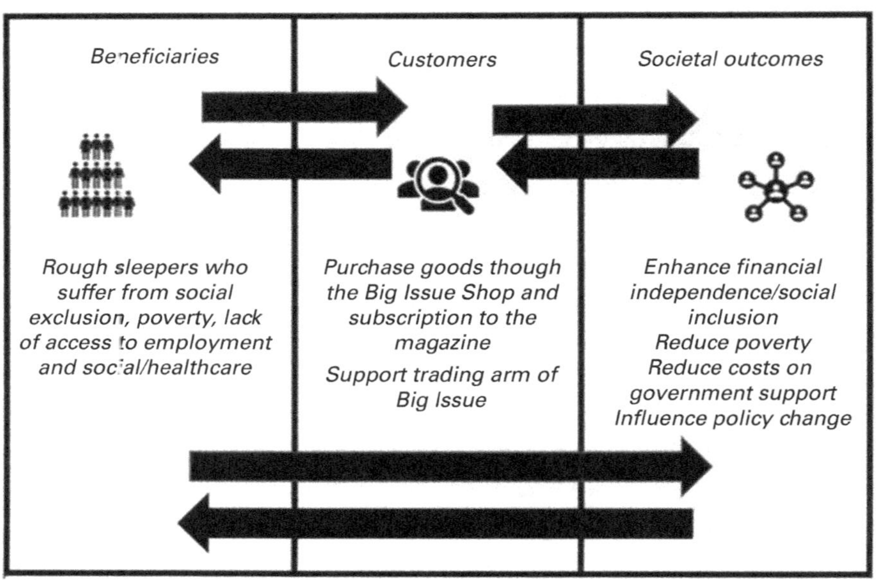

- **Customers:** While their main source of income comes directly from vendors' sales, the Big Issue also promotes social and ethical shopping through the Big Issue Shop – an online shopping platform that sells a range of ethical products and brands – and through subscriptions to the *Big Issue* magazine. Customers therefore play a key role in supporting their social mission by generating income. Their Impact Report (2022) highlights that approximately 3,189 customers made purchases through the Big Issue Shop, and 5,813 subscribed to the magazine. These purchases enabled them to reinvest revenues to support vendors and other social enterprise initiatives. The Big Issue Invest, an investment arm of the Big Issue, supports other SEs, charities and profit-with-purpose organizations to create social change. As of 2021, Big Issue Invest has supported 184 SEs and charities with approximately £40 million in investments and grants.
- **Social outcomes:** Based on the philosophy of 'self-help', the Big Issue supports rough sleepers to regain control of their lives and improve their financial independence and social inclusion. Beyond income generation, they contribute to broader social outcomes by facilitating access to skills training and moving rough sleepers off the streets into a home or a job training. The Big Issue Foundation, for instance, offers a range of services such as housing and resettlement support, training and education (e.g. computer skills), and services for drug or alcohol use. These support services help address systemic issues such as poverty, social inequality and discrimination. Furthermore, through their 'Big Futures' campaign, the Big Issue influences policy change in three key areas: housing, low wages and green jobs (Big Issue Impact Report, 2022).

## Summary and key learning points

In this chapter, we began by examining the conceptual debates related to social entrepreneurship. Although the term still suffers from a lack of a universal definition, it is commonly associated with addressing social and environmental problems through innovative approaches. We then explored the role social entrepreneurs play in the social entrepreneurial process. While many are driven by their social mission, others are influenced by antecedents or prior experience with the social problem. Next, we discussed the challenges of mission drift due to the tensions of social and business objectives. Since SEOs cannot be realized without the action of the social entrepreneur, we explored three stages of engaging with these opportunities: idea generation, experimentation and refinement. Finally, we examined the key components of an SVP that align the needs of beneficiaries, customers and the broader social and environmental outcomes.

The key takeaways are the following:

- Social entrepreneurship is broadly understood as a novel approach that addresses social and environmental problems.
- Unlike profit-driven entrepreneurs, social entrepreneurs are driven by their social mission over profit maximization.
- Due to the dual logics of social and business, social entrepreneurs can face tensions in reconciling them to create social value.
- Social entrepreneurs differ in how they discover SEOs, define their social mission and mobilize resources to act on these.
- Identification of SEOs is shaped by a range of factors, such as antecedents and prior experience with the social problem that influence how social entrepreneurs act upon these opportunities.
- Identifying SEOs often involves three stages: ideation (generating a number of solutions to the social problem), experimentation (gathering knowledge and resources) and refinement (creating meaningful social impact).
- Building a compelling SVP requires the alignment of three intersecting but distinct groups: beneficiaries (on whom the social mission is built), customers (who support the generation of revenues through their purchasing transactions) and the broader social or environmental outcomes – that is, generating positive social change.

## REAL-WORLD EXAMPLE INDICATIVE ANSWERS

1 What specific social problems did Oakleaf Enterprise identify in the local community which led to its foundation?

**Indicative answer**: Initially, you may want to watch the following video, https://www.youtube.com/watch?v=4g8OOAY01zw, which illustrates the specific social problem it addresses, namely mental health.

Oakleaf Enterprise was founded in response to mental health issues individuals face in the local community of Guildford. They sought to solve this problem through a range of tailored support services like well-being activities, pathways to work programmes, skills development in IT and gardening services, counselling services, and the Guildford Safe Haven to support those experiencing mental health crises. This demonstrates that Oakleaf Enterprise emerged from the recognition that those with mental health conditions are more often marginalized from mainstream society and face challenges including stigma, discrimination in the workplace, limited access to adequate care and difficulties in accessing social support and employment. Oakleaf Enterprise solves this problem by enabling clients to rebuild their lives, build their confidence, gain skills and engage in meaningful activities to integrate them into society.

2 How does Oakleaf Enterprise's social business model differ from charitable business models, and what are the advantages of embedding a social enterprise?

**Indicative answer:** Oakleaf Enterprise operates as a charitable business model to financially support its activities and deliver on its social mission – supporting those with mental health conditions. The charity relies on a variety of voluntary donation funding sources, including trusts and foundations, individuals, businesses, community groups and events. However, the charity also built a social enterprise business model to generate income through trading its gardening services. The beneficiaries actively participate in these activities as part of their training, which enables the charity to empower them and reintegrate them back into society. The business model of Oakleaf Enterprise aims for financial sustainability through a mix of donations and trading to achieve its social mission.

3 Using the SVP Canvas, who are the key beneficiaries of Oakleaf Enterprise? And how are their needs balanced with customers and the broader social outcomes?

**Indicative answer:** To explore Oakleaf Enterprise's social value proposition, revisit the example and **first** identify their key beneficiaries. Oakleaf Enterprise serves the needs of those with mental health conditions – that is, their beneficiaries, who are often socially marginalized and face a number of systemic barriers such as limited access to employment, social support and healthcare. Oakleaf Enterprise creates social value by addressing beneficiaries' needs through a range of interventions like well-being activities, pathway to work programmes, upskilling in IT and gardening, counselling services and a Safe Haven programme accessible for those experiencing mental health crises.

**Second**, identify their customer segment and their role within the social business model. While the charity generates most of its income from philanthropic sources such as donations from trusts and foundations, individual and business donors, and community groups and events, it also operates a social enterprise model by delivering services to paying customers (individuals or businesses). These customers help subsidise its training and well-being and employability programmes. In this regard, customers support the charity's broader social mission, which interplays with the broader social outcomes they create. As indicated in the Oakleaf Enterprise impact report, approximately 1,374 of their clients attended IT and gardening training courses, and 194 were supported by the Pathway to Work employment project, where a large number of their clients resumed volunteering roles, gained qualifications and found full- or part-time employment.

**Third**, identify the broader social outcomes generated by Oakleaf Enterprise. According to the World Health Organization (2022), poor mental health affects approximately 970 million people around the world and represents a significant global social challenge that impacts individuals, families, communities and the economy. While prevention and treatment options exist through traditional providers such as voluntary organizations and public health services, most people with mental health disorders do not have access to care. Oakleaf Enterprise addresses this gap by offering targeted interventions to improve clients' mental well-being, social inclusion and skills development. The tangible, broader social outcomes can be summarized as follows:

- **Improved well-being:** Effective mental health interventions can lead to improved well-being for those affected, and increased confidence and resilience.
- **Increased social participation:** Facilitate access to employment and upskilling opportunities (e.g. gardening/IT skills) to reduce barriers to social inclusion.
- **Reduced health inequalities**: Mental health care and support services accessible regardless of socio-economic background, which addresses disparity in mental healthcare.
- **Positive economic impact:** Improved mental health can lead to increased labour market productivity and lower demand on public healthcare providers, contributing to a more economically active workforce.

## CALL TO ACTION

We explored thus far the importance of building an SVP that aligns the needs of beneficiaries, customers and broader social outcomes. In this group activity, you are to develop a pitch deck to potential investors to demonstrate the components of your SVP when addressing the issue of food waste going to landfill.

In groups of two to four, follow the steps below:

- Clearly state **what problem** you are addressing: the issue of food waste going to landfill and why this is worth tackling.
- **Revisit the earlier section** and explain the type of research you conducted to understand the problem you have identified. It is a good practice to provide data to demonstrate the impact of food waste on the environment (e.g. greenhouse gas emissions).
- **Describe your solution** – this should articulate what the solution is and how well it addresses the problem identified.
- **Populate the SVP Canvas introduced in this chapter** and clearly articulate how your solution will meet the needs of beneficiaries (in this case, the environment), customers (your trading arm) and the broader social outcomes.

**USEFUL LINKS**

YouTube video: Reframing the problem: seeking social innovations by Shawn Smith: https://www.youtube.com/watch?v=u3Cc2QFVRJk

Schwab Foundation for social entrepreneurship: https://www.schwabfound.org/home

Forbes: How technology is being used for social good: https://www.forbes.com/councils/forbestechcouncil/2022/12/06/how-technology-is-being-used-for-social-good/

## References


Armstrong, R M and Grobbelaar, S S S (2023) Sustainable business models for social enterprises in developing countries: A conceptual framework *Management Review Quarterly*, 73(2): 787–40

Augsburg, B and Fouillet, C (2010) Profit empowerment: The microfinance institution's mission drift, *Perspectives on Global Development and Technology*, 9: 327–55

Austin, J, Stevenson, H and Wei-Skillern, J (2006) Social and commercial entrepreneurship: Same, different, or both? *Entrepreneurship: Theory & Practice*, 30: 1–22

Awaworyi, C S and Mishra, V (2017) Trust, social networks and subjective wellbeing in China, *Social Indicators Research*, 132(1): 313–39

Bacq, S and Alt, E (2018) Feeling capable and valued: A prosocial perspective on the link between empathy and social entrepreneurial intentions, *Journal of Business Venturing*, 33(3): 333–50

Bacq, S and Eddleston, KA (2018) A resource-based view of social entrepreneurship: how stewardship culture benefits scale of social impact, *Journal of Business Ethics*, 152: 589–611

Baldassarre, B, Calabretta, G, Bocken, NMP and Jaskiewicz, T (2017) Bridging sustainable business model innovation and user-driven innovation: A process for sustainable value proposition design, *Journal of Clean Production*, 147: 175–186

Bandura, A (2000) Exercise of Human Agency Through Collective Efficacy, *Current Directions in Psychological Science*, 9(75): 75–78

Bandura, A (2006) Toward a psychology of human agency, *Association for Psychological Science*, 1(2): 164–80

Baron, R A (2007) Behavioral and cognitive factors in entrepreneurship: Entrepreneurs as the active element in new venture creation, *Strategic Entrepreneurship Journal*, 1(1-2): 167–82

Battilana, J and Dorado, S ( 2010) Building sustainable hybrid organizations: The Case of commercial microfinance organizations, *Academy of Management Journal*, 53 (6): 1419–40

Battilana, J and Lee, M (2014) Advancing research on hybrid organizing – insights from the study of social enterprises, *Academy of Management Annals*, 8: 397–441

Begley, T M and Boyd, D P (1987) Psychological characteristics associated with performance in entrepreneurial firms and smaller businesses, *Journal of Business Venturing*, 2: 79–83

Big Issue Impact Report (2022) https://www.bigissue.com/wp-content/uploads/2023/05/BIGroup_Imapct-report_EXEC-SUMMARY_v2.pdf (archived at https://perma.cc/NQ8E-MXK5)

Brockhaus, R H Sr. (1980). Risk taking propensity of entrepreneurs, *Academy of Management*, 23(3): 509-520.

Brown, T (2016) Why social innovators need design thinking, *Stanford Social Innovation Review,* https://ssir.org/articles/entry/why_social_innovators_need_design_thinking# (archived at https://perma.cc/396H-F9HJ)

Budler, M, Zupič, I and Trkman, P (2021) The development of business model research: A bibliometric review, *Journal of Business Research*, 135: 480–95

Busenitz, L W, Gomez, C and Spencer, J W (2000) Country institutional profiles: Unlocking entrepreneurial phenomena, *Academy of Management Journal*, 43(5): 994–1003

Busenitz, L W and Lau, CM (1996) A cross-cultural cognitive model of new venture creation, *Entrepreneurship Theory and Practice*, 20(4): 25–40

Cagarman, K, Kratzer, J, von Arnim, L H, Fajga, K and Gieseke, M J (2020) Social entrepreneurship on its way to significance: The case of Germany, *Sustainability*, 12(21): 8954

Calò, F, Teasdale, S, Donaldson, C, Roy, M J and Baglioni, S (2018) Collaborator or competitor: Assessing the evidence supporting the role of social enterprise in health and social care, *Public Management Review*, 20(12), 1790–814

Casson, M and Yeung, B (2006) *Oxford Handbook of Entrepreneurship*, Oxford: Oxford University

Chell, E (2007) Social enterprise and entrepreneurship: Towards a convergent theory of the entrepreneurial process, *International Small Business Journal*, 25(1): 5–26

Chell, E (2010) Towards researching the 'opportunistic entrepreneur': A social constructionist approach and research agenda, *European Journal of Work and Organizational Psychology*, 9(1): 63–80

Corner, P D and Marcus, H (2010) How opportunities develop in social entrepreneurship, *Entrepreneurship, Theory and Practice*, 34(4): 635–59

Cornforth, C (2014) Understanding and combating mission drift in social enterprises, *Social Enterprise Journal*, 10(1): 3–20

Cunningham, J B and Lischeron, J (1991) Defining Entrepreneurship, *Journal of Small Business Management*, 29(1): 45–61

Dacin, P A, Dacin, M T and Matear, M (2010) Social entrepreneurship: Why we don't need a new theory and how we move forward from here, *Academy of Management Perspectives*, 24(3): 37–57

Dees, J G (2001) *The Meaning of 'Social Entrepreneurship'* Centre for the Advancement of Social Entreprreneurship, https://web.stanford.edu/class/e145/2007_fall/materials/dees_SE.pdf (archived at https://perma.cc/E4XC-XG7S)

Defourny, J and Nyssens, M (2006) Defining social enterprise. In M Nyssens (ed), *Social Enterprise: At the crossroads of market, public policies and civil society* (pp 3–26) Routledge

D'Espallier, B, Hudon, M and Szafarz, A (2016) Aid volatility and social performance in microfinance, *Nonprofit and Voluntary Sector Quarterly*, 46: 116–40

Di Domenico, M L, Tracey, P and Haugh, H (2010) Social bricolage: Theorizing social value creation in social enterprises, *Entrepreneurship Theory and Practice*, 34 (4): 681–703

Douglas, E and Prentice, C (2019) Innovation and profit motivations for social entrepreneurship: A fuzzy-set analysis, *Journal of Business Research*, 99: 69–79

Douglas, E J, Shepherd D and Venugopal, V (2021) A multi-motivational general model of entrepreneurial intention, *Journal of Business Venturing*, 36(4): 106–07

Ebrahim, A, Battilana, J and Mair, J (2014) The governance of social enterprises: Mission drift and accountability challenges in hybrid organizations, *Research in Organizational Behavior*, 34: 81–100

Ernst, D K (2011) *Heart over Mind: An empirical analysis of social entrepreneurial intention formation on the basis of the theory of planned behaviour*, Doctoral Dissertation Wuppertal Germany: University of Wuppertal

Farmer, J, De Cotta, T, McKinnon, K, Barraket, J, Munoz, S-A and Douglas, H (2016) Social enterprise and wellbeing in community life, *Social Enterprise Journal*, 12(2): 235–54

Fisher, K E and Julien, H (2009) Information behaviour, *Annual Review of Information Science and Technology*, 43(1): 1–73

Gartner, W B (1990) What are we talking about when we talk about entrepreneurship? *Journal of Business Venturing*, 5: 15–28

Gassmann, O, Frankenberger, K, Choudury, M and Csik, M (2020) *Business Model Navigator: The strategies behind the most successful organizations,* London: FT Publishing

Hafeez, K, Alghatas, F M, Foroudi, P, Nguyen, B and Gupta, S (2018). Knowledge sharing by entrepreneurs in a virtual community of practice (VCoP), *Information Technology and People*, 32(2): 405–29

Hagedoorn, J (1996) Innovation and entrepreneurship: Schumpeter revisited, *Industrial and Corporate Change,* 5(3): 883–96

Haugh, H (2007) Community–led social venture creation, *Entrepreneurship Theory and Practice*, 31(2): 161–82

Helliwell, J F and Putnam, R D (2004) The social context of well-being, *Philosophical Transactions of the Royal Society of London Series B: Biological Sciences*, 359(1449): 1435–446

Hockerts, K (2017) Determinants of social entrepreneurial intentions, *Entrepreneurship Theory and Practice*,1: 105–30

Human Rights Careers (2021) Ten Facts about Homelessness, https://www.humanrightscareers.com/issues/10-facts-about-homelessness/ (archived at https://perma.cc/Z9SU-9R5G)

Ibrahim, S, Marcella, R and MacLennan, A (2022) Indicative findings from a study of information behaviour in digital business ideation: Insights from the developing world, *IR Information Research*, 26(2), https://doi.org/10.47989/irisic2233 (archived at https://perma.cc/V4Q8-F6X6)

IDEO, (2016) Our approach: design thinking, https://designthinking.ideo.com/ (archived at https://perma.cc/EVP7-FJZA)

Ip, C Y, Liang C and Lai, H J (2021) Determinants of social entrepreneurial intention: An alternative model based on social cognitive career theory, *Nonprofit Management and Leadership*, 31(4): 737–60

Jack, S L and Anderson, A R ( 2002) The effects of embeddedness on the entrepreneurial process, *Journal of Business Venturing*, 17(5): 467–87

Jayawarna, D, Jones, O and Macpherson, A (2020) Resourcing social enterprises: The role of socially oriented bootstrapping, *British Journal of Management*, 31: 56–79

Kamaludin, M F (2023) Social sustainability within social entrepreneurship, *Technological Forecasting and Social Change*, 192: 122541

Kirzner, I (1979) *Perception, Opportunity and Profit,* Chicago: University of Chicago Press

Kraatz, M S and Block, E S (2008) Organizational implications of institutional pluralism, *The Sage Handbook of Organizational Institutionalism*, 840: 243–75

Lackéus, M (2018) What is value? A framework for analyzing and facilitating entrepreneurial value creation, *Uniped*, 41 (1): 10–28

Levi-Strauss, C (1966) *The Savage Mind*, London: Weidenfeld and Nicolson

Lockwood, T (2010) *Design Thinking*, NY: Alloworth Press

Low, M B and MacMillan, I C (1988) Entrepreneurship: Past research and future challenges, *Journal of Management*, 14(2): 139–61

Machlup, F (1980) *Knowledge and Knowledge Production*, Princeton: Princeton University Press

Mader, P (2013) Rise and fall of microfinance in India: The Andhra Pradesh crisis in perspective, *Strategic Change*, 22: 47–66

Mair, J and Noboa, E (2006) Social entrepreneurship: How intentions to create a social venture are formed. In: Mair, J, Robinson, J and Hockerts, K (eds) *Social Entrepreneurship*, London, UK: Palgrave Macmillan, pp. 121–135

Mair, J and Martí, I (2006) Social entrepreneurship research: A source of explanation, prediction, and delight, *Journal of World Business*, 41: 36–44

Mair, J and Schoen, O (2007) Successful social entrepreneurial business models in the context of developing economies: An explorative study, *International Journal of Emerging Markets*, 2: 54–68

Massetti, B L (2008) The social entrepreneurship matrix as a 'tipping point' for economic change, The First International Conference on Social Entrepreneurship, Systems Thinking, and Complexity USA: Adelphi University, April 24–26

McClelland, D C (1965) N achievement and entrepreneurship: A longitudinal study, *Journal of Personality and Social Psychology*, 1: 389–92

McDonald, R M and Eisenhardt, K M (2020) Parallel play: Startups, nascent markets, and effective business-model design, *Administrative Science Quarterly*, 65: 483–523

Mousavi, S M and Aghdaie, A S F (2021) Identifying the constructive elements of 'value proposition' and their impact on customers' satisfaction using sentiment analysis based on text mining, *Journal of Business Management*, 12(4): 1092–116

Munoz, S A, Farmer, J, Winterton, R and Barraket, J (2015) The social enterprise as a space of wellbeing: An exploratory case study, *Social Enterprise Journal*, 11(3): 281–302

Nambisan, S (2017) Digital entrepreneurship: Toward a digital technology perspective of entrepreneurship, *Entrepreneurship Theory and Practice*, 41(6): 1029–055

Nicholls, A and Cho, A H (2006) Social entrepreneurship: The structuration of a field. In *Social Entrepreneurship: New models of sustainable social change* (pp 99–118) Oxford: University Press

Osterwalder, A, Pigneur, Y, Bernarda, G, Smith, A and Papadakos, T (2014) *Value Proposition Design: How to create products and services customers want*, UK: Wiley

Ozgen, E and Baron, R A (2007) Social sources of information in opportunity recognition: Effects of mentors, industry networks, and professional forums, *Journal of Business Venturing*, 22(2): 174–92

Pansera, M and Sarkar, S (2016) Crafting sustainable development solutions: Frugal innovations of grassroots entrepreneurs, *Sustainability*, 8 (51): 1–25

Peredo, A M and McLean, M (2006) Social entrepreneurship: A critical review of the concept, *Journal of World Business*, 41(1): 56–65

Perrini, F, Vurro, C and Costanzo, L A (2010) A process-based view of social entrepreneurship: From opportunity identification to scaling-up social change in the case of San Patrignano, *Entrepreneurship and Regional Development*, 22(6): 515–34

Raiden, A B, Raiden, M, Loosemore, A and King, C G (2019) *Social Value in Construction*, Abingdon: Taylor and Francis

Ries, E (2011) *The Lean Startup: How today's entrepreneurs use continuous innovation to create radically successful businesses*, New York, NY: Crown Publishing Group

Roger, L M and Osberg, S (2015) *Getting Beyond Better: How social entrepreneurship works*, Massachusetts: Harvard Business Review Press

Sarason, Y, Dean, T and Dillard, JF (2006) Entrepreneurship as the nexus of individual and opportunity: A structuration view, *Journal of Business Venturing*, 21 (3): 286-305

Sarason, Y, Dillard, J F and Dean, T (2010) How can we know the dancer from the dance? Reply to 'Entrepreneurship as the structuration of individual and opportunity: A response using a critical realist perspective' (Mole and Mole, 2008), *Journal of Business Venturing*, 25(2): 238–43

Saunders, M N K, Lewis, P and Thornhill, A (2023) *Research Methods for Business Students*, 9th edition Harlow, UK: Pearson

Scarlato, M (2013) Social enterprise, capabilities and development paradigms: Lessons from Ecuador, *The Journal of Development Studies*, 49(9): 1270–283

Schaltegger, S, Beckmann, M and Hockerts, K (2018) Collaborative entrepreneurship for sustainability: Creating solutions in light of the UN sustainable development goals, *International Journal of Entrepreneurial Venturing*, 10(2): 131–52

Schultz, T W (1975) The value of the ability to deal with disequilibria, *Journal of Economic Literature*, 13: 827–46

Schumpeter, J A (1947) *Capitalism, Socialism and Democracy*, 2nd ed, New York: Harper and Bros

Scott, W (1995) *Institutions and Organizations*, Thousand Oaks, CA: Sage

Seelos, C and Mair, J (2005) Social entrepreneurship: Creating new business models to serve the poor, *Business Horizons*, 48(3): 241–46

Sevak, K Y and Baker, LT (2014) An interactionist approach to entrepreneurial opportunity: Combining discovery and creation theory, *Academy of Management Proceedings*, Academy of Management, Briarcliff Manor (p 13159)

Shane, S and Venkataraman, S (2000) The promise of entrepreneurship as a field of research, *The Academy of Management Review*, 25(1): 217–26

Shaw, E and Carter, S (2007) Social entrepreneurship: Theoretical antecedents and empirical analysis of entrepreneurial processes and outcomes, *Journal of Small Business and Enterprise Development*, 14(3): 418–34

Szreter, S and Woolcock, M (2004) Health by association? Social capital, social theory, and the political economy of public health, *International Journal of Epidemiology*, 33(4): 650–67

Tiku, N (2008) Do-gooder finance: How a new crop of investors is helping social entrepreneurs, *INC Magazine* (February) 29–30

Tomlins, R (2015) Uncaging Social Value Workshop, Presentation for the Homes and Communities Agency Investment Team, London

United Nations (2025) Everyone included – how to end homelessness, https://www.un.org/tr/desa/everyone-included-%E2%80%93-how-end-homelessness (archived at https://perma.cc/F2E9-DG5Z)

Ursache, M (2019) The problem statement canvas for startups and innovation teams, https://medium.com/disciplined-entrepreneurship/the-problem-statement-canvas-for-startups-and-innovation-teams-663364c1a951 (archived at https://perma.cc/L4HY-R3GB)

Weaver, R L (2018) Re-conceptualizing social value: Applying the capability approach in social enterprise research, *Journal of Social Entrepreneurship*, 9(2): 79–93

Weerawardena, J and Sullivan Mort, G (2006) Investigating social entrepreneurship: A multidimensional model, *Journal of World Business*, 41: 21–35

Weerawardena, J, Sullivan Mort, G and Carnegie, K (2003) Social entrepreneurship: Towards conceptualization, *International Journal of Nonprofit and Voluntary Sector Marketing*, 8(1): 76–88

Wirtz, B W, Pistoia, A, Ullrich, S and Gottel, V (2016) Business models: Origin, development and future research perspectives, *Long Range Planning*, 49(1): 36–54

Wolf, M and Mair, J (2019) Purpose, commitment and coordination around small wins: A proactive approach to governance in integrated hybrid organizations, *VOLUNTAS: International Journal of Voluntary and Nonprofit Organizations*, 30: 535–48

World Health Organization (2022) Mental Health, https://www.who.int/news-room/fact-sheets/detail/mental-health-strengthening-our-response (archived at https://perma.cc/5S69-KZ9M)

Wry, T and Haugh, H (2018) Brace for impact: Uniting our diverse voices through a social impact frame, *Journal of Business Venturing*, 33: 566–74

Wry, T and Zhao, E Y (2018) Taking trade-offs seriously: Examining the contextually contingent relationship between social outreach intensity and financial sustainability in global microfinance, *Organization Science*, 29: 507–28

Zahra, S A, Gedajlovic, E, Neubaum, D O and Shulman, J M (2009) A typology of social entrepreneurs: Motives, search processes and ethical challenges, *Journal of Business Venturing*, 24: 519–32

Zahra, S A, Wright, M and Abdelgawad, S G (2014) Contextualization and the advancement of entrepreneurship research, *International Small Business Journal*, 32(5): 479–500

Zhao, M (2020) Social entrepreneurship for systemic change: The case of Southeast and South Asian countries, *Journal of Asian Public Policy*, 14(2), 225–50

Zott, C, Amit, R and Massa, L (2011) The business model: Recent developments and future research, *Journal of Management*, 37(4): 1019–042

# 09 Social business modelling

SARAH PREEDY

## LEARNING OUTCOMES

By the end of this chapter, you should be able to:

- Describe what is meant by social business modelling.
- Examine some of the differing approaches to social business modelling.
- Critically discuss the balance of a socially and economically focused business model.
- Examine practical social business modelling tools with a specific focus on the Triple-Layered Business Model Canvas.
- Reflect on the practicalities of social business modelling approaches.
- Apply social business modelling considerations to a proposed business idea.

## REAL-WORLD EXAMPLE Pollenize – a social enterprise based in Plymouth, UK

Pollenize, a social enterprise founded in 2018, was originally founded to create better access to beekeeping equipment and local honey. However, it has since grown rapidly into a successful, thriving business with a wider aim to conserve the pollinator population (not just bees but also birds, bats, butterflies, moths, flies, beetles and wasps). The business describes its mission as bringing together 'the power of community and science to combat pollinator decline' (Pollenize 'About Us', 2023).

The social enterprise currently operates nine beehive sites (apiaries), which are accessible to the public through a subscription model, thereby further aiding the educational and research aspects of their mission. They have partnered with numerous businesses to help them host beehives at their locations, teach staff beekeeping, provide wildflower seeds and have shares of the honey. Their educational mission is important and includes providing free seed packets to schools across Plymouth through a crowdfunding project called the Seeds for Schools project to educate them regarding the importance of pollination and spread pollinator activity. In 2022, this crowdfunder saw 38,000 seed packets go to 90 schools in Plymouth.

Examples of innovative activity include their pioneering biodiversity tracking tool – Floradex. The Floradex software uses land data to strategically prescribe the next best planting solution for supporting on-site ecosystems. Pollenize feeds the vast amounts of data they gather into cloud-based technology, which uses AI and community experts to identify as many forms of insects and plants as possible. This innovation enables continuous improvements in the biodiversity of land and produces scientific, evidence-based reports.

Their work with Asian hornets is particularly topical. Asian hornets are considered a severe threat to native Western European honeybees. Their presence in non-native environments presents a real danger to crop production: bee-pollinated crops would produce £83 million less per year if the threat posed by this species is not met. They also have a very painful, venomous sting and attack humans if they feel threatened. Pollenize has developed **Hornet AI**, which utilizes automated camera bait stations loaded with AI-powered object detection computer vision models. The device will detect and monitor the presence of Asian hornets. Pollenize is now pursuing how to take the AI model and implement it onto an app to create a more citizen science-based approach and equip the beekeeping community with a mobile bait station, thus creating a mass monitoring approach that could be adopted for incoming challenges around Asian hornets. The outcome of the app is to aid in how government resources are used in the response to this invasive species.

Pollenize also operates an e-commerce site selling products to individuals and businesses, such as seed packets, craft kits, cards and merchandise for the brand. The company is now expanding into the neighbouring county of Cornwall.

Discussion questions (indicative answers at the end of this chapter):

1. What is the value proposition of Pollenize?
2. Plot the activities of Pollenize onto the social layer of the Triple-Layered Business Model Canvas, using their website (https://www.pollenize.org.uk/ (archived at https://perma.cc/7WXX-ZWJB)) to assist you in finding out more information. Are there any elements that were difficult to fill out? Why?
3. What challenges do you think the company faces in balancing revenue generation with their social and environmental aims?
4. With the rapid developments happening in the world of AI, how could Pollenize further expand its business activities?

# Introduction

In this chapter, we will be examining what is meant by a business model and, in particular, what is meant by a social business model. In the past century, the social impact of a business has become increasingly important (Collavo, 2023). Rather than starting up with the sole aim of making as much profit as possible, social enterprises (SEs) often have a strong social focus at their outset, as we have discussed throughout this textbook (Chahine, 2023). Economic considerations are important, but they must always be balanced against social considerations. This has implications for SEs at multiple levels: their structure, governance, and financing (Chahine, 2023; Collavo, 2023). Building an SE is, therefore, not easy. This chapter is designed to help you consider how you might build a socially focused business model of your own.

This chapter is structured as follows: in the next section, we outline a key challenge in social business modelling – the tensions that may exist when balancing a social mission with revenue generation. Then we establish what is meant by a business model and examine some common approaches. We explore why innovation is important in business modelling, and then examine the nuances of social business modelling by looking at some of the important contextual factors that may impact the business modelling process and critically discussing the tensions that may arise when considering social and economic goals for an SE. Following this, we review some of the practical social business modelling tools available, with a specific focus on the Triple-Layered Business Model Canvas (TLBMC). By way of a personal reflection, we encourage you to consider the practicalities when applying social business modelling approaches to an idea of your own. The final section summarizes the key arguments of the chapter and provides key learning points.

Throughout this chapter, we encourage you to consider any SEs you may use in your daily life, for example, those related to the clothes you wear, the food you eat and the way you get to and from work or university. Think carefully about their business models. What are the core features? How is profit balanced with social and/or environmental considerations? What challenges might SEs face? And what opportunities? By continually asking yourself such questions, you will become more comfortable with what a social business model looks like and how to understand its nuances.

# Balancing social mission with revenue generation

Throughout this textbook, we have been exploring the 'hybrid' model of SEs, meaning that they balance their profit considerations with their social mission (Bacq and

Alt, 2018). In this section, we explore the tensions that may exist when balancing a social mission with revenue generation.

As we have discussed in Chapters 1 and 5, traditionally, the primary goal of organizations has been to maximize shareholders' value with environmental and social initiatives moulded to fit their existing goals, to adhere to legislation or to attract consumers (Bansal and Roth, 2000). To achieve truly sustainable business models, this perspective of business modelling needs to be fundamentally transformed, with social and environmental impact at the core rather than the periphery (Stubbs and Cocklin, 2008). Socially focused business models have seen increasing popularity. When businesses prioritize present and future stakeholders, as opposed to shareholders, this means that their objectives consider the long-term impact of operations. This often leads to efforts to reduce their ecological footprint and adopt collaborative rather than purely competitive business strategies. When SEs balance profit generation with positive social and environmental impact, they can be seen to be subscribing to the Alter (2007) view of 'embeddedness'. Embeddedness refers to the level of integration between a social enterprise's social and business activities. Ideally, profit generation and social and environmental benefits are in harmony with one another.

## KEY RESEARCH

Kim Alter (2007) is a pioneer in formulating a typology of SEs. A typology refers to classifying information by types or categories to enable ease of understanding. In her work, she examined numerous SEs to look for commonalities and differences in how they were organized and operated. She found that SEs tended to fall broadly into the following 'types' according to how focused their business model was in relation to their social mission:

- Mission-centric: This is when an SE is created for the sole purpose of advancing a chosen social mission.
- Mission-related: When an SE creates social value, it is equally important to generate economic value to subsidize its social value activities.
- Unrelated to mission: The SE is not intended to advance the mission other than by generating income for its social activities and expenses.

What do you think of these three types? Can you think of any SEs that fit neatly into one of these 'types'? Or is it not always that simple?

Source: Alter, K (2007) *Social Enterprise Typology*, Virtue Ventures LLC, pp. 1–124

Despite the best of intentions, it is possible that SEs can struggle with 'mission drift', whereby they lose sight of their social mission in their efforts to generate revenue (Ebrahim et al, 2014) – first explored in Chapter 1. This is when the SE's core activity (essentially their business model) is misaligned with its intended mission. Mission drift is a phenomenon not specific to SEs but can be particularly problematic for them due to the tensions that can arise between commercial and social away from its original business model. How can a business navigate these tensions?

## Business modelling

Before we can turn our focus to social business modelling, we must ensure we understand what is meant by business modelling. This section outlines the meaning of business modelling, why it is necessary and some of the most common approaches.

There has been an explosion in business model research since the mid-1990s, with a prevailing consensus that business modelling is an approach to explaining how firms do business ( Zott et al, 2011). The concept of value has emerged as core to any business model (Gasparin et al, 2021; Teece, 2010), with successfully articulated business models being ones that clearly describe how an organization creates, delivers and captures value (Osterwalder and Pigneur, 2010). This requires the business to set out what it will *create* (the goods or services), how it will *deliver* those goods or services (reach its customers and/or beneficiaries) and how that value will be *captured* (measured and tangibly realized).

For SEs, the meaning of 'value' is often specific to their social mission and the sector in which they operate. Besides, SEs are required to clearly delineate what value means for their customers versus what it means for their beneficiaries (see the later section for a fuller discussion of customers and beneficiaries). For example, a social enterprise could aim to enrich the educational provision available for children living in poverty. Value is *created* for both customers and beneficiaries: value in the form of premium books or games for customers to purchase and the provision of free or discounted educational books and games for beneficiaries. *Delivery* of value may be through an e-commerce site that customers can easily access, and for beneficiaries, value may also be delivered online or through the physical distribution of books and games, depending on the level of access to the internet that they might have. *Capturing* value for customers might be customer satisfaction scores or reviews, and for beneficiaries, this might be a measurement of the positive impact on literacy rates.

The business model provides the roadmap for taking a business idea to market (Burns, 2020). Essentially, a business model, social or otherwise, describes how it plans to provide for its customers in a manner that is financially sustainable. It is important to understand that the *business idea* and the *business model* are connected but remain different entities. The *model* operationalizes the *idea* and, therefore, can be the reason a good idea may succeed or fail. There is no such thing as a 'best' business model, and numerous variants of business models exist (Zott et al, 2011). Crucially, the model needs to work with the idea and not against it. Although there are established types of business models that can be utilized and built upon, the most appropriate model is one that takes into account the specific circumstances and context of the idea. Common types of business models usually revolve around three key areas of consideration (Burns, 2020), which are discussed in turn below.

## Price

This refers to how low the cost of the product or service will be to customers. This can be a difficult model to sustain due to the challenges of keeping low business costs in order to sustain low selling prices. An example would be the 'value' products seen on the shelves in many supermarkets. These 'value', sometimes called 'basic', items usually have simple packaging and are made with cheaper ingredients than the more luxurious items on the shelves. Supermarkets will often describe such items as 'no frills' to effectively manage the expectations of customers. With costs kept to a minimum for production, packaging and marketing, this then enables low prices for customers.

## Customer relationships

Customer relationships are important for any business, regardless of its business model. However, different types of customer relationships can be cultivated. In a business model with customer relationships as central, customers are prioritized above anything else, and businesses will tailor their products and services according to their needs and wants. For instance, Chase Bank offers a similar service to other banking providers but has prided itself on a business model designed to make it easier for customers to manage their financial lives. A strong emphasis on the financial literacy and well-being of the customer marks them out as having a different type of relationship between bank and customer than has been traditionally the case.

## Differentiation

Differentiation often refers to specific features or a certain level of quality in a product or service. Apple is a well-known example of a business built on a model of differentiation. Apple products are not low-cost, and the company rarely discounts their products. The high price points are justified by the company's focus on offering premium-quality products. The customers buy from Apple because they want specific features that their products offer that may be difficult to find elsewhere. These specific features are often a result of innovation.

# Innovation

Innovation is an important element of business modelling. To gain a competitive advantage, the business needs to offer something new or different from its competitors in order to capture a share of the market. The type of innovation the business employs can vary; it may be incremental (Kirzner, 1973) – a slight adjustment to an existing product or service often in response to customer demand – or it may be radical (Schumpeter, 1942) – a complete change to the market the business operates in (Bessant and Tidd, 2018). This latter type, radical innovation, can be seen in relation to the business model itself. A well-known example is the multinational transportation company Uber, founded in 2009. Uber took a well-known service – taxis – and innovated on the business model by effectively changing who the 'users' of the service were. Rather than users being only those who needed transportation, they are now also the drivers. Uber is the platform for the drivers to operate on, which means that it also does not require its own fleet of vehicles like a traditional taxi company. This approach went against the dominant logic at the time but has been hugely popular. Today, Uber has over 32,000 employees and $33.8 billion in revenue (Forbes, 2023).

## KEY RESEARCH

Peter Drucker's seminal (1985) work on innovation outlines seven key sources of innovative opportunities. He encourages entrepreneurs to take a systematic approach to innovation, using these seven sources as a blueprint for discovering entrepreneurial opportunities.

The first **four** sources usually lie within the business or industry/sector itself (named internal sources):

- *The unexpected* – the unexpected success, the unexpected failure, the unexpected outside event. Most businesses will ignore these because they do not fit into an existing plan, but entrepreneurs should try to capitalize on the unexpected.
- *The incongruity* – between reality as it actually is and reality as it is assumed to be. Rather than accept the status quo, entrepreneurs question taken-for-granted assumptions.
- *Innovation based on process need* – when there is an obvious 'need' within the organization – here necessity is the mother of invention.
- *Changes in industry structure or market structure* – the emergence of new, fast-growing segments, such as home food delivery during the early stages of the Covid-19 pandemic in 2020.

The final **three** usually involve change outside of the business or industry/sector (named external sources):

- *Demographics* – changes in demography, such as the rising ageing population in the UK.
- *Changes in perception, mood or meaning* – changes in societal norms such as the enhanced focus on self-care and well-being post pandemic.
- *Access to new knowledge*, both scientific and non-scientific, opens up the scope for new ideas and products to emerge.

What do you think of these seven sources? Can you think of your own examples of types of businesses that have emerged as a result of one or more of these sources?

To read more about these seven sources, consult Drucker's seminal (1985) work, *Innovation and Entrepreneurship.*

Developing a business model often takes time and is usually an iterative process whereby customer feedback and/or market changes lead to adaptations (or pivots) to the model. Meanwhile, the business model must be consistent enough to provide a clear direction for the business. This can seem like a contradiction – having a model that is both flexible and consistent – but this balance is what can make an effective business model (or not).

## Social business modelling

This section explores the nuances of *social* business modelling. First, we explore what makes a social business model different from commercial business models. Second, we discuss whether a socially focused business needs a separate model. We also consider the contextual factors that play a role in formulating a social business model.

Social value creation is what underpins SEs and differentiates them from any other forms of organizations (Choi and Majumder, 2014). Without a social mission and a desire to create social value, the reason for an SE to exist disappears. The traditional focus on profit maximization is rejected for a focus on meeting a specified social aim or cause. This can range from helping people improve their vision, to helping disadvantaged communities in Eastern Africa and East Asia (see the case of 'Adventure Alternative' in Chapter 7).

## Beneficiaries and customers

As we have pointed out in Chapter 8, SEs must consider two key audiences: customers and beneficiaries. As for any business, a product or service must have a customer to sell to. The customer buys the value that the SE creates, thereby providing it with the funds needed to ensure its own survival. As SEs should generate the majority of their operating revenue through trade, it is crucial that they have a clearly identified customer base and can successfully sell their product or service to this base for a profit.

The beneficiaries are the individuals or groups that the social enterprise seeks to help. SEs should reinvest the majority of their profits in pursuit of a social mission, and the beneficiaries are those people or groups who benefit from the social mission. Beneficiaries are often those within society who could be considered vulnerable, marginalized or in a specific type of need, for example, people who are rough sleepers, young people leaving the care system, long-term unemployed people or those with drug dependence or addiction issues, to name a few. Value is delivered through the intervention the SE provides, which enables beneficiaries to improve their livelihood and the SE to deliver its core social mission.

Defining the differences between customers and beneficiaries may not always be simple. The relationship between the SE and its beneficiaries can vary considerably according to its business model. The SE may generate income from its customers separate from any interaction with the beneficiaries, as in the case of TOMS (see Chapter 3). Or the SE may generate income via direct involvement from the beneficiaries, as they are also its customers (often receiving goods or services at a low cost), its supplier (beneficiaries may produce goods/services that the SE pays for a premium for) or its employees (aside from pay, the SE may provide additional employee benefits related to the beneficiaries' education or health and well-being) (Kennedy, 2016). It is important to be aware of these different approaches as you are introduced to different examples of SEs.

## Vision and mission

For any business model, but particularly for a social business model, it is important to have a clear vision and mission. Having a clear vision and mission is important for creating a strong identity and direction for your social business (Burns, 2020).

Vision often refers to the long-term conception of what the business will be. Being clear on your vision for your SE provides a guiding light throughout the start-up process. It also communicates to others what your SE is doing and why. Your vision needs to convey *why* you are starting this SE. This can help bring together the founder (i.e. the social entrepreneur), employees, customers and stakeholders in a shared understanding of the future goals of the business.

The mission is much more practical in outlining the specific aims of the SE. The mission is what you hope to achieve (Chahine, 2023). It is often provided in a mission statement, which should clearly communicate to others what the purpose of the SE is and how it will achieve that purpose. The formulation of a business model and the establishment of your vision and mission are often an iterative process. What is crucial is that the vision and mission are in alignment with the business model. In essence, are you effectively balancing the beneficiary aspect (social) and the customer aspect (entrepreneurship)? However, in the meantime, it is worth considering the importance of the cultural context.

## Cultural context

As discussed in Chapters 7 and 8, contextual factors such as access to resources, legislative changes and cultural attitudes can all impact the business modelling process for an SE (Zahra et al, 2009). In many countries, SEs have access to subsidies or grants from public bodies to supplement their income generation, particularly in the start-up stage (Collavo, 2023). For example, in Belgium, SEs have benefited from a wealth of government support. Split into three social enterprise 'types' – associations, cooperatives, and mutuals; funding through public authority policies and donations; and social investment from philanthropic actors – they are important contributors to the social enterprise sector in this country (European Commission, 2020). While an entrepreneurial approach is encouraged in Belgium, SEs have been termed 'parastatal organizations' (European Commission, 2020), meaning that, although separate from the government, their activities can serve the state either directly or indirectly.

In other countries, such as the UK, there is the expectation that if a business is registered as a social enterprise (see Chapter 1 for further detail regarding legal structures for SEs), they operate a business model that covers their own costs through generating revenue. SEs in countries like the UK are expected to have a 'hybrid' social business model, adopting entrepreneurial practices to generate income to achieve societal and/or environmental objectives (Dees, 1998; Santos et al, 2015). There may be grants and loans available to assist (as there are for many small and medium-sized enterprises regardless of business type and particularly in the start-up stage), but this should not be the primary source of income for the business.

**STOP AND THINK**

Funding is a critical issue for all types of businesses, including SEs. If an SE requires access to additional sources of income to survive, does this signify a weakness in the business model itself? Or does such reliance on grants and donations become acceptable because of the social mission that underpins the business activities?

Discuss with a friend or colleague. What are your thoughts on additional sources of income?

By now, we have established what we mean by a social business model, how it differs from a business idea and important contextual factors to consider. In the following section, we will explore some of the practical tools that can be used for social business modelling.

## Social business modelling approaches

Although socially minded business approaches have grown in popularity, there remains a lack of research regarding business modelling for socially focused businesses (Gasparin et al, 2021). This section allows you to delve into the social business modelling approach and learn about a specific tool that you can use when generating a business model for an SE.

The use of a framework or tool can assist individuals at both the design and evaluation stages of the business journey by helping them visualize and articulate the business's activities (Burns, 2023; Chahine, 2023). One popular tool is the Business Model Canvas (BMC), pioneered by Osterwalder and Pigneur (2010), designed initially for use by larger businesses with established products and services as a means to visualize and communicate their business model (Burns, 2020). It has since been applied to a variety of business types, from start-ups to established ones, and recently triple bottom line thinking was incorporated.

**KEY RESEARCH**

Elkington's (1994) Triple Bottom Line model has been highly influential in the business world. This transformational framework helps businesses move towards a more sustainable future by considering the 'three Ps' – people, planet and profit. Elkington makes a clear case for businesses moving beyond a sole focus on profit to instead incorporate considerations for people and the planet. By doing this, a business can account for the full cost of doing business and is more likely to succeed in the long term.

For a fuller discussion of the triple bottom line, please refer to Chapter 6.

The merging of the BMC with triple bottom line thinking is called the Triple Layer Business Model Canvas (TLBMC). It is a particularly useful tool for social entrepreneurs wanting to start an SE due to their focus on social and/or environmental inputs and outputs. Joyce and Paquin (2016) argue that visually representing a business model through the economic, social and environmental layers supports social entrepreneurs in both developing and communicating a more holistic and integrated business model.

Having a layered format also helps users better understand the relationships between economic, social and environmental business decisions. Each layer of the TLBMC has nine sub-sections:

- The first layer, the economic layer, focuses on what the monetary inputs and outputs are to the business, i.e. cost structure, key resources and revenue streams.
- The other two 'layers' included, the environmental and social, are designed to help the user of the TLBMC explain how an organization creates, delivers and captures environmental and social value simultaneously with economic value (Joyce and Paquin, 2016).

## Social layer

The user of this approach is encouraged to consider the 'human' side of their business. This layer is an appropriate tool if you wish to start an SE to tackle a social issue. Each box is explained here:

- **Local communities:** This refers to social relationships that are built between the SE and other communities and groups, i.e. suppliers and local communities. The focus should be on maintaining mutually beneficial relationships.
- **Governance:** The organizational structure, decision-making process and leadership approach of the SE. Thought should be given to how fair and transparent the governance structures are.
- **Employees:** Employees are seen as core stakeholders in the business and not just a means to create and deliver the goods and services of the enterprise. Important considerations relate to issues such as diversity, working conditions and personal growth initiatives for people working for the SE.
- **Social value:** Consideration of the value that is created by the business beyond financial gain. This relates to the beneficiaries in particular and the value they derive from the SE.
- **Societal culture:** The potential effect the SE may have upon society as a whole (either positive or negative).
- **Scale of outreach:** The depth and breadth of the relationships the SE builds with its stakeholders. This will greatly depend on the reach of the SE, both geographically and digitally.
- **End-user:** This refers to the individuals or groups who consume the value created by the social enterprise: its customers. The SE needs to be concerned with how it addresses the needs of its end-users and contributes to their quality of life.

- **Social impacts:** What measurable costs (both positive and negative) the SE incurs through its activities. For example, positive community engagement or negative displacement within a supply chain.
- **Social benefits:** The positive social benefits that are created directly as a result of the SE's actions.

Below is a worked example for the social enterprise – Pollenize, a social enterprise founded in 2018, to protect and preserve pollinator populations (bees, butterflies, moths etc). Pollinators, such as bees, play a critical role in pollinating trees and flowers and maintaining healthy ecosystems, which are essential for our food production. On the surface, Pollenize may appear to be a business that is primarily concerned with the physical environment. However, their work has clear implications for humans. Pollinators play a pivotal role in maintaining a healthy ecosystem and are thereby essential in the provision of food for wildlife and humans. Without pollinators there would not be an adequate food supply to sustain our lifestyles. To understand further the social benefits of the social enterprise, Pollenize have aligned their activities against 13 of the 17 UN Sustainable Development Goals. More information can be found on the 'Our Mission and Values' page of their website.

Before plotting the activities of Pollenize on the social layer of the TLBMC, it is important to make the distinction between the social enterprise's beneficiaries and customers, as shown in Table 9.1.

Now the beneficiaries and customers are clear, each section of the social layer can be examined in turn. Figure 9.1 provides a visual of a worked example for the social layer:

- **Local communities** – Pollenize aims to inspire communities to 'think global, act local' by encouraging engagement and involvement in urban flower planting and beekeeping; this includes local schools and businesses in the Southwest of England. In 2023, 44 individuals joined the business of community beekeeping.

**Table 9.1** Beneficiaries and customers of Pollenize

| Beneficiaries | Customers |
|---|---|
| Current and future generations (enriched biodiversity which is essential for food production). | Farmers (utilize Pollenize technology to reduce pest and disease risk leading to enriched crop production). |
| Children and adults (enhanced knowledge and skills regarding healthy ecosystems). | Businesses (host beehives at their premises, track and improve on-site biodiversity via AI tools provided by Pollenize). |
| | Individuals (buy honey shares, beekeeping experiences and sowing packets). |

**Figure 9.1** Worked example of the social layer of the Triple Layered Business Model Canvas for real-world example Pollenize

<table>
<tr>
<td rowspan="2">LOCAL COMMUNITIES<br><br>Think global, act local</td>
<td>GOVERNANCE<br><br>Transparency, integrity</td>
<td rowspan="2">SOCIAL VALUE<br><br>Biodiversity and pollinator protection research</td>
<td>SOCIETAL CULTURE<br><br>Fostering environmental awareness through education</td>
<td rowspan="2">END-USER<br><br>Biodiversity tracking and improvement software</td>
</tr>
<tr>
<td>EMPLOYEES<br><br>Work-life balance</td>
<td>SCALE OF OUTREACH<br><br>Collaboration to promote eco-consciousness</td>
</tr>
<tr>
<td colspan="3">SOCIAL IMPACTS<br><br>Rewilding the land</td>
<td colspan="2">SOCIAL BENEFITS<br><br>Moving towards pesticide-free businesses</td>
</tr>
</table>

- **Governance** – Pollenize has built a governance structure on the values of transparency and integrity. A collaborative community approach means that members of the public can get involved and have a share of the honey crop each year.
- **Employees** – Pollenize encourages a working environment that promotes work/life balance.
- **Social value** – fund groundbreaking research into biodiversity and the protection of pollinator species. In 2020, it was estimated that over 400 pollinator species had been helped by the work of Pollenize.
- **Societal culture** – recognizing the importance of fostering environmental awareness in future generations, Pollenize offers engaging school programmes, and in 2022, 38,000 seed packets were given to school children via the Seeds for Schools project. From story reading to wildflower planting, bioblitz surveys and Q&A sessions with beekeepers, these interactive experiences spark a passion for pollinators and inspire young minds to become stewards of the environment.
- **Scale of outreach** – collaborates with numerous local educational institutions and businesses to promote eco-consciousness. Pollenize has partnered with a local waste plant that deals with non-recycled or non-composted waste from Plymouth, Devon and Torbay to host a Pollenize research apiary, providing a home for a colony of European native dark honeybees and enabling over 330 observations of 126 different plant species at the site.

- **End-user** – Floradex provides landowners, developers and businesses with an easy and effective solution to strategically track and improve on-site biodiversity.
- **Social impacts** – Pollenize offers wildflower seed packets, allowing individuals and organizations to create pollinator-friendly havens. Since 2018, 1.1k seed packets have been sown, which is 339.9 kg of carbon captured covering 738 square meters of land that has been rewilded across the UK.
- **Social benefits** – in spring 2023, Pollenize launched the Pesticide-Free Plymouth campaign, a city-wide movement aimed at raising awareness of the harmful effects of pesticide use on the environment. This resulted in 653 businesses pledging to become pesticide free.

There were many examples that could have been listed under each box, but the key highlights have been chosen to enable an effective visualization of the social layer for the SE Pollenize. As you can see, the use of statistics enables the scale and reach of the social aspects of this SE to be understood more tangibly.

**STOP AND THINK**

Having read the explanations for each box carefully and read through the given example, does considering the social layer of the TLBMC spark any additions or revisions to an idea for an SE that you might already have? If you do not currently have an idea for a SE, think of one that you admire, and what could be written in each box.

For further discussion and examples of the practical use of the social layer of the TLBMC, see Joyce and Paquin (2016).

## *Environmental layer*

This layer encourages the user to consider how their business may utilize and impact the physical environment, i.e. use of natural resources, air quality and recycling of materials. It is an appropriate tool if you wish to start a SE to tackle an environmental issue. As with the social layer, each box has been explained below:

- **Supplies and outsourcing:** The different material resources and production activities that the SE incurs outside of the core business activity. This could include supplies such as energy, either supplied in-house (such as solar power) or outsourced (such as gas). This relates strongly to the carbon footprint of the SE.
- **Production:** The actions the SE undertakes to create its product or service, particularly those that have a high environmental impact. For example, the transformation of raw materials into a higher-value product.

- **Materials:** These are the tangible resources required to create value, including consideration of where they come from and where they go to, i.e. waste streams.
- **Functional value:** This relates to the measurable quantities of physical output from the SE within a given timeframe.
- **End-of-life:** Consideration is given here to what happens when the customer and/or beneficiary decides to stop utilizing the product or service; for example, is it designed to be recycled? What might be required for it to be disassembled or destroyed?
- **Distribution:** The energy that is used in how the product or service is delivered to the end user. Factors such as distance travelled and types of transportation should be considered.
- **Use phase:** What energy is used in the consumption of the product or service. This includes consideration of what the customer and/or beneficiary may need to do for the product/service in terms of providing it with power or ensuring its maintenance.
- **Environmental impacts:** What tangible and therefore measurable impacts does the SE have upon the environment, and at what stage in the SE's activities may this occur? For example, $CO_2$ emissions from the manufacturing of a product or the use of natural resources in the use phase.
- **Environmental benefits:** This considers how the SE may provide ecological value, such as by reducing environmental damage or contributing to regeneration.

**Elvis and Kresse**, a social enterprise founded in 2005, was set up with the aim of rescuing raw materials from landfill and transforming them into luxury lifestyle accessories (handbags, belts, etc.) The social enterprise has grown from strength to strength, with its products stocked worldwide, and donates 50 per cent of its profits to charity (Djebali and Ciachir, 2021). Figure 9.2 is a worked example of the environmental layer of the TLBMC for this business:

- **Supplies and outsourcing** – Elvis & Kresse production activities are all fully powered by renewable energy, for example, the use of solar energy. Their main workshop, based in Kent, is within an environmentally restored mill.
- **Production** – heavy use of traditional craftsmanship, such as handmade techniques to make bags, lessens the use of machinery and thereby the need for energy sources to power heavy machinery.
- **Materials** – materials that would have otherwise gone to landfills, such as decommissioned fire hoses and parachute silk, are used to make the luxury products.
- **Functional value** – the company does not hold any discount days or participate in worldwide sales days (such as Black Friday) as they are not a fast-moving consumer goods brand (Elvis & Kresse, 2024). This decreases excessive physical output.

**Figure 9.2** Worked example of environmental layer of the Triple Layered Business Model Canvas for case study Elvis & Kresse

<table>
<tr>
<td rowspan="2">SUPPLIES AND OUTSOURCING<br><br>Use of solar energy</td>
<td>PRODUCTION<br><br>Traditional craftsmanship over guzzling machinery</td>
<td rowspan="2">FUNCTIONAL VALUE<br><br>Non-participation in discount and sales days</td>
<td>END OF LIFE<br><br>25-year repair guarantee to extend product life</td>
<td>USE PHASE<br><br>Maintenance via repair guarantee</td>
</tr>
<tr>
<td>MATERIALS<br><br>Repurposing materials destined for landfills</td>
<td>DISTRIBUTION<br><br>Lightweight product to lessen shipping burden</td>
<td></td>
</tr>
<tr>
<td colspan="3">ENVIRONMENTAL IMPACTS<br><br>Reclaimed packaging</td>
<td colspan="2">ENVIRONMENTAL BENEFITS<br><br>Reducing items sent to landfill</td>
</tr>
</table>

- **End-of-life** – all items have a 25-year repair guarantee to encourage customers to use products for longer and to reduce the number of items going to landfills.
- **Distribution** – although the company does offer international shipping, they try to minimize the bulk and weight of products and their packaging to lower the shipping burden.
- **Use phase** – the 25-year repair guarantee cuts down on the energy and resources needed to maintain the products.
- **Environmental impacts** – all packaging is reclaimed and made from materials such as old newspapers, coffee sacks and shoe boxes, thereby reducing the resources used in delivering the products to customers.
- **Environmental benefits** – repurposing materials that would otherwise go to landfills, such as decommissioned fire hoses, into high-end sustainable items has saved over 200 tonnes of material from landfills since 2005 (Dominguez and Bhatti, 2022).

**STOP AND THINK**

Since the first climate change emergency was declared in 2016, 2,355 jurisdictions in 40 countries have declared a climate emergency, which amounts to over 1 billion citizens (Climate Emergency Declaration, 2024). If you have an idea for a social enterprise, what can you add to each of the boxes to recognize your contribution to helping the environment?

As you can see from the inclusion of these layers, the social business model can become quite complex. If you utilize all three layers when considering your social business model, your SE must provide an economic, social and environmental rationale for its existence. Considering how to proceed with your SE can be challenging, as ideally the economic, social and environmental factors should be given near-equal consideration.

## Reflection on the application of social business modelling

In recognition of the challenges that can arise when using a business modelling tool such as the TLBMC, this section recounts an example of putting the social layer of the TLBMC to the test for a student's SE idea.

### *The proposed idea*

During the delivery of a final-year undergraduate enterprise module, where students were required to generate their own original business ideas, the author had an interesting conversation with one of their students. The student had a business idea for an SE, which was application (app)-based and aimed at reducing food waste by providing guidance and recipe ideas to families via their parents/guardians. The idea would generate profit through a freemium subscription model: monthly payments from customers using an advanced, tailored and ad-free version of the app, and then revenue from advertisers showcasing their goods and services on the more basic free version of the app. The freemium model has been highly successful, as exemplified by the likes of Spotify, Skype and Dropbox.

### *Customer segments*

When discussing the customer segments of the business model, without hesitation, the student stated that their key segment was 'busy working mothers'. Part of an educator's role is to encourage criticality, and therefore the author asked the student, 'Why only mothers?' to which the student appeared to be temporarily stumped. After a few minutes of reflection, the student explained that they wanted to target the segment of the market they thought would be most likely to use the app and therefore where the potential for the most profit lay. Statistically speaking, even in the 21st century, mothers still do most of the meal planning, preparation and cooking within the family home (Sieghart, 2022). If we see profit as the primary concern, then indeed the most logical approach is to target mothers as the main customer segment. However, their business model then appeared to be *profit first*, despite being an SE. There was a contradiction that needed further unpicking.

## Social versus economic considerations

The author encouraged the student to consider their idea with the social layer of the TLBMC in mind. In the year 2024, should we be following traditional ideas about parenting roles? Or should we be challenging them? This led to a discussion of whether perpetuating the stereotype of the working mother, who is also the primary meal prepper, planner and cooker, is in line with the social value of equality. Again, we came back to the profit conversation. Should we not target the audience that is going to be the easiest to market to? Who is most likely to be interested and therefore pay? The tension between the social mission of the SE and profit was apparent.

When looking at the social layer, it is important to consider what your business's *social value* will be. This requires consideration of the benefits created for society more broadly. Statistics show that a more equal distribution of household tasks between parents leads to better outcomes for family units as a whole (Sieghart, 2022). By recognizing that both parents are equally important in deciding the food intake of their household, the socially minded business model encourages this positive impact. In this case, surely both parents should have equal consideration? So, a social business model is not just about what we have to gain in terms of profit but also what the ripple effects of our business might be within the social world. A social business model ultimately wants to have a positive social value rather than a negative one. For example, perpetuating stereotypes could be considered a negative, whereas marketing an SE in a more inclusive manner in order to challenge stereotypes could be considered positive.

The student underwent a period of critical reflection following this conversation and was tasked with considering how we effectively balance social and economic considerations when formulating a business model for an SE. what had become clear to them was not only the need for balance between economic and social considerations but also how challenging this balance might be.

**STOP AND THINK**

Are you working on an idea for an SE? Stop now and write in two or three sentences what your 'social value' is. Remember, this is about the benefits your SE creates for society more broadly. The more developed your idea is, the more you may have to write here.

Can you see any tension between your social value and your proposed sources of revenue? What is the balance between profit and social considerations? Note down any tensions. You do not have to address each tension right now, but awareness is the first step in getting a better handle on the balance between the economic and social layers of your business idea.

## Summary and key learning points

As this textbook is designed to encourage a hands-on approach to learning, consider how you might apply the principles discussed in this chapter to a current or future SE idea. Reflect on how you might manage tensions between profit generation and reaching social goals. Consider any unintended social consequences that may arise from your idea and how you might mitigate them. Experiment with the practical business modelling tools that have been outlined, and seek feedback early on your idea to ensure you are sense checking as you go along.

The main learning outcomes:

- Rather than starting up with the sole aim of making as much profit as possible, SEs often have a strong social focus at their outset. Economic considerations are important, but they must always be balanced against social considerations.
- The hybrid model of SEs means that they balance their profit considerations with their social mission. SEs in countries like the UK are expected to have a 'hybrid' social business model, adopting entrepreneurial practices to generate income to achieve societal and/or environmental objectives.
- The concept of value is at the heart of a business model. For SEs, the meaning of 'value' will be specific to their social mission and the sector in which they operate. It will need to clearly delineate what value means for its customers versus what it means for its beneficiaries.
- For an SE, the customer buys the value that it creates, thereby providing it with the funds needed to ensure its own survival. The beneficiaries are the individuals or groups that the SE seeks to help. SEs should reinvest the majority of their profits in pursuit of a social mission, and the beneficiaries are those people or groups who benefit from the social mission.
- Common types of business models usually revolve around three key areas of consideration: price, customer relationships and differentiation.
- Innovation is an important element of business modelling. To gain a competitive advantage, the business will need to offer something new or different from its competitors in order to capture a share of the market.

- The use of a framework or tool can assist individuals at both the design and evaluation stages of the business journey by helping them visualize and articulate the business's activities. Such frameworks and tools greatly aid the business modelling process.
- Finding a balance between economic and social considerations requires reflection and criticality and is not always a straightforward task.

## SELF-CHECK QUESTIONS

1 What is the purpose of a business model?

2 How is a business model different from a business idea?

3 How does a social business model differ from a traditional business model?

4 Why is innovation important in a business model?

5 What is the purpose and value of using a social business modelling tool like the Triple Layer Business Model Canvas?

Responses to self-check questions can be assessed here:

1 A business model helps a business describe how it creates, delivers and captures value (Osterwalder and Pigneur, 2010). This requires the business to set out what it will *create* (the goods or services), how it will *deliver* those goods or services (reach its customers and/or beneficiaries) and how that value will be *captured* (measured and tangibly realized).

2 The business model is the roadmap for taking a business idea to market (Burns, 2020). The *model* operationalizes the *idea*. You can have a good idea but a bad business model and vice versa.

3 A social business model rejects a sole focus on profit maximization and instead aims to meet a specified social aim or assist a social cause. Social value creation is what underpins social enterprises and differentiates them from any other forms of organization (Choi and Majumder, 2014).

4 To gain a competitive advantage, a business will need to offer something new or different from its competitors. Being innovative enables a business to stand out from the competition and capture a share of the market.

5 The three layers of the TLBMC help the user to explain how an organization creates, delivers and captures economic, environmental and social forms of value simultaneously (Joyce and Paquin, 2016). Taking a layered approach also helps the user to understand the relationships between economic, social and environmental business decisions.

## REAL-WORLD EXAMPLE INDICATIVE ANSWERS

1 What is the value proposition of Pollenize?

**Indicative answer:** The value proposition of Pollenize lies in their ability to integrate environmental conservation, community education and innovative technology into a cohesive mission to combat pollinator decline. Pollenize combines environmental goals, education and technology in a sustainable, revenue-generating way.

2 Plot the activities of Pollenize onto the social layer of the Triple Layered Business Model Canvas, using their website (https://www.pollenize.org.uk/) to assist you in finding out more information. Are there any elements that were difficult to fill out? Why?

**Indicative answer:** The Triple Layered Business Model Canvas (TLBMC) examines business models across economic, social and environmental layers. Table 9.2 shows Pollenize's activities mapped onto the social layer.

**Table 9.2** Pollenize activities

| Element | Pollenize Activities |
|---|---|
| Social Value | Combating pollinator decline and biodiversity loss; empowering communities to support conservation. |
| Social Stakeholders | Schools, businesses, beekeeping communities, local residents, scientists and the government. |
| Scale of Outreach | Plymouth-based activities with plans to expand to Cornwall; national impact through innovative AI tools. |
| End-User/Beneficiaries | Local communities, schools (educational benefits), beekeepers and environmental organizations. |
| Social Activities | Seeds for Schools project, educational beehive hosting, partnerships with businesses for hive installation. |
| Impact Measurement | Tracking biodiversity improvements through Floradex; success of seed projects (e.g. 38,000 seed packets distributed). |
| Governance/Community Involvement | Collaboration with citizen scientists for pollinator monitoring; partnerships with local businesses and experts. |
| Challenges/Barriers | Balancing mission-focused work with financial sustainability; scaling operations while retaining social impact. |

Some elements, like impact measurement and social governance, could require more specific data. For example, exact metrics for biodiversity impact or user adoption rates of Hornet AI and Floradex. Similarly, while Pollenize's focus on education and innovation is evident, further details on governance processes (e.g. inclusion of stakeholders in decision-making) may be needed.

3 What challenges do you think the company faces in balancing revenue generation with their social and environmental aims?

**Revenue dependence**
Pollenize's reliance on crowdfunding, e-commerce sales and subscriptions could limit cash flow if there are fluctuations in consumer interest or funding availability.

**Mission drift**
As Pollenize expands into new regions like Cornwall or develops commercial tools (e.g. Hornet AI), they may face pressure to prioritize profit over environmental and social objectives.

**Scalability of impact**
Balancing the scalability of innovative tools (e.g. AI-powered monitoring) with their on-the-ground social impact (e.g. educational projects) requires careful resource allocation.

**Technological costs**
Investing in AI technologies (Floradex, Hornet AI) is expensive, and sustaining such innovations may strain resources, particularly for a small social enterprise.

**Stakeholder alignment**
Aligning the interests of schools, businesses, scientists and government bodies can be complex, particularly when coordinating large-scale projects.

**Public awareness**
Continued education and advocacy efforts are required to keep pollinator decline as a priority for the public and businesses.

4 With the rapid developments happening in the world of AI, how could Pollenize further expand its business activities?

Pollenize already demonstrates a strong foundation in AI with tools like Hornet AI and Floradex. Further AI-driven opportunities for expansion include:

**Global AI-powered monitoring network:**

- Develop Hornet AI into a scalable global citizen science tool, using the app-based approach to engage beekeepers and farmers worldwide.
- Aggregate real-time data to identify and predict patterns of invasive species like Asian hornets.

**Predictive biodiversity models:**

- Use AI to analyse historical and real-time land data to predict biodiversity risks and recommend planting solutions.
- Offer subscription-based consultancy for businesses or governments to optimize land use for pollinator support.

**AI-driven community engagement platforms:**

- Build an interactive app with AI features (e.g. plant identification, biodiversity scoring) that allows users to scan their environment and receive actionable conservation advice.
- Gamify the app to encourage schools and individuals to engage in pollinator-friendly practices.

**Smart beekeeping tools:**

- Develop AI-powered hive monitoring devices that analyse hive health, productivity and environmental threats (temperature, pests).
- This data can be sold to individual beekeepers or organizations as part of a subscription model.

**Collaborations with agri-tech companies:**

- Partner with agricultural businesses to integrate AI biodiversity tools into farming practices. AI could optimize crop pollination and provide metrics on ecosystem health.

**AI and policy advocacy:**

- Leverage AI-generated data to provide evidence-based reports to governments and environmental agencies, advocating for policies that combat invasive species and support pollinator populations.

## USEFUL WEBLINKS

https://www.strategyzer.com (archived at https://perma.cc/9F66-LUHD) – developed the Business Model Canvas and has additional business modelling tools to experiment with.

https://flourishingbusiness.org/ (archived at https://perma.cc/ZF85-UBVB) – with similarities to the TLBMC, the 'Flourishing Business Canvas' aims to provide users with a key tool to develop socially, environmentally and financially viable strategies.

# References


Alter, K (2007) *Social Enterprise Typology*, Virtue Ventures LLC, pp 1–124

Bacq, S and Alt, E (2018) Feeling capable and valued: A prosocial perspective on the link between empathy and social entrepreneurial intentions, *Journal of Business Venturing*, 33(3), pp 333–50

Bansal, P and Roth, K (2000) Why companies go green: A model of ecological responsiveness, *Academy of Management Journal*, 43(4): 717–36

Bessant, J R and Tidd, J (2018) *Entrepreneurship*, Glasgow: Bell and Bain Ltd

Burns, P (2020) *Corporate Entrepreneurship and Innovation*, 4th edition, London, UK: Red Globe Press

Burns, P (2023) *New Venture Creation: A framework for entrepreneurial start-ups*, London, UK: Palgrave Macmillan

Chahine, T (2023) *Social Entrepreneurship: Building impact step by step,* 2nd edition, New York, NY: Routledge

Choi, N and Majumder, S (2014) Social entrepreneurship as an essentially contested concept: Opening a new avenue for systematic future research, *Journal of Business Venturing*, 29(3): 363–76

Climate Emergency Declaration (2019) Climate emergency declarations in 549 councils cover 65 million citizens – Climate Emergency Declaration, https://climateemergencydeclaration.org/climate-emergency-declarations-cover-15-million-citizens/ (archived at https://perma.cc/RVR6-G4CZ)

Collavo, T (2023) *Foundations of Social Entrepreneurship: Theory, practical tools and skills*, New York, NY: Routledge

Dees, JG (1998) *The Meaning of 'Social Entrepreneurship*, The Kauffman Center for Entrepreneurial Leadership Kansas City, MO and Palo Alto, CA

Djebali, Z and Ciachir, C (2023) *Doing good through sustainable and ethical luxury fashion: The case of Elvis & Kresse*, Sage Publications, https://sk.sagepub.com/cases/doing-good-sustainable-ethical-luxury-fashion-case-elvis-kresse (archived at https://perma.cc/MT6L-T7K5)

Dominguez, M F O and Bhatti, Y A (2022) From waste to luxury fashion at Elvis & Kresse: A business model for sustainable and social innovation in the circular economy, *Sustainability*, 14, 11805, https://doi.org/10.3390/su141911805 (archived at https://perma.cc/PTK4-3VK4)

Drucker, P (1985) *Innovation and Entrepreneurship*, New York: Harper & Row

Ebrahim, I, Battilana, J and Mair, J (2014) The governance of social enterprises: Mission drift and accountability challenges in hybrid organizations, *Research in Organizational Behavior*, 34: 81–100

Elkington, J (1994) Towards the sustainable corporation: win-win-win business strategies for sustainable development, *California Management Review*, 36(2): 90–100

Elvis & Kresse (2021) Impact Report, www.elvisandkresse.com (archived at https://perma.cc/GXM4-GLWN)

Elvis & Kresse (2024) FAQS, https://www.elvisandkresse.com/pages/faqs (archived at https://perma.cc/K9WR-LL36)

European Commission (2020) Social enterprises and their ecosystems in Europe: comparative synthesis report, https://op.europa.eu/en/publication-detail/-/publication/4985a489-73ed-11ea-a07e-01aa75ed71a1/language-en (archived at https://perma.cc/49W8-YK9Z)

Forbes (2023) Uber, https://www.forbes.com/companies/uber/ (archived at https://perma.cc/K7V8-EWBY)

Gasparin, M, Green, W, Lilley, S, Quinn, M, Saren, M and Schinckus, C (2021) Business as unusual: A business model for social innovation, *Journal of Business Research*, 12: 698–709

Joyce, A and Paquin, R L (2016) The triple layered business model canvas: A tool to design more sustainable business models, *Journal of Cleaner Production*, 135, pp 1474–486

Kennedy, E D (2016) Positioning the beneficiary: The role of entwinement in social enterprise impact and performance management, Graduate Doctoral Dissertations Paper 244 University of Massachusetts Boston ProQuest Dissertations Publishing, 10118419

Kirzner, I (1973) *Competition and Entrepreneurship*, Chicago, Il, USA: University of Chicago Press

Osterwalder, A and Pigneur, Y (2010) *Business Model Generation: A handbook for visionaries, game changers, and challengers*, New Jersey, USA: John Wiley & Sons

Pollenize (2023) About us, https://www.pollenize.org.uk/about-pollenize (archived at https://perma.cc/3JEN-69F6)

Santos, F, Pache, A-C and Birkholz, C (2015) Making hybrids work: Aligning business models and organizational design for social enterprises, *California Management Review*, 57(3): 36–58

Schumpeter, J A (1942) *Capitalism, Socialism and Democracy*, New York, USA: Harper

Sieghart, M A (2022) *The Authority Gap: Why women are still taken less seriously than men, and what we can do about it*, W W Norton & Company

Stubbs, W and Cocklin, C (2008) Conceptualizing a 'sustainability business model', *Organization & Environment*, 2(2): 103–27

Teece, D J (2010) Business models, business strategy and innovation, *Long Range Planning*, 43: 172–94

Zahra, S A, Gedajlovic, E, Neubaum, D O and Shulman, J M (2009) A typology of social entrepreneurs: Motives, search processes and ethical challenges, *Journal of Business Venturing*, 24(5): 519–32

Zott, C, Amit, R and Massa, L (2011) The business model: Recent developments and future research, *Journal of Management*, 37(4): 1019–042

# 10 Social entrepreneurial learning

KELLY SMITH

## LEARNING OUTCOMES

By the end of this chapter, you should be able to:

- Understand key concepts relating to entrepreneurial learning.
- Recognize the importance of social and contextual learning for social entrepreneurship.
- Recognize the need to develop entrepreneurial competencies such as critical reflection, self-efficacy and emotional intelligence.
- Be able to seek out and take advantage of a range of mechanisms of entrepreneurial learning.

## Introduction to entrepreneurial learning

Although there is no single definition of entrepreneurial learning (Wang and Chugh, 2014), it is acknowledged to be a dynamic and continuous process where entrepreneurs develop the knowledge and skills necessary to start and manage new ventures (Politis, 2005), while seeking and recognizing opportunities (Rae, 2000), and reflecting on reactions to critical events through trial and error (Cope and Watts, 2000). Entrepreneurial learning has the power to change how the learner makes sense of events and connects past, present and future experiences relating to their social enterprise (Scheiber, 2016).

Engaging in entrepreneurial learning enables entrepreneurs to explore and develop knowledge about themselves, the business they are working on, the process of small business management, the environment within which their business sits, and the entrepreneurial networks and relationships needed for their business to survive and flourish (Cope, 2005). The ability to adapt to changing circumstances and learn from past experiences is crucial for entrepreneurial success and involves recognizing and responding to new opportunities and challenges as they arise (Hanage et al, 2024).

Amankwah-Amoah et al (2022) identified three stages of engagement with entrepreneurial learning: pre-founding, formation and development, and post-founding. In the first stage of pre-founding, entrepreneurs gather knowledge and resources from their past experiences and use this to shape new ventures. In the second stage, formation and development, entrepreneurs apply the lessons learned from previous failures to avoid past mistakes and improve their chances of success. Finally, in the post-founding stage, entrepreneurs engage in continuous learning and adaptation, refining their business strategies based on ongoing experiences and feedback. Similar mechanisms for learning can be used throughout the stages, but the focus will differ depending on the specific needs of each stage of personal and business development (Cope, 2005).

This chapter will explore the importance of entrepreneurial learning to your personal and emotional development as an entrepreneur, and the successful development of your social enterprise (SE). The next two sections in the chapter will present general theories and frameworks of entrepreneurial learning and discuss the importance of learning by doing, the need for social networks and how context frames what needs to be learned. The specific relevance of these concepts to entrepreneurial learning for social enterprise is then discussed with an emphasis on the social nature of learning. Later sections of the chapter explore how entrepreneurial learning leads to development of the competencies needed to drive forward a social venture. We introduce what these competencies are, and then take you through some of the key mechanisms available for you to take your learning forward. Some of the most useful learning opportunities for entrepreneurs emerge out of emotionally challenging critical incidents – both successes and failures. Tools for converting such incidents into meaningful knowledge and skills development, such as critical reflection and use of mentors, are discussed along with other mechanisms for learning, including formal education and taking advantage of incubators and accelerators, business coaches and advisors.

**STOP AND THINK**

Before reading on, think about how you like to learn. Do you prefer to learn theories first before trying things out, or do you throw yourself into doing and then use theories to make sense of what you have seen? Do you think about theories at all before you act?

# Experiential learning

Most theories of entrepreneurial learning are based on and extend concepts relating to experiential learning, proposed by Kolb (1984). Kolb's Experiential Learning Theory states that knowledge is created through the transformation of experience, with learners progressing through a four-stage learning cycle (Figure 10.1). The first stage of Concrete Experience involves learning through direct and hands-on experience where learners engage in a new experience or reinterpret an experience that they have previously been through. As we will see throughout this chapter, Reflective Observation is a critical stage in experiential learning (and, by extension, entrepreneurial learning). Here, learners reflect on their experiences from different perspectives, describing what they have seen and done and considering the positive or negative outcomes of their actions. In the third stage of the cycle, Abstract Conceptualization, learners use their reflections to develop generalizations or principles that can be tested through application to new real-world situations in the final stage of Active Experimentation. The experience of testing returns learners to the Concrete Experience stage, and further and deeper learning takes place.

## *Experiential learning and entrepreneurship*

One framework extending Kolb (1984)'s Experiential Learning Theory into the realm of entrepreneurship was put forward by Politis (2005); this is shown in Figure 10.2. Like Kolb, Politis emphasized the critical dimension of experience, which entrepreneurs need to acquire, or grasp, in order to transform learning into knowledge through reflection, analysis and application.

Entrepreneurial learning starts with recognition that entrepreneurs bring with them a level of relevant career experiences such as prior start-up experience, experience in

**Figure 10.1** Kolb's Experiential Learning Cycle

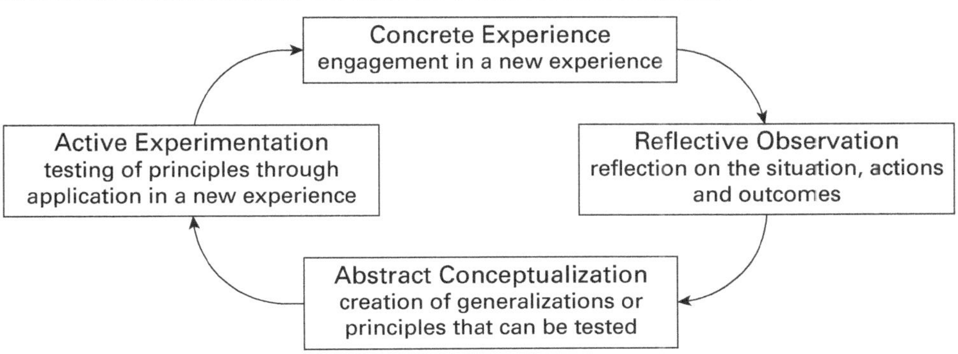


Adapted from Kolb (1984)

business management and experience in working within specific industries. Critical reflection on experiences of success or failure, the entrepreneur's predominant logic or reasoning style, and their career orientation lead them to favour exploration or exploitation routes to transform experiences into knowledge.

Similarly to Kolb (1984), Politis stresses that entrepreneurial learning is a continuous process, with entrepreneurs constantly improving their ability to adapt to new situations and developing their knowledge and skills. The dynamic nature of such learning involves continuous feedback loops where actions lead to new insights and adjustments in intentions (Hanage et al, 2024).

Predominant logic or reasoning in Politis's framework refers to an entrepreneur's preference for causation or effectuation as defined by Sarasvathy (2001). Entrepreneurs with a causation preference take a particular effect as a given and look to find the best means needed to create that effect (Sarasvathy, 2001). Politis suggests that causation-focused entrepreneurs are more likely to transform their experiences through exploitation, building on what they already know through selection, refinement and implementation (March, 1991; Politis and Gabrielsson, 2015).

In comparison, entrepreneurs with an effectuation preference consider the resources or means available to them and explore the possible effects that can be created with them (Sarasvathy, 2001; see Chapter 3). Here, effectuation is more likely to lead to a process of exploration whereby entrepreneurs experiment with new ideas and approaches, seeking out innovation and new opportunities (March, 1991; Politis, 2005). The choice of transformation process can change over time (El-Awad, 2023), with experience of failure increasing propensity for exploration and experience of success increasing exploitation (Politis, 2005).

Entrepreneurial learning in Politis's framework leads to two forms of entrepreneurial knowledge outcomes (Politis, 2005). Both learning outcomes – recognizing and acting on new business opportunities, and coping with liabilities of newness and the challenges involved with creating new ventures – are enhanced by the process of exploration (Politis and Gabrielsson, 2015). Exploitation is not positively associated with either learning outcome, however. Indeed, exploitation has been shown to be detrimental to an entrepreneur's ability to cope with newness, as entrepreneurs who prefer this learning style may be more comfortable and favour stable and predictable environments (Politis and Gabrielsson, 2015). Both opportunity recognition and coping with newness are enhanced through the acquisition of career experience (Politis, 2008; Politis and Gabrielsson, 2015).

Exploration of the entrepreneur's experience is core to the entrepreneurial learning theories described above. Starting and running commercial businesses and SEs, however, are collective endeavours, and effective learning requires more than an understanding of the experience of the individual entrepreneur alone. Entrepreneurial learning therefore needs to take into account the complex and dynamic interactivity between the individual and their business (Cope and Watts,

**Figure 10.2** Politis process of entrepreneurial learning

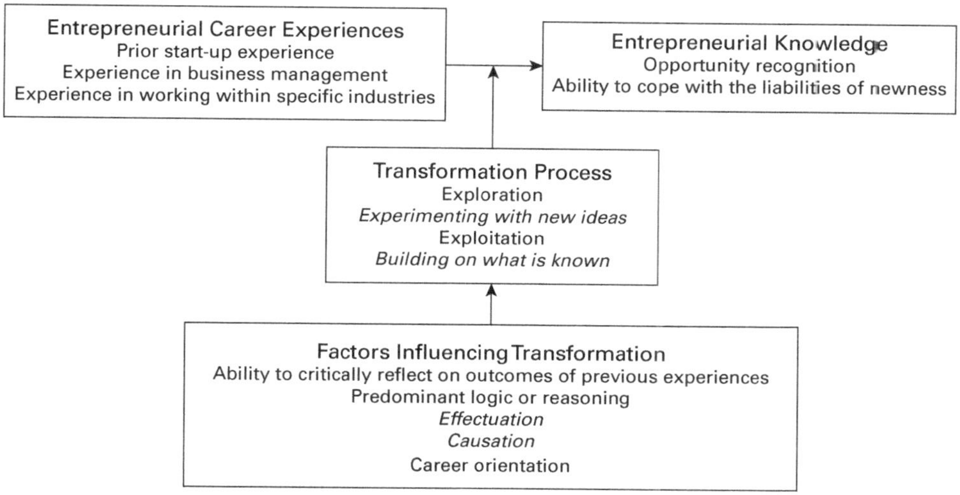


Adapted from Politis (2005)

2000) and the wider social and industry context in which the venture sits (Cope, 2005), including within entrepreneurial teams and organizations (Wang and Chugh 2014; Hanage et al, 2024).

**STOP AND THINK**

You will see the importance of critical reflection for entrepreneurial learning stressed throughout this chapter. Reflection is a powerful tool and a skill that needs to be developed and practised. How does this make you feel? How willing are you to put the time and effort into reflection that may be needed for effective entrepreneurial learning?

# The social nature of entrepreneurial learning

Rae (2000) provides a further framework stressing the importance of social interactions and the venture's specific context – such as the industry or market environment – on the entrepreneurial learning process. According to Rae, entrepreneurial learning has three key components:

- Learning by doing: related to Kolb's (1984) experiential learning theory with entrepreneurs learning through practical experience, experimentation and reflection.

- Social learning: recognizes the importance of social networks such as communities of practice (e.g. Lave, 1991) as described below.
- Contextual learning: interactions between the individual entrepreneur, their social networks and their industry context.

The critical elements for entrepreneurial learning proposed by Rae (2006) can be seen in Figure 10.3. Here, entrepreneurs construct their identity through autobiographical stories, taking into account social interactions and practical experiences. The development of identity can be challenging, with tensions occurring between the entrepreneur's current identity and future aspirations. Family is also important to personal and social emergence and can influence the entrepreneur's attitudes and actions. Skills, knowledge and the ability to recognize new opportunities are developed through immersion in the industry and social networks within which the entrepreneur and their venture sit. Industry-specific context can also facilitate the development of practical theories, which can inform entrepreneurial action.

Perhaps most important here, particularly for social entrepreneurship, is the recognition that ventures are created through collaborative efforts and shared beliefs, with cultures and practices developed through negotiation, and with roles and structures that develop over time as the business grows. Rae (2006) stresses the need to engage with diverse external networks as a mechanism to inform the negotiation process.

**Figure 10.3** The interaction of personal and social identity, negotiated enterprise and context

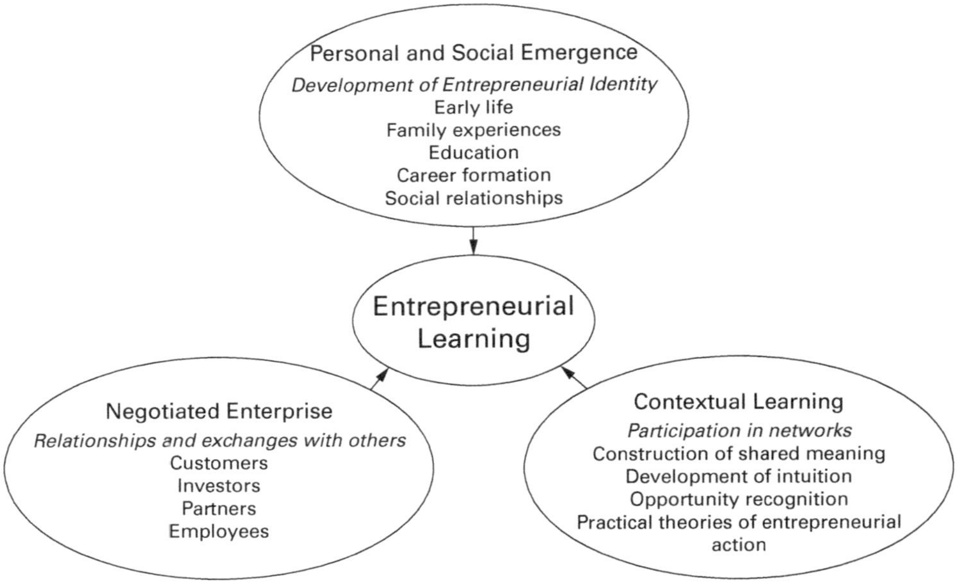


Adapted from Rae (2006)

Rae's concept of social learning was influenced by Bandura (1977) and Lave (1991). For Bandura (1977), social learning involves observing and modelling the behaviours of others. In order for learning through observation to occur, entrepreneurs need to pay attention to the behaviours they see and memorize them so that they can be replicated. The actions of observation and replication require focus and motivation, which can be influenced by anticipated rewards or punishments, the consequences of behaviours entrepreneurs have seen in others, and their own goals or needs.

Self-efficacy is an important concept in Bandura's social learning theory and refers to an individual's belief in their ability to perform a behaviour. Motivation is enhanced by self-efficacy, with higher self-efficacy leading to higher motivation to reproduce behaviours that have been observed in others (Bandura, 1977). Entrepreneurial self-efficacy is belief in abilities to perform on the various skill requirements necessary to pursue a new venture opportunity, such as developing new product and market opportunities, defining the venture's core purpose, coping with unexpected challenges and developing critical human resources (Chen, 1998; Jung et al, 2001).

Lave (1991) explored how learning takes place through communities of practice, defined as social structures for developing and sharing knowledge and made up of individuals bound by both formal or informal relationships who share common practices and activities. Communities of practice have three dimensions: mutual engagement, a negotiated enterprise and a repertoire of negotiable resources. These dimensions can be seen through sustained relationships, shared ways of doing things and the use of specific tools and artefacts such as local lore, shared stories and inside jokes.

The importance of the interplay between business context and social learning for social enterprise is highlighted by the work of Tauber (2021). Tauber explored entrepreneurial learning in Jordan as an example of an authoritarian context where challenges include bureaucratic obstacles, lack of legal registration options and reliance on personal connections. Although social entrepreneurs in Jordan often participate in entrepreneurship training programmes, bootcamps and mentorship schemes, many fail to achieve financial sustainability. Tauber suggests this indicates potential gaps in the effectiveness of programmes that are designed to teach business practices and sustainable strategies. They propose that more effective learning takes place through direct engagement with the communities in which social entrepreneurs sit, allowing them to understand the specific needs and challenges of their target populations.

Effective entrepreneurial learning in authoritarian contexts may therefore involve a combination of practical engagement, formal training and the formation of adaptive and innovative strategies to overcome systemic challenges and facilitate continuous adaptation to the political and economic landscape (Tauber, 2021). A further example of context-specific entrepreneurial learning is provided by Amankwah-Amoah et al, (2022), who describe how entrepreneurs in emerging markets need to learn to navigate weak institutions, corruption and a lack of infrastructure.

## Entrepreneurial learning for social enterprise

The vast majority of entrepreneurial learning literature focuses on traditional entrepreneurship with relatively little exploration of the social enterprise context (Nogueira, 2019; Wang and Chugh, 2014). One example – Tauber's (2021) research in Jordan – is presented above. Another notable contribution to social entrepreneurial learning is presented by Scheiber (2016), who explored how social entrepreneurs in Brazil acquired the skills, knowledge and motivation needed to address their selected societal problems. Scheiber's research emphasized the range and types of life events and prior experiences that social entrepreneurs bring to their learning. These include direct experience with inequality, volunteer work, social activism and interactions with religious institutions; social entrepreneurs also often identify as being part of their target populations themselves. Scheiber (2016) calls for the provision of opportunities for meaningful interactions with marginalized populations to foster a deeper understanding of social issues and increased commitment to addressing them.

Critical reflection is again seen as important for the enhancement of learning experiences for aspiring social entrepreneurs (Howorth et al, 2012; Scheiber, 2016). According to Scheiber (2016), reflection can help social entrepreneurs critically assess social injustices and develop strategies to address these, understand social power dynamics, foster their sense of social responsibility and increase motivation for action. Howorth et al (2012) add support to the contention that reflection is one of the most vital skills that a social entrepreneur can develop but caution that those working in deprived communities may prefer information sharing within a community of practice and see little value in reflective thinking. Communities of practice need to be cultivated with sufficient time made available to focus on learning and create feelings of trust and psychological safety, but also of excitement.

Table 10.1 presents a generalized summary of the differences between entrepreneurial learning for traditional and social enterprise business models. Although the table can be read as a dichotomy, it is important to recognize that there are overlaps between learning for traditional and social entrepreneurship, and there is huge diversity within each group (Howorth et al, 2012). Entrepreneurs with a traditional commercial focus may have strongly held social values that they wish to develop, and SEs may have a need to learn for growth, for example.

**Table 10.1** Generalized differences between learning for traditional and social enterprises

| | Traditional Entrepreneurship | Social Enterprise |
|---|---|---|
| **Primary goals for learning** | Profit maximization and business growth | Creating social or environmental impact |
| **Motivations for learning** | Driven by market opportunities, financial success and personal achievement | Driven by a desire to address societal issues, improve community well-being and contribute to the greater good |
| **Learning focus** | Business strategies, market analysis, financial management and innovation to gain competitive advantage and grow the business | Understanding social issues, stakeholder engagement, sustainable practices and innovative solutions to complex social problems |
| **Experiential learning processes** | Learning from business ventures, market interactions and financial outcomes | Learning from community interactions, communities of practice, social activism and volunteer work |
| **Relevant career and life experiences** | Career experiences such as start-up, management and industry-specific roles | Life experiences such as direct interaction with marginalized populations, involvement in social movements and intercultural interactions |
| **Critical reflection** | Engage with reflection on business successes and failures to refine strategies and improve performance | Engage in critical reflection to understand social power dynamics and develop strategies for social change |

## Development of entrepreneurial competencies

The stated outcomes of theories of entrepreneurial learning, such as those highlighted above, often relate to the development of knowledge (e.g. Politis, 2005). Although the term knowledge is used, it is clear that knowledge acquisition alone is not the end point of learning, with the implication that knowledge is necessary to drive action through the development of entrepreneurial skills, attributes and behaviours (Table 10.2) and an entrepreneurial mindset (Daspit et al, 2023). For Gibb (2008), for example, entrepreneurial learning should lead to the understanding and development of entrepreneurial ways of thinking, learning, doing, communicating, organizing and feeling about things.

More recently, there has been an emphasis on the need to develop competencies which combine the knowledge, skills, attributes and behaviours needed to enable an entrepreneur to perform tasks and take actions effectively. For example, Zheng et al (2023) suggest that both exploratory and exploitative learning (Politis, 2005; Politis

**Table 10.2** Social entrepreneurial skills, attributes and behaviours

| | Skills | Attributes | Behaviours |
|---|---|---|---|
| Definition | Specific abilities or expertise that can be learned through training and experience | Qualities or characteristics that an entrepreneur possesses | Observable actions or reactions of a social entrepreneur in various situations |
| Examples | Business planning, financial management, marketing, sales and negotiation, grant writing, community engagement, impact measurement | Honesty, empathy, resilience, passion, creativity, adaptability | Handling stress, interacting with others, building and maintaining relationships, responding to feedback |
| Focus | What a social entrepreneur can do | Who a social entrepreneur is | How a social entrepreneur acts |

and Gabrielsson, 2015) positively affect the development of competencies such as opportunity recognition, resource management and innovation capabilities, with exploratory learning additionally developing adaptability and exploitative learning strengthening abilities to organize and integrate resources.

EntreComp is a comprehensive tool originally developed by the European Commission to enhance the entrepreneurial capacity of European citizens and organizations, using a broad definition of entrepreneurship relating to the creation of cultural, social or economic value (Bacigalupo, 2016; EntreComp Europe, 2020). It consists of 15 competencies in three themes – ideas and opportunities, resources, and into action (Table 10.3) – with the full framework providing a detailed set of 442 learning outcomes across eight progression levels from foundation to expert. Competencies and learning outcomes that are explicitly relevant to social enterprise can be seen throughout the framework, such as the competency relating to ethical and sustainable thinking and a focus on community and helping or creating value for others.

One of the competencies seen in EntreComp relates to the concept of self-efficacy. In general, self-efficacy is an individual's confidence in their ability to accomplish a certain level of performance or achieve desired outcomes (Bandura, 1986). Entrepreneurial self-efficacy takes the concept further and refers to an individual's belief that they can successfully perform the various roles and tasks of entrepreneurship (Chen, 1998), including belief in abilities to develop new project and market opportunities, build an innovative environment, initiate investor relationships, define a core purpose, cope with unexpected challenges and develop critical human resources (De Noble and Ehrlich, 1998).

**Table 10.3** EntreComp framework's 15 competencies

| Ideas and Opportunities | Resources | Into Action |
|---|---|---|
| Spotting opportunities | Self-awareness and self-efficacy | Taking the initiative |
| Creativity | Motivation and perseverance | Planning and management |
| Vision | Mobilizing resources | Coping with uncertainty, ambiguity and risk |
| Valuing ideas | Financial and economic literacy | Working with others |
| Ethical and sustainable thinking | Mobilizing others | Learning through experience |

Entrepreneurial self-efficacy is positively associated with the intention to start an entrepreneurial venture, leads to a stronger conviction in entrepreneurial judgement and stronger feelings of passion, and increases task effort and commitment to goals (Newman et al, 2019). According to Rae (2001), confidence and self-belief are central to entrepreneurial learning, driving the connection of learning points to the resultant achievements.

Another important concept that can be seen in the detailed EntreComp learning outcomes relates to the development of emotional intelligence. First proposed by Salovey and Mayer (1990), emotional intelligence is the ability of an individual to assess and manage their own emotions and the emotions of others (Goleman, 2020). The benefits to entrepreneurs of emotional intelligence and the related concept of empathy were explored by Humphrey (2013), who stated that emotional intelligence helps entrepreneurs become more emotionally resilient when facing obstacles, enables them to manage intense emotions, facilitates effective leadership, gives an advantage in developing products and services that customers will want, and improves an entrepreneur's effectiveness in negotiating with funders, suppliers and employees.

More recently, emotional intelligence has been shown to lead to better performance in family businesses through the management of conflicts caused by family emotions and by facilitating the building and maintaining of strong relationships with customers and suppliers (Gilani and Aydin, 2024). Interestingly, Pathak and Muralidharan (2024) found cultural differences in the influence of emotional intelligence competencies on commercial versus social enterprise choices, with an emphasis on social well-being and sociability increasing the likelihood of social enterprise formation, and an emphasis on hedonic well-being, adaptability and self-control more likely to lead to commercial enterprise formation. As we will see below, emotional events are strong drivers of entrepreneurial learning, and the ability to be aware of your emotions – and the causes of them – is key to this.

**STOP AND THINK**

Consider the 15 EntreComp competencies presented in Table 10.3. Which competency do you feel most confident that you can demonstrate at this point in time? Which competency do you think you need to develop the most?

# Mechanisms of learning

The importance of entrepreneurial learning and competency development have been discussed above, but what can an entrepreneur do to assess their current abilities and drive their learning?

## *Critical reflection*

One of the most important aspects of entrepreneurial learning highlighted throughout this chapter is the need to fully engage with critical reflection as a purposeful activity undertaken to analyse experiences and responses to them in order to learn and improve knowledge, skills and abilities. As Gibbs (1988) states, it is not sufficient to simply have an experience to learn; reflection is needed to prevent an experience from being forgotten and to draw out its full learning potential.

The concept of reflective practice was first put forward by Dewey in 1993 (Ryder and Downs, 2022), gathering momentum with further development and application in the 1980s through work by Kolb (Figure 10.1), Schön (1983) and Gibb (2008), with a later commonly used framework for reflection proposed by Driscoll (2007). Criticisms of these frameworks include that they are 'boring' to use and risk being seen as a 'tickbox' exercise (Ryder and Downs, 2022). They remain widely used, however, and will be described here with a call for those looking to reflect to engage fully and deeply with the reflective process, recognizing that reflection is a skill that requires commitment and practice to develop and use meaningfully.

Schön's (1983) model of reflection encourages learners to reflect before, during and after an experiential event. Before taking part in an experience that is known to be about to occur, reflectors are asked to consider what they think might happen, what the challenges they face might be and what they need to know or do to be best prepared. During the experience itself, notes can be made to track what is happening as decisions are made and consider if the experience is working out as expected and if the reflector thinks they are dealing with the challenges well.

Additionally, during the experience, the reflector can consider if there is anything they can do, say or think to make the experience successful and is encouraged to explicitly think about what is being learned. The final section of the framework takes place immediately after the experience, later when there is more emotional distance from the event, or at both time points. Here the reflection focuses on how the experience went, what was particularly valuable to the reflector, what they would do before or during a similar event and what they think they learned.

Driscoll (2007) put forward a simpler framework for reflection with three components: What? So What? Now What? Here, the first stage of What? requires the reflector to provide a description of the event so that selected aspects of the experience can be purposefully considered in the reflection. In So What?, the reflector analyses the experience to discover what learning has taken place. Finally, in Now What?, proposed future actions are made based on the learning that has taken place.

Perhaps most useful for social entrepreneurial learning, with its emphasis on feelings and emotions, is Gibbs' Reflective Cycle 1988 (Figure 10.4). For Gibbs, reflection on feelings and thoughts leads to the development of generalizations and the generation of concepts that enable the effective tackling of new situations. Of particular note is the need to provide a factual description of the situation being experienced and the emotions felt without further commentary; this comes later. An understanding of how the situation and feelings relate to the reflector's values – an important consideration for social entrepreneurs in particular – can be brought in at the evaluation stage.

**Figure 10.4** Gibbs' Reflective Cycle

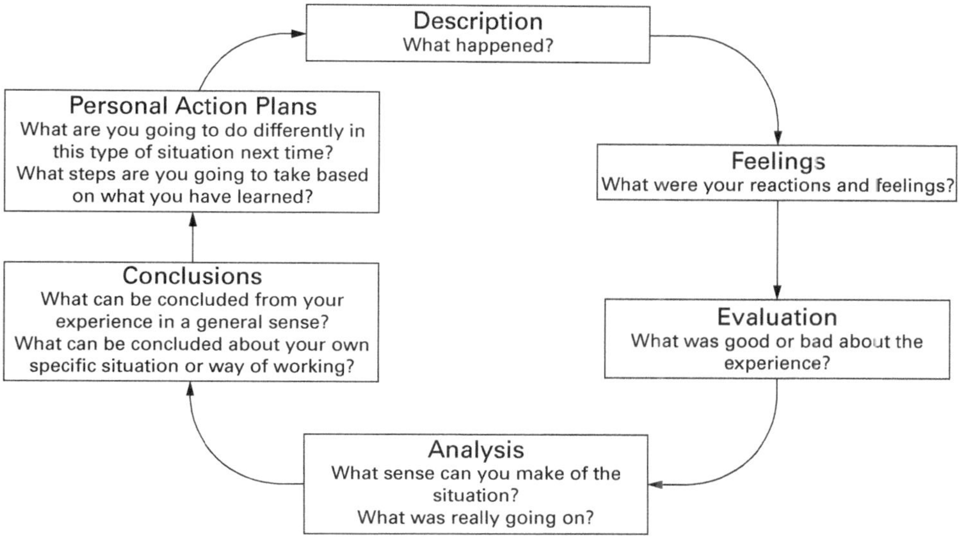


Adapted from Gibbs (1988)

## Learning from success and failure

Critical learning events – both positive and negative – are significant experiences that trigger higher-level learning. Such events can be complex in nature, prolonged and traumatic, involving social and emotional dimensions that need to be explored to fully capitalize on the learning opportunity (Cope and Watts, 2000; Cope, 2005). Such emotional events are associated with the development of competencies such as entrepreneurial identity, self-efficacy, tolerance of uncertainty and self-awareness (Lackéus, 2014).

Entrepreneurs often learn about themselves, their ventures, networks, relationships and venture management through failure. Critical reflection on failure, where core beliefs and assumptions are challenged and reassessed, can lead to significant learning, which is transformative and future-oriented with the potential to enhance entrepreneurial preparedness (Cope, 2003; 2011). Learning from mistakes can also enable entrepreneurs to develop resilience and adaptability (Amankwah-Amoah et al, 2022).

Failure is an example of a discontinuous experience (Cope, 2003; 2011). It impacts financial, emotional, physiological, social, professional and entrepreneurial aspects of life. The emotional impact of failure is significant and linked to changes in entrepreneurial identity, social costs and feelings of responsibility towards others (Cope, 2011; Fisch and Block, 2021). Recovery from failure and the resultant impacts involves a gradual healing process, starting with a hiatus from activity followed by a period of critical self-reflection and then re-engagement in new activities (Fisch and Block, 2021). Social reparation – repairing personal and professional relationships – is crucial for recovery (Cope, 2011). Although professionally and emotionally challenging, failure can elicit important learning outcomes for entrepreneurs, such as an increased self-awareness with a better understanding of their own strengths and weaknesses, an enhanced ability to be resilient, and an improved understanding of how to manage relationships and networks. Critical reflection enables entrepreneurs to develop insights into the reasons for business failure, leading to improved abilities to assess a venture's strengths and weaknesses and manage and anticipate challenges in the future (Cope, 2011).

## Mentoring, business advice and coaching

Entrepreneurs and social entrepreneurs have a range of external sources of advice and support available to them that can be categorized as mentoring, business advice and coaching. Each type of support has different aims and forms of implementation (Table 10.4), but all are based on the need to provide a supportive and trusted relationship to support personal and professional development with the intention to enhance business success and potential for growth.

**Table 10.4** Mentoring, business advice and coaching

| | Mentoring | Business Advice | Coaching |
|---|---|---|---|
| Focus | Provision of guidance, advice and support based on the mentor's own experiences | Provision of expert solutions to specific questions or challenges | Support to achieve specific personal or professional goals |
| Time scale | Long-term | Short-term or one-off | Time-bound |
| Relationship | Personal | Transactional | Collaborative |
| Paid or voluntary | Usually voluntary | Usually paid | Usually paid |

Mentoring pairs a more experienced or knowledgeable person (the mentor) with someone who is earlier in their development and in need of advice and support (the mentee). Through mentoring, the mentee explores their personal and professional situation and looks to develop strategies or goals to drive their business venture forward. The role of the mentor is to encourage the mentee to reflect on their explorations. The mentor shares their own knowledge and experiences, making sure not to tell the mentee what to do; the focus here is to enable the mentee to develop their own resourcefulness and to solve the problems they experience for themselves (Lowbridge et al, 2011).

Good mentoring support at the early stages of an entrepreneur's development can enhance creativity and persistence, develop their entrepreneurial identity and ability to acquire resources, and lead to a successful venture launch (Ahsan et al, 2018). It can also positively influence the development of entrepreneurial self-efficacy (Newman et al, 2019). For more established ventures, mentoring can be particularly useful in helping entrepreneurs to interpret critical incidents as learning experiences, increasing the power of the learning outcomes (Cope and Watts, 2000). Mentors are usually volunteers and unpaid but can benefit from the process themselves, informing their own entrepreneurial learning through the conversations they had with their mentee, finding a renewed commitment to their own ventures and developing additional skill sets (Walmsley and Nabi 2024).

Business advice can focus on transactional, day-to-day operational matters such as regulation, health and safety and legal issues, or transformational strategy development including growth enhancement activities such as innovation, exporting and new product or business model development (Brown et al, 2024; Łobacz et al, 2016). Specialist advice for social enterprise start-up, funding and growth may also be made available through national social enterprise support agencies and organizations in addition to local providers. Examples of social enterprise-specific support organizations include the UK's UnLtd, and Ashoka, which started in India in 1981 and now supports social entrepreneurs in more than 90 countries across the globe.

Recent research suggests that accessing business advice improves performance on a number of different entrepreneurial outcome measures, including increased levels of innovation and productivity (Brown et al, 2024). Entrepreneurs may feel reticent in asking or paying for advice, however, with those most in need perhaps least likely to ask for it (Łobacz et al, 2016).

Where mentoring and business advice tend to focus on the development of the business idea and implementation, coaching in this context focuses on the entrepreneur themselves. It can benefit the entrepreneur – and through them, their business – by developing personal competencies such as self-awareness and self-efficacy, emotional intelligence, communication skills, problem-solving and critical thinking. Coaching can also improve goal setting and attainment and strategic planning (Brinkley, 2018). An often-unstated issue within entrepreneurship is the importance of health and well-being. Coaching can again help here with discussions around work-life balance, job satisfaction and mental health (Brinkley, 2018).

## Formal education

Formal education has long been thought to be associated with entrepreneurial outcomes, with engagement in either general or entrepreneurship-specific programmes of study positively associated with venture creation (Weaver et al, 2006) and a positive relationship between the level of general education of the entrepreneur and venture performance (Sluis, 2005). One of the reasons for this relationship is thought to be the opportunities provided by higher levels of education to develop greater levels of knowledge, skills and competencies – also known as human capital (Martin et al, 2013, Millán et al, 2014). Of specific relevance here, high levels of educational attainment are found to provide social entrepreneurs with the skills and knowledge necessary for their initiatives (Scheiber, 2016).

There has been an increasing focus on the benefits of entrepreneurship-specific programmes on student entrepreneurial outcomes and activity, particularly within higher education (Anubhav and Aashish, 2024). Systematic reviews of published evidence generally suggest that engagement with entrepreneurship education at university leads to positive impacts on entrepreneurial intent (Pittaway and Cope, 2007; BIS, 2013, Martin et al, 2013; Nabi et al, 2017), development of knowledge, skills and competencies (BIS, 2013; Martin and Kay, 2013, Nabi et al, 2017) including self-efficacy (Rideout and Gray, 2013), and venture start-up and performance outcomes (BIS, 2013, Martin et al, 2013; Rideout and Gray, 2013; Nabi et al, 2017, Smith et al, 2022). Social entrepreneurship-specific learning in higher education, with a focus on soft or transversal skills, can help students feel more capable in relation to their social entrepreneurship potential (García-González and Ramírez-Montoya, 2021).

The success of formal entrepreneurship education programmes in encouraging and supporting entrepreneurial outcomes is likely to depend on a number of factors including: the levels of experiential learning opportunities that are embedded into the programme; the strength of focus on reflection, reflexivity and learning from emotions; and the provision of opportunity for social interaction, for example, through assessed teamwork or access to mentors.

Reflexivity here moves beyond reflection by encouraging learners to develop understanding to shape future practice through everyday interactions and conversations with fellow students, educators and entrepreneurs. It encourages learners to become more aware of their practices and the social contexts that shape them (Higgins, Smith and Mirza, 2013) and to critically examine their values, assumptions and socio-economic context of their entrepreneurial activities (Karatas-Ozkan et al, 2023).

The need to embed socialized learning opportunities within entrepreneurship education programmes is again highlighted by Williams Middleton et al (2019), who call for the inclusion of co-curricular, informal learning activities such as mentoring or university business support provision. Student-led enterprise societies may also have a key role to play in developing students with entrepreneurial attributes and facilitating the development of relevant competencies outside a programme's core curriculum (Preedy and Jones, 2015).

## Networking

The importance of networks for social learning has been discussed throughout this chapter, particularly in relation to Lave's (1991) work on communities of practice and Rae's contextualized learning through participation in networks. We have also explored how entrepreneurs' learning from failure can lead to an improved understanding of how to manage relationships and networks (e.g. Cope, 2011).

Networking is a key activity for entrepreneurs, enabling them to learn how to build social capital and use connections to help navigate challenges and seize opportunities in dynamic environments (Wu et al, 2021; Amankwah-Amoah et al, 2022). Networking groups often function as communities of practice where entrepreneurs can collaborate, support each other, and share and develop knowledge through interaction with a diversity of experience (Wasim et al, 2024). Reflection and trust are again important here, with entrepreneurs using their networks to reflect on their experiences (Soetanto, 2017) and valuing honest feedback from trusted individuals (Wasim et al, 2024).

## Incubators and accelerators

The final mechanism for learning we will explore in this chapter looks at incubation and acceleration. Both incubators and accelerators support entrepreneurs in their business development but differ in several key aspects, as summarized in Table 10.5.

**Table 10.5** Generalized differences between incubators and accelerators

| | **Incubation** | **Acceleration** |
|---|---|---|
| Focus | Helping early-stage start-ups develop into viable businesses | Rapid start-up or scale-up |
| Timescale | Longer term with variable start dates | Short and intense with fixed start date |
| Common resources | Space, mentorship, business advice, workshops and training, networking opportunities | Structured guidance, mentorship, funding, access to investors, networking opportunities |
| Cost | None or fees-based | Equity transfer |
| Funding availability | Limited; some offer grants or small seed investments | Typically provide seed funding in exchange for equity stake |
| Equity stake required | None or small | Often 5% to 10% |
| Selection criteria | None or based on specific offer focus | Usually competitive, often looking for high growth potential |

Incubators are often provided by organizations such as educational institutions or funded by local government and aim to support early-stage start-ups with low-cost access to a range of resources and services. Accelerators are usually privately run, providing intense support over a shorter period of time to businesses with high growth potential looking to rapidly start or scale up. They usually take out an equity stake in the business being supported in exchange for the support provided, which often includes access to investors through a 'demo day' at the end of the accelerator programme where entrepreneurs pitch for investment to fund further development and growth.

Although generalizations can be made, incubator and accelerator offers and use of programme names vary widely. For example, the term 'accelerator' can be used to describe a programme that is free with no equity stake required but has a fixed start date and is time-limited, and some incubators charge rent for office space. It is important that entrepreneurs look carefully at the exact offer and assess how this fits with the stage and nature of their venture, what the selection and graduation policies are, if the programme fits with the entrepreneur's mission and sector focus, and what networks of advisors, mentors, strategic partners and potential investors are built in (Isabelle, 2013).

One of the most powerful aspects of incubator or accelerator provision with respect to entrepreneurial learning is the entrepreneur's access to internal networks with other programme beneficiaries. Such networks positively affect entrepreneurial learning by promoting trust and the building of strong relationships, facilitating knowledge transfer and encouraging mutual learning opportunities (Isabelle, 2013; Wu et al, 2021). It is therefore recommended for programme applications to consider if and how the programme facilitates community of practice formation through shared space, workshops or internal networking opportunities, for example. For all entrepreneurs, but perhaps for social entrepreneurs in particular, the reputation of the incubator or accelerator should also be considered (Isabelle, 2013).

## Summary and key learning points

Entrepreneurial learning is a multifaceted and dynamic process that is essential for the personal and professional development of social entrepreneurs. This chapter has explored various theories and frameworks that underscore the importance of experiential learning, social interactions and contextual understanding in the entrepreneurial journey.

The key takeaways are the following:

- The experiential learning theories introduced highlight the continuous nature of entrepreneurial learning, where experiences are transformed into knowledge through reflection, analysis and application. This cyclical process enables social entrepreneurs to adapt to new situations, recognize opportunities and develop the necessary skills to navigate the complexities of starting and managing a venture.
- The role of social learning further illustrates the significance of social networks and communities of practice in shaping entrepreneurial identity and fostering the acquisition of practical knowledge. These interactions not only provide support and motivation but also facilitate the sharing of experiences and best practices, which are crucial for the growth and sustainability of social enterprises.
- Critical reflection emerges as a pivotal tool in entrepreneurial learning, enabling entrepreneurs to derive meaningful insights from both successes and failures. The ability to critically assess experiences, understand social power dynamics and develop strategies for social change is particularly vital for social entrepreneurs who aim to address societal issues and create a positive impact.
- The chapter also underscores the importance of entrepreneurial self-efficacy and emotional intelligence in driving entrepreneurial intentions, resilience and effective leadership. These competencies, along with the development of specific skills, attributes and behaviours, form the foundation of an entrepreneurial mindset that is essential for achieving both commercial and social objectives.

In conclusion, entrepreneurial learning is not a linear process but a continuous and iterative journey that involves a complex interplay of individual experiences, social interactions and contextual factors. For social entrepreneurs, this journey is further enriched by a deep commitment to addressing societal challenges and creating sustainable impact. By seeking out learning opportunities and embracing the principles of experiential learning, entrepreneurs can enhance their ability to innovate, adapt and thrive in an ever-changing environment.

## REAL-WORLD EXAMPLE Driving social change through arts

Calico is a Birmingham-based social enterprise co-founded by Daz Scott and Martha Harrison in May 2021 whilst in their final year of study at the University of Birmingham. Inspired by the high-profile murder of Sarah Everard in March the same year, Calico focuses on using arts and activism to combat gendered violence and has a mission to drive social change through creative means such as theatre, film and virtual reality. They strive to create safer, more inclusive public spaces and foster a culture of respect and empathy, and have received funding for their efforts from Innovate UK and the Commonwealth Games legacy project. The enterprise is youth-led, with a team entirely under 25, emphasizing the strength and activism of young people.

Though Calico, Daz and Martha aim to amplify voices and influence policies; they collaborate with local communities and organizations such as the Moseley & Kings Heath Neighbourhood Policing Team, West Midlands Combined Authority, and Transport for West Midlands in order to co-create artistic campaigns. Examples of Calico's projects include Curfew, seeking to address public street harassment. Curfew evolved into Curfew VR, an empathy training tool that simulates the experiences of women in public spaces to foster understanding and reduce violence against women and girls. Another recent project, Look Sharp, focuses on campaigns for the criminalization of needle spiking.

As students and latterly graduates of the University of Birmingham, Daz and Martha were eligible to apply for exclusive entrepreneurial learning support from the University's Be Enterprising team and Elevate accelerator. They took full advantage of the opportunities offered to help them develop their ideas and start up their social enterprise.

Located at The Exchange in Birmingham city centre, Elevate provides a supportive environment for developing entrepreneurial ventures. The programme offers a multifaceted approach, including workshops, events, mentoring and business planning advice, aimed at fostering growth and innovation. Participants also benefit from access to dedicated incubation space, a wide range of networking opportunities through the university's alumni network and regional business support schemes, and access to funding opportunities, such as the Startup Scholarship, which offers financial support to help scale business ideas.

Discussion questions:

1. What aspect of the Elevate offer do you think would first attract entrepreneurs such as Daz and Martha?
2. What aspect of the Elevate offer do you think would best drive entrepreneurial learning?
3. What key skill or competency would you recommend Daz and Martha prioritize for development to help them get the most out of their learning experiences?

## REAL-WORLD EXAMPLE INDICATIVE ANSWERS

1 What aspect of the Elevate offer do you think would first attract entrepreneurs such as Daz and Martha?

**Indicative answer:** The honest answer here is that most applicants to schemes such as these will be first attracted by the offer of funding. Perhaps disappointingly to those putting together a vibrant and varied range of learning opportunities, potential applicants often look to see if there are any grants or other routes to funding the time they need to concentrate on the development of their venture, to test ideas and to help them start to collect resources. Here, we would encourage entrepreneurs to look beyond immediate financial benefits and consider engagement with entrepreneurial learning as an investment worth making, whether it is complemented by funding opportunities or not.

2 What aspect of the Elevate offer do you think would best drive entrepreneurial learning?

**Indicative answer:** Elevate offers a range of activities and opportunities specifically designed to support entrepreneurial learning, including workshops, events, advice and mentoring, and networking opportunities. Workshops, events and business planning advice provide training and support for technical skills and competency development. Mentoring by and networking with those you trust can aid critical reflection, sharing of knowledge and mutual support. Each mechanism for entrepreneurial learning can or will be 'best' depending on the specific needs of the entrepreneur at the time and their stage of development. Engagement with every opportunity on offer should be encouraged.

3 What key skill or competency would you recommend Daz and Martha prioritize for development to help them get the most out of their learning experiences?

**Indicative answer:** You will have seen reference to critical reflection as key to entrepreneurial learning throughout this chapter. Reflection is a skill that takes practice, concentration and commitment to be fully effective, but it is so important to getting the most out of entrepreneurial learning that putting effort into developing your ability to reflect is very strongly recommended.

## CALLS TO ACTION

1. Revisit Table 10.3 and the 'Stop and Think' box presented in the section 'Development of Entrepreneurial Competencies'. For a more detailed exploration of the EntreComp visit the EntreComp (2020) practical guide. Make a list of the competencies you feel you most need to develop to take an entrepreneurial idea forward.
2. Select the mechanisms you think would best help you develop your competencies from those presented in this chapter.
3. Plan how you will develop your critical reflection skills.

# References

Ahsan, M, Zheng, C, DeNoble, A and Musteen, M (2018) From student to entrepreneur: How mentorships and affect influence student venture launch, *Journal of Small Business Management*, 56(1): 76–102

Amankwah-Amoah, J, Khan, Z, Ifere, S, Nyuur, R and Khan, H (2022) Entrepreneurs' Learning from Business Failures: An Emerging Market Perspective, *British Journal of Management*, 33(4): 1735–756

Anubhav, K, Dwivedi, A and Aashish, K (2024) Entrepreneurship education in higher education (2002–2022): A technology-empowered systematic literature review, *The International Journal of Management Education*, 22(3): 100993

Bacigalupo, M, Panagiotis, K, Punie, Y and Van den Brande, G (2016) *EntreComp: The Entrepreneurship Competence Framework*, Luxembourg, Publications Office of the European Union

Bandura, A (1977) *Social Learning Theory*, Englewood Cliffs, NJ: Prentice Hall

Bandura, A (1986) *Social Foundations of Thought and Action: A social cognitive theory*, Englewood Cliffs, NJ Prentice Hall

BIS (2013) *Enterprise Education Impact in Higher Education and Further Education*, London: Department for Business, Innovation and Skills

Brinkley, M-L and le Roux, I (2018) Coaching as a support function for potential entrepreneurs, *The Southern African Journal of Entrepreneurship and Small Business Management*, 10(1): a99

Brown, R, Cowling, M and Sun, H (2024) *Advice and SMEs: Who takes it and what happens thereafter?* ERC Research Paper Series Coventry, UK, Enterprise Research Centre **112**

Chen, C, Greene, P and Crick, A (1998) Does entrepreneurial self-efficacy distinguish entrepreneurs from managers? *Journal of Business Venturing*, 13(4): 295–316

Cope, J (2003) Entrepreneurial learning and critical reflection, *Management Learning*, 34(4): 429–50

Cope, J (2005) Toward a dynamic learning perspective of entrepreneurship, *Entrepreneurship Theory and Practice*, 29: 373–97

Cope, J (2011) Entrepreneurial learning from failure: An interpretative phenomenological analysis, *Journal of Business Venturing*, 26(6): 604–23

Cope, J and Watts, G (2000) Learning by doing: An exploration of experience, critical incidents and reflection in entrepreneurial learning, *International Journal of Entrepreneurial Behavior & Research*, 6(3): 104–24

Daspit, J, Fox, C and Findley, K (2023) Entrepreneurial mindset: An integrated definition, a review of current insights, and directions for future research, *Journal of Small Business Management*, 61(1): 12–44

De Noble, A, Jung, G and Ehrlich, S (1998) Entrepreneurial self-efficacy: The development of a measure and its relationship to entrepreneurial action, *Frontiers for Entrepreneurship Research. Waltham*, MA, P&R Publication Inc: 73–78

Driscoll, J (2007) Supported reflective learning: The essence of clinical supervision? Chapter 2 in *Practising Clinical Supervision: A reflective approach for healthcare professionals* (2nd edition) London: Bailliere Tindall, pp 27–50

El-Awad, Z (2023) Explore or exploit? Unpacking the situational conditions and cognitive mechanisms underlying entrepreneurial learning in the new venture development process, *Entrepreneurship & Regional Development*, 35(1–2): 162–86

EntreComp Europe (2020) EntreComp: A Practical Guide, EntreComp Europe

Fisch, C and Block, H (2021) How does entrepreneurial failure change an entrepreneur's digital identity? Evidence from Twitter data, *Journal of Business Venturing*, 36(1): 106015

García-González, A and Ramírez-Montoya, S (2021) Social entrepreneurship education: Changemaker training at the university, *Higher Education, Skills and Work-Based Learning*, 11(5): 1236–251

Gibb, A (2008) Entrepreneurship and enterprise education in schools and colleges: Insights from UK practice, *International Journal of Entrepreneurship Education*, 6(2): 101–44

Gibbs, G (1988) *Learning by Doing: A guide to teaching and learning methods*, London: FEU

Gilani, H, Mena, J and Aydin, G (2024) Longevity through emotional intelligence: A relationship marketing approach in family businesses, *Journal of Family Business Management*, 14(1): 225–44

Goleman, D (2020) *Emotional Intelligence: Why it can matter more than IQ*, London: Bloomsbury

Hanage, R, Davies, M, Stenholm, P and Scott, J (2024) Extending the theory of planned behavior: A longitudinal study of entrepreneurial intentions, *Entrepreneurship Research Journal*, 14(3): 1223–258

Higgins, D, Smith, K and Mirza, M (2013) Entrepreneurial education: Reflexive approaches to entrepreneurial learning in practice, *The Journal of Entrepreneurship*, 22(2): 135–60

Howorth, C, Smith, S and Parkinson, C (2012) Social learning and social entrepreneurship education, *Academy of Management Learning & Education*, 11(3): 371–89

Humphrey, H R (2013) The benefits of emotional intelligence and empathy to entrepreneurship, *Entrepreneurship Research Journal*, 3(3): 287–294

Isabelle, D (2013) Key factors affecting a technology entrepreneur's choice of incubator or accelerator, *Technology Innovation Management Review*, 3(2): 16–22

Jung, D, Ehrlich, S, de Noble, A and Baik, K (2001) Entrepreneurial self-efficacy and its relationship to entrepreneurial action: A comparative study between the US and Korea, *Management International*, 6: 41–53

Karatas-Ozkan, M, Ibrahim, S, Ozbilgin, M, Fayolle, A, Manville, G, Nicopoulou, K, Talti, A and Tunalioglu, M (2023) Challenging the assumptions of social entrepreneurship education and repositioning it for the future: Wonders of cultural, social, symbolic and economic capitals, *Social Enterprise Journal*, 19(2): 98–122

Kolb, D (1984) *Experiential Learning: Experience as the source of learning and development*, Englewood Cliffs, NJ, Prentice-Hall

Lackéus, M (2014) An emotion-based approach to assessing entrepreneurial education, *International Journal of Management Education*, (Elsevier Science) 12(3): 374–97

Lave, J, Etienne, W (1991) *Situated Learning: Legitimate peripheral participation*, Cambridge, Cambridge University Press

Łobacz, K, Głodek, P, Stawasz, E and Niedzielski, P (2016) Utilisation of business advice in small innovative firms: The role of trust and tacit knowledge, *Entrepreneurial Business and Economics Review*, 4(2): 117–38

Lowbridge, R, Dudman, A and Stevens, P (2011) *Introduction to Enterprise Mentoring*, County Durham, SFEDI

March, J G (1991) Exploration and exploitation in organizational learning, *Organization Science*, 2(1): 71–87

Martin, C, McNally, J and Michael, K (2013) Examining the formation of human capital in entrepreneurship: A meta-analysis of entrepreneurship education outcomes, *Journal of Business Venturing*, 28(2): 211-224

Millán, M, Congregado, E, Concepción, R, van Pragg, M and van Stel, A (2014) The value of an educated population for an individual's entrepreneurship success, *Journal of Business Venturing*, 29(5): 612–32

Nabi, G, Liñán, F, Fayolle, A, Krueger, N and Walmsley, A (2017) The impact of entrepreneurship education in higher education: A systematic review and research agenda, *Academy of Management Learning & Education*, 16(2): 277–99

Newman, A, Obschonka, M, Schwarz, S, Cohen, M and Nielsen, I (2019) Entrepreneurial self-efficacy: A systematic review of the literature on its theoretical foundations, measurement, antecedents, and outcomes, and an agenda for future research, *Journal of Vocational Behavior*, 110: 403–19.

Nogueira, F (2019) Entrepreneurial learning: What do we mean by it? *The Learning Organization*, 26(6): 560–73

Pathak, S and Muralidharan, E (2024) Contextualizing emotional intelligence for commercial and social entrepreneurship, *Small Business Economics*, 62(2): 667–86

Pittaway, L and Cope, J (2007) Simulating entrepreneurial learning: Integrating experiential and collaborative approaches to learning, *Management Learning*, 38(2): 211–33

Politis, D (2005) The process of entrepreneurial learning: A conceptual framework, *Entrepreneurship Theory and Practice*, 29(4): 399–424

Politis, D (2008) Does prior start-up experience matter for entrepreneurs' learning? *Journal of Small Business and Enterprise Development*, 15(3): 472–89

Politis, D and Gabrielsson, J (2015) Modes of learning and entrepreneurial knowledge, *International Journal of Innovation and Learning*, 18(1): 101

Preedy, S and Jones, P (2015) An investigation into university extra-curricular enterprise support provision, *Education + Training*, 57(8/9): 992–1008

Rae, D (2000) Understanding entrepreneurial learning: A question of how? *International Journal of Entrepreneurial Behaviour and Research*, 6: 145–59

Rae, D (2006) Entrepreneurial learning: A conceptual framework for technology-based enterprise, *Technology Analysis & Strategic Management*, 18(1): 39–56

Rideout, C, Gray, E and Denis, O (2013) Does entrepreneurship education really work? A review and methodological critique of the empirical literature on the effects of university-based entrepreneurship education, *Journal of Small Business Management*, 51(3): 329–51

Ryder, M and Downs, C (2022) Rethinking reflective practice: John Boyd's OODA loop as an alternative to Kolb, *The International Journal of Management Education*, 20(3): 100703

Salovey, P and Mayer, D (1990) Emotional intelligence imagination, *Cognition and Personality*, 9(3): 185–211

Sarasvathy, S (2001) Causation and effectuation: Toward a theoretical shift from economic inevitability to entrepreneurial contingency, *Academy of Management Review*, 26(2): 243–63

Scheiber, L (2016) How social entrepreneurs in the third sector learn from life experiences, *VOLUNTAS: International Journal of Voluntary and Nonprofit Organizations*, 27(4): 1694–717

Schön, D A (1983) *The Reflective Practitioner: How professionals think in action*, London: Routledge

Sluis, D V J (2005) Entrepreneurship selection and performance: A meta-analysis of the impact of education in developing economies, *The World Bank Economic Review*, 19(2): 225–61

Smith, K, Rogers-Draycott, M and Bozward, D (2022) Full curriculum-based venture creation programmes: Current knowledge and research challenges, *International Journal of Entrepreneurial Behavior & Research*, 28(4): 1106–127

Soetanto, D (2017) Networks and entrepreneurial learning: Coping with difficulties, *International Journal of Entrepreneurial Behavior & Research*, 23(3): 547–65

Tauber, L (2021) Beyond homogeneity: Redefining social entrepreneurship in authoritarian contexts, *Journal of Social Entrepreneurship*, 12(1): 50–68

Walmsley, A and Nabi, G (2024) Entrepreneurship mentoring in higher education: How does the mentor benefit? *Journal of Small Business and Enterprise Development*, 31(7): 1279–301

Wang, L and Chugh, H (2014) Entrepreneurial learning: Past research and future challenges, International, *Journal of Management Reviews*, 16(1): 24–61

Wasim, J, Youseff, M, Christodoulou, I and Reinhardt, R (2024) *The path to entrepreneurship: The Role of social networks in driving entrepreneurial learning and education*, *Journal of Management Education*, 48(3): 459–93

Weaver, M, Dickson, P and Solomon, G (2006) Entrepreneurship and education: What is known and not known about the links between education and entrepreneurial activity, *The Small Business Economy for Data Year 2005: A Report to the President*, Washington, DC

Williams Middleton, K, Padilla-Meléndez, A, Lockett, N, Quesada-Pallarès, C and Jack, S (2019) The university as an entrepreneurial learning space, *International Journal of Entrepreneurial Behavior & Research*, 26(5): 887–909

Wu, W, Wang, H and Wu, Y (2021) Internal and external networks, and incubatees' performance in dynamic environments: Entrepreneurial learning's mediating effect, *The Journal of Technology Transfer*, 46(6): 1707–733

Zheng, X, Yang, Y, Zhang, Q and Yang, J (2023) Linking entrepreneurial learning to entrepreneurial competencies: The moderating role of personality traits, *Current Psychology*, 42(14): 11597–612

# 11 | Social financing

EKATERINA MURZACHEVA

**LEARNING OUTCOMES**

After reading this chapter, you should be able to:

- Appraise various funding options and models for social enterprises given the role in balancing social and economic value creation.
- Understand the role and applications of socially focused financial instruments in both primary and secondary financial markets.
- Analyse the implications of the social financing lifecycle in accordance with the financial needs of social enterprises.
- Outline the barriers and challenges that social enterprises face when seeking funding.

## Introduction

Entrepreneurs face many hurdles when starting a new business, with raising funds and financial management being the most challenging ones (OECD, 2022; Reficco et al, 2021; Smith et al, 2012). This is true for any type of venture, let alone social enterprises (SEs), as they are caught between a rock and a hard place, trying to prove their economic sustainability without compromising the social mission, which is at the heart of their activities (see Chapter 1).

Yet, most social enterprises appear not to be aware of the full range of funding opportunities available in the market (European Commission, 2019; Ozdemir et al, 2016; Reficco et al, 2021). Over the last decade, the financial system has been rapidly evolving, giving rise to diverse and accessible finance options for start-ups (British Business Bank, 2021/2022; Cumming et al, 2019; Kraemer-Eis, 2022). However, many start-ups still do not reach out to external finance and mainly rely on bootstrapping (see later section), informal support or other internal resources (BDRC Continental, 2016; BMG Research, 2013; Department for Business, Innovation and Skills, 2015, 2016; Smith and Besharov, 2019). Bank lending is the dominant source of cash when entrepreneurs reach out for capital externally (e.g. start-up loans and personal lending), and only around 1 per cent of small businesses have used equity finance – an exchange of the company's shares for investment, as further explained later in the chapter (British Business Bank, 2014; Business Angel Institute, 2021).

These observations can be explained both from demand and supply perspectives. First, entrepreneurs tend to either overestimate the difficulties associated with raising finance or underestimate the level of preparation, commitment, rigour and the extent and depth of the due diligence processes. Second, the level of risk of new ventures exceeds the expected levels of returns for funders due to uncertainty and volatility (Aldrich, 1999; Cassar, 2004). As a result, internal sources of finance are more likely to be utilized at the start of any entrepreneurial journey (Baldock and Mason, 2015; North et al, 2013).

When looking at social enterprises specifically, these challenges become even more exacerbated. Like any other enterprise, they compete against all other types of businesses to get access to the same financial markets. Meanwhile, the lack of emphasis on economic returns might be an additional barrier to securing mainstream forms of funding. Nevertheless, there are finance options in the market particularly tailored for 'social good' in new social start-ups. This 'social good' could include the sustainability agenda, compliance with the UN Sustainable Development Goals, 'ethical' business, 'green' business or the widely adopted corporate social responsibility initiatives (see Chapter 5). These sources open additional funding choices for new social start-ups:

- government or corporate grants
- legal schemes to support social missions (e.g. tax incentives)
- social impact funding
- social impact bonds
- many other instruments tailored specifically to social enterprises (all those instruments are discussed in detail in this chapter)

However, this part of the market is equally saturated by 'profit for public good' organizations, and even 'profit for shareholders' businesses, which are extending their activities to generate social impact. Besides, not all these funding sources that are designed to support social good are potentially beneficial since they are dependent on the activity of the social start-up. For example, working towards securing a particular government grant may tilt the focus over to the social mission side, forgoing economic value creation. Equally, bidding for a social impact fund could divert the focus from the activities where the impact is more challenging to capture.

This chapter unravels these trade-offs and opportunities by delving into the peculiarities of the financing options available for new social start-ups. It also evaluates their advantages and limitations and elaborates on what it means for social start-ups in terms of their focus and strategy to successfully secure the type of funding that would maximize dual value creation. First, we review what is available in contemporary markets and outside them, covering bootstrapping, traditional finance methods and alternative finance markets. Next we explore blockchain applications in social finance. Further finance instruments tailored specifically for social start-ups are discussed, such as social impact investment and the latest derivatives in the secondary finance markets. The implications of different funding models are considered in the long term, something that we refer to as the social financing lifecycle. Finally, the last section outlines the key barriers and challenges and evaluates the potentially suitable financing options for different types of social start-ups.

## Key finance sources for social enterprises

As we have discussed throughout this textbook, the underlying goal of social enterprises is to create social value for their beneficiaries and to get access to funding markets on par with 'profit for shareholders' organizations. However, they do need to demonstrate their financial viability and compete for resources (Haugh, 2007; Vestrum, 2016). Like any entrepreneurial venture, social enterprises therefore tend to consider a wide range of financing sources, broadly categorized into five main groups (Cosh et al, 2009):

1. internal finance
2. grants and donations
3. debt finance
4. equity finance
5. alternative finance

A summary and a more detailed classification of these funding sources are presented in Figure 11.1. This is followed by a detailed overview of the key categories. As the finance markets and organizational needs develop, new opportunities for raising money to launch or sustain organizational activities also emerge. In this way, the first four categories represent the so-called 'traditional' funding market. Although these forms of funding have been available for decades, they are also subject to innovation. For example, bank products have extended far beyond the common product types, such as overdrafts, invoice finance or business credits, tapping into blockchain technologies, such as blockchain-based cross-border instant payment solutions, first introduced by Bank ABC in the Gulf region. Therefore, although everything that is not covered within the 'traditional' sector falls into the so-called 'alternative funding markets', many of those alternative applications get into the conventional banking and equity finance sectors as well. The following sections consider more in-depth blockchain applications, social impact investments and financial instruments in the secondary market, potentially benefiting social entrepreneurs.

**Figure 11.1** The map of social finance

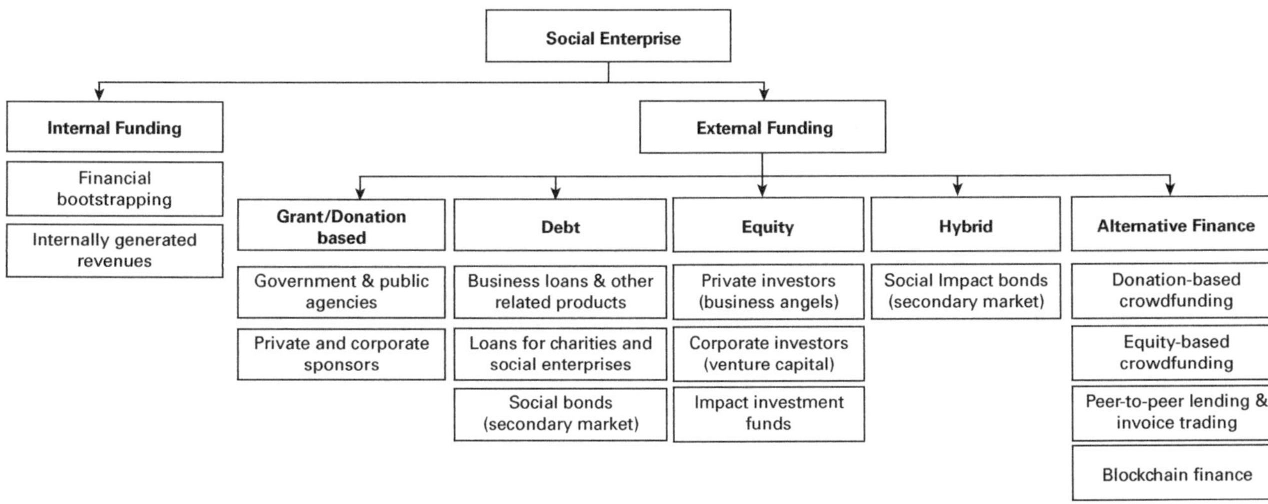

*NB: this chapter mainly considers primary market financial instruments, except for social bonds and social impact bonds as specific examples of secondary market securities, potentially suitable for social enterprises.*

## Internal finance sources

These mainly include personal savings, contributions from friends and family, and internally generated revenue streams. Entrepreneurs may also employ other tactics to acquire resources or secure savings. These may include leveraging accessible internal means (e.g. working from home or utilizing their credit card for business purposes), encouraging early cash payments (e.g. through discounts and rewards), minimizing fixed costs (e.g. the 'dropshipping' business model), or exploiting available partnerships and connections (e.g. utilizing university premises for business meetings). This is known as 'financial bootstrapping' – the term describes the use of methods to meet the need for resources without relying on external finance (Ozdemir et al, 2016; Reficco et al, 2021; Winborg and Landström, 2001).

Financial bootstrapping is a resource-acquisition strategy adopted widely by start-ups to overcome the constraints they face. It includes a set of capabilities (a developed skillset that enables organizations to achieve certain outcomes) that aim to address the need for finance (or resources broadly) at the lowest cost possible (Ozdemir et al, 2016). This is particularly relevant for social enterprises, which often face higher barriers to securing external funding. Financial bootstrapping can therefore be beneficial for social start-ups to achieve their social mission, the so-called 'socially-oriented bootstrapping' (Vestrum, 2016; Winborg and Landström, 2001).

For example, social enterprises are likely to serve vulnerable, under-represented communities and markets that are often not targeted by traditional finance providers (Corner and Ho, 2010). They also appear to develop activities to tackle challenging issues and conditions, which often require an innovative approach not only to generate impact but also to source and sustain it (Fujimoto et al, 2014). To illustrate this, imagine a social enterprise where beneficiaries are involved in the creation of a product (service) that generates revenues, and who are positively affected because of this experience. This would illustrate the bootstrapping practices that decrease labour costs, ultimately reducing the need for finance (see the box below for further examples and the theoretical explanation behind bootstrapping).

**KEY RESEARCH**

Socially-oriented bootstrapping: social exchange and signalling theories

To explain how social enterprises approach resourcing their activities while pursuing social value creation, two theories could be helpful: social exchange theory and signalling theory (Jayawarna et al, 2020). Broadly, these theories describe the relationships between two parties (the party could be either an individual or an organization) and the conditions under which these relationships evolve to pursue certain outcomes.

Social exchange theory focuses on the interaction between the two parties, represented as a sequence of transactions. During these transactions, resources are exchanged based on the principle of reciprocity, and the outcome of such an exchange is driven by the quality of the relationship, characterized by trust, flexibility, openness and commitment (Cropanzano et al, 2017).

Signalling theory, on the other hand, is concerned with the information asymmetry between two interacting parties, where the achievement of a certain outcome is dependent on the availability and disclosure of the information necessary for decision-making (Connelly et al, 2011). For example, the bond with the community, sympathy for the social challenge and connections with the beneficiaries serve as signals for a social enterprise to manifest its credibility to prospective funders (signalling theory). At the same time, leveraging community resources to deliver a positive intervention can be viewed as a social exchange. In both cases, this leads to bootstrapping practices that allow social enterprises to benefit from resources under more favourable conditions than otherwise would be available to them.

The emphasis on reciprocal arrangements to secure resources necessary to benefit the communities that also supply these resources, proposes a fit with the social exchange theory. It further highlights the importance of such relationships for social enterprises. Living up to the community/beneficiaries' expectations (e.g. in terms of public appearance and adhering to carbon-reduction practices) sends signals to create trust, openness and commitment to the cause to facilitate further access to resources.

## *Grants and donations*

These are typically provided by governments (see later in this chapter for examples of government programmes), agencies, private (individual or corporate) donors and other types of organizations when the activity of the social enterprise aligns with their social and/or environmental agenda. The purpose is to stimulate research and development, support emerging industries, underrepresented groups and disadvantaged communities, facilitate innovation or create social impact (Beaton and Dowin Kennedy, 2021; Reficco et al, 2021; Smith et al, 2012). While donations are often characterized by their philanthropic nature, grants are mainly driven by a specific purpose (agenda) to achieve public good (Bosma et al, 2016; OECD, 2022; Smith and Besharov, 2019). The latter is usually available on a competitive basis, for a specific purpose with no formal obligations to return it, but with the anticipation of the intended impact/outcome associated with a positive change or follow-up longer-term arrangements. Both options represent the first stepping stones for social enterprises to get external funding, as they do not involve any payback.

## Debt finance

This mainly refers to the services of financial institutions (e.g. banks) or, broadly, the exchange between the funding provided (loan) and the contractual agreement to pay it back at a price (interest rate) within a certain time (payback period). Quite often, such arrangements require an existing track record and collateral to secure the loan (or any other financial product – e.g. the repayment of an invoice, an overdraft or managing trade flows to cover short-term liquidity gaps). With the occurrence of the recent financial crisis caused by Covid-related disruptions, political tensions (e.g. Russia-Ukraine conflict, Gaza-Israel conflict, US-China strategic competition) and economic supply-related challenges worldwide, credit conditions have become even tighter (Khan, 2022). Besides, despite various initiatives undertaken by financial institutions to make their products more accessible, funding gaps are still widely prevalent. For example, in Europe, there is a slowdown in bank lending to businesses due to the monetary tightening in the economy overall and an increase in demand for external finance. This resulted in a notable financing gap, especially among small and medium enterprises (SMEs), reaching 6 per cent in 2023 (European Central Bank, 2023). Similarly, in the United States, the share of firms that sought bank financing and were successful had been declining up until 2021 (from 50 per cent in 2019 to 30 per cent in 2021) with just around half of the companies getting the intended outcomes (The Federal Reserve, 2022). The situation is further exacerbated in developing countries, with an estimated 40 per cent of SMEs (including micro-firms) having a funding gap of $5.2 trillion every year (The World Bank, 2023). Debt finance often has financial implications – the more debt, the less financially stable a firm is deemed to be. This is due to the focus being inadvertently directed on debt management rather than development and growth. Hence, it is more likely the firm will adopt strategies that involve reducing costs and seeking further external finance.

## Equity finance

Equity finance serves a different purpose to debt finance. It is mostly used by businesses to boost growth in the long term. It is an exchange of the company's stake (share) for funding, where ownership and control become the 'collateral', while the value of the company and profit sharing contribute to the return on investment. There are various forms of equity funding that can be used in combination with debt funding (e.g. hybrid securities such as convertible bonds and equity releases for debt consolidation traded in secondary markets). It can be provided by the following investors:

- angel investors: certain wealthy individuals who engage in investment activities professionally (private equity capital)
- networks and syndicates (e.g. European Business Angels Network, Business Angel Network of Southeast Asia)
- institutional/corporate venture capital that comes from financial institutions (e.g. investment banks)
- large corporates (e.g. Google Ventures, Unilever Ventures)

Corporate venture capital, although not accessible to a wide range of organizations, is still considered to be a key driver for innovation and growth. It has significantly increased in the last few decades, reaching $73.1 billion in 2020. In comparison, outstanding business loans in the US alone accounted for $833 billion in 2020, while the angel investment market was estimated at $26 billion a year earlier in the US and Canada (Business Angel Institute, 2021; Logman, 2021; OECD, 2022). If debt finance providers are mainly concerned with debt management, equity investors are driven by (economic) growth potential. This restricts the pool of 'eligible' start-ups and potentially compromises the ownership structure.

## Alternative finance

This is an umbrella term that aggregates all the remaining funding sources outside the 'traditional' methods mentioned above (Ziegler et al, 2021). With the digitalization and decentralization of financial marketplaces, the first forms of alternative funding included crowdfunding platforms. These range from reward-based and donation models to other alternative products, replicating and extending traditional options such as debt-based crowdfunding (peer-to-peer lending, invoice trading) and equity crowdfunding. Donation-based crowdfunding (e.g. Just Giving, SimplyGiving, Crowdfunder, GoFundMe) and reward-based crowdfunding models (e.g. Indiegogo, Kickstarter) have proved to be the most popular ways for social enterprises to fundraise (Chandna, 2022).

As the name suggests, donation-based crowdfunding models are driven by donations from the public, who are attracted to the cause of the social enterprise, or who are the potential beneficiaries of its product or service. Reward-based platforms are particularly suitable for social enterprises, which can provide 'tangible gifts' (rewards) in return for funding received. These could include small tokens of appreciation (e.g. a shout-out on social media), promotional merchandise (e.g. t-shirts with printed drawings created by refugee children) or a free sample of the product (e.g. a 'root-growing kit' to promote healthy living). In all cases, success is dependent on the time and effort spent to build your networks and deliver a message that is both appealing and realistic for achieving the set goals. For those reasons, despite the wide proliferation, funding rates for such campaigns remain quite low (Farhoud et al, 2021).

The development of blockchain technologies and tokenization platforms has emerged most recently (e.g. NYALA) as a form of alternative finance market. New means of funding are also available in secondary alternative finance market options that allow the reselling of shares, invoices, debts or digital tokens initially obtained on the primary markets. The key principles of these developing virtual funding spaces are rooted in accessibility and decentralization. With accessibility, more 'agents' can now be involved in financing activities, thus increasing opportunities for businesses to be funded. Decentralization implies that no singular agent (such as a bank or a venture capitalist) is in control of decision-making and, subsequently, deal management and rewards harvesting.

Despite being an attractive option for those start-ups who are often rejected or discouraged from the 'traditional' forms of funding, alternative finance is not without risks and downsides:

- First, accessibility also means enhanced competition, and the need to differentiate and stand out to attract the 'crowd'.
- Second, decentralization potentially drives the dilution of ownership (e.g. equity crowdfunding) and increased risks associated with the increased exposure to a wider market (e.g. secondary markets) therefore affecting the potential stability of the organization.
- Third, the lack of a single decision-maker can also be deceptive, as the control is still contained by a particular group of entities with potentially conflicting interests (for example, short-term gain versus longer-term growth).

Alternative finance also covers non-digital 'niche' solutions, for example, lending cooperatives, social impact funds, schemes and programmes run as part of corporate activities to meet certain objectives (e.g. Virgin Start-up, accelerators, networks).

## Blockchain applications in social finance

The fast-paced development in the financial markets has implications for social enterprises as well. One of the most current technologies that has made possible the increasing volumes of 'social good' is blockchain. Blockchain is a digital ledger (a public record book) that stores all transactions, and connections among them, in organized 'blocks' of data, forming a 'chain' (Devine et al, 2021; Zachariadis et al,

2019). While this technology has found use in various industries and markets, it has substantially affected access to capital for new ventures in general. One of the ways to raise finance using this technology is through an ICO (initial coin offering). Companies issue their own digital currency (known as 'tokens') and sell it to potential investors or other partners. As with any currency, it captures the value that drives its supply and creates demand for it (i.e. the price that the tokens can be traded for). This value can be (Schückes and Gutmann, 2021):

- future payments made by customers for particular products or services provided by the company that issues those tokens (so-called, 'utility tokens')
- voting rights to take part in the decision-making of the company that is funded through the tokens
- assets/usage rights, such as the opportunity to access or store data, the assets, contracts and equity shares

The different forms of value that back up the tokens determine their type (e.g. utility tokens). To issue a token, a company would normally use an existing network (such as Bitcoin or Ethereum) to facilitate this process. The meticulous record of all these transactions and their transparency provides security to users, enabling them to easily prove their identities, verify transactions and protect ownership of digital assets at a relatively low cost (Yang et al, 2019). As a result, users can achieve certain outcomes that traditional funding methods are struggling to demonstrate without facing high risks and costs.

For example, the fact that funds can be easily traced could make it possible to monitor aid distribution more accurately. Moreover, the ability to send money anywhere to anyone, securely and easily, makes it cheaper and more reliable to send funds across borders, natural disaster zones or even war zones. Finally, managing identities securely allows people like those from disadvantaged communities, who would otherwise struggle to interact with established financial institutions (e.g. banks), to get access to funding (Stanford Graduate School of Business, 2019).

Blockchain technology also has indirect funding implications for social enterprises. Its key advantages revolve around the transparency of data, identities and decisions, which facilitate trust. The latter is essential for a social enterprise to secure funding, especially from a social impact investor – see the next section (Devine et al, 2021; Prashar et al, 2020). For example, its non-monetary implications can facilitate tracking throughout the supply-chain system by collecting, monitoring and managing data for each operation, stakeholder and time point – from the farmer in the field to the processing facility and distribution.

At the same time, existing organizations and finance providers have also started funding social businesses in cryptocurrency. For example, the UNICEF CryptoFund invested in eight social enterprises in seven countries. The aim was to solve local and global challenges around education access to young children, hunger, mental health and medical diagnostics targeting those in poverty, those with physical impairment and wider populations from disadvantaged communities (UNICEF, 2020). For example, Cireha, a social enterprise based in Argentina, used the funding to scale the reach of their app to help children with speech impairments communicate using symbols. Avyantra, based in India, leveraged the investment to upgrade its health app, which uses data science to support front-line health workers in the early diagnosis of neonatal sepsis.

## *Blockchain in social finance: limitations and additional considerations*

As with any decision, the use of blockchain technology to finance or facilitate funding in a social enterprise cannot be made without thorough consideration. Regardless of the 'disruptiveness' of blockchain technology, we have not yet witnessed its wide proliferation. For example, Deloitte estimated that the chance for a blockchain project to survive (as a business application) is less than 15 per cent (Deloitte Insights, 2021). While the number of cryptocurrencies in the world peaked in February 2022 (tipping over 10,000), they reduced by 20 per cent by the same month in 2023: 31 per cent of sampled companies reported the use of blockchain technology in payments/trading processes worldwide, 34 per cent in financial flow traceability and 44 per cent in digital currency (Statista, 2023). The reasons for that boil down to the following:

1. Adopting blockchain solutions adds a certain layer of complexity to the already complex social business model, where the level of confidence and readiness to embrace new technologies tend to be a dominant factor preventing one from their utilization (Platt et al, 2021). Therefore, building collaborations with more experienced partners through knowledge-exchange programmes (e.g. reaching out to universities, business hubs and governmental initiatives) could be a way to ease adoption.
2. Data transparency has its downside, given that the regulation is yet to be advanced to manage the rising conflicts around sensitive information like customer data and financial information (Rossi et al, 2019; Sedlmeir et al, 2022).
3. The inability to delete any data entry posits another limitation, which contradicts GDPR's 'right to be forgotten' where any user can request to remove the information related to them (Schellinger et al, 2022).
4. Depending on the scope of integration and use, blockchain technology might turn out to be an expensive stream of activities to maintain, especially when applied to scaling (Mahjoub et al, 2022), which is particularly discouraging for social start-ups.

# Social impact investment

Social impact is a key metric that needs to be captured for a social enterprise, regardless of the way it is financed or what types of funding it is looking to attract. It serves as the key beacon guiding social enterprise activities and their further development (Rawhouser et al, 2019). Therefore, social impact becomes even more important when accessing tailored types of funding to support social enterprises, and where social returns on investment become equally important, if not more, compared to economic returns. Social impact funding is one such instrument that is designed to provide capital that would generate specific social and environmental returns as well as financial returns for investors. As such, it is a form of equity funding (see earlier section) that incorporates social value generation on par with economic value.

The already substantial funding gap for SMEs worldwide has been exacerbated in recent years due to global disruptions (e.g. Covid-19 pandemic, war conflicts and weather-related emergencies). A $4.2 trillion funding gap has been identified in fulfilling the commitments to achieve Sustainable Development Goals (SDGs) by 2030 (OECD, 2021). Despite this striking number, it is equivalent to only 1.1 per cent of all assets held by all institutional financial organizations (see corporate venture capital as defined earlier). At the same time, the latest estimates of the size of the impact investing market suggest nearly $1.3 trillion across the world. Western, Northern and Southern Europe generate 55 per cent of the impact, while 37 per cent is from the US and Canada (Hand et al, 2022). The majority of impact investment in Europe comes in the form of private debt and private equity – 83 per cent in total; the third place is taken by real assets – 11 per cent (e.g. social housing), followed by EU funding (5 per cent) and other types of organizations and individuals. In particular, financial institutions (28 per cent) represent the majority of capital providers, followed by individual investors (26 per cent) (Gianluca Gaggiotti, 2022). According to the same source, the most popular SDGs targeted by impact investors (in terms of the volume of impact capital provided) in 2022 were Decent Work and Economic Growth (8), Reduced Inequalities (10) and Climate Action (13), while the least served targets are Peace, Justice and Strong Institutions (16), Life Below Water (14) and Life on Land (15).

Following the guidelines of the European Impact Investment Consortium in an attempt to further boost market growth, three principles known as 'The Triad of Impact' or 'Impact Investment Pillars' were suggested to be adhered to when it comes to capturing social impact for feasibility estimations of social impact investment (Gianluca Gaggiotti, 2022):

1 *Intentionality* – implies an original intention (conscious and deliberate choice) outlined at the outset of an investment deal to serve a particular social (or environmental) purpose and achieve an impact, which is manifested through a positive effect or change for a pre-defined group of beneficiaries.

2 *Measurability* – refers to the quantification of the impact, starting from specific objectives to the deliverables that are captured within a metrics system, which could include both quantitative and qualitative measures.

3 *Additionality* – characterizes the add-on benefits of the investment to the targeted social (environmental) impact. It is a quality attributable to the investment itself, suggesting that without this investment, the anticipated impact (in terms of its measurable objectives) could not have been achieved, or the likelihood of its occurrence is significantly less.

An example of capturing the social impact and working out the returns on the social impact investment is presented in the box below.

**KEY RESEARCH**

How to measure social return on impact investment?

*Addressing the problem of isolation and the lack of sense of belonging among women refugees.*

For this fictional case, which represents a cluster of social enterprises in developed economies, Wellsprings Ltd is working with women refugees who were forced to flee their country, seeking shelter and a new start in life. Through their London-based centre, they provide social and emotional support to their beneficiaries on an individual and group basis, generating revenues through the sale of bakery products, produced collaboratively by those women.

As a result, we will consider this case in terms of the 'Triad of Impact' outlined above.

*1. Intentionality*

Two streams of impact are declared to be achieved for the target group of beneficiaries:

- reduced feelings of isolation
- a sense of belonging

*2. Measurability*

To develop a metrics system to measure the stated objectives, the following indicators are being monitored throughout the duration of the programme:

- self-evaluation of the feelings associated with being understood, belonging to the community, having friendships and trusting others (client survey, Likert scale)
- actual number of 'quality' friendships/acquaintances made (client survey, Likert scale, conversations with staff)

- engagement in voluntary community activities as part of the programme (staff observations, registry)

*3. Additionality*

To determine that the sought-for outcomes have been driven by the activities of Wellsprings Ltd, the comparisons with the baseline evaluations (the initial evaluation, followed by bi-weekly and monthly evaluations) were made.

**Table 11.1** Capturing social value (for a year)

| Outcomes (Metrics) | Feeling of Isolation | Sense of Belonging | Sources/Assumptions |
|---|---|---|---|
| 1. Average % increase in positive feelings compared to initial evaluation | 28% | 46% | Based on the Client Survey – indirect impact further leads to measurable outcomes 2 and 3. |
| 2. Average increase in meeting friends/ acquaintances per week (%) | 50% | | Increase in meeting friends/ acquaintances/family from once/twice per week to most days is equivalent to £15,500 a year, or £535 per 1% increase (Powdthavee, 2008). |
| 3. Average % increase in community activities engagement | | 15% | A 1% increase in the community activities generates 6% increase in revenues (historical data), which is equivalent to £2,021 (annual revenue is £33,680). |
| Estimated value per year | £26,750(50 x £535) | £30,315(15 x £2,021) | |

NB: The inflation indices and the correction for the 'severity' of the cases have not been taken into account.

*Return on social impact investment*

- The overall outcome evaluation equals: £26,750 (feeling of isolation) + £30,315 (sense of belonging) + £33,680 (revenues generated) = £60,425.
- The overall input costs are estimated as: £17,622+£13,456+£6,675+ £3,751 = £41,504.

**Table 11.2** Input costs (for a year)

| Category | Description | Evaluation |
|---|---|---|
| Women-support activities | • Salary to a professional worker (0.5 FTE)<br>• Rental and utility costs | £17,622 |
| Bakery activities | • Chef (0.6 FTE)<br>• Ingredients, regulatory compliance expenses | £13,456 |
| In-kind contributions | Marketing, packaging, baking equipment and some ingredients and furniture (donations) | £6,675 |
| Volunteer contributions | Volunteer time (360 hours a year at £10.42p/h) | £3,751 |

- The estimated return on social impact investment: **£60,425/£41,504** = **£1.46** (per each £ invested into this social enterprise, the total value that is to be generated is £1.46).
- The estimated return on social value: (**£26,750** (feeling of isolation) + **£30,315** (sense of belonging))/**£41,504** (total costs) = **£1.37** (per each £ invested into this social enterprise, the social value that is to be generated is equivalent to **£1.37**).

As with the economic return on investment, an indicator that is greater than 1 suggests a positive return on social value, meaning that the social impact investment (the money spent) generates an 'excess' of social value expressed in monetary terms. Based on the demonstrated evaluations, the social impact investment into Wellsprings Ltd generates **£0.37** of 'extra value' per each **£1** invested (after covering for all the costs). This proposes a successful use of investment that justifies (and outperforms) the capital obtained to achieve the sought-for outcomes.

### Additional considerations

**Attribution of value:** for more accurate representation, it is important to acknowledge other factors outside the activities provided by the social enterprise that contributed to (or slowed down) social value generation. For example, the longer the women stay in the country, the more likely they are to be settled and form connections outside 'Wellsprings Ltd', which would lead to positive outcomes. So not necessarily all the positive change could be attributed to this particular social enterprise.

**The life-long value of benefit:** the current evaluation captures the quality and strength of the connections and experiences, leading to a positive change. As the programme is restricted in time, which is essential for its continuity in accommodating new beneficiaries, it is not clear whether the documented positive change will continue taking place once the interaction with this social enterprise is over. Moreover, there is also a potentially diminishing effect here, where the impact could be at its highest at the initial stages while levelling off or even being reduced towards the end of participation in the programme.

**Addressing the root cause**: the quality of the impact could also be considered by taking into account the extent to which the root cause of the problem is addressed. While the refugee women might have experienced an increased sense of belonging and started feeling less isolated, the solutions have not addressed the problem of them having to leave their country and family behind, causing life-long distress and a sense of unsettlement.

**SOURCE**: the case is partially based on materials published by https://www.wellspringsforwomen.com (archived at https://perma.cc/WJ3U-HDLW)

## Social bonds and social impact bonds

Securities that are derived from the original (primary market) transactions are traded both in the debt and equity finance markets (see earlier section). They represent a form of contract between a finance provider and the recipient of the funding. This 'contract' specifies the terms of a financial transaction, such as the amount of funding and its conditions (e.g. interest rate, payback period), which could be further sold on the secondary markets for immediate financial benefit.

For example, on the primary market, a company receives a bank loan that totals \$1,000 and needs to be paid back in a year with a 10 per cent interest rate. Alternatively, the same company could issue a bond (a type of security), which specifies the need for the same \$1,000 under the same conditions, and can be traded on the secondary market (i.e. stock exchange). If an investor buys this bond, the company will get \$1,000 and will commit to paying the interest and the payback amount. However, if this investor decides to resell this bond to get the money back sooner than in one year, they could get \$900 now (depending on the price that the bond is being traded at), and the new investor will have the right to claim the interest and the payback from the company that issued this bond. In this way, a bond is a debt-based security that seals the deal between the debt provider (the principal) and the recipient (the agent) on payment terms, where the principal provides the loan, and the agent is responsible for its repayment in the future.

Bonds are particularly widespread among larger, more established organizations that seek to leverage finance on a larger scale, diversifying the pool of their creditors. With the proliferation of alternative finance markets, bonds can also be traded on certain crowdfunding platforms, which specialize in peer-to-peer lending. This is known as a secondary market option compared to the original setup, where loans could be directly issued to the recipient.

## Social bonds

These secondary markets also trade a series of bond-type securities that aim to support positive social and environmental causes, where the International Capital Market Association (ICMA) issued a set of principles, differentiating among Social Bonds, Green Bonds and Sustainability Bonds. The main distinction refers to the type of cause (ICMA, 2023):

- **Social bonds** should attract funding specifically for projects/activities that aim to address a particular social issue and seek to achieve positive social outcomes (e.g. affordable basic infrastructure, access to essential services, affordable housing, food security).
- **Green bonds** are linked to 'green projects' that contribute to environmental objectives related to climate change, the use of natural resources, conservation of biodiversity and tackling pollution.
- **Sustainability bonds** should target a combination of social and environmental causes.

The guidance also recommends the issuer (e.g. a social enterprise) of such bonds maintain full financial and social impact disclosure, regular reporting, independence of financial accounts and external verification for quality assurance. This has proved to be an attractive finance instrument for growing social enterprises, where the global market for social bonds reached nearly $150 billion in 2020, skyrocketing compared to the previous year (Asian Development Bank, 2021; Hilbrich, 2021).

## Social impact bonds

Social bonds are not to be confused with another instrument, Social Impact Bonds (first introduced in the UK in 2010), which is an agreement between social enterprises (or other not-for-profit organizations) and funding providers (often governments or other institutional investors – corporate venture capital) to deliver a pre-defined social outcome in return for the finance provided in line with the predefined terms and conditions (OECD, 2016, 2021; Social Finance, 2012). However, this agreement works quite differently compared to the bonds, as has been described so far. Usually the first 'tranche' is provided to cover the operating costs associated with the activities that aim to deliver the pre-agreed social outcome. If the objective is achieved, the issuer of the bond (the social enterprise) receives the rest of the payment (Social Finance, 2012). As a result, the agreement works as a future contract rather than a bond in its traditional understanding, which can further be sold at the financial markets for risk and profit management purposes. This form of growth capital for social enterprise has found recognition worldwide, reaching $1 trillion in 2021, mainly as one of the most effective tools to achieve 'public good' objectives set out by governments. Europe, the Middle East and Africa have been leading the issuance of social impact bonds, followed by the Asia-Pacific Region and the United States (Wong, 2022).

### *Social bonds and social impact bonds: limitations*

As with any financial security, these forms of funding are not without limitations:

- First, due to the nature of financial obligations, new and smaller social enterprises are less likely to be able to take advantage of them (and meet the eligibility criteria).
- Second, while securitization facilitates the management of financial risks associated with the failure of the agreement (which can happen from both sides), those cannot be eliminated (OECD, 2016).
- Third, due to the complexity of the infrastructure, which often involves intermediaries (Tortorice et al, 2020), it is not a cheap financing option.
- Fourth, the challenges around measuring social (or environmental) impact, and transparency around the activities pose additional barriers for funding providers to select the 'worthy' project.
- Fifth, potentially conflicting objectives pursued by social enterprises and finance providers (the buyers of the bonds) hinder the way to the optimum resolution, achieving fair conditions and the expected outcomes (European Commission, 2023; Pequeneza, 2019). For example, the objectives of local authorities or governmental bodies may not necessarily align with the objectives of a particular social enterprise while dealing with the same social/environmental issue and targeting the same population group.

## Social enterprise funding model

With the ongoing development of funding markets as well as the ever-growing need to meet social and environmental objectives, new instruments are emerging that are becoming more accessible for social enterprises. Yet, the success of a social enterprise depends not only on the quality and reach of the social value that it is delivering to beneficiaries but also on its financial viability, which is essential to sustaining and growing its operations. Considering the importance of the financial aspect, social enterprises have to develop a competitive business model (see Chapter 9), like any market-driven organization, or a 'funding model' as suggested by Foster et al (2009), given their main focus on the social value proposition. This funding model should include the revenue-generating stream and also bring together other finance sources at each stage of business development. The choice of those sources, aligned with activities and objectives, is crucial for the financial sustainability of social enterprises. As such, multiple factors need to be taken into consideration:

## 1. The stage of business development and its financial needs across the timeline

As illustrated, start-ups, and social enterprises in particular, are often constrained in their choices, and most are 'hungry' for cash. However, even within a limited range of options, the decision at this stage can significantly shape the future development of the social enterprise. These decisions can either foster its social impact or trigger the 'mission drift' tensions (Lumpkin et al, 2013) (see Chapter 1). Any funding application, bid, pitch or transaction requires a significant amount of time and certain skills. This suggests that any effort should be thought through and pre-evaluated, rather than based just on opportunistic decision-making. The stage of business development is closely associated with product/service readiness and track record – the fundamental factors for any debt financing. The nature and scope of the social/environmental impact are more likely to drive equity-based funding, which requires rigour, due diligence and quite often external evaluations to capture and validate the anticipated outcomes.

## 2. The internal organizational structure

In technical terms, the legal form of the business (as illustrated in the next section) can define the eligibility of a business for funding opportunities. From a more conceptual point of view, the composition of the team, the employees (if applicable) and their profile (e.g. full-time versus hourly paid) would also drive the need for finance and potentially be key in determining its accessibility (e.g. impact investors would want to evaluate the suitability of the 'team' and the impact that is set out to be achieved, as shown earlier).

## 3. The 'entrepreneurial' capital

Entrepreneurial capital typically encompasses financial, human, social, cultural and physical capital (Erikson, 2002). This capital would establish the presence of collateral for the majority of debt finance products. It will also determine the success of the equity-based funding sources, where the relationships with the beneficiaries and intermediaries that facilitate the scope and delivery of social value are of importance. The competencies of the team, affiliations, sponsorships, networks, education and professional background can drive success in engaging with more complex digital solutions, ranging from crowdfunding to blockchain finance (see the example of blockchain applications earlier).

## 4. The nature of the business and its social/environmental course

As noted in this chapter, certain funding sources available to social enterprises are often tailored to specific initiatives, objectives, geographical areas and groups of beneficiaries. This is often driven by higher-level policy and guidance documents (e.g. SDGs), but can also vary at the local level, depending on topical priorities or situational context. Institutional and, even more so, private investors (within both primary and secondary markets) could have their preferences and areas of professional expertise, favouring projects that fit those the most.

## 5. The internal funding mechanisms.

The internal funding model, or the way revenues are generated in the social enterprise, will also determine the eligibility for particular sources, as well as the attractiveness of certain types of funders. For example, the availability of a stable inflow of cash, driven by the large-scale customer base, can potentially deter social impact investors. However, it will most certainly secure debt financing and facilitate success in digital public-centred platforms. The niche customer profile, closely aligned with social objectives, could, on the contrary, serve as a positive signal for equity-based finance.

## 6. Short-term objectives and longer-term aspirations

The entrepreneurial proclivity of the founder (or key decision makers) would also play a significant role in the process of finance acquisition. High risk tends to be associated with better, more attractive conditions, for example, social (impact bonds), blockchain finance and equity-based financial instruments. The risks are linked with the success of securing the deal (versus the cost, time and resources spent to achieve it) and also with the success of achieving the anticipated result. For example, reaching the set target in the crowdfunding campaign, attracting a sufficient number of users in blockchain finance or seeing the fulfilment of the deal from the funder's side in social impact bonds. The future of the organization, in terms of its long-term growth and aspiration, is also an important factor for equity-driven investments, as illustrated earlier in the chapter.

### 7. *External environment*

The contextual surroundings should not be neglected either, ranging from macroeconomic conditions affecting, for example, interest rates, stock markets and social-demographic developments, to more granular environmental aspects relevant to the decision-making. The latter could include political and monetary incentives (e.g. tax relief schemes), market conditions (e.g. competition) and the relevance or importance of social or environmental outcomes concerning local matters. Notably, the supply of funding sources would be equally subjected to all those factors, which will in turn shape the funding availability and conditions.

Taking all those factors into consideration, it becomes evident that the funding model is not a linear representation of a particular sequence of funding sources (Lyon and Owen, 2019). With each iteration of social enterprise development, with each pivot (which could include lack of success in securing the sought-after funding source), the need for finance comes in again. The difference is that each time it comes at a different starting point. This can be due to a more advanced product/service development, a different situational setting, increased entrepreneurial capital, an adjusted social value proposition or even a changed founder's outlook on the problem/issue and the case of running a social enterprise. As a result, we can witness a social financing lifecycle (see Figure 11.2) that is dynamic, fluid and contextual. However, it is still based on the key pillars of social financing decisions covered in this chapter: the demand perspective represented by the social venture, the supply perspective, the fit between the two, and the context-specific attributes.

## The choice factors of social finance and key challenges

When considering sources of finances, several factors need to be considered that inform decision-making.

First, 'information asymmetries' between entrepreneurs and financial providers (Hirsch and Walz, 2019). The latter will never have full information about the business that they are supporting, and having to deal with uncertainties and assumptions would be forced to create conditions to minimize those. From the entrepreneur's stance, these conditions are substantial barriers that they need to break through by demonstrating their business potential, financial sustainability and credibility. These obstacles are manifested through high interest rates, the demand for an increased stake in the company, restrictive contractual agreements, the necessity of collateral or the existing track record of successful operations (Cumming and Binti Johan, 2008).

**Figure 11.2** Social financing cycle

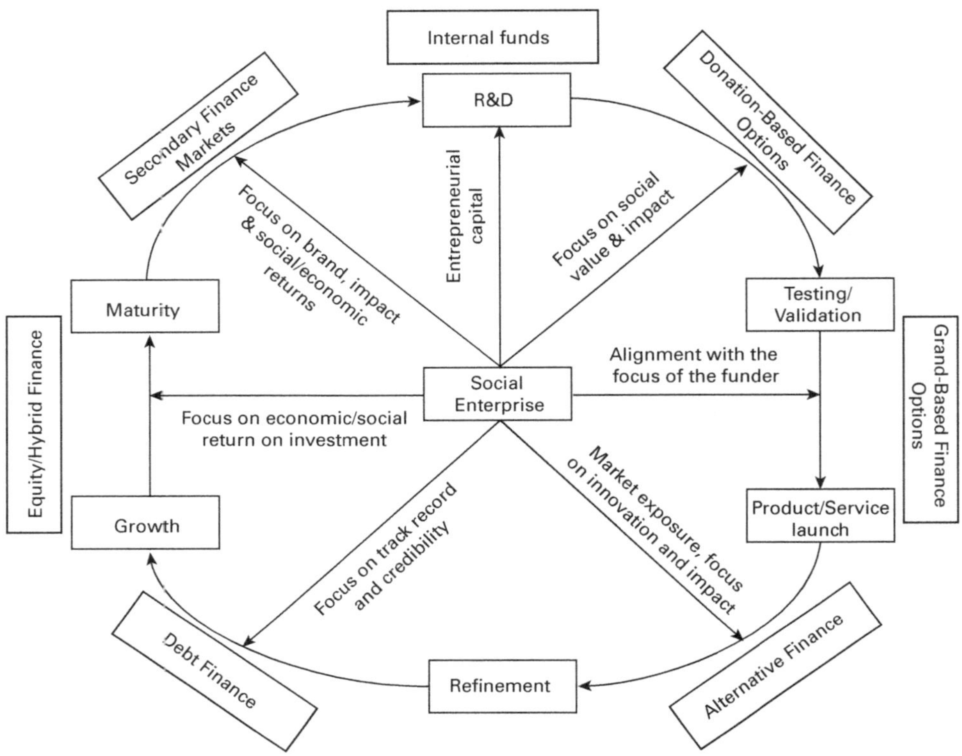


Second, 'liability of newness' implies not only the struggle to get out to the market but also to obtain other non-financial resources, such as social and human capital (by accessing networks, knowledge and skills), reputation and legitimacy (Block et al, 2019; Bonini & Capizzi, 2019). This also has implications on decision-making for entrepreneurs, who are to think strategically about how access to finance can serve as a bridge to all other necessary resources to facilitate business success. For example, securing a bank loan can signal either positively or negatively on the firm's financial structure (depending on its position concerning other sources). It will potentially affect its attractiveness in the eyes of private equity investors, who in turn might provide valuable strategic advice and open up networks (Doherty et al, 2014; Vickers et al, 2017). Developing a crowdfunding campaign might yield disappointing results. However, if accompanied by careful consideration of the marketing plan, it can add value in terms of user engagement, customer feedback and extensive market exposure (Wald et al, 2019).

While these two factors relate to all types of ventures and are, in most cases, applicable to new entrepreneurial firms, social enterprises also have to deal with the fact that their activities develop around their beneficiaries and communities. Those are already, by definition, less resourceful than communities with developed business and public infrastructure, high employment rates and higher levels of welfare. As a result, social enterprises are more likely to operate in areas (within communities) where the resources are already limited, posing further difficulties in funding their activities (Miller et al, 2012; Peredo and McLean, 2006). Social enterprises have unique features, for example, the secondary role of the economic value stream, targeting vulnerable groups of customers who are often restricted in financial terms, positioning themselves in less competitive markets compared to mainstream commercial organizations. Those characteristics make them even less attractive for 'traditional' external finance providers such as debt finance and equity finance, whose aims, structures and processes are not aligned with this (Bacq & Eddleston, 2018; Jayawarna et al, 2020; Vestrum, 2016). As a result, social enterprises are left with bootstrapping, grants and donations, and alternative finance options, which have also evolved into socially oriented forms specifically to meet the needs of the ever-growing social enterprise market. To tackle these challenges, social enterprises ought to be innovative to identify new ways to secure funding or minimize the need for it by still striving to maximize the social value that they create.

## Social finance landscape: additional considerations

At the same time, there have been some positive developments in the financial markets worldwide, boosting the supply of finance for social enterprises. In the first place, these funds are driven by government programmes in the realization of the need to address the social and environmental challenges proliferating in our societies and the increased pressure to tackle them. Examples of such programmes include:

- The European Social Fund + (ESF+) is one of the European Union's largest funds (€99.3 billion for the period 2021–2027) to aid employment, social and educational inequalities, culminating post- Covid-19 pandemic. In particular, one of its initiatives, the ESF Social Innovation+, provides grants to validate and scale social innovation across Europe, while also building networks to facilitate knowledge exchange through the European Social Innovation database and Competence Centre for Social Innovation.
- In the UK, among various other schemes, the Social Enterprise Boost Fund, which runs from 2023 to 2025 (with a total funding available of £4.1 million) provides small-scale grant funding to social enterprises in six disadvantaged areas of England.
- The Office of Community Services (OCS), within the US Department of Health and Human Services Administration for Children and Families, funds social businesses to facilitate economic development in low-income communities.

The options extend beyond the grant funding into lending and investment opportunities as well (Lyon and Owen, 2019). These funds range from various social lending forms (e.g. subsidized loans, microfinance) to specialized equity-based instruments (e.g. philanthropic venture capital, social impact bonds, impact investments). While these 'niche' forms of funding are still liable to the same advantages and challenges as the traditional types of debt and equity financing, there are some additional considerations that shape the decision-making when it comes to social enterprises. These include:

- First, the 'legal visibility' of social enterprises in the market, which would be identified by the adopted legal form, the definitions of which vary significantly across different countries (see Chapter 1).
- Second, the governance structure, and the positioning of the social and economic value streams, will define the eligibility for more specialized funding sources. For example, the Thrive Together Fund (TTF) in England offers a mix of loan and grant funding to specifically defined social enterprises, which must fall into one of the specific categories and be registered as an incorporated business. The US Department of Agriculture's Farm Service Agency (FSA) offers guaranteed loans to for-profit cooperatives. Unincorporated associations, trusts and even some forms of limited companies are unlikely to attract impact equity funding, while some specialized legal forms (e.g. Community of Interest Companies in the UK, Social Purpose Corporation in the US, Social Purpose Company in Belgium) are designed to be adopted by social enterprises seeking the benefits of equity investments while maintaining the emphasis on social purpose.
- Third, another important factor is associated with the transparency and measurement of social impact, which is further translated into the reporting and, even more, certification/ratings. This increases the accountability of social enterprises for their activities in front of potential funders across various stages – from the initial screening or pre-evaluation (utilized by impact investment funds) to incorporating specific requirements imposed by the funder. Examples of such requirements could be targeting specific groups of beneficiaries or managing and using funds in a specifically pre-determined way that is to be monitored and measured (which is likely to be expected for grant funding). For specialized debt-based programmes targeting social enterprise specifically, the expectation of financial sustainability and economic resilience is common. Thus, reiterating the need to balance social and economic streams, social ventures ultimately face a double-whammy challenge compared to traditional profit-driven organizations, especially when it comes to seeking and securing funding.

## Summary and key learning points

In this chapter, we started by considering various funding sources available in the market, discussing their key peculiarities, differences and application to social enterprises. We further delved into specific forms of finance, tailored particularly to fill in the gap in financial capital for social enterprises in response to the rising social and environmental challenges: blockchain applications, social impact investments and social (impact) bonds. Finally, the chapter concluded with considerations of the factors shaping the social enterprise funding model and the choice of suitable finance sources.

The key takeaways are the following:

- The specific nature of the social enterprise, having to balance the social and economic sides of their business models, determines the accessibility of finance sources in the market, where financial bootstrapping, internal means of funding, grants and donations are the starting points for most social enterprises.
- Social impact investments and social (impact) bonds are instruments specifically designed to facilitate social change, where the transparency and measurability of social impact are of paramount importance.
- Emerging financial instruments (e.g. blockchain applications) could be an attractive alternative for entrepreneurs looking to embrace new technologies for social good, given the right combination of entrepreneurial capital.
- The need for funding and the suitability of sources would vary depending on the stage of the business development, the type of social venture and the particular situational context, where re-evaluation is required at each step, in line with the strategic outlook of the organization.
- Apart from the challenges that any start-up would face, social enterprises also have to deal with additional barriers, associated with the nature of their activities, their legal structure and challenges around capturing social impact.

### DISCUSSION QUESTIONS

The questions below do not have right or wrong answers, and aim to explore various contingencies and contextual situations where certain answers would be more helpful than others:

1 Think of the suitable funding sources for your social venture. What do you need to demonstrate to your potential funder to maximize your chances of securing this funding? What are the downsides of securing it?

**Indicative answer:** Your answer will be based on the consideration of the sources reviewed in this chapter, and your own research in your region in terms of various programmes, policies and initiatives available at local, national and even international levels. The chapter gives you an overview of the key choice factors that you might want to consider. Their relevance to your case would be determined by the nature of your social enterprise, its stage of development, the state of the current macroeconomic and local environment, and your own background and aspirations in relation to your social venture.

2 Search online for some examples of social impact funds, social bonds and/or social impact bonds in your region. Would your social venture fit the criteria of any of them? How successful could you be in securing this investment based on your financial forecasts and the evaluation of the social impact? Why?

**Indicative answer:** Your examples would vary, depending on where you are, and what is available at the time of your search. This area is constantly evolving, and depending on the market environment and government priorities various funds will emerge and disappear. Your priority should be to check their focus and whether your social mission fits it. They might have further requirements in relation to your stage of development, involvement of other partners and funders, legal form and other things that could determine your eligibility. Finally, you need to be mindful about their expectations, and how realistic, viable and – more importantly – compatible with your social purpose they are. Social impact evaluation is likely to be the key feature of a potential agreement. Therefore, the data collection needs to be embedded in your organizational practices and accounted for in your decisions. Remember the concept of 'mission drift' – this is the area where it is often observed.

3 Explore further various sources of alternative finance in the market, such as crowdfunding and blockchain applications in social finance. Consider what you need to have in place to successfully utilize them. How viable do you think it is for you to adopt one of these sources for your social venture?

**Indicative answer:** For crowdfunding sources, your marketing efforts, the size of the user base, the extent of the social impact and the appeal to the public (or potential other funders) should be your main considerations. It is also a very competitive environment, so the chances of success would also depend on the size of your existing network and your ability to grow and leverage it. The advantage is that you can visit such crowdfunding platforms and do your own research into social enterprises similar to yours to understand what contributed to the success of their campaigns. At the time of this book's publication, the adoption rate for blockchain finance is very low. It has to do with the level of technological readiness – of both the social enterprise and the community – the development of the infrastructure and, more importantly, trust in this instrument. Yet, it is expected this area will be developing quickly, where partnerships are most likely to be the first step for social enterprises to utilize this source. Again, checking the most recent examples and cases will help you understand the requirements in your particular situation.

## CALLS TO ACTION

1 Review Figure 11.1 and the explanation provided. Research the examples of the funding providers in your local area/region/country for each of the categories. Evaluate their suitability (and accessibility) for social enterprises, based on your understanding of the concept so far.

2 Identify a social enterprise in your local area, and using the information available online, or even your conversations with the founders (if possible to be arranged), note which funding sources (methods) they have used so far, and which opportunities they have potentially missed out on based on your review in Action Point 1.

3 Building on the Social Financing Cycle model shown in Figure 11.2, outline the next steps towards funding opportunities for the selected social enterprise.

## USEFUL LINK

OECD Social Entrepreneurship and Social Enterprises: https://web-archive.oecd.org/temp/2023-12-11/566784-social-entrepreneurship.htm (archived at https://perma.cc/87SP-QXYB)

# References

Aldrich, H E (1999) *Organizations Evolving*, Sage

Asian Development Bank (2021) Promoting social bonds for impact investments in Asia, https://www.adb.org/publications/social-bonds-impact-investments-asia (archived at https://perma.cc/C7MK-PNXW)

Bacq, S and Eddleston, K A (2018) A resource-based view of social entrepreneurship: How stewardship culture benefits scale of social impact, *Journal of Business Ethics*, 152, 589–611

Baldock, R and Mason, C (2015) Establishing a new UK finance escalator for innovative SMEs: The roles of the enterprise capital funds and angel co-investment fund, *Venture Capital*, 17(2): 1–28

BDRC Continental (2016) SME Finance Monitor, http://bdrc-continental.com/wp-content/uploads/2016/03/BDRCContinental_SME_Finance_Monitor_Q4_2015.pdf (archived at https://perma.cc/U5BP-SFNP)

Beaton, E E and Dowin Kennedy, E (2021) Responding to failure: The promise of market mending for social enterprise, *Public Management Review*, 23(5): 641–64

Block, J H, Fisch, C O, Obschonka, M and Sandner, P G (2019) A personality perspective on business angel syndication, *Journal of Banking & Finance*, 100, 306–27

BMG Research (2013) Small Business Survey 2012: SME employers, https://www.gov.uk/government/uploads/system/uploads/attachment_data/file/193555/bis-13-p74-small-business-survey-2012-sme-employers.pdf (archived at https://perma.cc/R7ZV-L4B2)

Bonini, S and Capizzi, V (2019) The role of venture capital in the emerging entrepreneurial finance ecosystem: Future threats and opportunities, *Venture Capital*, 21(2–3), 137–75

Bosma, N, Schutjens, V and Volker, B (2016) Local social entrepreneurship and social capital. In *Handbook of Social Capital and Regional Development* (pp 55–81) Edward Elgar Publishing

British Business Bank (2014) SME Journey Towards External Finance (BMG Research, http://british-business-bank.co.uk/wp-content/uploads/2014/12/Final-BMG-SME-Journey-Research-Report.pdf (archived at https://perma.cc/Q9HQ-EWQJ)

British Business Bank (2021/2022) Small Business Finance Markets, https://www.british-business-bank.co.uk/wp-content/uploads/2022/02/Small-Business-Finance-Markets-Report-2022-FINAL.pdf (archived at https://perma.cc/W2J2-QVDA)

Business Angel Institute (2021) Angel investments in figures – the US vs Europe, https://businessangelinstitute.org/blog/2021/04/15/angel-investments-in-figures/ (archived at https://perma.cc/K9TD-3CDV)

Cassar, G (2004) The financing of business start-ups, *Journal of Business Venturing*, 19(2), 261–83

Chandna, V (2022) Social entrepreneurship and digital platforms: Crowdfunding in the sharing-economy era, *Business Horizons*, 65(1), 21–31

Connelly, B L, Certo, S T, Ireland, R D and Reutzel, C R (2011) Signaling theory: A review and assessment, *Journal of Management*, 37(1): 39–67

Corner, P D and Ho, M (2010) How opportunities develop in social entrepreneurship, *Entrepreneurship Theory and Practice*, 34(4): 635–59

Cosh, A, Cumming, D and Hughes, A (2009) Outside entrepreneurial capital, *The Economic Journal*, 119(540): 1494–533

Cropanzano, R, Anthony, E L, Daniels, S R and Hall, A V (2017) Social exchange theory: A critical review with theoretical remedies, Academy of Management Annals, 11(1), 479–516

Cumming, D and Binti Johan, S A (2008) Preplanned exit strategies in venture capital, *European Economic Review*, 52(7), 1209–241

Cumming, D, Deloof, M, Manigart, S and Wright, M (2019) New directions in entrepreneurial finance, *Journal of Banking & Finance*, 100, 252–60

Deloitte Insights (2021) Deloitte's 2021 Global Blockchain Survey: A new age of digital assets, https://www.deloitte.com/ie/en/services/audit-assurance/research/deloitte-2021-global-blockchain-survey-deloitte-ireland.html (archived at https://perma.cc/2K6D-ML3L)

Department for Business, Innovation and Skills (2015) Small Business Survey 2014: SME employers, *BIS Research Paper 214*, https://assets.publishing.service.gov.uk/media/5a7563f4e5274a467f7e426c/bis-15-151-small-business-survey-2014-sme-employers_v1.pdf (archived at https://perma.cc/6SSH-2ASP)

Department for Business, Innovation and Skills (2016) Longitudinal Small Business Survey Year 1 (2015): SME employers, *BIS Research Paper 289*, https://assets.publishing.service.gov.uk/media/5a803033e5274a2e8ab4eb2f/bis-16-227-sme-employer-report.pdf (archived at https://perma.cc/Q5CT-UK4G)

Devine, A, Jabbar, A, Kimmitt, J and Apostolidis, C (2021) Conceptualising a social business blockchain: The coexistence of social and economic logics, *Technological Forecasting and Social Change*, 172, 120997

Doherty, B, Haugh, H and Lyon, F (2014) Social enterprises as hybrid organizations: A review and research agenda, *International Journal of Management Reviews*, 16(4): 417–36

Erikson, T (2002) Entrepreneurial capital: The emerging venture's most important asset and competitive advantage, *Journal of Business Venturing*, 17(3): 275–90

European Central Bank (2023) Survey on the access to finance of enterprises (SAFE), https://www.ecb.europa.eu/stats/ecb_surveys/safe/html/ecb.safe202306~58c0da48c6.en.html (archived at https://perma.cc/3ZEV-L4J5)

European Commission (2019) A recipe book for social finance, https://ec.europa.eu/social/main.jsp?catId=738&langId=en&pubId=8251&furtherPubs=yes (archived at https://perma.cc/RJJ2-EFWW)

European Commission (2023) Strengthening clarity in social finance: Scaling up social bonds, https://finance.ec.europa.eu/system/files/2023-12/231204-ipsf-social-bonds-report_en.pdf (archived at https://perma.cc/E9QC-ZT6Z)

Farhoud, M, Shah, S, Stenholm, P, Kibler, E, Renko, M and Terjesen, S (2021) Social enterprise crowdfunding in an acute crisis, *Journal of Business Venturing Insights*, 15, e00211

Foster, W L, Kim, P and Christiansen, B (2009) Ten nonprofit funding models, *Stanford Social Innovation Review*, 7(2): 32–39

Fujimoto, Y, Rentschler, R, Le, H, Edwards, D and Härtel, C E (2014) Lessons learned from community organizations: Inclusion of people with disabilities and others, *British Journal of Management*, 25(3): 518–37

Gianluca Gaggiotti, A G, Raffaella De Felice (2022) Accelerating Impact: Main takeaways from the first harmonised European impact investment market sizing exercise, https://www.impacteurope.net/sites/www.evpa.ngo/files/publications/EVPA_Accelerating_Impact_2022.pdf (archived at https://perma.cc/RH9P-X2YX)

Hand, D, Ringel, B and Danel, A (2022) Sizing the impact investment market 2022, https://thegiin.org/publication/research/impact-investing-market-size-2022/ (archived at https://perma.cc/36VM-6UFV)

Haugh, H (2007) Community-led social venture creation, *Entrepreneurship Theory and Practice*, 31(2): 161–82

Hilbrich, S (2021) What is social finance? Definitions by market participants, the EU taxonomy for sustainable activities, and implications for development policy, https://www.idos-research.de/uploads/media/DP__29.2021.pdf (archived at https://perma.cc/44B7-28UE)

Hirsch, J and Walz, U (2019) The financing dynamics of newly founded firms, *Journal of Banking & Finance*, 100, 261–272

ICMA (2023) *Guidance Book*, https://www.icmagroup.org/assets/documents/Sustainable-finance/2023-updates/The-Principles-Guidance-Handbook-November-2023-291123.pdf (archived at https://perma.cc/LAX8-5F96)

Jayawarna, D, Jones, O and Macpherson, A (2020) Resourcing social enterprises: The role of socially oriented bootstrapping, *British Journal of Management*, 31(1): 56–79

Khan, S U (2022) Financing constraints and firm-level responses to the COVID-19 pandemic: International evidence, *Research in International Business and Finance*, 59, 101545

Kraemer-Eis, H, Botsari, A, Gvetadze, S, Lang, F and Torfs, W (2022) *The European Small Business Finance Outlook* (Working Paper 2022/84) https://www.eif.org/news_centre/publications/eif_working_paper_2022_84.pdf (archived at https://perma.cc/RYZ5-V53G)

Logman, B (2021) Most Active Corporate Venture Funds in the UK, Beauhurst, https://www.beauhurst.com/blog/corporate-venture-funds-uk/ (archived at https://perma.cc/KZ38-UEX5)

Lumpkin, G T, Moss, T W, Gras, D M, Kato, S and Amezcua, A S (2013) Entrepreneurial processes in social contexts: how are they different, if at all? *Small Business Economics*, 40, 761–83

Lyon, F and Owen, R (2019) Financing social enterprises and the demand for social investment, *Strategic Change*, 28(1), 47–57

Mahjoub, Y I, Hassoun, M and Trentesaux, D (2022) Blockchain adoption for SMEs: opportunities and challenges, IFAC-PapersOnLine, 55(10)L: 1834–839

Miller, T L, Grimes, M G, McMullen, J S and Vogus, T J (2012) Venturing for others with heart and head: How compassion encourages social entrepreneurship, *Academy of Management Review*, 37(4): 616–40

North, D, Baldock, R and Ullah, F (2013) Funding the growth of UK technology-based small firms since the financial crash: Are there breakages in the finance escalator? *Venture Capital*, 15(3): 237–60

OECD (2016) Understanding social impact bonds, https://www.oecd.org/en/publications/understanding-social-impacts-bonds_7e48050d-en.html (archived at https://perma.cc/2L8H-82R8)

OECD (2021) Global outlook on financing for sustainable development 2021: A new way to invest for people and planet, https://www.oecd.org/en/publications/global-outlook-on-financing-for-sustainable-development-2021_e3c30a9a-en.html (archived at https://perma.cc/4M2M-2ELV)

OECD (2022) Financing SMEs and entrepreneurs 2022: An OECD scoreboard, https://www.oecd.org/cfe/smes/financing-smes-and-entrepreneurs-23065265.htm (archived at https://perma.cc/SJ5P-A5LJ)

Ozdemir, S Z, Moran, P, Zhong, X and Bliemel, M J (2016) Reaching and acquiring valuable resources: The entrepreneur's use of brokerage, cohesion, and embeddedness, *Entrepreneurship Theory and Practice*, 40(1): 49–79

Pequeneza, N (2019) The downside of social impact bonds, *Stanford Social Innovation Review*

Peredo, A M and McLean, M (2006) Social entrepreneurship: A critical review of the concept, *Journal of World Business*, 41(1): 56–65

Platt, M, Hasselgren, A, Román-Belmonte, J M, De Oliveira, M T, De la Corte-Rodríguez, H, Olabarriaga, S D, Rodríguez-Merchán, E C and Mackey, T K (2021) Test, trace, and put on the blockchain? A viewpoint evaluating the use of decentralized systems for algorithmic contact tracing to combat a global pandemic, *JMIR Public Health and Surveillance*, 7(4): e26460

Powdthavee, N (2008) Putting a price tag on friends, relatives, and neighbours: Using surveys of life satisfaction to value social relationships, *The Journal of Socio-Economics*, 37(4): 1459–480

Prashar, D, Jha, N, Jha, S, Lee, Y and Joshi, G P (2020) Blockchain-based traceability and visibility for agricultural products: A decentralized way of ensuring food safety in India, *Sustainability*, 12(8): 3497

Rawhouser, H, Cummings, M and Newbert, S L (2019) Social impact measurement: Current approaches and future directions for social entrepreneurship research, *Entrepreneurship Theory and Practice*, 43(1): 82–115

Reficco, E, Layrisse, F and Barrios, A (2021) From donation-based NPO to social enterprise: A journey of transformation through business-model innovation, *Journal of Business Research*, 125, 720–32

Rossi, M, Mueller-Bloch, C, Thatcher, J B and Beck, R (2019) Blockchain research in information systems: Current trends and an inclusive future research agenda, *Journal of the Association for Information Systems*, 20(9): 14

Schellinger, B, Urbach, N, Volter, F and Sedlmeir, J (2022) Yes, I do: Marrying blockchain applications with GDPR, *e-government*, 19, 22

Schückes, M and Gutmann, T (2021) Why do startups pursue initial coin offerings (ICOs)? The role of economic drivers and social identity on funding choice, *Small Business Economics*, 57(2): 1027–052

Sedlmeir, J, Lautenschlager, J, Fridgen, G and Urbach, N (2022) The transparency challenge of blockchain in organizations, *Electronic Markets*, 32(3): 1779–794

Smith, B R, Cronley, M L and Barr, T F (2012) Funding implications of social enterprise: The role of mission consistency, entrepreneurial competence, and attitude toward social enterprise on donor behavior, *Journal of Public Policy & Marketing*, 31(1): 142–57

Smith, W K and Besharov, M L (2019) Bowing before dual gods: How structured flexibility sustains organizational hybridity Administrative Science Quarterly, 64(1): 1–44

Social Finance (2012) Social Impact Bonds: An Overview, https://www.socialfinance.org.uk/assets/documents/A-New-Tool-for-Scaling-Impact.pdf (archived at https://perma.cc/8UCA-R5FL)

Stanford Graduate School of Business (2019) Blockchain for Social Impact, https://humanrights.wbcsd.org/project/blockchain-for-social-impact-2019/ (archived at https://perma.cc/D2ED-TEC7)

Statista (2023) Top use cases for blockchain technology 2021, https://www.statista.com/statistics/982566/worldwide-top-use-cases-blockchain-technology-by-market-share/ (archived at https://perma.cc/37TS-6U9U)

The Federal Reserve (2022) Availability of Credit to Small Businesses, https://www.federalreserve.gov/publications/2022-october-availability-of-credit-to-small-businesses.htm (archived at https://perma.cc/H7VD-TG3H)

The World Bank (2023) Small and Medium Enterprises (SMEs) Finance: Improving SMEs' access to finance and finding innovative solutions to unlock sources of capital, https://www.worldbank.org/en/topic/smefinance (archived at https://perma.cc/FKK5-LUEV)

Tortorice, D L, Bloom, D E, Kirby, P and Regan, J (2020) A theory of social impact bonds https://papers.ssrn.com/sol3/papers.cfm?abstract_id=3623102 (archived at https://perma.cc/JW7G-USU9)

UNICEF (2020) UNICEF Cryptocurrency Fund announces its largest investment of startups in developing and emerging economies, https://www.unicef.org/press-releases/unicef-cryptocurrency-fund-announces-its-largest-investment-startups-developing-and (archived at https://perma.cc/4CTH-5Z7D)

Vestrum, I (2016) Integrating multiple theoretical approaches to explore the resource mobilization process of community ventures, *Journal of Enterprising Communities: People and Places in the Global Economy*, 10(1): 123–34

Vickers, I, Westall, A, Spear, R, Brennan, G and Syrett, S (2017) Cities, the social economy and inclusive growth: A practice review, https://www.jrf.org.uk/neighbourhoods-and-communities/cities-the-social-economy-and-inclusive-growth (archived at https://perma.cc/V5XM-JM2J)

Wald, A, Holmesland, M and Efrat, K (2019) It is not all about money: Obtaining additional benefits through equity crowdfunding, *The Journal of Entrepreneurship*, 28(2): 270–94

Winborg, J and Landström, H (2001) Financial bootstrapping in small businesses: Examining small business managers' resource acquisition behaviors, *Journal of Business Venturing*, 16(3): 235–54

Wong, A B M (2022) Impact Bond Analysis: Examining trends across global markets, https://www.ice.com/article/impact-bond-analysis (archived at https://perma.cc/95WN-D4JR)

Yang, M-H, Lee, T-R and Chang, T-C (2019) Key success factors of blockchain platform for micro-enterprises, *The Journal of Asian Finance, Economics and Business*, 6(3): 283–93

Zachariadis, M, Hileman, G and Scott, S V (2019) Governance and control in distributed ledgers: Understanding the challenges facing blockchain technology in financial services, *Information and Organization*, 29(2): 105-117

Ziegler, T, Shneor, R, Wenzlaff, K, Odorović, A, Hao, R and Ryll, L (2021) The 4th European alternative finance benchmarking report, https://papers.ssrn.com/sol3/papers.cfm?abstract_id=3772260 (archived at https://perma.cc/LBC9-BLRH)

# 12 Conclusions and future directions for social entrepreneurship

**ZEINEB DJEBALI**

**LEARNING OUTCOMES**

- To be able to communicate the basic principles of this textbook.
- To explain the key differences between social enterprises and other types of organizations.
- To explain the key challenges involved in creating a social enterprise.
- To explain how future emergent trends might influence the evolution of social enterprises.

## Introduction

The key objective of this textbook is to provide you with a 'hands-on' approach to starting a social enterprise (SE), both at the pre-and post-phases. Inevitably, we acknowledge that many other factors, such as gender, educational background and the broader social, cultural and institutional context in which you are embedded, may influence your social entrepreneurial intentions (Bacq et al, 2016; Bacq and Alt, 2018). However, the principles outlined in this textbook offer you a strong basis for developing a sustainable social enterprise that creates social value for the beneficiaries you intend to serve alongside financial sustainability. Social entrepreneurs play a critical role in addressing the most pressing social and/or environmental problems (Dees, 2001; Mair and Martí, 2006; Martin and Osberg, 2007; Peredo and McLean, 2006), and to this end, learning how to build a hybrid social enterprise – one that is founded on a dual logic of social and business – is the starting point for new social venture creations (Doherty et al, 2014).

First, we summarize the core themes addressed in this textbook. These include the key theoretical debates shaping the field and the emergence of hybrid social enterprises that balance a social mission with business objectives. Next, we examine the regulatory environment that is shaping the development of social enterprises (SEs), followed by exploring the process of starting up a social enterprise, including opportunity recognition, problem definition, social value proposition and social business modelling. We explore some of the key challenges facing SEs, with a particular focus on access to capital and measuring social impact. Finally, we offer our forward-looking perspective on the evolving nature of social entrepreneurship, looking at the growing relevance of 'corporate social intrapreneurs' – individuals who can leverage entrepreneurial strategies within existing organizations to create social impact – and the influence of emerging technologies on empowering social entrepreneurs to address social and environmental challenges through tech-driven solutions.

## Current state of social entrepreneurship – theoretical debates

Social entrepreneurship has gained increasing attention as a field of academic enquiry, practice and policy. Despite its growing prominence, the field continues to suffer from a lack of a universal definition and multiple conceptualizations (Peredo and Mclean, 2006; Weerawardena and Sullivan Mort, 2006). As such, in Chapter 1, we examined the historical emergence of social entrepreneurship, tracing its roots to the English Industrial Revolution (1760–1840). Not-for-profit organizations (NFPs), such as cooperatives, charities and mutual societies, emerged as a response to unmet social needs. Cooperatives in particular, due to their principles of collective action, trade of goods and services to fund their social mission, and limited profit generation, can be seen as an early form of modern social enterprise (Bailly et al, 2017; Biekart, 1998; Green and Matthias, 1997; Haugh, 2006; Perotin, 2012).

As social entrepreneurship developed across Europe towards the end of the 20th century, taking a major role in tackling social problems that traditional governmental players were unable to meet, scholars took an interest in the concept and sought to define the field (Bacq and Janssen, 2011; Choi and Majumdar, 2014; Dacin et al, 2011; Dwivedi and Weerawardena, 2018; Stevens et al, 2015). A key point of interest was to determine how social entrepreneurship distinguished itself from other socially-aligned constructs like charitable giving, corporate philanthropy (Acs et al, 2013) and corporate social responsibility (CSR) (Mair and Martí, 2006; Nicolopoulou, 2014).

Research also examined the intrinsic traits of social entrepreneurs compared to their profit-oriented counterparts (Austin et al, 2006). Social and profit-oriented entrepreneurs share common characteristics such as risk-taking, innovativeness, opportunity recognition and resourcefulness (Peredo and McLean, 2006; Santos et al, 2021; Tiwari et al, 2020; To et al, 2020). Where social entrepreneurs differ from their profit-oriented counterparts, however, is that they often identify opportunities to solve an unmet social need rather than maximizing shareholder value (Zahra and Wright, 2016). A growing body of research has also examined the concept of antecedents, factors that shape social entrepreneurial intentions (SEIs). Antecedents such as integrity, compassion, altruism and personal values are key drivers of SEIs (Bacq and Alt, 2018; Douglas and Prentice, 2019; Douglas et al, 2021). So too has research examined the influence of gender, education, prior experience with the social problem and the socio-economic and cultural contexts in which individuals are embedded on SEIs (Hockerts, 2017; see Chapters 3 and 8).

Countering the research focus on social entrepreneurs as individuals, an emerging body of research has instead focused on the organizational structure of SEs as their distinctive characteristic (Dacin et al, 2011; McMullen and Warnick, 2016; Mair and Schoen, 2007), resulting in the formation of two different schools of thought. The first is the 'social innovation' school, which, as described, emphasizes the critical role social entrepreneurs play in developing innovative approaches to social and/or environmental problems (Dees, 2007; Leadbeater, 1997). The second is the 'hybrid school', which focuses on the hybrid organizational structure of SEs that adopt business practices to address social and/or environmental challenges (Seelos and Mair, 2005; Pache and Santos, 2013).

Whilst SEs share common goals with profit-for-shareholder organizations committed to CSR actions, their approaches diverge (see Chapter 5). For corporations, CSR has evolved from a voluntary philanthropic practice into a strategic organizational practice that is aimed at demonstrating corporations' social and environmental responsibility (Garriga and Melé, 2004; Carroll, 1991; Freeman, 1984). Regulatory frameworks, such as the United Nations Global Compact (UNGC), Integrated International Reporting Framework (IIRF), Global Reporting Initiative (GRI) and Environmental, Social and Governance (ESG) metrics, serve as mechanisms that guide corporations to disclose their social impact. Nevertheless, CSR crucially remains secondary to their primary objective of maximizing profits and enhancing shareholder value (Carroll and Shabana, 2010), and has been criticized as enabling greenwashing activities whereby corporations may exaggerate or misrepresent their social and/or environmental impact to enhance their competitive advantage (Dahl, 2010; Jahdi and Acikdilli, 2009; Li et al, 2022; Nemes et al, 2022; Torelli et al, 2019).

In contrast, SEs prioritize their social mission over profits. SEs exist at the intersection of profit-for-shareholders organizations that focus on economic value creation, and NFPs that give priority to their social mission (Doherty et al, 2014). As such, they are defined by the following characteristics:

- **Social value creation** for the beneficiaries on whom the social mission is built (Santos et al, 2015). The beneficiaries may directly receive goods or services or may be embedded into the broader social mission.
- **Blending of social and commercial activities** (Alter, 2006; Battilana and Dorado, 2010; Dohrmann et al, 2015). SEs utilize for-profit revenue generation logics to achieve financial sustainability, and often reinvest profit (if any) back into their social mission.

The above research strands have significantly advanced our understanding of social entrepreneurship as a field of scholarly enquiry and practice. They have also brought valuable insights into the role social entrepreneurs play in the social entrepreneurial process. Although the absence of an agreed definition continues to shape the field (Dwivedi and Weerawardena, 2018; Stevens et al, 2015), a common theme that unifies the various definitions is social value creation (Doherty et al, 2014; Pache and Santos, 2013; Tracey et al, 2011) – that is, how social entrepreneurship is shaped by solving social and/or environmental problems that provide benefits to those affected.

## Regulatory and policy environment for SEs

As discussed in Chapter 1, SEs are characterized by their dual social and business logics (Battilana et al, 2015; Mair and Martí, 2006; Santos et al, 2015). Despite there being no universal legal structure, a number of countries across Europe have introduced legal frameworks to accommodate the hybrid nature of SEs. The UK was among the first countries in Europe to formalize such a legal framework with the introduction of the Community Interest Company (CIC) in 2005. The CIC is structured similarly to private businesses but is subject to two key constraints to safeguard the SEs' social mission. First, the **asset lock provision** restricts the transfer of assets, allowing transfers only to other socially driven organizations such as another CIC or a charity. Second, dividend payouts are regulated through a **dividend cap**, limiting them to approximately 35 per cent of distributable profits (Brackman-Reiser, 2010). The CIC offers a robust governance framework but is only one of many possible legal structures which can be adopted depending on the social mission of the SE and its approach to trading.

In Chapter 2, we explored the broader context in which SEs operate, highlighting how social innovation emerged as a new paradigm to respond to unmet social and/or environmental needs (Mulgan et al, 2007; Mulgan, 2006). This chapter, while not dealing specifically with regulatory frameworks, highlighted several defining characteristics of SEs, such as an explicit social mission, innovation, stakeholder engagement, ethical governance and social impact measurement.

In Chapter 6, we examined how the concept of social value is quantified and regulated through **social impact measurement**. Social value has gained increasing policy attention as organizations of all types are increasingly mandated to demonstrate how their actions contribute to society, the environment and the economy (Elkington, 1994; Kroeger and Weber, 2014; Stevens et al, 2015; Ruskin et al, 2016). Governments in Europe increasingly legislate for consideration of social value as part of the public contracting process, signalling its importance in policy and practice. In the UK, for instance, the Public Services (Social Value) Act 2012 requires public authorities and providers of public services to consider social value when awarding contracts. As such, methods of measuring social value have become a way of demonstrating social impact while ensuring accountability.

One of the many frameworks explored in this chapter is the Social Return on Investment (SROI). This framework not only allows SEs to quantify the broader social impact they create but also to make better-informed decisions about where to strategically allocate their resources and prioritize those that generate the most significant value. It also serves as a tool to engage with social impact investors who are increasingly interested in blended returns on investment: financial and social/environmental outcomes (Salverda, 2024). Moreover, SROI data can be leveraged by SEs to advocate for policy changes or secure additional funding. Nevertheless, despite its applicability, it is not without its challenges. SROI is built on quantifiable outcomes, meaning it assigns monetary value to otherwise subjective social outcomes, risking the devaluation of less tangible outcomes such as improvements to well-being or empowerment. As such, the accuracy and compatibility of the data obtained can be put into question.

## The process of starting up a social enterprise

A growing body of research has examined the process of social venture creation. Findings suggest that the social entrepreneurial process often involves three interrelated stages: identification and exploitation of social entrepreneurial opportunities (Austin et al, 2006; Zahra et al, 2008); resource mobilization, often achieved through bricolage due to resource constraints (Meyskens et al, 2010); and the development of innovative approaches to address social and/or environmental challenges (Luke and Chu, 2013; Peredo and McLean, 2006). As explored in Chapter 8, whereas profit-oriented entrepreneurial opportunities are primarily driven by economic value creation to maximize shareholder value, social entrepreneurial opportunities arise from unmet social needs or market inefficiencies that fail to address existing social or environmental challenges (Corner and Ho, 2010; Thompson et al, 2000).

Nevertheless, recognizing and exploiting social entrepreneurial opportunities is insufficient for the creation of a social enterprise. As discussed in Chapter 10, entrepreneurial learning is key, enabling *aspiring* social entrepreneurs to acquire the relevant knowledge, skills, self-efficacy, emotional intelligence and key competencies necessary to start and manage their social start-up (Politis, 2005). Importantly, **social** entrepreneurial learning has also been identified to play a key role in shaping social entrepreneurial identities, which can be facilitated through experiential learning opportunities. We identified that in general, entrepreneurial learning is a dynamic and interactive process that involves reflection and learning through experience (Cope and Watts, 2000).

To facilitate this learning, Chapter 7 examined the foundational skills and processes involved in starting a social enterprise, with a focus on problem identification and opportunity recognition. This chapter introduced the 'Problem Statement Canvas' (Ursache, 2019) as a tool to assess the nature, context and root causes of the problem, facilitating the design of effective solutions that meet the needs of target beneficiaries. The benefits of this approach are twofold: first, it helps avoid the fallacy of providing a one-size-fits-all solution, and second, it enables nascent social entrepreneurs to target their solution to the beneficiaries who are experiencing the most significant problems.

The chapter also highlighted the significance of community engagement, collective approaches and cultural sensitivity to ensure the relevance of the solution and its impact on those affected (Aquino et al, 2018; Civera et al, 2019; Voorberg et al, 2014). Additionally, the chapter underscored the importance of recognizing that the initial understanding of the problem and the proposed solution are based on untested assumptions. Hence, it is critical to fully research the problem by collecting *primary* data from those affected or using reliable *secondary* data from industry reports and studies to gain an understanding of the broader impact of the problem on those experiencing it (Saunders et al, 2023).

In Chapter 8, we examined the role social entrepreneurs play in the social entrepreneurial process. Social entrepreneurs, impacted by antecedents such as empathy, moral obligations, ethical fibre, personal values and prior experience with the social problem, all influence social entrepreneurial intentions (SEIs) and determine how they define their social mission (Massetti, 2008; Zahra et al, 2009). The chapter also introduced the social entrepreneurial opportunity (SEO) identification process, which involves three stages: ideation, experimentation and refinement (Hafeez et al, 2018; Jayawarna et al, 2020; McDonald and Eisenhardt, 2020). Finally, the chapter introduced the social value proposition (SVP) framework that aligns the needs of three distinct but interrelated groups: beneficiaries, customers and broader social outcomes (Perrini et al, 2010). First, the SVP must clearly define the specific value generated for the target beneficiaries. Second, it must engage with customers who are either directly served by the social enterprise or who contribute financially to its mission by purchasing products or services. Finally, it must demonstrate the broader social or environmental outcomes.

Building on this, Chapter 9 explored the concept of social business models. While the concept draws from profit-driven business models (Osterwalder and Pigneur, 2010) that demonstrate how organizations create and deliver value to customers and capture value – that is, generate revenues (Afuah, 2004; DaSilva and Trkman, 2014; Mahadevan, 2000; Masanell and Ricart, 2010) – a social business model mixes two institutional logics: a social mission with commercial goals. It therefore offers two sorts of value: social, by addressing pressing social and/or environmental problems; and commercial, to ensure financial sustainability (Canestrino et al, 2019). The chapter also introduced the Social Triple Layer Business Model Canvas (Joyce and Paquin, 2016). This model incorporates three core layers: the social or environmental mission, trading activities and revenue streams, and organizational resources and cost structures. These layers illustrate how SEs create value for beneficiaries, deliver that value through their activities, and generate revenues to sustain themselves.

## Challenges ahead for nascent social entrepreneurs

Despite the growth of SEs as a vehicle for addressing complex social and/or environmental problems, a number of challenges continue to hinder their growth and scalability. In the sections below, we focus on two key challenges: access to capital and measuring social impact.

### *Access to capital*

As highlighted in Chapter 11, a range of funding sources can be leveraged, ranging from **internal** sources, such as bootstrapping, donations and grants, to **external** sources, such as social impact investments, social impact bonds and emerging technologies like blockchain and crowdfunding. Furthermore, philanthropic institutions, such as the Rockefeller Foundation, Skoll Foundation, Gates Foundation and UnLtd (UK-based), provide grants aimed at nascent social entrepreneurs that can demonstrate measurable social impact. Recent data from the Global Impact Investing Network (2025), for instance, reflects the growing interest among investors, venture capitalists and private equity firms in investments that generate both financial returns and social impact. For example, in 2024, d.light, founded by Peace Corps volunteer Sam Goldman in 2014, secured approximately US$176 million to support its PayGo loan programme across three African countries (Kenya, Tanzania and Uganda) to provide off-grid solar solutions to low-income households that lack access to electricity (Yuen, 2024).

Like any other startup, social entrepreneurs are required to mobilize the necessary resources (human, financial, technological and others) to launch their social enterprise (Austin et al, 2006). However, nascent social entrepreneurs may face unique challenges in securing funding despite the above developments. This can be attributed to the conceptual ambiguity related to social entrepreneurship, which means different things across regional and national contexts (Kerlin, 2006), complicating efforts in establishing common criteria for funding. Impact investors, who more often place emphasis on measurable outcomes, may be unwilling to support early-stage start-ups as they have limited financial history, no funding and unproven impact metrics (Adekunle et al, 2017). Traditional investment opportunities such as banks may also be deterred, since in many contexts the formation of a venture is categorized as either a charity or a commercial business with little room for hybrid SE structures. This is further exacerbated by the common lack of a revenue stream or sufficient collateral to take out loans.

## Measuring social impact

Measuring social impact has become critical for SEs, as it not only enables them to set realistic impact objectives, guide their resource allocation and enhance organizational effectiveness, but also attracts funding and can influence policy change (Alomoto et al, 2022; Buckland and Hehenberger, 2021; Islam, 2022). The European Commission (2014) defines social impact measurement as a mechanism to assess whether an SE's activities create the intended social outcomes. Others describe it as the identification and quantification of changes experienced by individuals or the environment resulting from a specific intervention, as well as the degree to which the agent – that is, in this context, the social entrepreneur – contributes to these changes (e.g. San Pedro and Ballesteros, 2021).

Despite its critical role, measuring social impact remains a challenge. Some argue that often the indirect nature of social impact is difficult to measure accurately (e.g. Buckland and Hehenberger, 2021). Others point out that impact may not be observable immediately, as it can occur over a long-term timescale, and many SEs lack the financial or human resources to measure impact that requires longitudinal data (e.g. Gonul and Senyuva, 2020). Besides, the absence of standardized frameworks and clear guidelines on which methodology to adopt makes it challenging to provide comparable data across organizations and sectors. These challenges ultimately hinder SEs from communicating the social value they create to their stakeholder groups, particularly investors, making it difficult to secure the required financial support to scale their social impact (Bloom and Smith, 2010; Choda and Teladia, 2018).

## Forward-looking perspectives on the evolving nature of social entrepreneurship

As highlighted in previous sections, much of the extant literature on social entrepreneurship has predominantly focused on examining social entrepreneurship from individual and organizational perspectives. Despite invaluable insights into the role social entrepreneurs play in solving social problems, as well as the process by which social ventures are created, there is relatively little attention paid to the role 'corporate social intrapreneurs' (CSIs) play in driving organizational change. Of equal importance, while emerging technologies such as artificial intelligence (AI), data analytics and crowdfunding platforms are increasingly being leveraged to access funding, enhance efficiency and scalability, or measure social impact, little is explored on how these technologies can contribute to the future development of social entrepreneurship, particularly among nascent or emerging social entrepreneurs.

### *The rise of corporate social entrepreneurship*

Despite its growing relevance, corporate social entrepreneurship (CSE) has yet to emerge as a separate field of study due to the prominence of other fields such as corporate or social entrepreneurship as well as CSR, all of which have attracted wider scholarly and policy attention (Carroll, 1991; Googins and Rochlin, 2006). Mair and Martí (2006) argued that CSE is a practice that applies the principles of social entrepreneurship but within a corporate context. The root of this can be traced back to Schumpeter (1947; see Chapters 1 and 2), who predicted that the entrepreneurial process of innovation and creative destruction is more likely to shift from individual entrepreneurs to corporations that have the necessary resources, technology and research and development (R&D) capabilities to innovate and sustain a competitive advantage. CSE can therefore be defined as the process of discovering, evaluating and exploiting social entrepreneurial opportunities within established corporations, leading to social and/or environmental value creation (Covin and Miles, 1999; Donald et al, 2017). Crucially, CSE is undertaken by specific individuals that the research has termed corporate social intrapreneurs (CSIs).

Whereas social *entrepreneurs* start a social enterprise to fulfil their social mission, CSIs have been defined as change agents who advocate for the integration of social and economic value into an already-existing corporation's core mission, organizational processes and operations. They often create innovative, impactful solutions that challenge the status quo (Austin et al, 2005) and build their internal legitimacy by communicating the relevance of social action with the corporation's strategic priorities. In this regard, CSE can be understood as a mechanism by which established corporations cultivate an entrepreneurial environment that enables CSIs on two levels: 1) renewing the corporation from within to simultaneously create social and economic value (Austin et al, 2006), and/or 2) introducing innovative products and services to tackle pressing social and/or environmental challenges.

Given the rising global issues, including climate change, pandemics, economic inequality, political instability, resource scarcity and gender inequality, with nearly 700 million people still living in extreme poverty (World Bank, 2024), CSE offers a promising avenue for corporations to rethink their strategies and cultivate a culture that empowers CSIs to lead change and generate economic and social value. Whereas the notion of creating social value within a corporate environment is not new – Dees (2001) tells us that social entrepreneurship can occur in profit-for-shareholder organizations as well as hybrid SEs and NFPs – it has typically remained confined to limited-in-scope CSR practices that remain secondary to the primary mission of generating profits and maximizing shareholder value (Googins and Rochlin, 2006). As such, to fully leverage the impact of CSIs on corporations' strategic objectives, a new form of corporation is required, one that shifts away from traditional CSR practices towards innovative entrepreneurial strategies that cultivate an environment open to change, experimentation, risk-taking and a leadership that is not focused on profit maximization but on empowering CSIs to transform social responsibility into a key part of a corporation's structure (Austin et al, 2005; Emerson, 2000, 2003; Emerson and Bonini, 2003).

## *Emerging technologies for social good*

According to the United Nations, more than 600 million people worldwide are projected to face hunger (SDG 2) by 2030, and approximately 2.2 billion people still lack access to clean drinking water (SDG 6) (www.sdg.org). So too do the challenges facing modern societies today, such as climate change, environmental degradation, global healthcare and economic/social inequality, underscore the need for tech-driven solutions that solve these challenges at scale. Emerging technologies, including AI, data analytics, e-commerce, digital media, social networking and crowdfunding, are revolutionizing how social entrepreneurs address social and environmental challenges (Chen et al, 2012; McAfee and Brynjolfsson 2023; Jiwat and Zang, 2022). These technologies are not only reshaping how social entrepreneurs create value for their beneficiaries or society at large but also enable scalability of social impact and improve efficiency. For instance, innovations such as 3D printing have enabled the development of low-cost prosthetic mobility solutions for those underserved, as well as off-grid solar panels and portable wind turbines that address issues of energy in impoverished communities. Advances in biotechnology have also facilitated the development of affordable products that tackle hunger and malnutrition. While these technologies are not without their challenges, they can empower social entrepreneurs to develop innovative solutions, as this section will outline.

## Automation to enhance efficiency and scale

As discussed, one of the most significant barriers facing social entrepreneurs is measuring and scaling social impact due to limited financial, human and technical resources. In this context, automation, particularly through AI and machine learning, can provide opportunities to automate processes and scale social impact at reduced cost (Jean et al, 2016; OECD, 2019). For instance, **telemedicine technologies** that employ AI chatbots can enable beneficiaries to consult with healthcare providers and access either basic health support or track their health. These tools can help social entrepreneurs extend healthcare solutions to underserved communities, offering a cost-effective solution in comparison to in-person services. As will be discussed next, automation can also help with social impact measurement, a topic that remains an ongoing challenge for SEs due to its complexity. Nonetheless, the adoption of these technologies would require significant upfront investments, technical expertise and ongoing maintenance, which may constrain uptake, particularly among social entrepreneurs who lack financial capital.

## Data analytics – tracking and enhancing social impact

The rapid growth in computing capabilities, open data sources, IoT, generative AI and mobile connectivity, including smartphone devices, has enabled organizations to leverage the vast amount of human and machine-generated data to build their competitive advantage and create value for their target customers. Machine-generated data can be found in autonomous systems, such as robotics, environmental/weather-related sensors and supply chain tracking devices. Human-generated data, in contrast, emerges from social media activity, mobile phone usage, online forums, consumer searches and purchasing activities. As a result, data analytics has become a valuable tool for corporations to collect, manage and analyse data that enables them to gain market insights to guide their decision-making and improve their market performances (Chen et al, 2012; Jiwat and Zhang, 2022). A report published by the Harvard Business Review (2023) revealed that 53 per cent of high-performing organizations actively leverage data analytics to drive business outcomes (Eboigbe et al, 2023). Furthermore, according to IDC (2024) forecasts, global data is expected to grow by approximately 60 per cent annually, increasing tenfold every five years. This exponential growth presents opportunities for organizations to leverage data available to them to enhance their value (Klee et al, 2021; Ranjan and Foropon, 2020).

Data analytics for social entrepreneurs offers, therefore, a unique opportunity to track and analyse the impact of their interventions in real time and provide evidence of the positive outcomes they create. For instance, a social enterprise that focuses on clean water provision can use health and demographic data to assess its impact on the well-being of those affected. An environmental social enterprise can equally use sensor-driven data to track environmental changes and respond to issues of climate change. The McKinsey Global Institute (2018) also believes that AI has a high potential to support tackling the SDGs, offering examples such as using AI on satellite data to map and predict the progression of wildfires (SDG 13) or personalized and adaptive learning technologies that facilitate education for underserved communities (SDG 4).

## Gamification to drive awareness

Tech-driven solutions such as gamification can offer new avenues for social entrepreneurs to drive social change (Dhiman, 2023; Schreiner, 2008). Gamification, which refers to the practice of integrating game design and interactive features, can motivate individual and collective behaviour, enhance engagement and raise awareness of complex social and/or environmental issues (Marin et al, 2021; Spanellis and Harviainen, 2021). Examples of gamification include awarding points, badges, or discounts when certain tasks are completed; leaderboards that inspire competition among users; and progress visualization that gives a sense of completion and achievement. When these features are combined with a socially driven mission, gamification can encourage users to adopt prosocial behaviours like reducing consumption, recycling or supporting community initiatives. Gamification can also serve as an educational tool by raising awareness about social issues, using rewards and discounts to attract a larger user base that may not have been initially interested in social impact activities. Platforms such as **GoodGuide**, which rewards users for sustainable shopping choices, **ShareTheMeal**, which enables users to donate meals for people in need, and **Google One Today**, which facilitates daily micro-donations to diverse social causes, are all examples of platforms that use gamification to not only educate the public but also incentivize changes in behaviour and participation.

## Democratizing access to capital: blockchain and cryptocurrency for social good

Decentralized technologies such as cryptocurrency and blockchain are significantly democratizing access to funding, particularly for social entrepreneurs located in remote areas with unstable banking systems (Bartoletti et al, 2018; Pisa and Juden, 2017). Blockchain-based platforms, as discussed in Chapter 11, offer transparent records of financial transactions, enhancing accountability and trust among donors and other stakeholders. The **GiveCrypto** project, for instance, founded by Brian Armstrong, has demonstrated how decentralized financial transfers can reach individuals in poverty without the mediation of traditional banking systems. This not only increases efficiency but also removes barriers for those requiring credit history and collateral for banks. Further, blockchain technology, which is based on transparent proof ledgers, can enhance SEs' governance by making the allocation and use of resources and funds auditable and verifiable. Donors can track in real time how their contributions are being utilized, thereby strengthening legitimacy and stakeholder confidence.

## *Crowdfunding as an inclusive financing mechanism*

Crowdfunding platforms emerged as a novel alternative to conventional financing, particularly for nascent social entrepreneurs who often face challenges in accessing capital through traditional financial channels such as banks or venture capital firms. According to the World Bank (2013), the global crowdfunding market is expected to reach a valuation of $300 billion by 2025, underscoring the growing importance of digital and smart technologies in reshaping financial ecosystems (Baumgardner et al, 2017; Profatilov et al, 2014; Poetz and Schreier, 2012; Tan et al, 2024). As already covered, the diversity of crowdfunding platforms, including donation-based (e.g. JustGiving and GoFundMe), reward-based (e.g. Indiegogo and Kickstarter), loan-based (e.g. BabyLoan) and equity-based (e.g. Crowdcube and Seedrs), enables nascent social entrepreneurs to access funding and minimize the constraints existing with traditional investment methods. These platforms also reduce transaction costs and connect social entrepreneurs to global networks of individual backers, thereby expanding their reach and engagement. **Kiva**, for instance, co-founded by Matt and Jessica Flannery in East Africa, leverages crowdfunding to connect individual lenders with social entrepreneurs in developing regions. In 2005, Kiva made its first loan – a $500 investment to a female entrepreneur in Uganda to expand her fishmongering business. By 2010, Kiva had lent more than $100 million, predominantly to women in underserved communities, illustrating the importance of alternative digital financial solutions (Kiva, 2019).

Diversity of crowdfunding platforms:

- **Donation-based:** raising funds from individuals who are motivated by philanthropy or social causes.
- **Reward-based:** providing financial backers with early access to the project.
- **Loan-based:** borrowing money from investors who receive interest payments.
- **Equity-based:** selling shares to investors who receive a percentage of the profits.

### *Limitations of emerging technologies*

Despite these substantial benefits, the adoption of emerging technologies by nascent social entrepreneurs is not without its limitations (Buhmann and Fieseler, 2021; Shams et al, 2023). Some of the key barriers include digital literacy and skills gaps, as some nascent social entrepreneurs may lack the technical expertise required to effectively deploy and manage these emerging technologies. Limited access to digital technologies in underserved communities can widen the digital divide between them and other social entrepreneurs who are embedded in more favourable ecosystems (Bentley et al, 2024). AI and blockchain infrastructures are also costly, which can prohibit their adoption. Finally, data privacy and algorithm bias can pose significant ethical challenges (Roche et al, 2023). Hence, the successful integrations of these technologies require not only technical capabilities but also time, resources and a deep understanding of the context in which these solutions are deployed.

## Concluding reflections for aspiring social entrepreneurs

We embarked on this journey of writing this textbook with the firm belief that social entrepreneurship plays a critical role in building a more equitable and sustainable world. Thus, we believe that as an aspiring social entrepreneur, you can play a key part in contributing to the evolution of social entrepreneurship and in addressing the mounting social and/or environmental challenges we experience. We acknowledge that all types of entrepreneurs, whether social or commercial, operate in an uncertain environment. Changes in the macro-economic landscape, evolving consumer behaviour and the disruptive impact of emerging technologies are obviously affecting the way we do business. However, we believe that social entrepreneurs specifically face additional complexities inherent in their social business model due to the need to balance their dual objectives as well as the difficulties in quantifying their impact. We therefore require a shift in societal attitudes to encourage social entrepreneurship as a viable career pathway for those with the passion to contribute to social good, rather than favouring conventional business models that focus on profit maximization.

This textbook has been designed with a practical approach to equip you with the knowledge, skills and competencies needed to create meaningful change. Inevitably, this will start from your own passion, motivation and personal values. But so too is careful evaluation and planning a necessary part of becoming a successful social entrepreneur. Once you decide to embark on your social entrepreneurial journey, we encourage you to evaluate the resources you would require, how you might monetize your social value proposition in a way that is sustainable while avoiding mission drift, and how to create a long-lasting impact. Having a viable social business model will not only build your legitimacy with your key stakeholders, such as governments, profit-for-shareholder organizations and investors, but will also support you in developing your social mission to its fullest potential.

## References

Acs, Z, Boardman M and McNeely C (2013) The social value of productive entrepreneurship, *Small Business Economics*, 40: 785–96

Adekunle, D N A, Haezendonck, E and van Balen, M (2017) The role of governments in the business and society debate, *Business & Society*, 56(4): 527–544

Afuah, A (2004) *Business Models: A strategic management approach*, New York: McGraw Hill

Alomoto, W, Niñerola, A and Pié, L (2022) Social impact assessment: A systematic review of literature, *Social Indicators Research*, 161: 225–50

Alter, S K (2006) Social enterprise models and their mission and money relationships. In Nicholls, A (Ed), *Social entrepreneurship: New models of sustainable social change*, Oxford: Oxford University Press, pp 205–232

Aquino, R S, Lück, M and Schänzel, H A (2018) A conceptual framework of tourism social entrepreneurship for sustainable community development, *Journal of Hospitality and Tourism Management*, 37: 23–32

Austin, J, Stevenson, H and Wei-Skillern, J (2006) Social and commercial entrepreneurship: Same, different, or both? *Entrepreneurship: Theory & Practice*, 30: 1–22

Austin, J, Herman, L, Reficco, E and Wei-Skillern, J (2005) Social Entrepreneurship: It's for corporations, too. In *Social Entrepreneurship: New paradigms of sustainable social change*, edited by A Nicholls Oxford, GB: Oxford University Press

Bacq, S and Alt, E (2018) Feeling capable and valued: A prosocial perspective on the link between empathy and social entrepreneurial intentions, *Journal of Business Venturing*, 33(3): 333–50

Bacq, S, Hartog C and Hoogendoorn B (2016) Beyond the moral portrayal of social entrepreneurs: An empirical approach to who they are and what drives them, *Journal of Business Ethics*, 133: 703–18

Bacq, S and Janssen, F (2011) The multiple faces of social entrepreneurship: A review of definitional issues based on geographical and thematic criteria, *Entrepreneurship & Regional Development*, 23: 373–403

Bailly, F, Chapelle, K and Prouteau, L (2017) Wage differentials between conventional firms and non-worker cooperatives: Analysis of evidence from France, *Competition & Change*, 21(4): 321–41

Bartoletti, M, Cimoli, T, Pompianu, L and Serusi, S (2018) Blockchain for social good: A quantitative analysis, *Goodtechs 18: Proceeding of the 4th International Conference on Smart Objects Technologies for Social Good*, (pp 37–42) https://doi.org/10.1145/3284869.3284881 (archived at https://perma.cc/A8QR-55Z8)

Battilana, J and Dorado, S (2010) Building sustainable hybrid organizations: The case of commercial microfinance organizations, *Academy of Management Journal*, 53: 1419–440

Battilana, J, Sengul, M, Pache, A C and Model, J (2015) Harnessing productive tensions in hybrid organizations: The case of work integration social enterprises, *Academy of Management Journal*, 58: 1658–685

Baumgardner, T, Neufeld, C, Huang, PC-T, Sondhi, T, Carlos, F and Talha, M A (2017) Crowdfunding as a fast-expanding market for the creation of capital and shared value, *Thunderbird International Business Review*, 59: 115–26

Bentley, S V, Naughtin, C K and McGrath, M J (2024) The digital divide in action: How experiences of digital technology shape future relationships with artificial intelligence, *AI Ethics*, 4: 901–15

Biekart, K (1998) The Politics of Civil Society Building: European private aid agencies and democratic transitions in Central America, *International Books/Transnational Institute*, Utrecht, 1998

Bloom, P N and Smith, B R (2010) Identifying the drivers of social entrepreneurial impact: Theoretical development and an exploratory empirical test of SCALERS, *Journal of Social Entrepreneurship*, 1(1): 126–45

Brackman-Reiser, D (2010) Blended enterprise and the dual mission dilemma, *Vermont Law Review*, 35: 105–16

Buckland, L and Hehenberger, L (2021) Measuring social impact can help foster a stronger European social economy, Stanford Social Innovation Review, https://doi.org/10.48558/T7W2-YR13 (archived at https://perma.cc/DG65-65XC)

Buhmann, A and Fieseler, C (2021) Towards a deliberative framework for responsible innovation in artificial intelligence, *Technology in Society*, 64: 101475

Canestrino, R, Ćwiklicki, M, Di Nauta, P and Magliocca, P (2019) Creating social value through entrepreneurship: The social business model of La Paranza, *Kybernetes*, 48(10): 2190–2216

Carroll, A B (1991) The pyramid of corporate social responsibility: Toward the moral management of organizational stakeholders, *Business Horizons*, 34 (4): 39–48

Carroll, A B and Shabana, K M (2010) The business case for corporate social responsibility: A review of concepts, research and practice, *International Journal of Management Reviews*, 12(1): 85–105

Chen, H, Chiang, R H L and Storey, V C (2012) Business intelligence and analytics: From Big Data to big impact, *MIS Quarterly*, 36(4): 1165–188

Choda, A and Teladia, M (2018) Conversations about measurement and evaluation in impact investing, *African Evaluation Journal*, 6(2): 1–11

Choi, N and Majumdar, S (2014) Social entrepreneurship as an essentially contested concept: Opening a new avenue for systematic future research, *Journal of Business Venturing*, 29: 363–76

Civera, C, De Colle, S and Casalegno, C (2019) Stakeholder engagement through empowerment: The case of coffee farmers, *Business Ethics: A European Review*, 28(2): 156–4

Cope, J and Watts, G (2000) Learning by doing – an exploration of experience, critical incidents and reflection in entrepreneurial learning, *International Journal of Entrepreneurial Behavior & Research*, 6(3): 104–24

Corner, P D and Ho, M (2010) How opportunities develop in social entrepreneurship, *Entrepreneurship: Theory & Practice*, 34: 635–59

Covin, J and Miles, M P (1999) Corporate entrepreneurship and the pursuit of competitive advantage, *Entrepreneurship Theory and Practice*, 23(3): 47–63

Dacin, M T, Dacin, P A and Tracey, P (2011) Social entrepreneurship: A critique and future directions, *Organization Science*, 22: 1203–213

Dahl, R (2010) Greenwashing: Do you know what you're buying? *Environmental Health Perspectives*, 118 (6): 246–52

DaSilva, C M and Trkman, P (2014) Business model: What it is and what it is not, *Long Range Planning*, 47 (6): 379–89

Dees, J G (2001) *The Meaning of 'Social Entrepreneurship'*, Centre for the Advancement of Social Entrepreneurship

Dees, J G (2007) Taking social entrepreneurship seriously, *Society*, 44: 24–31

Dhiman, B (2023) Games as tools for social change communication: A critical review, *Global Media Journal*, 21(61): 1–4

Doherty, B, Haugh, H and Lyon, F (2014) Social enterprises as hybrid organizations: A review and research agenda, *International Journal of Management Reviews*, 16: 417–36

Dohrmann, S, Raith, M and Siebold, N (2015) Monetizing social value creation: A business model approach, *Entrepreneurship Research Journal*, 5: 127–54

Donald, F, Kuratko, D F McMullen, J S, Hornsby, J S and Jackson, C (2017) Is your organization conducive to the continuous creation of social value? Toward a social corporate entrepreneurship scale, *Business Horizons*, 60 (3): 271–83

Douglas, E and Prentice, C (2019) Innovation and profit motivations for social entrepreneurship: A fuzzy-set analysis, *Journal of Business Research*, 99: 69–79

Douglas, E J, Shepherd D and Venugopal, V (2021) A multi-motivational general model of entrepreneurial intention, *Journal of Business Venturing*, 36(4): 106–107

Dwivedi, A and Weerawardena, J (2018) Conceptualizing and operationalizing the social entrepreneurship construct, *Journal of Business Research*, 86: 32–40

Eboigbe, E O, Farayola, O, Olatoye, F O and Chinwe, N O (2023) Business intelligence transformation through AI and data analytics engineering, *Science & Technology Journal*, 4(5): 285–307

Elkington, J (1994) Towards the sustainable corporation: Win-win-win business strategies for sustainable development, *California Management Review*, 36(2): 90 –100

Emerson, J (2000) The nature of returns: A social capital markets inquiry into elements of investment and the blended value proposition, Working Paper, Division of Research, Harvard Business School, Boston, MA

Emerson, J (2003) The blended value proposition: Integrating social and financial returns, *California Management Review*, 45(4): 35–51

Emerson, J, and Bonini, S (2004) The Blended Value Map: Tracking the intersects and opportunities of economic, social and environmental value creation, https://www.blendedvalue.org (archived at https://perma.cc/QQY6-MH9U)

European Commission (2014) Proposed approaches to social impact measurement, https://ec.europa.eu/social/BlobServlet?docId=13401&langId=en (archived at https://perma.cc/4SSQ-TTUV)

Freeman, R E (1984) *Strategic Management: A stakeholder approach*, Boston: Pitman

Garriga, E and Melé, D (2004) Corporate social responsibility theories: Mapping the territory, *Journal of Business Ethics*, 53: 51–71

Global Impact Investing Network (2025) https://thegiin.org/ (archived at https://perma.cc/37KK-6PV9)

Gonul, O O and Senyuva, Z (2020) How social entrepreneurs can create impact for a better world, *Entrepreneur & Innovation Exchange*, DOI: 10.32617/459-5e69faa31fceb (archived at https://perma.cc/LFT2-3NAQ)

Googins, N K and Rochlin, S A (2006) *Corporate Citizenship: Top to bottom*, Westport, CT: Praeger

Green, A and Matthias, A (1997) *Non-Governmental Organizations and Health in Developing Countries*, UK: Palgrave

Hafeez, K, Alghatas, F M, Foroudi, P, Nguyen, B and Gupta, S (2018) Knowledge sharing by entrepreneurs in a virtual community of practice (VCoP), *Information Technology and People*, 32(2): 405–29

Haugh, H (2006) Nonprofit social entrepreneurship, In S Parker (ed) *The Life Cycle of Entrepreneurial Ventures: International handbook series on entrepreneurship*, pp 401–36

Hockerts, K (2017) Determinants of social entrepreneurial intentions, *Entrepreneurship Theory and Practice*, 1: 105–130

IDC (2024) Worldwide Big Data and Analytics Software Forecast, 2024–2028, https://my.idc.com/getdoc.jsp?containerId=US52421424 (archived at https://perma.cc/4676-YYPE)

Islam, S M (2022) Social impact scaling strategies in social enterprises: A systematic review and research agenda, *Australian Journal of Management*, 47(2): 298–321

Jahdi, K S and Acikdilli, G (2009) Marketing communications and corporate social responsibility (CSR): Marriage of convenience or shotgun wedding? *Journal of Business Ethics*, 88 (1): 103–113

Jayawarna, D, Jones, O and Macpherson, A (2020) Resourcing social enterprises: The role of socially oriented bootstrapping, *British Journal of Management*, 31: 56–79

Jean, N, Burke, M, Xie, M, Davis, M A, Lobell, D B and Ermon, S (2016) Combining satellite imagery and machine learning to predict poverty, *Science*, 353(6301): 790–94

Jiwat, R and Zhang, Z (L) (2022) Adopting big data analytics (BDA) in business-to-business (B2B) organizations: Development of a model of needs, *Journal of Engineering and Technology Management*, 63: 1–20

Joyce, A and Paquin, R L (2016) The triple layered business model canvas: A tool to design more sustainable business models, *Journal of Cleaner Production*, 135: 1474–486

Kerlin, J (2006) Social Enterprise in the United States and Europe: Understanding and learning from the differences, *Voluntas*, 17(3): 246–62

Kiva (2019) How we got to $1 billion: A look at Kiva's history, https://www.kiva.org/blog/how-we-got-to-1-billion-a-look-at-kivas-history (archived at https://perma.cc/57JP-ZBEJ)

Klee, S, Janson, A and Leimeister, JM (2021) How data analytics competencies can foster business value: A systematic review and way forward, *Information Systems*, 38(3): 200–217

Kroeger, A and Weber, C (2014) Developing a conceptual framework for comparing social value creation, *Academy of Management Review*, 39: 513–40

Leadbeater, C (1997) The Rise of the Social Entrepreneur, DEMOS, https://demos.co.uk/wp-content/uploads/2023/03/theriseofthesocialentrepreneur.pdf (archived at https://perma.cc/WJ3U-HDLW)

Li, W, Li, W, Seppänen, V and Koivumäki, T (2022) Effects of greenwashing on financial performance: Moderation through local environmental regulation and media coverage, *Business Strategy and the Environment*, 32(1): 820–41

Luke, B and Chu, V (2013) Social enterprise versus social entrepreneurship: An examination of the 'why' and 'how' in pursuing social change, *International Small Business Journal*, 31: 764–84

Mahadevan, B (2000) Business models for Internet-based e-commerce: An anatomy, *California Management Review*, 42(4): 55–69

Mair, J and Martí, I (2006) Social entrepreneurship research: A source of explanation, prediction and delight, *Journal of World Business*, 41: 36–44

Mair, J and Schoen, O (2007) Successful social entrepreneurial business models in the context of developing economies: An explorative study, *International Journal of Emerging Markets*, 2: 54–68

Marin, S, Lee, V and Landers, R N (2021) Gamified active learning and its potential for social change. In Spanellis, A and Harviainen, J T (eds) *Transforming Society and Organizations Through Gamification*, Palgrave Macmillan, https://doi.org/10.1007/978-3-030-68207-1_11 (archived at https://perma.cc/Y3FK-52EF)

Martin, R L and Osberg, S (2007) Social entrepreneurship: The case for definition, *Stanford Social Innovation Review*, https://ssir.org/articles/entry/social_entrepreneurship_the_case_for_definition (archived at https://perma.cc/5MQM-NUT2)

Masanell, R C and Ricart, J E (2010) From strategy to business models and onto tactics, *Long Range Planning*, 43(2–3): 195–215

Massetti, B L (2008) The social entrepreneurship matrix as a 'tipping point' for economic change, The First International Conference on Social Entrepreneurship, Systems Thinking and Complexity USA: Adelphi University, April 24–26

McAfee, A and Brynjolfsson, E (2023). Big Data: The management revolution, *Harvard Business Review,* https://hbr.org/2012/10/big-data-the-management-revolution (archived at https://perma.cc/UNL5-TBQN)

McDonald, R M and Eisenhardt, K M (2020) Parallel play: Startups, nascent markets, and effective business-model design, *Administrative Science Quarterly*, 65: 483–523

McKinsey Global Institute (2018) Applying artificial intelligence for social good, https://www.mckinsey.com/featured-insights/artificial-intelligence/applying-artificial-intelligence-for-social-good (archived at https://perma.cc/5YVG-ALYU)

McMullen, J S and Warnick, B J (2016) Should we require every new venture to be a hybrid organization? *Journal of Management Studies*, 53: 630–62

Meyskens, M, Robb-Post, C, Stamp, J A, Carsrud, A L and Reynolds, P D (2010) Social ventures from a resource-based perspective: An exploratory study assessing global, *Ashoka Fellows Entrepreneurship: Theory & Practice*, 34: 661–80

Mulgan, G (2006) The Process of Social Innovation, *Innovations: Technology, Governance, Globalization*, 1(2): 145–162

Mulgan, G, Tucker, S, Ali, R and Sanders, B (2007) *Social Innovation: What it is, why it matters and how it can be accelerated*, Young Foundation

Nemes, N, Scanlan, S J, Smith, P, Smith, T, Aronczyk, M, Hill, S, Lewis, S L, Montgomery, A W, Tubiello, F N and Stabinsky, D (2022) An integrated framework to assess greenwashing, *Sustainability*, 14(8): 4431

Nicolopoulou, K (2014) Social entrepreneurship between cross-currents: Toward a framework for theoretical restructuring of the field, *Journal of Small Business Management*, 52: 678–702

OECD (2019) Artificial Intelligence in Society, https://www.oecd.org/en/publications/artificial-intelligence-in-society_eedfee77-en.html (archived at https://perma.cc/X4Q2-ZYPD)

Osterwalder, A and Pigneur, Y (2010) *Business Model Generation: A handbook for visionaries, game changers and challengers*, New Jersey, USA: John Wiley & Sons

Pache, A and Santos, F (2013) Inside the hybrid organization: Selective coupling as a response to competing institutional logics, *Academy of Management Journal*, 56: 972–1001

Peredo, A M and McLean, M (2006) Social entrepreneurship: A critical review of the concept, *Journal of World Business*, 41: 56–65

Perotin, V (2012) The performance of workers' cooperatives. In Battilani, P and Schröter, H G (Eds) *The Cooperative Business Movement 1950 to Present*, Cambridge: Cambridge University Press, pp 195–221

Perrini, F, Vurro, C and Costanzo, L A (2010) A process-based view of social entrepreneurship: From opportunity identification to scaling-up social change in the case of San Patrignano, *Entrepreneurship and Regional Development*, 22(6): 515–34

Pisa, M and Juden, M (2017) Blockchain and Economic Development: Hype vs Reality, CGD Policy Paper, Washington, DC: Center for Global Development, https://www.cgdev.org/publication/blockchain-and-economic-development-hype-vs-reality (archived at https://perma.cc/C7DH-YRRS)

Poetz, M K and Schreier, M(2012)The value of crowdsourcing: Can users really compete with professionals in generating new product ideas? *Journal of Product Innovation Management*, 29 (2): 245–56

Politis, D (2005) The process of entrepreneurial learning: A conceptual framework, *Entrepreneurship Theory and Practice*, 29(4): 399–424

Profatilov, D A, Bykova, O N and Olkhovskaya, M O (2014) Crowdfunding: Online charity or a modern tool for innovative projects implementation? *Asian Social Science*, 11(3): 146–51

Ranjan, J and Foropon, C (2020) Big data analytics in building the competitive intelligence of organizations, *International Journal of Information Management*, 56, 102231

Roche, C, Wall, P J and Lewis, D (2023) Ethics and diversity in artificial intelligence policies, strategies and initiatives, *AI Ethics*, 3(4): 1095–1115

Ruskin, J, Seymour, R G and Webster, C M (2016) Why create value for others? An exploration of social entrepreneurial motives, *Journal of Small Business Management*, 54: 1015–037

Salverda, M (2024) Social return on investment, https://www.betterevaluation.org/methods-approaches/approaches/social-return-investment (archived at https://perma.cc/AP3Y-KXAA)

San Pedro, P and Ballesteros, C (2021) Proposals for social impact measurement and management, https://files.griddo.comillas.edu/abstract-proposals-for-social-impact-measure-management.pdf (archived at https://perma.cc/7RKM-9GPN)

Santos, F, Pache, A and Birkholz, C (2015) Making hybrids work: Aligning business models and organizational design for social enterprises, *California Management Review*, 57: 36–58

Santos, S C, Nikou, S, Brännback, M and Liguori, E W (2021) Are social and traditional entrepreneurial intentions really that different? *International Journal of Entrepreneurial Behaviour & Research*, 27(7): 1891–911

Saunders, M N K, Lewis, P and Thornhill, A (2023) *Research Methods for Business Students*, 9th edition, Harlow, UK: Pearson

Schreiner, K (2008) Digital Games Target Social Good, *EEE Computer Graphics and Applications*, 28(1): 12–17

Schumpeter, J A (1947) *Capitalism, Socialism and Democracy*, 2nd ed, New York: Harper and Bros

Seelos, C and Mair, J (2005) Social entrepreneurship: Creating new business models to serve the poor, *Business Horizon*, 48: 241–46

Shams, R A, Zowghi, D, Bano, M (2023)AI and the quest for diversity and inclusion: A systematic literature review, *AI Ethics*, https://doi.org/10.1007/s43681-023-00362-w (archived at https://perma.cc/8SV2-QFPL)

Spanellis, A and Harviainen, J T (2021) an introduction to societal transformation through gamification. In Spanellis, A and Harviainen, J T (eds) *Transforming Society and Organizations through Gamification*, Palgrave Macmillan, https://doi.org/10.1007/978-3-030-68207-1_1 (archived at https://perma.cc/47B8-YCEZ)

Stevens, R, Moray, N and Bruneel, J (2015) The social and economic mission of social enterprises: Dimensions, measurement, validation, and relation, *Entrepreneurship Theory & Practice*, 39: 1051–1108

Sustainable Development Goals (2025) End hunger, achieve food security and improved nutrition and promote sustainable agriculture, https://wonderfoundation.org.uk/sdg-series-sustainable-development-goals-2025-report-highlights-wonders-role/?gad_source=1&gad_campaignid=22166330394&gclid=Cj0KCQjwxL7GBhDXARIsAGOcmINuPN6Mwqcl9y63ZOoz7XhKKZkCGyPBB36IzkjeqQTOo57sidppJzcaAo2mEALw_wcB (archived at https://perma.cc/3X57-FN4U)

Tan, X, Abbas, J, Al-Sulaiti, K, Pilař, L and Shah, S A R (2024) The role of digital management and smart technologies for sports education in a dynamic environment: Employment, green growth, and tourism, *Journal of Urban Technology*, 23(5): 1–32

Thompson J, Alvy, G and Lees, A (2000) Social entrepreneurship: A new look at the people and the potential, *Management Decision*, 38: 328–38

Tiwari, P, Bhat, A K and Tikoria, J (2020) Mediating role of prosocial motivation in predicting social entrepreneurial intentions, *Journal of Social Entrepreneurship*, 13(1): 118–41

To, C K, Martínez, J M and Orero-Blat, M (2020) Predicting motivational outcomes in social entrepreneurship: Roles of entrepreneurial self-efficacy and situational fit, *Journal of Business Research*, 121: 209–22

Torelli, R, Balluchi, F and Lazzini, A (2019) Greenwashing and environmental communication: Effects on stakeholders' perceptions, *Business Strategy and the Environment*, 29 (2): 407–21

Tracey, P, Phillips, N and Jarvis, O (2011) Bridging institutional entrepreneurship and the creation of new organizational forms: A multilevel model, *Organization Science*, 22: 60–80

Ursache, M (2019) The problem statement canvas for startups and innovation teams, https://medium.com/disciplined-entrepreneurship/the-problem-statement-canvas-for-startups-and-innovation-teams-663364c1a951 (archived at https://perma.cc/L4HY-R3GB)

Voorberg, W, Bekkers, V and Tummers, L (2014) The key to successful co-creation: An explanation of causal processing, presented at EGPA conference 10-12 September Speyer (Germany)

Weerawardena, J and Sullivan Mort, G (2006) Investigating social entrepreneurship: A multidimensional model, *Journal of World Business*, 41: 21–35

World Bank (2013) Crowdfunding's Potential for the Developing World, https://documents1.worldbank.org/curated/en/409841468327411701/pdf/840000WP0Box380crowdfunding0study00.pdf (archived at https://perma.cc/4QLG-MED5)

World Bank (2024) Addressing a Multitude of Global Challenges, https://www.worldbank.org/en/about/annual-report/addressing-multitude-global-challenges (archived at https://perma.cc/34UM-4GKC)

Yuen, S (2024) D.light closes US$176 million new financing for off-grid offerings in Africa, https://www.pv-tech.org/d-light-closes-us176-million-new-financing-for-off-grid-offerings-in-africa/ (archived at https://perma.cc/LRD4-UVUG)

Zahra, S A, Gedajlovic, E, Neubaum, D O and Shulman, J M (2009) A typology of social entrepreneurs: Motives, search processes and ethical challenges, *Journal of Business Venturing*, 24(5): 519–32

Zahra, S A, Rawhouser, H N and Bhawe, N (2008) Globalization of social entrepreneurship opportunities, *Strategic Entrepreneurship Journal*, 2: 117–31

Zahra, S A and Wright, M (2016) Understanding the social role of entrepreneurship, *Journal of Management Studies*, 53: 610–29.

# INDEX


academia 45
Action Funder 167
Acumen 39
Adventure Alternative (AA) 179–80, 184
Africa 218, 304
agreeableness 70
AI chatbots 329
AI. *See* artificial intelligence (AI)
Alt, E 184
Alter, Kim 238
Altinay, L 182
Amankwah-Amoah, J 262, 268
Annan, Kofi 131
anthropology 35
Apple 240
Aravind Eye Hospital 218
Armstrong, Brian 330
artificial intelligence (AI) 118, 327, 328, 330
Ashoka Foundation 39
Asia-Pacific Region 304
Astbury, Mike 70, 82–83
Australia 105–06
Avyantra 297

Bacq, S 42, 184
Bandura, A 9, 267
Bangladesh 7
BANI. *See* brittle, anxious, nonlinear and incomprehensible (BANI)
Barendsen, L 74
Barney, Jay 40
Bate, Gavin 179–80, 184, 186
Belgium *16*, 244
Bell, G G 42
Bezos, Jeff 79
Bhatt, P 182
Bhawuk, D 193
Bielefeld, W 182
Big Five 70
Big Issue 8, 29–30, 223–25, *224*
*Big Issue* (magazine) 8, 29–30, 74
Big Society Capital 15
Bio Bean 79
biodiversity loss 132
Bird, John 29–30, 74
Blair, Tony 13–14
Blockbuster 6
Bloom, P N 42
Blumenthal, Neil 117
BMC. *See* Business Model Canvas (BMC)
Bowen, Howard 120
brand loyalty 129

Brexit 158
bricolage 70, 79–80, 81, 323
brittle, anxious, nonlinear and incomprehensible (BANI) 153
Brown, Tim 36, 214–15
Burns, Paul 71
Business Model Canvas (BMC) 245

Calico 280
Cameron, David 15
Canada 294, 298
*Capitalism, Socialism, and Democracy* (Schumpeter) 35–36
career experience 264
Carroll, A B 121–22
Carter, S 73
CDFIs. *See* Community Development Finance Initiatives (CDFIs)
Chandra, Y 72
Chase Bank 240
Chatterji, A K 42
Chell, E 182
Chesbrough, Henry 36
Chevron 130–31
Christensen, Clayton 36
CIC. *See* Community Interest Company (CIC)
ClickFix 39
climate change 132, 207, 328, 330
Coca-Cola Company 130
commercial entrepreneurs 9, 73, 81, 83, 94–95
  social entrepreneurs vs 71, 77, 78
commercial goals 210, 325
communication patterns 46, 48
communication skills 276
communication tools 38, 45
Community Development Finance Initiatives (CDFIs) 15
community ecosystems 47
Community Empowerment (Scotland) Act (2015) 157
Community Interest Company (CIC) 15, 17, 18 19, 322
Co-ops UK 14
corporate philanthropy 320
corporate social entrepreneurship (CSE) 327–28
corporate social responsibility (CSR) 2, 34, 91, 320
  challenges 129–32
  differences between SEs and 125–29, *128*
  greenwashing 130–32
  introduction 119–20, 121–25
  *see also* SEs (social enterprises)

Costco 118, 136
Covid-19 pandemic 97, 149, 241
Crane, A 123
cross-functional teams 150–51
cryptocurrency 296, 330–31
CSE. *See* corporate social entrepreneurship (CSE)
CSIs (corporate social intrapreneurs) 327–28
CSR. *See* corporate social responsibility (CSR)
customer feedback 242, 308
customer loyalty 129
customer relationships 19, 240, 254

d.light 218, 325
data analysis 151, 186
data analytics 327, 328, 329–30
data privacy 332
debt financing 305, 306
Dees, J. Gregory 7
Defourny, J 50
Deloitte Insights 297
Department of Trade and Industry (DTI) 14
design thinking 148–49, 151, 152–53, 168
Development Trust Association (DTA) 14
Devon 248
Dewey, John 272
Di Domenico, M 208
digital assets 296
digital currency/tokens 295, 296, 297
digital media 328
digital technologies 38, 332
Divine Chocolate 39, 218
Doherty, B 31, 34
Drayton, Bill 6
Driscoll, J 272, 273
Dropbox 252
Drucker, Peter 35 36, 241 42
DTA. *See* Development Trust Association (DTA)
DTI. *See* Department of Trade and Industry (DTI)
Dyck, B 42

East Asia 242
Eastern Africa 179, 242
economic equilibrium 6, 209
economics 35, 39
Eddleston, K A 42
effectuation 70, 80, 81, 264
Elevate 280
Elkington, J 155, 245
Elvis & Kresse 250, *251*
emotional intelligence 73, 76, 271, 276, 324
employee loyalty 129
England 50, 156, 158, 247, 310
English Industrial Revolution (IR) 3, 9, 10, 22, 120, 320
EntreComp 270–71, *271*
entrepreneurial identity 77, 274, 275
entrepreneurial learning
  critical reflection 272–73, *273*
  development of competencies 269–71, *269*, *270*, *271*
  experiential learning theory 263–65, *263*, *265*
  formal education 276–77
  incubators and accelerators 277–79, *278*
  introduction 261–62
  learning process 274
  mechanisms of learning 272–79
  mentoring, business advice and coaching 274–76, *275*
  networking 277
  social nature 265–68, *266*
environmental disasters 122
environmental pollution 10, 132, 135
Environmental, Social and Governance (ESG) 92, 131–32, 154, 321
equity funding 293–94, 298, 310
ESF Social Innovation+ 309
ESF+. *See* European Social Fund + (ESF+)
ESG. *See* Environmental, Social and Governance (ESG)
EssilorLuxottica 118, 136
ethical fibre 210, 212, 214, 219, 324
ethical governance 323
EU (European Union) 125, 158
Europe 3, *16–17*, 155, 293, 320
  impact investment 298
  issuance of social impact bonds 304
  social entrepreneurship emergence 13–16
European Commission 123, 159, 270, 326
European Environmental Agency 121
European Impact Investment Consortium 298–99
European Social Fund + (ESF+) 309
Evenbreak 222
external stakeholders 43

financial bootstrapping 291, 311
financial crisis 293
financial institutions 52, 53, 293, 296, 298
financial metrics 41, 160
financial value 3, 209
financial viability 32, 33, 107, 289, 304
Five Factor Model 70
FixMyStreet 39
Floradex 249
Freeman, R E 16
FSA (Farm Service Agency) 310
full-time-equivalent (FTE) 156

Gardner, H 74
Gartner, W B 22, 93–94
Gates Foundation 325
gender inequality 207, 328

Generation Z 77
generative AI 329
Ghana 218
GHG. *See* Greenhouse Gas (GHG)
Gibb, A 269, 272
Gibbs, G 272–73
Gilboa, Dave 117
GiveCrypto project 330
Glasgow's Regeneration Agency (GRA) 168
Global Entrepreneurship Monitor 76
Global Impact Investing Network (2025) 325
global warming 122
Good-Faith Learning 80
GoodGuide 330
Google One Today 330
government agencies 45, 47, 126, 150
GRA. *See* Glasgow's Regeneration Agency (GRA)
Grameen Bank 7, 32, 39, 213
Greenhouse Gas (GHG) 130
GRI (Global Reporting Initiative) 124, 132, 134, 321
Grohs, S 35, 50
Guclu, A 189, 191
Guo, C 182

HACT Social Value Bank 166
'Hands Across America' 6
Harrison, Martha 280
Harvard Business Review (2023) 329
healthcare services 3, 91–92, 150
Heinze, K 191
Henry, Colette 45
Hetzler, William 146
Hill, R C 81
Hockerts, K 184, 210
Howorth, C 268
Humphrey, H R 271
Hunt, Andy 117

ICMA. *See* International Capital Market Association (ICMA)
ICO (initial coin offering) 296
ICT. *See* Information and Communication Technologies (ICT)
Identity Theory (IT) 169–70
IIRC (International Integrated Reporting Council) 124
IIRF (International Integrated Reporting Framework) 124, 132, 134, 321
Indarti, N 169
India 218, 275, 297
informal relationships 46, 48, 267
Information and Communication Technologies (ICT) 122, 135
innovation channels 47
interest rates 307
International Agency for the Prevention of Blindness Report (2024) 118
International Capital Market Association (ICMA) 303
Italy 12, *17*, 182

Jordan 267, 268
Joyce, A 245, 249

Kerlin, J A 50
key influencers 46
Kiva 39, 331
Kolb, D 263, 264, 272
Kropp, F 183–84, 188

labour rights 122, 124, 127–28
Lave, J 267, 277
LEGO Group 137
Levenhagen, M 81
Lévi-Strauss, Claude 79, 212
Living Wage Foundation 158
Long, W 81
Luddite Movement 37

Mair, J 184, 210, 327
MAKE CIC 80
market conditions 40, 95, 149, 307
Martí, I 327
Martin, J S 192
Massetti, B L 210–11, 212
Matten, D 123
Mayer, D 271
McKinsey Global Institute (2018) 330
McLean, Malcolm 38
McMullan, W E- 81
Meaton, J 193
mentorship schemes 267
microloans 213
Middle East 304
Middleton, Williams 277
Miller, T 71–72
minimal viable product (MVP) 217
moral obligations 210, 212, 324
Moving Mountains (MM) 179–80
Muralidharan, E 271
Mycoskie, Blake 68–69, 78

National Vision 118
National Vision Inc. 118
Netflix 6
neuroticism 70
Newth, J 51
NFPs ('not-for-profit' organizations) 3–4, 13, 91, 95, 148, 320
  priority to social mission 207, 212, 322
  reliance on government 208
  social innovation collaboration 150
  SROI impacts on 164
NGOs (non-governmental organizations) 2, 3, 13, 96, 102, 123

Noboa, E 184, 210
Northern Ireland 45, 158
Novicevic, M 192
Nyssens, M 50

Oakleaf Enterprise 203–07, *205–06*, 216
OCS (Office of Community Services) 309
Office for Civil Society and Innovation 32
One-for-One model 68–69
online forums 329
Organization for Economic Co-operation and Development (OECD) 125, 147–48, 149, 154
organizational structures 6, 34, 48
Osterwalder, A 220, 245
'Our Mission and Values' 247
Owen, Robert 11

Pache, A 34
pandemics 122, 328
Paquin, R L 245, 249
Patagonia 129, 130, 217–18
Pathak, S 271
PayGo loan program 325
Peace Corps 325
Penrose, Edith 40
Perrini, F 182
personal characteristics 69, 70
personal drivers
 achievement, autonomy and influence 72
 compassion 71–72
 critical moments 74–75
 education support 73–74
 embeddedness 73
 traits theory 70–71
personal experiences 72, 183
personal savings 291
personality traits 70, 72, 83, 93
Pigneur, Y 245
Pinheiro, P 133
political science 35, 39
political tensions 293
Pollenize 235–36, 247–49, *247*, *248*, 256–58, *256*
pollution 10, 122, 303
Principles for Responsible Investment (PRI) report 131
private investors 306
Procurement Act (2023) 158–59
Procurement Reform (Scotland) Act (2014) 157
psychological safety 268
psychology 35, 39
Public Services (Social Value) Act (2012) 155–56

R&D. *See* research and development (R&D)
Rae, D 265–67, 271, 277
Raider, Jeff 117
research and development (R&D) 327
*Research Methods for Business Students* (Lewis, Saunders, Thornhill) 190
Rinaudo, Keller 146
Rio de Janeiro 121
Rochdale Society of Equitable Pioneers 11
Rockefeller Foundation 325
Roddick, Gordon 29–30
Rose, Alison 76
Rwanda 147, 173

Sahlins, M D 193
Salovey, P 271
Santos, F 34
Sarason, Y 209–10
Sarasvathy, Saras 80, 264
SBS. *See* Small Business Service (SBS)
Scheiber, L 268
Schön, D A 272
School of Social Entrepreneurs (SSE) 14
school of thought
 alternative research streams 8–9
 social innovation and hybrid 6–8
Schumpeter, Joseph 6, 35–36
Schwab Foundation for Social Entrepreneurship 7
Scotland 50, 157, 158
Scott, Daz 280
Scott, Richard 48–49
Scottish Futures Trust (SFT) 157
Seanor, P 193
SEIs (social entrepreneurial intentions) 207, 210, 212, 321, 324
self-awareness 274, 276
SEOs (social entrepreneurial opportunities) 207, 210, 214
SEs (social enterprises)
 accreditations 101–06
 business logics 12–13
 conceptual traditions 208–09
 engagement principles and tools 191–95
 entrepreneurial learning 268–69, *269*
 growth models and sustainability 107–11
 hybridity 33–35
 institutional theory and 48–53
 key drivers for 91–95
 key financing sources 289–95
 legal structures 16–19, *16–17*, *19–22*
 network theory and 46–48
 opportunity recognition 188–91
 problem identification 183–84
 problem statement canvas 184–88, *185*, *187*
 RBV principles 40–42
 social impact measurement 132–34, 326
 social innovation and 148–53
 social start-up skills 181–82
 social vs commercial context 95–99

stakeholder theory and 43–46, *43*
unique characteristics 4–5, *4*, *5*
*see also* entrepreneurial learning
Shang, L 72
ShareTheMeal 330
Shaw, E 73
Single Market Act (2011) 159
Skoll Foundation 7, 325
Skype 252
Small Business Service (SBS) 14
SMEs (small and medium enterprises) 293, 298
Smith, B R 71
social business modelling
contextual factors 244–46
customers and beneficiaries 243
environmental layer 249–52, *251*
innovation 241–42
recognition of challenges 252–54
social layer 246–49
vision and mission 243–44
social costs 274
social drivers 75–77
Social Enterprise Boost Fund 309
Social Enterprise Coalition 14
Social Enterprise Partnership 45
Social Enterprise World Forum 149
social entrepreneurs
commercial entrepreneurs vs 71, 77, 78
entrepreneurial opportunities 213–20
experimentation stage 215–16
idea generation 214–15
key challenges 325–26
refinement stage 216–19, *217*
role in the entrepreneurial process 209–12
social finance
blockchain applications 295–97
choice factors and key challenges 307–10, *308*
funding model 304–07
introduction 287–89
key sources 289–95, *290*
social bonds and social impact bonds 302–04
social exchange and signalling theories 291–92
social impact investment 298–302, *300*, *301*
Social Firm UK 14
social injustices 122, 268
Social Investment Tax Reliefs 15
Social Network Analysis 46
social networks 41, 47–48, 262, 266, 279
social norms 52, 127, 193, 196, 210
*Social Responsibilities of the Businessman* (Bowen) 120
Social Return on Investment (SROI) 133, 154, 323
Social Role Valorization (SRV) 169–70
social start-ups 98, 103, 288–89, 291
Social Value Act (2013) 91
Social Value Model 156
social value
co-created monetary proxies 167–70
identification process 55
impacts on public procurement 157–59
monetary proxies 162–67
role in public policy and practice 155–57
SROI 162–65, *163*, 323
storytelling 160–62
tensions in creation 212–13
sociology 35, 39
Spinning Jenny 37
Spotify 252
SROI. *See* Social Return on Investment (SROI)
SSE. *See* School of Social Entrepreneurs (SSE)
Stearns, Stephen 37
Steckler, E 81
stock markets 307
Sustainable Development Goals (SDGs) 298
SVP (Social Value Proposition) 207, 324
components and definition 220–21, *221*
interplay between beneficiaries and social outcomes 221–22, *222*
interplay between beneficiaries, customers and social outcomes 223–25
interplay between customers and social outcomes 222–23

Tauber, L 267
TCFD (Task Force on Climate-related Financial Disclosures) 159
Thatcher, Margaret 13
theory of change (ToC) 15–16, 133
Theory of Planned Behaviour (TPB) 75
3D printing 328
TLBMC. *See* Triple-Layered Business Model Canvas (TLBMC)
TOMs (Themes, Outcomes and Measures) 157
TOMS Shoes 39, 68–69, 222–23
Torbay 248
TPB. *See* Theory of Planned Behaviour (TPB)
'Triad of Impact' 298–300
Triple Bottom Line 154, 160, 170, 245–46
triple bottom line 154, 160, 170, 245–46
Triple-Layered Business Model Canvas (TLBMC) 237, 245–46, 252
Trivedi, R 73
TTF (Thrive Together Fund) 310

Uber 241
UK (United Kingdom) 13–14, 17–19, 244, 309, 322, 323
UK Cabinet Office 156
UN Sustainable Development Goals 122, 167, 247, 288
UNFCCC (UN Framework Convention on Climate Change) 121
UNGC (United Nations Global Compact) 124, 132, 134, 321
UNICEF CryptoFund 296–97

United Nations 9, 328
United Nations Development Programme (2016) 127
United States 6, 293, 294, 298, 304
UnLtd 275, 325
user engagement 308
Ushahidi 39

Visionworks of America Inc. 118
von Hippel, Eric 36
VUCAH (volatile, uncertain, complex, ambiguous and hyperconnected) 153

Waddock, S 81
Wales 50, 156, 158
Warby Parker 117–19, *118*, *119*, 135–36
Weerakoon, W 80
Wellsprings Ltd 299–302
Wernerfelt, Birger 40
Westerveld, Jay 130
WHO-5 166
Woods, C 51
workforce conditions 122–23
work-life balance 276
World Bank 125, 331
World Economic Forum (2023) 130
Wyrobek, Keenan 146

Yitshaki, R 183–84, 188
Yudarwati, G A 194
Yunus, Muhammed 7

Zahra, S A 211–12
Zheng, X 269–70
Zipline 146–47